£10.

ECONOMIC HISTORY

DEVELOPMENT STUDIES AND COLONIAL POLICY

D0101094

Development Studies
and
Colonial Policy

Edited by

BARBARA INGHAM and **COLIN SIMMONS**

Deptartment of Economics, University of Salford

FRANK CASS

First published 1987 in Great Britain by
FRANK CASS & Co. LTD.
Gainsborough House, Gainsborough Road,
London, E11 1RS, England

and in the United States of America by
FRANK CASS & CO. LTD.
c/o Biblio Distribution Centre
81 Adams Drive, P.O. Box 327, Totowa, N.J. 07511

This Collection Copyright © 1987 Frank Cass & Co. Ltd.

British Library Cataloguing in Publication Data

Development studies and colonial policy.
1. Commonwealth of Nations—Economic
conditions   2. Developing countries—
Economic conditions
I. Ingham, Barbara   II. Simmons, Colin
330.9171'241   HC246

ISBN 0-7146-3231-7

Library of Congress Cataloging-in-Publication Data

Development studies and colonial policy.

1. Economic development. 2. Great Britain—Colonies—
Economic conditions.   I. Ingham, Barbara.   II. Simmons,
Colin.
HD82.D395 1987   338.9171'241   87-6562
ISBN 0-7146-3231-7

Typeset by Williams Graphics, Abergele, North Wales
Printed and Bound in Great Britain by
A. Wheaton & Co. Ltd., Exeter

CONTENTS

NOTES ON CONTRIBUTORS

Dr C. Christensen's research was carried out in the Department of History at the University of Leicester.

Dr Barbara Ingham is Lecturer in Economics at the University of Salford, and Director of the University's Centre for Development Studies.

Dr Frederick Nixson is Senior Lecturer in the Faculty of Economic and Social Studies at the University of Manchester. His special area is the economics of developing countries.

Dr Robert Pearce is a Lecturer in the Department of History at St. Martin's College, Lancaster. He is an authority on the history of colonial West Africa.

Martin Rudner is Associate Professor of Development Studies in the Norman Paterson School of International Affairs at Carleton University, Ottawa, Canada.

Dr Colin Simmons is a Senior Lecturer in the Department of Economics at the University of Salford, with special interests in Third World history, and the economic history of India.

Dr A. Webster is a Lecturer at Basingstoke College of Technology. His research on Southeast Asia was undertaken at the University of Birmingham.

Dr Nicholas Westcott carried out his research at the University of Cambridge, and is now employed in the Foreign Office.

PREFACE

This volume is the product of a number of meetings held by the Third World History and Development Study Group, which is one of several study groups sponsored by the Development Studies Association. The Group was formed in 1978 at the Development Studies Association Conference held at the University of Strathclyde, Glasgow. It comprises people who for one reason or another wish to raise the status of historical work within development studies, seeking to redefine the scope and enlarge upon its role.

The present collection of essays represents research which has been done both on procedures and methodology in development studies, and on colonialism as a historical process relevant to the study of underdevelopment. The volume is divided into two parts. The first part focuses directly on the question of how to define 'development' and 'development studies', placing the commitment to historical work within this important theoretical context. The second part comprises six individual contributions on colonial policy between 1750 and 1945. These explore a range of issues, reappraising the relationship between metropolitan economies, principally Britain; various phases of overseas expansion; and development and change in peripheral areas. The framework of the book is designed to overlap both history and development studies, and it is hoped that 'developmentalists' and 'historians' alike will draw upon it in a mutually reinforcing fashion.

The editors are most grateful to the Development Studies Association for the support it has provided, both for the research workshops and for the preparation of this volume. We wish to express our gratitude too, to the contributors who have demonstrated great forbearance, and who have suggested a number of changes which we have tried to incorporate into the book. Colleagues at the University of Salford have commented on various drafts. Secretarial assistance has been provided by Salford University Department of Economics, and we also thank the Department of Geography for preparation of maps and diagrams.

B.I. and C.S.

PART ONE

1

Economic Development and Economic History

COLIN SIMMONS

INTRODUCTION

In the aftermath of the Second World War and within the general context of de-colonisation the modern discipline of Development Economics and its offshoot — the rather wider inter-disciplinary field of Development Studies — became established. During their first quarter century or so both subjects expanded at a very rapid rate and first in the West and then subsequently in many parts of the emergent 'Third World', a Liberal-Orthodox development tradition came into being. The rise of this tradition is briefly examined in the first part of this paper, and although I make no claim to provide a comprehensive review of its many component parts, I do seek to highlight what I take to be its basic ethos. Now partly as a result of a whole series of perceived development failures, over the last decade a growing sense of disillusionment and questioning has characterised the orthodox development profession. Both from within as well as from without the tradition there has been a growing challenge to the earlier consenses, and these pressures are explored in Part II. I argue that the current state of the art is highly unsatisfactory on many counts and in particular there is now a great deal of confused thinking about the meaning, relevance and measurement of many of the key concepts — especially the central notion of economic development itself. Finally, in Part III I suggest how it might be possible to clarify the major issues, reconcile some of the different approaches and point a way forward out of the impasse. The burden of the argument rests upon the proposition that a long-run perspective is required if we are to understand the underlying causes of 'late-', 'less-' or 'under-' development and then go on to identify its manifestations. Although the injunction of an explicit historical dimension inclines us more towards explanation and development education than the current preoccupations with prescription would seem to allow, far from being a source of weakness or even withdrawal, it is contended that without it the very basis upon which various policy strategies and pronounce-ments are made, is both inadequate and unsound.

I

FAITH, HOPE AND CHARITY:
DEVELOPMENT ECONOMICS, c. 1945–1975

The emergence of the modern discipline of Development Economics and its offshoot, the somewhat broader field of Development Studies, can be proximately dated to the decade following the end of the Second World War. Irrespective of whether we can meaningfully trace back its theoretical antecedents to the writings of the Classical Political Economists[1] (or, with François Quesnay's *Tableau* in mind, perhaps even earlier),[2] relevant sections of the work of Marx and Schumpeter,[3] the efforts of those civil servants involved with the promotion of 'development' during the late colonial period,[4] the reports of various international economic agencies responding to the Great Depression,[5] or the seminal articles by Paul Rosenstein-Rodan on the industrialisation of Eastern Europe pub-lished over 1943/4,[6] it was really not until the late 1940s and early 1950s that the subject we recognise today became established. The basic condition for its birth and subsequent growth was, of course, the dismantling of the major colonial empires (a process which, when we bear in mind the experience of the full-range of erstwhile possessions, has been highly uneven over space and time), and the creation of a still rising number of formally autonomous states throughout Asia, the Pacific, Africa, the Middle East, the Caribbean and parts of South and Central America.

The most obvious common characteristic of these countries was the poverty, absolute as well as relative, of the great majority of their inhabitants, and the energies of the local political leaders were soon directed – at least on paper in a whole panoply of five-year plans – towards 'developing' the respective economies. Now depending upon the prevailing ideological persuasion of the particular ruling elite – which, more often than not, was the direct outcome of the way in which independence was achieved – the preferred choice of development route was generally a variant of either the perceived Western or Soviet models (or, in some notable instances such as Pandit Nehru's India and Kwame Nkrumah's Ghana, some sort of combination of the two laced with 'relevant' doses of indigenous values and re-vamped institutions).[7] Since such strategies were in some fundamental sense replicatory, and given the fact that the pool of appropriate development 'knowledge' was thin on the ground, it was but natural that financial assistance, technical advice and even expert guidance should be sought from without — though for under-standable reasons of national honour this latter point, if not handled sensitively, was something of a touchy issue in the early days.

As it happens, a ready and welcoming reception was accorded to such overtures — indeed it was frequently the case that these services were offered well in advance of their being solicited — by govern-ments and academics in Western and Eastern hemispheres alike. A fortunate conjunction of circumstances — political, economic, strategic and scholarly — had paved the way for the appearance of a Development Establishment keen to attain official or quasi-official status and become professional.[8] In the Western democracies the opportunity to expunge some of the feelings of guilt which had begun to build up as a result of past imperial activity was too good to be missed, and the apparent success of the Marshall Aid Programme[9] in revitalising the war-ravaged European economies, offered plenty of scope (in association with the theoretical implications stemming from the Harrod—Domar formulations) for thinking that a similar disbursement of funds would perform the same sort of task for the capital-scarce societies of the 'less developed' world. Further, the triumph of Keynesian Economics among other things legitimised a degree of purposeful state intervention, and this was consistent with the stated intention of many, if not most, 'Third World'[10] govern-ments to perform much more than a purely night-watchman role.

There was also the question of competition with the Soviet bloc for influence amongst the emergent nations because they too were extremely anxious to ply their own version of development: once 'Socialism in One Country' had perforce been buried by virtue of the acquisition of Eastern Europe, the Kremlin became highly receptive to the need to court the governments and people of what they insisted on referring to as the 'victims of capitalist imperial-ism'.[11] After all, it was alleged, only two decades of national plan-ning had had a dramatic effect in propelling the USSR from a state of abject backwardness into an advanced industrial power — and this was precisely what articulate voices in the Third World were demanding. They were not prepared to accept a gradualistic unfolding of a laissez-faire style of development: no, in view of the urgency of the domestic poverty problem and the not-unconnected issue of 'national strength', there seemed to be a patent need to telescope far-reaching change to the fabric of society and economy in as short a span of time as possible. Of course once the revelations about the human costs of the Soviet crash development programmes became widely disseminated following Stalin's death, even those governments overtly sympathetic to the USSR were quick to distance themselves from these 'negative' aspects. But as Stephen Clarkson and others have shown,[12] disillusionment was not total and the feeling lingered that somehow it was possible to abstract selective parts of the package and that, with the design of appropriate safeguards, important lessons could still be learnt and hence the uncontested material benefits emanating from such a policy framework would be unsullied. The onset of the Cold War heightened the rather unsavoury spectacle of both sides attempting to score points off each other in terms of who held the 'key' to development, and this tended to bid up promises of aid, all manner of assistance and, of course, military hardware. Both sides, too, became ever firmer in the conviction that they alone could provide the ideological and intellectual answer to the question of how best to bring about development, and both were prepared to back their respective cases with increasing allocations of resources.

In this way, through an untidy admixture of humanitarian idealism, the pragmatic quest for strategic hegemony and spheres of influence, and frank self-interest,[13] Development Economics received the necessary motivation, justification and essential wherewithal to flourish. If the impetus initially derived from national considerations, it was not long before a cadre of experts emerged to fill an expanding number of positions in the international agencies: the various arms of the UN and the array of financial institutions born at Bretton Woods began to recruit suitable (i.e., predominantly Western) staff, and so cause a second tier of professional developmentalists to come into existence.[14] Finally, and to complete the picture, after a comparatively short time-lag, the Third World began producing a home-spun supply of personnel. At first recourse was made to acquiring development education and training abroad (again mainly in the West), but soon universities and other specialist centres (frequently manned by expatriates in the early phases) appeared, and hence by the late 1950s the discipline had put down roots all over the world.

For the first 25 years or so of its existence, Development Economics enjoyed a tremendous spurt of growth and prestige. A heady atmosphere of hope and optimism was built up. There was widespread consensus upon underlying values, fundamental principles and a whole series of composite issues including the derivation of a general explanation for the state of 'less' or 'late' development, the evolution of suitable analytical tools and techniques for studying its incidence, forms and manifestations, the identification of the most promising directions of research activity, the laying out of policy options, and the refinement of procedures to monitor and evaluate particular development projects. In the West, and shortly afterwards in many of the 'client' Third World countries, this basic agreement permitted the formation of a Development Orthodoxy – one which was essentially Liberal in outlook.[15] By this I mean that it (*a*) rejected the brand of Marxist-Leninism currently being peddled by the Soviet Bloc and its Western apologists as 'sterile' and 'outdated'; (*b*) was highly selective in its appropriation of neo-Classical theory – indeed after a sequence of 'litmus tests' the bulk of such theory was considered to be lacking in relevance, realism and significance: the economics of the 'special case' (i.e. the contemporary Western societies) as Dudley Seers once put it,[16] was too far removed from the Third World to be of much consequence; (*c*) positively encouraged the promotion of a mixed private and public enterprise economy in the Third World, placing a considerably greater emphasis upon state planning[17] and 'gap-filling' entrepreneurship[18] than was currently being advocated for the West.

Thus safely distanced from both Left and Right, and riding upon the crest of a new wave of interest in the social sciences (flush with infusions of real cash), the Liberal-Orthodox 'developmentalists' were able to construct a substantial institutional edifice and inspire a great deal of academic work – work which was highly respected (perhaps even envied in some quarters) and apparently taken very seriously at the highest levels of government and administration.[19]

From the myriad of development centres, specialist institutes and departments of universities and other higher educational establishments, came a veritable flood of text-books, monographs, edited readings, journals, periodicals, manuals, guides and commissioned reports.[20] New packages of courses were designed to cater for increasing numbers of overseas and domestic students, and curriculum experimentation proceeded apace. The media were naturally not slow to become (selectively) involved, and in the wake of dramatic presentations (particularly if they were vividly pictorial) of disaster and distress, many charitable organisations were either freshly founded or suitably reconstituted. Home governments responsible for aid disbursement began to play one sort of role, and private consultancies – then at the other end of the spectrum – commenced to set up shop. 'Development decades' were declared, and at frequent intervals impressive-sounding international conferences and symposia were convened. An environment characterised by genuine intellectual excitement and real advance prevailed, and those whom one commentator has rather unkindly dubbed 'the jet-set proletariat'[21] roved the Third World to and fro carrying around a baggage that could well have been labelled 'faith' (in development progress), 'hope' (that the advice would be implemented) and 'charity' (promises of aid, grants and low-interest credits).

Although it would be quite absurd to attempt to convey the variegate nature of development thinking over these halcyon years in a few sentences — to do that adequately one would require a great deal of space, and certainly much more considered thought than recent exercises conducted in this vein would suggest[22] — I believe that it is possible to capture its essential thrust. Shorn of the details, and without engaging in too much parody and caricature, we can reduce the Liberal-Orthodox position to the following basic elements.

First, economic development came to mean a process of structural change resulting from a sustained rise in per capita incomes. An acceleration of the growth rate would lead to a declining share of the primary sector (usually excluding extractive mining activity) in N.D.P. and labour resources, and a substantial enhancement of the secondary sector (especially manufacturing) — with the tertiary sector remaining roughly neutral in the 'first phase' and then rising quite rapidly thereafter. The method of measuring growth and development derived from national income accounting, and extensive use was made of the three-sector classificationary model as pioneered by Irving Fisher, Colin Clark and Simon Kuznets. This pattern — but not of course the timing — of development was predicated upon Western experience.

Second, the prognosis for the Third World was optimistic but conditional upon certain types of direct action. If Third World governments would begin to usher in an ethos of 'modernisation' by encouraging or inculcating a spirit of 'improvement'; if Western states would offer to supply capital and expert personnel on 'soft' terms; and if a liberal international trading framework could be negotiated into effect, then internal, bilateral and multilateral obstacles to development would be progressively removed.

Third, although development economists were reluctant to yield up their supposed theoretical primacy and pivotal position, ground was gained by other social scientists (with the occasional assistance of the technologists) consequent upon the growing realisation that economic factors did not exist in some sort of socio-cultural-political-geographical vacuum. The age of interdisciplinary effort had, it seemed, now dawned. Armed with these three crucial foundation stones — concordance on the definition, meaning and measurement of development; the holding out of real hope that it was an eminently feasible thing to aim for an engineer; and the emergence of a co-operative spirit of scholarly enquiry — work proceeded apace.

Of course it would be an exaggeration to claim that the entire community of interested developmentalists subscribed to this overall view, and even more of a simplification to argue that all Third World regimes were in sympathy with — and correspondingly keen to digest and then actually implement — the prescriptive implications that followed. Apart from those countries formally pledged to the collectivist route, there were others which began to look favourably upon some of the insights being thrown up by a new Radical or neo-Marxian group of scholars (mainly Western based). Following the publication of Paul Baran's work on underdevelopment in the mid-1950s[23] − written from an unashamedly reformist Marxist standpoint − a number of intellectuals began the daunting task of updating the classical Marxian theory of imperialism. This source of criticism from without can be contrasted with the elements of disquiet from within the Liberal-Orthodox tradition. Two such lines of thinking (both connected together) may be readily identified since neither could be easily countered and have, in fact, come to greater prominence in recent years. First of all the tendency to equate simple rises in per capita incomes with unambiguous 'progress' and certain welfare gain caused a great deal of unease. Aside from the obvious qualification concerning its social and spatial distribution, the advances made in Welfare Economics led by Kenneth Arrow and others were not 'matched' by any corresponding work of substance appraising the analytical worth of the national income index itself. In the second place, doubts about the applicability of the methods and conventions deployed by the national income accounting prac-titioners to measure − in as precise a manner as possible − the economic growth rate in the Third World started to surface almost from the outset of detailed enquiry. This induced an improvement in the processing and presentation of a data base which was invariably sketchy, inaccurate and subject to wide margins of errors[24] (not least because of weak Central Statistical Offices and state bureauc-racies and, more substantively, the problem of how to value non-monetary and black-market transactions). It also led some economists and statisticians to search for other indices (such as school enrolments, radios and telephones per capita and the output of 'modern' products such as steel and automobiles)[25] which could be used in conjunction with − but not as surrogates for − income.

Such work paved the way for a relatively early entry of econometrics into development (via regression analysis); stimulated a greater awareness of the difficulties of comparing the income level of the same country over time (weights, price deflators, base years) and over space between different countries (exchange rate distortions adjusted by purchasing power parities);[26] and prompted a 'quality of life' set of criteria in place of the hitherto dominant income approach.[27] But although these caveats and criticisms were poten-tially important, and in some cases have had far-reaching effects, it would surely be erroneous to overstate their ability to inflict serious damage on the credibility of the subject in general or to pierce the self-confidence of the most directly vulnerable authors. Adverse commentary from 'outside' (neo-Marxism) could be marginalised or ignored relatively easily, and worries from 'within' could either be subsumed into the orthodoxy by relegating them to the status of qualificationary statements, or bypassed altogether on the ground that 'warts and all' income was still the most convenient and least objectionable indicator available. In any event, the economic growth record over c. 1950–75 for the LDCs as a group[28] was not only unprecedentedly high in relation to the historical experience of both West and 'South', but seemed to be impressive with respect to manufacturing performance – the key to structural change and hence 'fully-fledged' development. This 'delivery of the goods' was – at least at first (and apparently still is for those inclined towards Bill Warren's version of Marxism)[29] – a powerful argument in support of the case being propounded by the developmentalists.

II

1975–1985:
A DECADE OF DOUBT, DISSENT, PESSIMISM AND RETREAT

If it is fair to characterise the first quarter century of Development Studies in general and Development Economics in particular as being time of great expansion, widespread consensus and a reasonably optimistic prognostication for Third World economies, then the essential hallmarks of the last decade (c. 1975–1985) have been doubt, dissent, pessimism and – certainly as far as the Liberal-Orthodox position is concerned – retreat. According to some of the most widely-known, well-respected and influential academic figures, the contrast between the two periods can scarcely have been greater. Whereas the first phase had witnessed 'a remarkable outpouring of fundamental ideas and models', the 'generation of controversies that contributed much to its liveliness' (Albert Hirschman),[30] had seen 'exciting times of ferment' full of 'intellectual pioneering' (Paul Streeten),[31] and was replete with 'vigorous optimism' (Dudley Seers);[32] the same authors opined that the tide had decisively turned during the latter, and had given way to profound disagreement, theoretical aridity, gloom, and a decline in funding, interest and public image. Most extreme of all, Professor Seers contended that not only had the subject 'proved less useful than was expected', that in some circumstances it 'may well have aggravated social problems', but that 'there are reasons to doubt whether it will survive much longer'.[33] Even Arthur Lewis – one of the founding fathers and still a staunch defender of the faith – in his recent Presidential Address to the American Economics Association was forced to acknowledge that Development Economics ('however defined'), is 'said to be now in the doldrums'; that 'it has been deserted by American Ph.D. students'; that 'it no longer competes' as a career; that 'foreign aid has been cut'; that 'the multilateral institutions cannot keep up with inflation'; and − the final ignominy! − that 'the Ford Foundation has changed its priorities'.[34]

Indeed, over this ten-year period − and at a seemingly remorselessly accelerating pace − there has been an extraordinary amount of questioning and critical re-examination, re-assessment and re-appraisal of the state of the art.[35] Fundamental values, standard premises and assumptions, theoretical frameworks, units of analysis, key concepts and the very meaning of the basic terms have all been put under an increasingly searching microscope − and many have been found to be either wanting and in need of drastic surgery, or requiring substantial qualification, modification and revision. Opinion and pronouncement upon the current health − or otherwise − of the subject, and speculation about its future are now commonplace, and there has been something of a stampede into conferences and symposia in order to air this disquiet.[36] In part, of course, this probing and taking stock is a reflection of a perfectly normal desire to review the progress of a young discipline which is, after all, barely out of its adolescence; but the very breadth and depth of the critique is surely indicative of a more general sense of dissatisfaction and malaise. In my view what is now surfacing is serious misgiving about the utility of Liberal-Orthodox formulations with respect to both of its principal objectives, i.e., to comprehend and explain the complexities of contemporary Third World 'reality', and to provide an adequate and feasible prescriptive basis for policy-making (including its implementation).

In retrospect, it now seems abundantly clear that these were − and still are − Herculean tasks to even begin to approach (let alone 'solve'); but in the euphoric circumstances of the time, the first generation of developmentalists − both academic and actual practitioners − obviously did not consider such expectations to be over-ambitious or their perceptions to be hopelessly naive. Also, to be fair, few academics (but not so few Third World governments) thought that any 'real' type of sustained growth and development could be achieved in the short-to-medium term since they were well aware of the significance of potentially damaging forces that were either exogenous to the nation state and hence beyond the control of planners (such as fickle primary product markets), or lay deeply embedded within given social structures (a range of so-called 'non-economic' variables) and which were therefore not easily amenable to the kind of root-and-branch change − via appropriate market signals or even direct state action – that was considered necessary. Thus only the most confident and sanguine members of the profession – plus a host of governments with promises to keep – were predicting a relatively rapid and painless transition: the majority, with cooler and perhaps wiser heads,[37] were fully alive to the possibility of a slow haul – and one which could well be (*a*) highly uneven over space and between different social groups; (*b*) politically troublesome – if not explosive – and (*c*) subject to occasional reversibility. But that admitted, I think that even the most cautious and far-sighted of the Liberal-Orthodox academics remained fairly committed to the basic principles of 'progress' and – the vogue word – 'modernisation', which were being enunciated (albeit often more by implication than in an explicit way) in the ever-growing number of tracts on and around this subject: many became enmeshed in what used to be called a Kuhnian 'paradigm'[38] of development. I suspect that most developmentalists of 40, 30 and perhaps even 20 years ago would have been surprised at current (mid-1980s) levels of world poverty, hunger and malnutrition (affecting an estimated one billion people) and material deprivation of all kinds;[39] that not many would have anticipated the state of international, inter-regional and inter-personal inequalities;[40] and that fewer still would have expected to witness the catastrophic famines now stalking the Sahel and large segments of sub-Saharan Africa, claiming the lives of millions and casting a blighting influence over immense areas of terrain. So although it is exceedingly difficult to accurately gauge and succinctly convey a sense of mood, it is certain that the intellectual pendulum has now swung far away from its cautiously confident and somewhat smugly comforting original point. But of course like all shifts of this order of magnitude,[41] it did not happen precipitately: rather it was a process which only began to get underway when it was no longer tenable to either square empirical observation and on-the-ground reality with theoretical prediction, or to continue to find suitable extenuating factors (such as stubborn and recalcitrant Third World governments and bureaucracies) that impeded the realisation of even the best-laid development ideas and plans.

One of the earliest assaults on the Liberal-Orthodox modernisation edifice arose from the ranks of those economists who felt increasingly unhappy at the supposedly intimate connection between economic growth and economic development. Until well into the 1960s – if not later – it would be fair to say that most academic development economists had worked on the assumption that 'growth' and 'development' were complementary processes and that sooner or later the former would inevitably 'lead' to the latter. Indeed those who have closely examined the literature of the period from this particular focus[42] have shown that not only did these terms become inextricably linked together but, more often than not, were used either interchangeably – almost 'for the sake of stylistic variety',[43] or simply as convenient synonyms. Donald Gould took great exception to this apparent carelessness and bemoaned the 'debasement' and 'impoverishment' of the English language – whilst at the same time noting that colleagues on the other side of the Channel in France, Germany and Italy also failed to properly discriminate between the two 'concepts'.[44] He and Professor Arndt also suggested that two of the leading text-books of the day, *viz.* Arthur Lewis's *The Theory of Economic Growth* (London, 1955) and Walt Rostow's *The Stages of Economic Growth, a non-Communist Manifesto* (Cambridge, 1960) were obviously mistitled since they were really referring to 'development' (structural change) rather than to 'growth' (defined in terms of change in per capita incomes).[45] Furthermore, Robert Flammang who is perhaps less concerned about semantics than the other critics, maintains that the failure to make the distinction between the two crystal clear has had deleterious consequences for both theory and policy analysis, and goes on to say that 'if people really mean to communicate effectively with each other' then it is absolutely necessary to be as precise as possible with their respective deployment.[46] All three reviewers were inclined to the opinion that it had been highly unfortunate that Joseph Schumpeter's early theoretical distinction between 'Growth' and 'Evolution' ('development') and perhaps even Marx's original formulations,[47] had been either forgotten or ignored by post-World War Two writers.[48]

Now whatever reservations we may harbour today about the importance – or otherwise – of distinguishing between the two,[49] it is not difficult to understand the reasoning behind the feelings of dissatisfaction of those who complained about the conflation of growth and development. Following a reasonably thorough and detailed investigation of the course of recent economic change in the West African state of Liberia, Robert Clower and his team of associates (G. Dalton, M. Harwitz and, surprisingly, A. A. Walters) chose to draw attention to the need to separate out growth and development by deliberately entitling their study *Growth without Development – An Economic Survey of Liberia* (Evanston, 1966).[50] Directly building upon the work of the slightly earlier traditions of dualism (pioneered by J. H. Boeke)[51] and economic enclaves (H. Myint and Jonathan Levin),[52] they sought to demonstrate the proposition that there had been substantial growth but insignificant development. Their 'principal conclusion' was that the 'rapid growth in production ... had little developmental impact on Liberia or Liberians'; and they went on to demonstrate how 'enormous growth in primary commodities ... had been unaccompanied either by structural changes to induce complementary growth or by institutional changes to diffuse gains in real income among all sectors of the population'.[53] Although this was a trenchant and powerful frontal attack on the conventional wisdom it seemed to cause few immediate ripples: to the extent that it was acknowledged at all,[54] the mainstream could easily shrug Liberia off as being something of a special case. Not only was the country particularly dominated by American influence, capital and multinational enterprises[55] (because of its unusual heritage, i.e. its long anti-slavery affiliation with the USA); it was relatively small, seemingly obscure and far removed from the contemporary preoccupation with the so-called archetypal 'less developed' cases such as India and Brazil. Nevertheless, in retrospect the Clower volume − though not a catalyst in itself − can be regarded as being something of a symbolic landmark in that from that time on the foundations of the Liberal-Orthodox position began to be subjected to close scrutiny and we can detect the beginnings of a monumental shift of its intellectual ground.

Irrespective of whether economic growth in the Third World was being accompanied by structural change (*a*) in the 'right' direction (i.e. a diversification away from primary activity); (*b*) of the 'correct' order of magnitude (so that, for example, the country in question would not end up with a bloated or hypertrophied tertiary or urban 'informal' sector); and (*c*) at the 'appropriate' speed (in accordance, say, with planned targets), many observers started to draw attention to the fact that neither the domestic poverty problem nor the gap between rich and poorest countries seemed to be noticeably diminishing.[56] These unpalatable empirical findings had a large number of very serious implications, but for the purpose of our argument here, we choose to highlight just three. First, the meaning of 'development' (whether prefixed by 'economic' or not) underwent a radical and far-reaching alteration. From being somewhat narrowly − but specifically − identified with structural change, it widened out to embrace a bewilderingly large − and apparently ever-expanding − range of eminently 'desirable' qualities including, inter alia, (*i*) reductions in poverty, inequality, unemployment, underemployment, disease, the rate of population growth, malnutrition, technological 'vulnerability', cultural dependence, illiteracy and slums; and (*ii*) enhancements to diet, educational opportunity, life-chances, health, social services, 'self-esteem' (i.e. identity, dignity, respect, honour, recognition), freedom, leisure, contemplation, beauty ... and Uncle Tom Cobley.[57] The most cursory perusal of the relevant literature of the last ten years would reveal the elasticity of the term 'economic development', and it is difficult to find agreement among authors even on 'core' constituents.[58] Moreover, if we extend our horizons to include the work of non-economists then the confusion multiplies.[59] Our conclusion must therefore be that adherents to the Liberal-Orthodox tradition are now in something of a dilemma: on the one hand, the early meaning seems to have been discredited by events, was therefore jettisoned and today can no longer be easily resurrected – even if there was the will to do so; but on the other, the changing and slippery quality of the 1970s and early to mid-1980s formulations, with their ever-widening normative premises, their medley collections of worthy concerns, the plea of international peace, disarmament and environmental protection (B. Hettne, 1984) and sometimes their embarrassingly obvious vacuity ('to create more options for more people' – Emmanuel de Kadt, 1985) threaten the clarity of the central concern.

The second implication – and one that directly follows the first – is that economic growth could not be construed as being a sufficient – or even necessary – condition to bring about economic development (which, for the moment, and purely for the sake of expositional convenience, we will define in terms of poverty reduction). Perhaps the earliest and clearest recognition of the need to change overall strategy came in the guise of the now celebrated 1972 ILO Report on the Kenyan Economy.[60] Although primarily addressed to the issue of employment creation, it was really the progenitor of the Structuralist-inspired 'Redistribution with Growth' concept.[61] With hindsight we can see that R.W.G. was an important transitory position between the 'growthmanship' of the early years and the now dominant 'Basic Needs' approach.[62] This current appeal to a direct amelioration of poverty levels has thus provided the Liberal-Orthodox school with a means to achieve a sort of logical symmetry in development thinking. With growth now shunted out of the way, the 'new' idea about 'development' can now be pursued with vigour. Unfortunately, however, there are almost as many normative, utopian and politically unrealistic dimensions to this line[63] as there are to the current crop of ideas on 'economic development', and this has now even been acknowledged – albeit only half-heartedly – by the High Priest of Basic Needs, Paul Streeten himself.[64]

The third implication derives from the observation that the actual record of growth and development (conventionally defined) over the post-War period has been extremely mixed. Despite the unease which some of the early developmentalists harboured about lumping the Third World states together into a single analytical category and deploying a set of general principles to cover very different areas there was, nevertheless, a tendency to assume that it was still very useful to consider the 'economics of less developed countries' in a holistic manner. But with the passage of time it became increasingly obvious that not only was the Indian experience quite different from that of, say, the Gambian, but that the elements which were common were perhaps of much less importance than the distance between them. The pitfalls of treating the myriad of developing (!) countries that constituted the Third World as some sort of homogeneous block rapidly became manifest. Indeed, as far as how the LDCs saw themselves is concerned, even at the level of political proclamations and high-sounding rhetoric, the euphoria of Non-Alignment (adopted at the famous Afro-Asia Conference convened at Bandung in 1955)[65] and of continental unity (the Conference of Independent African States – the precursor of the OAU – held at Accra in 1958)[66] turned sour all too soon; and though it would be a mistake to dismiss such gestures as effervescent pipe-dreams it would be equally wrong to suggest that they provided the foundation stones necessary for reconciling important inter-state and inter-continental differences.

Furthermore, the growing realisation that the experience of the LDC groupings that were set up to counter some of the pressures stemming from the changes in the international economy in general and of alterations in the pattern of international trade in particular, have not proved to be anything like as successful or enduring as was hoped. Granting the fact that exogenous forces have had an important and generally hostile influence (notwithstanding the pious 'mutality of North–South interests' argument put forward in the two Brandt Commission Reports – which anyway have sunk like the proverbial stone in the Western economies),[67] few observers would be able to deny the significance of the 'internal' obstacles in the way of establishing and then effectively prosecuting such things as custom union areas, common markets, regional associations for furthering closer economic co-operation, commodity groupings (exclusive of the special case of OPEC), the Group of 77 within UNCTAD and, most recently, the union of debtor countries. The fanfare of the present North–South dialogue – culminating in the demand for a 'New International Economic Order' – can hardly disguise the deep divisions within the Third World, and the series of embarrassingly inconclusive top-level summits over the past quinquennium or so only underlines the fact that there simply is not a single LDC voice on any issue of real substance.[68] The rise in the price of petroleum-based products on the one hand, and the export-led successes of the Newly Industrialising Countries (especially the four 'Asian Tigers' – South Korea, Taiwan, Hong Kong and Singapore)[69] drove several crucial wedges between the LDCs – a trend that even the World Bank was belatedly compelled to concede in successive World Development *Reports* (low-income economies – with China and India given a special sub-category, lower-middle income, upper-middle income and high-income oil exporting economies).[70] In sum it is now something of a fiction to refer to 'the economics of the less developed countries': Third World economic structures and problems are too diverse to permit all but the most common-sense sort of generalities.

As a result of these accumulating doubts, the distressing succession of unpalatable political and social upheavals (especially military dictatorships) in the client regimes, and the subsequent shifts of ground, the intellectual hegemony of the Liberal-Orthodox School began to wilt and then crumble away. The attack on its position arose from two[71] main sides, notably from the resurgent neo-Classical and more latterly Supply-Side economists, and from the ranks of the neo-Marxists. To be sure, criticism from these quarters did not suddenly appear in the 1970s: as we have seen, from the Left Paul Baran's trenchant critique dates back to the early 1950s,[72] and from the other wing, the views of that recently ennobled seer P. T. Bauer were first adumbrated nearly 30 years ago.[73] But the tide then running in favour of the Liberal-Orthodox movement was far too strong to be checked, and such sniping action was regarded by the majority as no more than an annoying nuisance. However, for a variety of reasons which lie well beyond the remit of this chapter – and relate more to developments inside the congeries of Western nations (such as the demise of Keynesian Economics) than to Third World matters *per se* – these critiques gained great momentum. From their very different perspectives and in their distinctive ways both approaches started to question the premises, assumptions, models and prescriptions of the dominant tradition, and to provide their own alternatives.

Now although this is not the place to rehearse the respective arguments, perhaps it is worthwhile to point out that whereas the Right has by and large managed to present a generally consistent line, the neo-Marxian position is far more difficult to tie down and characterise. This is because there are almost as many disagreements within the canon as between it and the other two. Thus the nucleus of the neo-Classical view is fairly straightforward and may be conveniently summarised as 'getting the prices right' (to borrow a phrase from Martin Wassell's Preface to Deepak Lal's recent IEA-sponsored Hobart Paperback);[74] in other words it is a plea for the market – rather than the state – solution to resource allocations. The belief in the power of market forces, together with the familiar assumptions of a universally rational utility-maximising economic man, the possibility that such individuals can substitute at the margin, and the use of 'second-best' welfare economics have long featured in the neo-Classical commentary, and indeed many upholders of the 'true faith' have even denied that there is such a thing as a distinctive 'economics of development'. For writers like Deepak Lal,[75] Milton Friedman,[76] Harry Johnson[77] and Peter Bauer,[78] 'good' economics holds whether one is referring to the rural jungles of Amazonia or the concrete jungles of Chicago.[79]

In the recent past the critique centred upon many of the key elements of the Liberal-Orthodox position including dualism, ECLA- and later Structuralist-inspired import substituting industrialisation strategies, protectionism, over-valued currencies, 'inappropriate' technological choice, balanced growth, 'surplus' extraction from agriculture, the alleged zero marginal productivity of farming labour, and two sector models, etc. But over the last 15 years or so, most attention has been specifically directed to a re-examination of the role of the state in the promotion of development. It is possible to identify three sorts of direction to this ensuing research. First, the success of the (varying number[80] of) newly industrialising countries has aroused much interest. Little, Scitovsky and Scott,[81] followed by Jagdish Bhagwati and Padma Desai,[82] Bella Belassa,[83] Louis Turner and N. McMullan,[84] and Ian Little (independently)[85] have all recognised that the case for the Export Promotion growth strategy has necessarily involved both an actively interventionist government and even a first-stage ISI programme.

Second, those members of the Chicago School most interested in the issue of how to effect a fundamental transformation of Third World agricultural and agrarian sectors − primarily associated with the work of Theodore Schultz − have acknowledged a legitimate role for State action.[86] They would countenance intervention in order for the State to make appropriate infrastructural investments in human capital (especially in the sphere of elementary education), to further the dissemination of information (particularly with respect to the biochemical components of Green Revolution technology), to provide complementary non-physical inputs that would normally not be available because their private rates of return are inadequate and are certainly less than their social rates (such as rural extension services) and, where necessary, to purposefully free input and final product markets from natural imperfections and government-made distortions.

Finally, and perhaps closer to the original copy, there are the implications for the Third World arising from the emergence of the new supply-side economics.[87] According to this view governments have been unwise to raise the fiscal burden in order to subsidise (mistaken) development efforts (especially those geared towards fostering industrialisation). Keith Marsden, for example, has endeavoured to show that those Third World countries with relatively low levels of taxation 'outperformed' – in terms of per capita growth rates – 'similar' economies with relatively higher ones;[88] and – more significantly – the IMF has recently arrived at the same sort of conclusions.[89] Now although there are some important elements of contradiction between these ideologically akin areas of study, the basic thrust of the neo-Classical argument is still clear enough, and the Tradition has come a long way from the essentially static and general equilibrium mode of theorising that so displeased the emerging breed of development economists over c. 1945–70. The standing of the new-Right has also immeasurably improved and is not simply confined to pro-Thatcher or pro-Reagan political alignments. Thus the gushingly favourable reception afforded to Deepak Lal's tirade against the *dirigiste dogma* (that he claims has dominated the whole of the development profession) which appears in a recent review in the *Economic Journal* attests to the growing acceptance of this general viewpoint: Walter Elkan's praise is clear enough – the 127-page Hobart Paper is, in his opinion, a 'major contribution to the literature on the problems facing Third World countries', is 'a brilliant display of theory' showing 'an extraordinary mastery of the literature and the facts', and not only does it contain a 'superb' discussion of the debate on planning, but is 'one of the most stimulating books that have appeared for years'.[90] It is doubtful if such an accolade would have been penned (and published in this forum) ten or even five years ago.

For their part, since the mid-1960s the neo-Marxists have spawned a large number of contributions.[91] Following Baran (and not in any real chronological order) we may identify the following approaches: the Dependency School (important aspects of which, of course, derived from the Structuralist perspective)[92] at first dominated by Latin American scholars such as T. Dos Santos, F. Cardoso, O. Sunkel and C. Furtado – but now extended to Africa and the Caribbean; the 'development of underdevelopment' associated with the early[93] best sellers of André Gunder Frank; the core-periphery analysis of Samir Amin; the theory – or rather theories – of unequal exchange whose best-known exponent is A. Emmanuel; the 'World System' theory of Immanuel Wallerstein and his colleagues at the F. Braudel Centre, New York; the rise of the modern TNC as the agent of a new form of imperialism (Hugo Radice and many more); the 'Modes of Production' school (John Taylor, Hamza Alavi and a host of others); the 'New International Division of Labour' school (originally triggered off by Frobel, Heinrichs and Kreye); the Marxian (rather than neo-Marxian) re-emphasis of the importance of class struggle and production relations analysis (Robert Brenner, E. Laclau); the 'Internationalisation of Capital' approach (R. Jenkins, W. Andreff, P. Khvoinik and C. Palloix);[94] the return to a pre-Leninist Marxism which stresses the progressive role of imperialism and capitalist industrialisation (Bill Warren and J. Schiffer); the implications that have been drawn for development studies from the famous 'Transition from Feudalism to Capitalism' Debate;[95] and finally there are a number of sturdily 'independent' Marxist scholars who, crudely speaking, share one important common outlook − a great sense of dissatisfaction with many of the arguments contained in the above-named viewpoints (one is thinking here of writers such as Geoffrey Kay, Nicos Mouzelis, Gavin Kitching, Colin Leys and Henry Bernstein).

The sense of confusion that such an array of diversity invariably provokes would be further compounded if we were also to take proper cognisance of ongoing work in related areas which has an indirect bearing upon our brief − such as that of the philosophers (notably the Althusserians), the structuralist anthropologists (especially French Marxists such as Claude Meillassoux and P. P. Rey), the political scientists (such as E. Laclau and N. Poulantzas) and the more applied batch of studies on the economies of the newer parts of the Communist bloc. Now although only the most ideologically hostile of observers would be reluctant to concede that this outpouring of literature offered many valuable insights into the range of problems that confront the Third World, the very proliferation of competing ideas must surely be a source of genuine confusion to 'insiders' as well as to sympathetic 'outsiders'. This is recognised all too clearly by several writers from within the Tradition: Anthony Brewer, Colin Leys, Nicos Mouzelis, Phil Leeson, Peter Worsley and Henry Bernstein − to name but six − have all gone on record to express their dismay at the failure of neo-Marxism to present a coherent and unambiguous point of view.[96] Indeed the last-named author has greatly regretted the tendency to advance a bewilderingly large number of 'concepts and means of explanation' such as 'advanced underdevelopment, ultra-under-development, unequal development, lumpen development, dependent development, dependent bourgeoisie, lumpen bourgeoisie, comprador bourgeoisie, semi-colonial, neo-colonial, post-colonial, neo-imperialism, sub-imperialism, sub-metropole, semi-periphery',[97] etc., etc. That said, however, it remains true that the neo-Marxian and Marxian assault on Liberal-Orthodoxy (and, of course, neo-Classical economics in general)[98] has not only gained many fresh adherents − witness the popularity of Frank's books − but has left a deep imprint on the general course of development studies.

How have the Liberal developmentalists reacted to this two-pronged broadside, and how has it affected their claim to Orthodoxy? First of all we should note that to date there is little evidence of a constructive interchange between the opposing sides. Dispute has not so much led to debate and lively controversy − perhaps because the gulf between the respective positions is too deep to allow for genuine dialogue − as it has to what Phil Leeson calls 'stultifying defensiveness'.[99] Nor, in my view, has it caused a 'congruence' of traditions as Dudley Seers once argued.[100] What has happened, however, is that those academics interested in writing text-books have either had to openly nail their colours to the mast and forward an internally consistent argument from one or other vantage point, or to try to somehow present a 'balanced' picture of the respective Traditions. Neither course of action is entirely satisfactory and the (potential) student readers may be forgiven for feeling rather bemused.[101] Indeed, any claim to authentic 'text-book' status at this juncture seems to me to be extremely dubious. This, of course, is hardly unique to Development Studies or Development Economics as the clutch of Radical 'anti-'type texts − which have been a feature of social sciences since the late 1960s − attests. What is different though is that the hitherto dominant Liberal-Orthodox Tradition does not seem strong enough to put up as effective centre-ground resistance as it has managed to do elsewhere (e.g. in mainstream economics). Moreover, on account of its long-standing prescriptive orientation, the resulting uncertainty reaches far beyond the confines of academic disputation. It is a matter of no little consequence that instead of being in a position to celebrate the entry into a fifth decade of existence by adumbrating solid achievements, parading a record of successes and evincing evidence of intellectual strength-in-depth, the Liberal developmentalists are short on confidence and still facing an unremitting barrage of criticism which is proving difficult to deflect − let alone effectively answer.

Two further influences gnawing away at the Liberal position may be identified. In the first place the link between the different development subject disciplines has begun to look increasingly tenuous. In the early days the case for mounting an interdisciplinary effort seemed logical, sensible and perfectly feasible. Writers such as Bert Hoselitz (who pioneered the explicitly inter-disciplinary journal *Economic Development and Cultural Change*),[102] Everett Hagen, Gunnar Myrdal and Albert Hirschman argued that the process of economic change in the LDCs could hardly be seriously studied without recourse to understanding the given socio-cultural milieu. They therefore recommended that it was desirable either to engage the services of interested social scientist colleagues and form a team of researchers, teachers and project consultants, or for economists to learn new skills and develop a familiarity with specific aspects of other relevant disciplines. (It was never, of course, suggested that this should include highly technical subject areas like agronomy, climatology, hydrology, ecology and all types of engineering.) However, although some real progress was made on a number of fronts – particularly development education – the formidable methodological and practical difficulties that such exercises invariably throw up have never been satisfactorily resolved: and sceptics such as Michael Lipton and Colin Leys have, in their very different ways, demonstrated the inherent weaknesses of the actual inter-disciplinary road.[103] Perhaps it is worthy of mention too that this failure has not only been a feature of the Liberal Tradition: there have not, at least to my mind, been many conspicuous examples of cross-disciplinary work emanating from the Radicals.[104]

The second 'undermining' factor is rather more recent in origin, largely exogenous to the discipline and, without a doubt, the most damaging. I refer, of course, to the changing climate of opinion within the West – especially in the UK and the USA – towards the Third World in general and to Development Studies in particular. Following the lurch into recession in the mid-1970s, there has been a notable lack of enthusiasm with regard to even maintaining the earlier level of resource flows into all forms of economic aid[105] and the funding of academic research. Mirroring the downgrading of the Overseas Development Portfolio, there has been a substantial reduction in the amount of public money being earmarked for a large number of institutions and causes which are devoted – in one way or another – to the development effort itself, and to its study. This has threatened the viability of both the specialist centres of learning such as the Institute of Development Studies at Sussex[106] and also the work of many individuals and programmes based elsewhere. Problems 'closer-to-home' now have a prior and favoured claim to financial allocations, and the research councils have a conscious bias towards supporting only those projects which are deemed to be 'relevant' for the particular country's own (short-term) interests.[107] Furthermore, the widespread tendency to attribute the de-industrialisation of parts of Europe and America to the 'unfair' competitive pressures emanating from the Third World (or rather a small part thereof) does not bode well for future allocations of resources. If the reaction of the central government (in the UK) to the visibly horrific scenes of mass starvation in Ethiopia, the Sudan and Chad over 1984–5 has been profoundly disappointing (which goes well beyond the failure to waive the VAT levy on the Band Aid record and on tickets for the Live Aid concert!), there is not much room for optimism with respect to the future treatment of the academic development lobby.

Faced with these sorts of growing pressures the Liberal (now not so Orthodox) School has been forced to retreat[108] and re-group. This has taken several forms. First there has been a wide-ranging enquiry into the history of this Tradition. In my opinion the basic purpose of these forays[109] is to determine what has gone wrong and why, and whether anything can be salvaged − rather than being a disinterested attempt to obtain 'knowledge for its own sake'. Second, there has been a 'branching-off' effect. After having declared the 'death' of Development Economics (as it was over 1945−75) Professor Seers − one of the intellectual spearheads of the field, a founder-member of the IDS, an advisor to many Third World governments, and a key figure in the creation of the UK Ministry of Overseas Development − together with some of his colleagues in Sussex and elsewhere, have argued that the way forward is to apply some of the tools and techniques of the Tradition to the states on the 'periphery' of Europe (especially Iberia, Greece, Yugoslavia and even Wales, Scotland, N. Ireland and Eire).[110] Third, a desire to 'return to the fold' of neo-Classical and perhaps Keynesian economics has begun to surface. In recent years distinguished developmentalists such as Sir Arthur Lewis, Ian Livingstone, Paul Streeten and Sanjay Lall have suggested that the discipline may have lost its moorings due to its concentration upon the special features and unique characteristics of Third World economies; and they have also started to rethink the parallel notion that much standard economic theory was inapplicable to non-Western settings simply because it had been born elsewhere.[111] Fourth, apart from the movement to the Basic Needs approach, a number of new research orientations has emerged. Among the most noteworthy have been Lance Taylor's work on Structuralist Macroeconomics;[112] A. K. Sen's generalised theory of exchange entitlements;[113] and Irma Adelman's rather convoluted ADLI (i.e., agricultural, demand-led industrialisation) strategy.[114] It is clearly too early to say whether any one − or combination − of these and other such initiatives can reinvigorate Liberal Development Economics, but one suspects that the omens are not promising − if only because they do not seem to me to possess the necessary breadth or the 'kiss of life' quality that now seems to be required to effect an all-round resuscitation of the ailing patient.

What then are we to conclude from all this? It is my contention that a widely defined Development or Underdevelopment Economics is now in a state of virtual hiatus. Since so much intellectual capital has been sunk into it, and given the fact that there is still an important − though declining – effective demand for it both at home and in the Third World itself it seems probable that it will continue to survive – but not I suspect in its present confused form. Not only do we have three competing theoretical traditions (of which at least two are unwieldy aggregations of several separate threads), but we also have a curious mixture of positive, normative, prescriptive, idealistic, quasi-Eurocentric, narrowly technical, extremely universalistic, materialistic, qualitative and quantitative entities to juggle with.[115] The task of clarifying and ultimately moving towards some sort of resolution to the conflicts, divisions and conundrums that have been mentioned above is daunting – and no one person can hope to get very far. So it is in the spirit of furthering the debate that I offer what I see as one of the most promising ways forward which, paradoxically, takes us back towards an investigation of long-run historical forces.

III

THE CASE FOR A 'HISTORICAL DIMENSION'

1. *Preliminary Observations*

Before I commence to argue the case for the entry of an explicitly 'historical dimension' into the lexicon of Development Studies in general and Development Economics in particular, let me first offer a brief definition – to be further elaborated later on – of what I take the term to mean, and then follow this up with a number of important disclaimers. Since the general spirit of this essay is suggestive rather than didactic, and given the enormity and complexity of the literature addressed to probing the question of 'what is history?',[116] it is not my intention to embark upon a long metaphysical disquisition on the subject of what precisely constitutes a 'historical dimension'. Instead let me propose a simple – but I hope not simplistic – working definition along the following lines. To my mind there are two crucial components of such a dimension which, as a first approximation, are most easily labelled as the 'materialist' and the 'idealist' – or, to put the distinction in terms less offensive to the professional philosophers, 'events' and 'ideas'.[117] In our particular context, the former involves a critical consideration of the major changes that have taken place in the world – and specifically the Third World – economy over the last two centuries or so; and the latter refers to the manner in which such changes have been perceived and analysed. This loose – but open – formulation can be further reduced to being a study of modern economic history allied with a purposeful enquiry into the history of economic thought and doctrine as it relates to the causes, the course, and the consequences of long-run change. Put in this way, the major historical controversies revolving around, *inter alia*, the nature of the inter-relationship between 'action' and 'thought', the role of the individual, and the primacy − or otherwise − of economic forces (the substructure in the Marxian nomenclature) over the political, legal, social, cultural and diplomatic (superstructural) ones,[118] may be conveniently sidestepped − at least for the purpose of this exercise.

If − by the title of the paper, or by the implications of the views that have so far been advanced, or even by the section heading itself − I have given the impression that an injection of a historical dimension will somehow act as a *deus ex machina*, let me start with an immediate disclaimer. However we might choose to characterise the nature of the economic problems that now confront the underdeveloped world, what is reasonably clear − at least to all but the most dogmatic ideologues [119] − is that they cannot be quickly, easily or painlessly 'solved'. Now although academic study and discourse undoubtedly has an important − albeit indirect[120] − role to play, given the host of 'internal' factors at work such as the confused state of the tradition with the greatest claim to Orthodox status, the pronounced scholarly divisions and the swingeing financial cutbacks − as well as the play of more 'external' forces such as the rise of new forms of economic nationalism, the growth of 'self-reliant' development strategies (which occasionally, as in Ne Win's Burma, Seke Toure's Guinea and Pol Pot's Cambodia, verges on autarchy), and the natural desire of indigenously-trained scholars to forge independent paths 'specifically relevant' to particular countries in the Third World itself, Liberal Development Economics is unlikely to exert the same kind of sway that it enjoyed during the halcyon period of c. 1945−1975. Thus any fresh scholarly initiative − such as the one being proposed here − is no more likely to tackle the real on-the-ground issues than it is to completely resolve the intellectual and ideological differences: indeed one can well sympathise with any latent resistance to the parading of yet another potential fashion − whatever its merits may be. Furthermore, far from attracting greater infusions of scarce research funds, the proposal outlined below is probably more likely than not to fall upon unresponsive ears since, in the present climate at least, there is an emphasis upon the practical, the problem-solving, and the technocratic 'solutions' which are thought to yield an immediate pay-off (not least for the Western economies).

In addition to this fundamental *caveat emptor*, it is necessary to clear the ground of a number of other possible misconceptions. First, however elastically we may choose to define a historical dimension, and however sympathetic some of us may be towards the 'history as a servant of the present' view, it obviously cannot be regarded as a narrowly operational subject with its own distinctive 'box of tools'. Let us imagine we can eavesdrop on a committee meeting of some typical project planning forum in an LDC. The constitution of the membership is unlikely to include a historian *qua* historian. Besides the administrators and political nominees, and depending upon the precise purpose of the authority in question, there might be civil engineers, accountants, hydrologists, agronomists, soil scientists, ecologists, health planners, micro-economists, etc. etc. Each of these − with the possible exception of the first two − would be able to bring to bear on the deliberations a bank of specialist knowledge and an array of highly specific skills. But should the professional historian be co-opted to serve, it is doubtful if he/she would be in a position to contribute to the proceedings in the same way as the technocrats. Not only would the institution of itself be rather foreign, but the usually narrow terms of reference would exclude the kind of general 'input' that I hope to show is at least as important to the overall realisation of 'development' as any of the other subjects mentioned above. Clearly the role will be different in that it focuses more upon developing a comprehension of change over the long run − and is therefore closer to peer disciplines such as Social Anthropology, which also adopts a 'perceptive' rather than a 'curative' approach.[121]

Second, I do not see a historical dimension as being a substitute for abstract reasoning, theorising and model-building. As Donald McCloskey has argued in another − but analogous − context (that of economic history to neo-Classical economic theory),[122] both types of approach can be considered as being complementary − and not competitive − paths towards one common goal. Third, I do not subscribe to the view that the study of history yields up a set of immutable 'lessons' which are valid for all time and all places.[123] Irrespective of whether this sentiment is expressed openly or more subtly, or whether it is couched in the guise of a series of unilinear 'stages' or in terms of the cruder sort of economic determinism associated with at least one branch of the Marxian tradition (to wit that based in the USSR's Academy of Economic Science), I suspect that few modern historians feel comfortable with it. The rejection of 'historicism' does not, of course, imply that no general pattern of change can be gleaned from a study of history − especially one which deliberately starts out with a specific purpose in mind. Fourth, and this is directly related to the last point, I am not advocating a

casual 'appropriation of history' by those who merely seek to add
credence to a given view that has already been long developed. What
I principally have in mind here are the 'grand theories' – such as
those of Walt Rostow originating from the modernisation (and anti-
communist) school, and those of the likes of André Gunder Frank
from the Radical Left – which, by their appeal to a very selective
sort of history, purport to be of direct contemporary relevance. As
I hope to show, this kind of work has probably had a counter-
productive effect, and in my view has done no little damage to the
cause of legitimising a historical dimension.

It should now be clear that I am not advancing the argument that
a historical dimension is some sort of panacea, and that it is capable
of resolving all the problems we have discussed. On the contrary,
I believe that the study of 'development' – like 'development' itself
– is a hard slog, however we view its basic essence and whatever
its various manifestations. A historical dimension offers no short
cut: indeed its main value may well be the insight that 'development'
is invariably a long, arduous, uphill struggle.[124] But before we turn
to a consideration of its utility in a more formal and explicit sense
let us review the way in which those concerned with development
have used, abused, or simply ignored the historical dimension. Let
us begin with a short discussion of those in the driving-seat of the
development effort, i.e., the Third World politicians. Rather than
attempt to generalise over the entire spectrum, and given the fact
that comparatively little work has been done on identifying the
intellectual origins of the development nostrums of the major political
figures, parties and groupings as they relate to the 'social function
of the past' (to paraphrase from Eric Hobsbawn),[125] let us concentrate upon the area with which I am most familiar, that of India.

2. *The Case of India*

In point of fact, even if we put convenience to one side, this is an
extraordinarily useful case to highlight since many of the most
powerful subcontinental politicians of this century have been acutely
'aware' of history. In large measure of course this consciousness
derived from the very length of time of foreign rule and the relative
venerability of the consequent anti-colonial struggle. Indeed, the first
stirring of a vocal and coherent stream of Nationalist writing even
pre-dates the establishment of the Indian National Congress (which
celebrated its centenary in December 1985). As long ago as 1871 that
'Grand Old Man of Indian Nationalism', Dadabhai Naoriji, published
his seminal study of the causes of Indian poverty[126] and this marked
the start of a veritable flowering of work – surely the earliest example

of a now voluminous genre — addressed to what we might nowadays call the 'economics of long-run development failure'. It was upon the foundation stones laid by the likes of Naoriji's successors — L.S.G. Tilak, M.R. Ranade, R.C. Dutt, William Digby and others — that the Nationalist School and the INC built up their case.[127] By the early twentieth century the argument had been extended, refined and had become a crucial part of the political process — finding expression in the *Swadeshi* (boycott of imported manufactures) and *Swaraj* (self-government) Movements, and subsequently in Gandhi's famous campaigns.[128] Of course the claims of these writers did not go unchallenged: in view of their damaging and potentially explosive political implications a clear-headed defence of the economic record of the Raj was called for — with the chorus of rebuttal being led by no less a figure than the then Viceroy, Lord Curzon.[129] In this way 'history' itself became politicised and for a time the battle between Nationalists and Apologists (with the Marxists also entering the lists a bit later on)[130] raged almost as much over the interpretation of the past as it did about the analysis of the present and future; and not surprisingly in such circumstances polemics tended to take precedence over scholarship. Thus when Independence was finally gained in 1947 the INC leadership had already been exposed to many decades of fiercely partisan historical disputation. It was therefore almost inevitable that 'history' should somehow figure in modern development thinking — especially because the Party in general and the Nehru 'dynasty' in particular exerted such a degree of dominance at all levels of India's body politic.[131] I think that it is possible to clearly identify a number of important general perceptions about the past which undoubtedly influenced both the choice and form of development strategy taken after 1947. These include the following notions:

1. On the eve of her Independence India's lack of 'all-round' economic development and the resultant poverty problem was largely attributable to the longevity and nature of colonial rule.

2. The pre-British period was regarded as being something of an economic 'Golden Age': thus for Romesh Chandra Dutt, writing at the turn of the twentieth century, India had been 'a great manufacturing as well as a great agricultural country, and the products of the Indian loom supplied the markets of Asia and Europe';[132] and for a more modern Nationalist, R.S. Sharma, 'before the advent of the Europeans, especially during the 17th and 18th Centuries, India was the industrial workshop of the world'.[133] For Mahatma Gandhi, of course, the relevance of many — but not all[134] — of the pre-colonial economic institutions (such as

agricultural self-sufficiency, the spinning-wheel, decentralised government, harmonious patron–client relationships) for the brave new world that was to follow, was self-evident.[135]

3. Even after the achievement of political sovereignty a great many of the structures (e.g. the land tenure system), organisations (such as the managing agency firms), and attitudes (the anti-business bias of the ICS and its successor, the IAS) long regarded as inimical to long-run development necessarily carried over and, because they had taken root over many years, were extremely difficult to eradicate or change as swiftly as the early planners would surely have liked.

4. Both the Partition settlement itself – the culmination of the divide-and-rule policy – and the untidy and ultimately divisive arrangements concerning the integration of the erstwhile Princely States into the Union (especially pronounced in the cases of Kashmir and Hyderabad) had negative long-run as well as disruptive short-term consequences, witness the military hostility between India and Pakistan and the expensive pension rights meted out to the former maharajas, nawabs, etc.

5. The idea that the market had proved to be a wholly inadequate vehicle for effecting development in that:

(i) internally, the laissez-faire stance of the nineteenth-century state had greatly inhibited the potential of the economy to grow and develop along the lines say of Prussia/Germany, Meiji Japan or even late-Czarist Russia, and indeed was responsible for the 'de-industrialisation' of the economy;[136] and that the limited interventionism after 1919 (the Government of India's new 'industrial policy' for example)[137] had been 'too little, too late' to propel India into an industrial revolution.

(ii) Externally, the Free Trade policy of the last two-thirds of the nineteenth century[138] had transformed India's economy in that (*a*) the commodity and geographical pattern of India's trade had been changed so that she became the classic exporter of primary produce and raw materials and an importer of finished manufactured goods (mainly from Britain); (*b*) her balance of trade surpluses allowed for a 'massive outflow of funds'[139] which went towards meeting the foreign obligations of the East India Company and later the Government of India – the infamous 'Home Charges' element of the 'drain' of wealth;[140] and (*c*) making India a key component of Britain's entire pre-1914 international payments system;[141] and that when a degree of tariff autonomy was granted after the First World War via the policy of discriminating protection,[142] it had been totally inadequate to generate a healthy, balanced and sustainable industrial base.

6. The INC were highly dubious of the net benefits that allegedly accrued to India as a result of unrestricted foreign inflows of capital, and of foreign ownership, control and management of her industries and commerce. Amongst other things it was alleged that this had led to:

   (*a*) the highly uneven spread of modern industry – with most of the factories and plant being largely confined to the Presidency towns;

   (*b*) the 'wrong' choice of investment in the social overheads – with 'too much' going to the railways and 'too little' to irrigation;

   (*c*) the fact that the railways were more orientated towards overseas – rather than internal – markets;

   (*d*) the bias in favour of the purchase of stores from abroad, especially from the country supplying the bulk of the capital investment – the UK.

7. The lack of indigenous control over the determination of the exchange rate had worked against both Indian industry and commercial-crop producers.

8. That through various direct and indirect mechanisms the imperial authority had not only practised a form of discrimination between Europeans and the indigenous population, but had deliberately helped to create an extraordinarily wealthy and powerful entrenched class of monopoly capitalists (such as the Parsis) in both industry and trade.

9. The contention that the agricultural sector had been grievously damaged over the entire imperial epoch as a result of a combination of mistaken policies (the propping-up of a parasitic class of compliant, quasi-feudal landlords and their functionaries), a ruinously high and rigidly inflexible fiscal burden (the Land Revenue demand), the absence of an effectual and humane position on famines (with regard to both its prevention and mitigation) and, not least, sheer neglect (as evinced, say, in the failure to promote any substantive programme of agronomic research).

The reason why I have thought it worthwhile to parade these ideas at some length – although this summary hardly does proper justice to a complex tradition of thought[143] – is that either directly or indirectly and in one form or other they all found their way into the key development nostrums of the post-Independence period. Those reasonably familiar with the immediate post-Independence history of India (say up to the end of the Second Five-Year Plan) will not find it difficult to recognise the source of inspiration of a great many of the basic principles and characteristic policies of that era.[144] Most of these notions had some sort of prescriptive correlate and could be readily translated into a set of tasks to be done – or things to be avoided. Thus numbers 1, 3, 4 and 9 could always be wheeled out to provide an excellent excuse/justification for development failure, frustration, or its slow, halting progress;[145] no. 2 could be deployed to appeal to some pre-colonial 'norm' in order to legitimise a distinctively indigenous form of development,[146] and also to pump resources into the ailing handicraft sector; no. 4 could be used to justify heavy expenditure upon defence; no. 5 (i) meant planning – especially for heavy and machinery-to-make machinery industrialisation strategies; no's. 5 (ii), 6 and 7 authorised controls and licensing; no. 8 demonstrated the need to regulate the activities of the likes of the Tatas and the Birlas; and no. 9 was catholic enough to warrant sweeping land reforms (to the Zamindary system for instance) and, paradoxically, a squeeze on the sector to obtain the surplus currently being 'squandered', and – later on – a massive infusion of fresh resources in the hope of promoting technological change (a Green Revolution). The policies that India did adopt then influenced – to varying degrees – many of the countries that gained their independence after her, and so the rather unique degree of historical awareness exhibited by the INC transcended – albeit in a diluted way – the subcontinental experience *per se.*

However, I am not suggesting that the version of history as put out by the Nationalists and the INC is the most reliable and accurate. Indeed, once independence had been won and the decks cleared of politically inspired dispute it became possible to study the past in a fuller and altogether less encumbered intellectual environment. Since 1947 an increasing (that is until quite recently) number of scholars both in India and around the world are devoting their careers to researching and ultimately challenging the interpretation of Indian economic and social history as put forward by Nationalist (and other) writers.[148] Monographs,[149] specialist journals,[150] bibliographical studies,[151] guides to the sources, archives and statistical data banks,[152] occasional symposia and regular conferences[153] and, most recently, the publication of the *Cambridge Economic History of India*[154] all testify to a growing curiosity and a deeper sense of professionalism. Influenced by the considerable theoretical advances and new techniques that have been developed over the last two decades or so, historians and some social scientists are starting to do the necessary empirical spadework, to critically re-examine traditional viewpoints, to expose shibboleths, and to pose entirely new sets of questions. As the scope, scale and sophistication of these endeavours gathers momentum a firmer, better anchored and more balanced picture has emerged, and already there are signs that many of the older views are no longer really tenable and cannot now be accepted.[155] Indeed, since the appearance of Morris David Morris's iconoclastic article in the *Journal of Economic History* in the early 1960s[156] and the succeeding furore generated by his attempt to re-interpret much of the Nationalists' position[157] – a debate which gave a major fillip to research enquiry and which is by no means dead today[158] – the proliferation of work has been so marked as to warrant a flurry of publications seeking to take stock of the new insights and to place specialist advance within a much broader context.[159] By its very nature these newer and certainly more dis-interested versions do not lend themselves nearly as readily to partisan appropriation as the older: the purpose, method of approach, depth, thoroughness, statistical knowledge and the entire writing environ-ment now differ enormously from that pertaining during the first half of the century.

But this, of course, is only a variant of the common generation-gap problem that everywhere faces historians of all types of persuasion. By the time a more precise interpretation of the past does become available the issues have long since lost their immediacy and general importance – at least as far as most contemporary politicians are concerned. As we approach the 40th anniversary of India's indepen-dence it seems most unlikely that Rajiv Gandhi and his colleagues[160] should regard the events and ideas of the 1950s and 1960s – much less the pre-1947 period – with anything other than passing interest and attention. Quite simply the well researched history of, say, the colonial era is perceived to be of little or no practical or operational significance: after all the problems of the present (whatever their origins) are considered to be formidable enough – and occupy so much scarce time and personnel – as it is. We therefore arrive at the predictable conclusion that even in the somewhat atypical case of India non-polemical history plays relatively little part in the development thinking of most Third World politicians. We next turn to consider whether this contrasts with the academics.

3. *Development Paradigms and History*

(a) *Neo-classicism*

Let us first examine the neo-Classical position since this is the least ambiguous and the most easily dealt with. The basic point must surely be that the Tradition has always been consciously ahistorical. From its commencement in the 1870s the essential orientation of the work of the heirs to Leon Walras, Carl Menger and Stanley Jevons has been deductive theorising. Now although progressively fewer numbers of modern students are aware of the reasons for this – history of economic thought courses are unfortunately no longer a standard part of the undergraduate diet – in one respect at least they are germane to our purposes here. The founding fathers of what has become known as the Marginalist Revolution set their sights upon the economics of short-run equilibrium analysis mainly because they considered that the long-run development problem had been solved (at least for the countries of Western Europe and the USA), and so for them the fear of the coming of the 'stationary state' had long since been banished. Thus the issues which had so preoccupied the Classicals and, of course, Karl Marx, were no longer thought to be very important. Later on, and as the Tradition evolved after Alfred Marshall, something of a split opened up between those economists primarily interested in theory and those who sought to apply the most recent theoretical postulates to particular economies and particular situations. Most of the applied work was directed at the Western experience but gradually a set of propositions emerged which – their authors claimed – transcended national frontiers and even 'historical time' – thus Professor John Hicks was able to elaborate what he called *A Theory of Economic History*,[161] and Professors North and Thomas have recently focused on a very long time horizon.[162]

As we have seen, it was this claim of universality which so offended those post-1945 economists who began to specialise in the economics of the emerging Third World states. Their rejection of many neo-Classical ideas has in turn now been challenged, and it is interesting to note that one element (admittedly occupying only a relatively small part) of the recent critique of Development Economics has involved a focus upon the historical record. Such stalwarts of the neo-Classical stance as Deepak Lal, Ian Little and Theodore Schultz have tried to show that 'history on their side' in the sense that an examination of certain aspects of the past fully vindicates the more important neo-Classical precepts. Thus both Lal[163] and Little[164] quite independently have made brief excursions into the course of modern history in order to demonstrate the developmental virtues of free markets and to refute those 'historical perceptions' which 'are the product of influential rationalist and Marxist writings'.[165] In view of what we have said earlier about the importance of the Indian case it is no accident that both authors have chosen to cast their respective eyes upon the subcontinent. They contest the charge that the free trade regime operative in India during the nineteenth century had thwarted or even partially limited the process of industrialisation; they adamantly deny the de-industrialisation thesis as it applies to the handicraft sector; and they maintain that the inter-war policy of discriminating protection grievously damaged the growth potential of the factory-based industries. As a flavour of the argument we may quote Lal who writes that 'the fortunes of the Indian textile industry, which under laissez-faire and free trade had so triumphantly turned the tables against Lancashire in the second half of the 19th century, provide one of the best cautionary tales to illustrate the central message of this *Hobart Paper*';[166] that the tariff of the 1920s and 1930s resulted in a 'waste of resources' and 'imposed lower growth in both employment and industrial output than was feasible';[167] and, warming to one of his major preoccupations, he goes on to claim that 'the troubles of the Indian textile industry arose from the introduction in 1881 ... of legislation to protect industrial workers from perceived abuses ... and whereas the Japanese textile industry was built on using female labour working two shifts a day, the Bombay industry was hamstrung by labour laws which forbade such long working hours'.[168] So, in just four and a half short pages and relying upon a carefully selected and tiny sample of the total number of possible reference sources[169] — including a draft manuscript written by Lal himself entitled *Cultural Stability and Economic Stagnation — India c. 1500 B.C. — 1980 A.D.*[170] — our 'authority' has made enormously sweeping claims (some of a counter-factual nature which have never been argued through anywhere — and least of all here), ridiculed the work of many scholars (whom, on the basis of what appears in this publication one doubts he has ever taken the trouble to read) and ignored the work of those with whom he patently disagrees: in short, he has abandoned all the accepted standards of scholarship. To offer an interpretation of history based upon a close, balanced, and reasonably comprehensive perusal of the available secondary literature is one thing; but to engage in this sort of 'history' is surely folly of the first order and can only be counter-productive. Thus Lal's 'refutation' of artisal de-industrialisation is utterly simplistic and altogether unconvincing — not only has he failed to appreciate the problematic and ambiguous nature of the primary evidence, but he has totally disregarded the findings of modern research.[171] The same could be said for his assertions on the tariff and the question of labour conditions in the textile mills.[172] Professor Little's foray into the subject, though a mite longer and written in a more circumspect manner, suffers from similar blemishes.[173]

Similarly, but in a slightly different context, Professor Schultz has also invoked the (Indian) past in order to pour scorn upon development economics in general and the notion of unemployed and underemployed rural labour in particular.[174] For Schultz the proposition that the marginal productivity of labour tends towards zero collapses when subjected to the acid test of empirical verification. He argues that the prediction of the Lewis and the Ranis and Fei models[175] is found seriously wanting when set against the historical experience of Indian agriculture following the influenza epidemic of 1917–18. However, as A.K. Sen and others have shown,[176] a fuller investigation of the events following the outbreak does not disprove the notion at all: a more careful perusal of the data yields a quite different perspective and that – at best – Schultz's test is 'quite inconclusive'.[177] These observations on this mini-controversy are designed neither to uphold nor reject the original hypothesis (indeed so much water has passed under the surplus labour bridge since the mid-1960s that it would now be quite absurd to judge the issue on this particular case): rather it is meant to suggest that in this instance Schultz's use of history is deeply problematical and highly tendentious. This is a rather unfortunate verdict on two counts. First, his pioneering work on human capital formation has undoubtedly enriched the potential conceptual framework and even vocabulary of those engaged in full-time historical research, and second, in his recent writing – including the Nobel Lecture delivered in December 1979[178] – Schultz has placed on record his lament that many economists have, to their – and our – cost, neglected economic history. Certainly I would wholeheartedly concur with his view that

> Understanding the experience and achievements of poor people over the ages can contribute much to our understanding the problems and possibilities of low-income countries today. That kind of understanding is far more important than the most detailed and exact knowledge about the surface of the earth, or of ecology, or of tomorrow's technology.[179]

And again, I have little to quarrel with the statement that

> Historical perception is also lacking with respect to population. We extrapolate global statistics and are horrified by our interpretation of them, mainly that poor people breed like lemmings headed toward their own destruction. Yet that is not what happened looking back at our own social and economic history when people were poor. It is equally false with respect to population growth in today's poor countries.[180]

But whilst I would readily second Theodore Schultz's eloquent pleas for a greater input of economic history into the neo-Classical frame of reference – echoed elsewhere by Professors Henry Phelps-Brown, Douglass North and Donald McCloskey[181] (in order to provide, *pace* the last named authority, 'more economic facts'; 'better economic facts'; 'better economic theory'; 'better economic policy' and 'better economists'),[182] and also accept that this application has clearly yielded some useful – if rather limited – insights (such as the demonstration that in some countries at certain points of time in the past, and in a variety of different circumstances, peasants have responded in the 'predicted way' to change in product prices),[183] I have two interrelated reservations about this call. First and most obviously, if history is 'taken up' in a cavalier and quite unsystematic way (*pace* Deepak Lal) and deployed to simply try to validate a given *a priori* argument (Schultz), there are real dangers of the record being grossly distorted. Further problems occur if history is interpreted within a very narrow conspectus – be it in terms of either a very short time horizon or with respect to a set of Western norms. Examples of what I have in mind here include the recent focus upon the NIC phenomena (which has been largely restricted to the last two decades and in the case of South Korea and Taiwan – the two flagships – without much recognition of either the crucial role played by Japanese imperialism or the important state-building initiatives of the 1940s and 1950s),[184] the tendency to concentrate upon those areas and issues which have an unimpeachable data base,[185] and the Eurocentrism of Schultz's agricultural and demographic models of development change.[186] My second reservation concerns the inherent limitations of the neo-Classical methodology. Though the tradition prides itself upon its theoretical ubiquity, in my view it is not at all clear that non-altruistic behaviour, utility maximisation 'rationality', individual free exchanges, harmony of interests between different classes (on a national basis let alone as between different countries at very different stages of development at the international level), perfect certainty, automatic market clearing mechanisms, the possibility of effecting a multitude of marginal transactions and adjustments, the existence of a clear division between economic and non-economic activity, and all the other postulates of the canon, are generally valid over long periods of historical time and in specifically Third World environments. This of course was at the root of the departure from the Orthodoxy led by the early developmentalists; and it remains an even more telling issue as far as most historians are concerned.

(b) *Marxism and Neo-Marxism*

If I am correct in thinking that the study of history has had only a very minor role to play in the evolution of neo-Classical doctrine, and if the application of such doctrine to illuminate the past has really only just begun to be deemed respectable (largely through the work of the New Economic Historians or Cliometricians on selected aspects of the growth of the Western – rather than the Third World – economies), then the contrast with the Marxian and neo-Marxian tradition can scarcely be greater. From Marx and Engels onwards the very starting point of enquiry has been dialectical materialism, and the classification and analysis of different historical stages remains an integral part of the methodology.[187] As is well known, according to this approach it is necessary above all to delineate those underlying forces revolving around the ownership and control of the means of production which exist in the history of all societies in order to determine the manner in which they function and evolve. For many Marxists the notion that different social formations can be most meaningfully analysed through the development of a mode of production is a key part in laying bare the forces which operate in a constant process of reproduction. The interplay of a mode's two constituent parts (which vary in relative importance depending upon the particular stage of development), namely, the forces of production – mankind's fashioning of the natural environment – and the relations of production – the relationship between the class that owns the means of production and the rest – provides the explanation of the fundamental structures and relations underpinning all societies throughout known history. This framework has been deployed to examine a variety of pre-capitalist modes and the rise of capitalism (in its various Merchant, Industrial and Monopoly-Imperialist phases). The process whereby one stage gives way to another (culminating of course in communism) is called 'development' – and in our context it is important to stress that this meaning differs sharply from that of the other traditions. So in principle at least there can be no divide between history and development: indeed quite the contrary, development *is* history. Moreover, by its very nature, this history and development cannot be artificially chopped up into 'economic', 'political', 'diplomatic', 'social', 'dynastic', etc., segmentations: though material changes are at the base of all other types of change, they articulate together within a holistic frame of reference.

Now while it is incontrovertible that most Marxists and neo-Marxists regard historical materialism as central to their work, the application of the method to the study of the history of the Third World has by no means proved to be very straightforward. Without going into this longstanding and rather thorny question in any real depth,[188] I would argue that there are probably three main reasons for this. First, the rather high level of abstraction informing the various modes of production has given rise to a great variety of different – and not infrequently conflicting – readings of concrete situations. Thus within the general debate concerning the whole mode of production controversy[189] – perhaps the classic instance of internal division – there is a basic lack of clarity and an overall sense of uncertainty with regard both to theoretical issues, and to more applied ones such as the characterisation of Indian agriculture,[190] and the notion of a specifically 'colonial' mode of production.[191] Despite many attempts to reconcile the differences between the respective contributors to both the debates, fundamental divisions remain profound. Second, and clearly related to the first issue, is the seemingly endless seam of controversy surrounding the Asiatic Mode of Production. Though an enormous literature has now built up on and around Marx's original formulation[192] (which of course geographically transcends Asia itself) it seems to me that we are still a very long way from achieving anything like consensus on its meaning, its core characteristics, its historical 'accuracy', its generality and least of all its significance. Third, the basic division between 'paleo-' and neo-Marxism has important and ongoing implications for historical analysis. Specifically, the early twentieth century Marxist theories of imperialism developed by Kautsky (1902– 1909),[193] Luxemburg (1913),[194] Bukharin (1915),[195] Lenin (1916),[196] and, much later, Paul Sweezy (1942)[197] only briefly touched upon the particular experience of the then less developed colonial world. For them the paramount phenomenon that required extended analysis was the very fabric of monopoly capitalism – especially how the system has changed since Marx's day – and hence most attention was devoted to the economics of the 'motor' countries which then, of course, were almost exclusively located in the Western hemisphere.[198] With the honourable – but still partial – exception of Chapters 27–31 of Luxemburg's *Accumulation of Capital* and, stretching the point further, Trotsky's notion of 'uneven and combined development',[199] the coverage of the international spread or 'outreach' of capitalism signally failed to incorporate a distinctive Third World dimension. Aside from the quite perfunctory attempt by the Third International and the Comintern to address this issue within the admittedly far wider political content of whether or not to lend support to various struggles of national liberation, there was little sustained thought given to this subject: clearly the minds of the Marxist intelligentsia during this period were concentrated upon the formidable internal problems that faced the USSR. Thus right up to the 1950s the only real source of guidance open to the (few) Marxists who could spare more than a passing interest in Third World affairs was that contained in Marx's own rather casual and scattered writings on the colonial world (mainly penned in mid-century and largely confined to India, China and Ireland). Those theorists who may have been (inwardly) reluctant to simply follow Stalin's shallow and somewhat vacillatory line were therefore faced with the daunting tasks of trawling through the entire works — many of which were not freely available at that time; relating the applied observations to the theoretical core of the analysis; developing an internally consistent position from the early and late periods; and finally confronting the sort of ambiguities which modern research has only recently begun to unearth and grapple with.[200]

All this, of course, is reasonably well known and many of today's authorities have acknowledged the fact that this lacuna had left an important imprint upon the neo-Marxist approach to the Third World.[201] But what has perhaps not been sufficiently appreciated as yet is that this legacy has had significant implications for the study of historical change in general and that of the evaluation of the Third World in particular. To begin with, we may refer to the uneasy co-existence — under the one Marxist umbrella — of two quite separate groups of theory. Thus in his recent survey of the theory of imperialism Antony Brewer points to 'those that concentrate on the progressive role of capitalism in developing the forces of production, and conversely those that present capitalism as a system of exploitation of one area by another',[202] and Ronald Chilcote in his review refers to the 'dichotomy' that opened up between 'progressive and regressive' interpretations of the impact of capitalism on the Third World.[203] So we may now identify, on the one hand, that body of thought which re-asserts the overriding need to study the 'laws of motion' of capitalism, highlights its unique historic mission as an agency for change, concentrates upon traditional class analysis and relations of production, and seeks to point out the latter-day phenomenon of the internationalisation of capital;[204] whereas on the other, there is the Dependency and World-System's inspired notion of the 'development of underdevelopment' which places the blame for the perceived ills of the Third World squarely on capitalism via the 'unequal' exchanges underlying the market relations between centre and periphery, and a process of surplus extraction.[205] Both claim to be the true modern-day heirs of Marx and Engels (the former group in an almost literal sense, the latter in terms of the 'spirit' of the analysis and what Marx might well have come to rather more explicitly had he lived a little longer) but end up with very different interpretations of past and present. This tension — which can hardly be reduced to being one of differing degrees of emphasis — has been responsible for producing many fundamental disagreements, hostile exchanges and counter-critiques.[206] At the polar ends we may observe the proponents of an essentially externally orientated explanation of underdevelopment as opposed to those who espouse a more internally centred set of courses; but there are also many theorists who occupy 'intermediate' positions and who would adamantly reject the label of being either 'Eurocentric' or 'Third Worldist'.[207] As yet – and despite the efforts of self-styled synthesisers such as Samir Amin – integration has proved impossible and we are therefore left with what one commentator (John Saul) has recently called a situation of competing 'Marxisms'.[208] This vying for pride of explanatory place has demonstrably hindered the derivation of a generally acceptable framework for historical enquiry. A second implication flowing from the long neglect of the Third World in its own right within the corpus of Marxist thinking is that work on many branches of theory has tended to be focused upon mature or late capitalist society, and hence seems increasingly distant from past and present reality pertaining in the underdeveloped world.[209] Theoretical discourse in Marxist economics – partly occasioned by the rise of neo-Ricardianism – has developed a momentum of its own, and controversy over issues such as the measurement of capital, the labour theory of value, and the tendency of the rate of profit to fall are now far removed from our area of concern – even, I suspect, in an indirect sense.[210] In this context perhaps it is also worth pointing out two associated issues – both spilling over from a common source, namely, Althusserian Marxism. The first, relating to historical methodology, is that a great deal of energy has been expended on the dispute between the 'empiricists' and the 'abstractionists' – but neither side has had much to say about the Third World.[211] The second – which is ostensibly connected with the nature of Third World formations – concerns the mode of analysis adopted by many of the post-1945 Marxist Sociologists and Social Anthropologists. This school has – of course – been heavily criticised from many sides, and one of the greatest areas of disquiet centres upon the gap between theoretical and empirical work; indeed Peter Worsley has been moved to deliver a sweeping broadside at what he calls the 'metatheoretical procedures' that 'reflect the insulated position of intellectuals ... drawn as they are, overwhelmingly, from upper class backgrounds, with minimal knowledge of or involvement in the daily life of the poor. They are, in a word, elitist theories ... from the penthouse and the university office'.[212] If this sentiment is held to be fair comment upon this particular stream of writing and also of much of this type of work in general then it would be reasonable to conclude that, in the main, theory has not been a conspicuously helpful servant either to Marxist praxis with respect to the contemporary Third World, or to the scientific exploration of its history. This verdict, however, should not be taken to mean that the Marxist historiography of the Third World has contributed little to our understanding: on the contrary it has many important achievements to its credit,[213] and even the somewhat loose and slipshod work of Frank[214] has been instrumental in posing fresh sets of questions and developing new insights. Rather, I would agree with Hardach, Karras, and Fine, that 'there can be no simple leap from general theoretical abstractions (even when these are correct) to an understanding of complex and concrete developments'.[215]

(c) The Liberal Orthodoxy

Let us draw this review of the place of historical enquiry within the main intellectual traditions to a close by considering the Liberal-Orthodox school. During the early phases − say up to the mid-1960s, there can be little doubt that history did inform the discipline in a number of different and useful ways. Perhaps we need do little more than refer to the work of such influential pioneers of the subject as Simon Kuznets, Gunnar Myrdal, Arthur Lewis, Ragnar Nurkse, Walt Rostow and Bert Hoselitz to appreciate this point; and then to peruse the contents of texts such as those contributed by Gerald Meier and Robert Baldwin (1957) − which, incidentally, the authors claim was the 'first "real" textbook in economic development',[216] Benjamin Higgins (1959)[217] and, of course, Rostow's best seller of 1960.[218] In sharp contrast to many of the younger generations of economists who have been given scant encouragement or incentive to study any form of history,[219] these early scholars were not only exposed to the discipline during their undergraduate and postgraduate training and therefore, in my view, enjoyed the benefits of a more all-round education, but were sufficiently interested and competent to make important specialist contributions to the subject during the course of their respective careers.[220] Thus there was no question of there being a divorce between history and development theory; indeed the two went hand-in-hand, and often the former was a key ingredient in the making of the latter. A few examples may clarify this point. For Kuznets, an examination of the long-run growth and social distribution of per-capita incomes yielded many fertile insights which were then deployed to evolve a series of general hypotheses about the course, timing and pattern of past, present and even future development paths;[221] for Myrdal, the 'differences in initial conditions' between those in the LDCs and those pertaining in the West on the eve of its modern development were crucial in determining the choice of appropriate development path;[222] for Lewis, an understanding of the nature and dynamics of savings and investment behaviour − and hence of the 'necessary' levels of capital formation during the Industrial Revolution − was vital in establishing planning strategy;[223] for Rostow, the entire stages approach was predicated upon the modern history of the 'advanced' countries;[224] for Nurkse, a knowledge of international capital flows during the classical Gold Standard era underlay his views of the development requirements and specific needs of the LDCs within a reformed world economic environment;[225] and for Hoselitz, since the modern problems of entrepreneurship in the developing nations could only be appreciated within the wider context of the play of non-economic variables, the nineteenth and early twentieth century experience offered an instructive and invaluable guide to problems and options.[226] Of course, in the light of more modern methods of study and more up-to-date research findings on these and related topics, we may be justified in being somewhat sceptical of accepting their versions of history,[227] and given that today we would undoubtedly have reservations about the Eurocentric flavour of a great deal of this writing,[228] it can scarcely be denied that history figured prominently in their overall conception of development processes and problems.

I suspect that this would not be true of the vast majority of their intellectual followers. Although the general influence of the ideas of the pioneers has been acknowledged – and indeed still remains an integral part of our collective body of thought – particular elements, such as the interest in and concern with history, have not been taken up and built upon further. I do not think that it would be much of an exaggeration to say that such explicitly historical work began to dry up in the 1960s and then came to a rather precipitate end around the end of that decade. Among the subsequent crop of development economists it is something of a rarity to find anyone who seems comfortable grappling with this historical dimension – and even rarer, of course, to stumble across someone who feels sufficiently motivated or confident to undertake the kind of broadly-based study that appeared to come so naturally to the likes of the earlier generation. That this is true of more mainsteam economists – witness the drying-up of the source of influence (Lord Keynes?) responsible for producing academics such as Henry Phelps-Brown, Alec Cairncross, Robin Mathews and the late Thomas Balogh,[229] who seem to me to be almost as at home with history as with current issues and theories – indicates that this regrettable trend in the field of development is by no means exceptional. The background to this demise is the coming of the social science revolution which unleashed forces generally hostile to this mode of work; indeed so pervasive and all-conquering was the movement that historians themselves began to take on board new methodologies borrowed from their efflorescent and proselytising colleagues[230] – and, as Alan Bullock has noted, 'the most obvious' case was that of the economic historians who 'learned to employ econometric models and sophisticated statistical and analytical techniques derived from economics'.[231]

Admittedly this has yielded significant and long-run gains, but we would surely be unwise to ignore the cost which, as far as the pre-occupations of this essay are concerned, has involved the virtual freezing out of purposeful historical enquiry. We should also note the fact that not only was economic and social history ignored in the new alignment of subjects that constituted the acceptable inter-disciplinary mixture of development studies in the 1960s, but also that because these disciplines themselves were changing as a result of the infusion of the new methods, they too were moving away from history. The classic instance of this is Sociology after Parsons: but soon the trend took root in Human Geography, Political Science and Social Anthropology.[232]

The repercussions of these forces have been such that over the last two decades or so an explicit and clearly defined historical dimension has been absent from Liberal-Orthodox work on economic develop-ment. It is now quite usual for someone to become an expert on Development Economics – and Development Studies – without being exposed to more than a casual acquaintanceship with historical knowledge. Of course, history has not entirely disappeared altogether from this tradition, but it seems to me that it features in only the loosest and *ad hoc* manner. Any fair-minded survey of the field – which would take in the current scope of development research; the standard textbooks, collected 'readings' and monographs on develop-ment economics; the range of articles which appear in the specialist journals; the structure and curricula of development education at all levels; the occasional papers and development manuals issued by official and quasi-official institutions; national economic develop-ment plans; the informed media; and the deliberations of the Development Studies Associations – would clearly demonstrate that the great bulk of the work completed, planned or in progress, is essentially ahistorical.[233]

The insertion of the adverb 'essentially' in the preceding sentence denotes that some qualification to this claim is called for. If Gerald Meier is correct in arguing that in the 1950s the pioneers of develop-ment economics looked to economic history in order to tackle such central tasks as the determination of 'the sources of growth' and even the delineation of the appropriate 'strategies of development',[234] then by the end of the following decade, history had been relegated to a much lower division. It seems to me that in those instances where history did receive more than a passing mention, it was deployed to perform three minor functions.

First, and most common, it served as a provider of 'background' to the 'real' issues. This has taken several all-too-predictable general forms. We note the almost obligatory mention of colonisation and imperialism;[235] the reference to the ideas of a clutch of past economists, notably Smith, Malthus, Marshall, Schumpeter and Keynes;[236] the indication that there is an 'alternative' intellectual tradition stemming from the Left and hence Marx, Baran and the Dependency writers are alluded to;[237] there is a thumb-nail sketch of the evolution of the Western – especially the British – economies since the Industrial Revolution, and this is sometimes accompanied by a cursory glance at the Soviet Union after 1917;[238] and finally, in the treatment of the standard individual topics – population, migration, urbanisation, agriculture, etc., – historical experience is sometimes evoked.[239] But needless to say, these historical manifestations would hardly satisfy the historians; not only are there the twin dangers of superficiality and distortion to consider, but also the fact that serious injustice may be done to the richness and complexity of both history 'proper' and the history of ideas when abstracted for essentially tendentious purposes.

Second, history has been used to derive hypotheses and, rather more infrequently, as a testing ground for the application of theory and econometric prediction. In principle this procedure has much to commend it, and certainly many of the first generation of developmentalists relied heavily upon this method. Indeed it is possible to cite a large number of studies ranging over several different problem areas which have proved to be illuminating – either on account of their own inherent merits or by virtue of the controversies that arose in their wake. Thus the debate concerning the role of overseas trade in promoting development – 'engine' or 'handmaiden'? – the discussions about the role of capital investment, and the question of the 'primacy' of industrialisation and its corollary – a 'supportive' role ascribed to agriculture – all contained important historical dimensions. Unfortunately the alleged failure of development strategies based upon an application of this work seems to have been a factor in the general turning away from history.[240] With a few honourable exceptions such as Sen's work on famines and the series of articles by Adelman and Tuffs on poverty typologies,[241] the modern developmentalists seem increasingly reluctant to draw upon the historical record for ideas, for improving upon the quality of assumptions they make, or for confirmation (refutation) of predictive models. Today, and mirroring the trend in mainstream economics, 'history' seems to mean little more than post-1945 experience, and then be largely restricted – at least in an analytical sense – to those countries possessing suitable time-series data of the requisite and readily quantifiable variables.

Third, in order to meet a perceived need for imparting context, the tradition has taken on board a selection of those ambitious formulations contained in the works of writers such as Rostow and Frank (and, much more occasionally, Gerschenkron, Barrington Moore, Jones, Kitching, Wilkinson, Maitra, Guha and Olson).[242] In my view one of the main reasons why the studies of Rostow and Frank have been co-opted and appear regularly in the literature[243] is that they appear to offer universal generalisations about the complex historical processes of development/underdevelopment, and provide the kind of broad sweep that is so noticeably lacking from many of the modern studies. Now though developmentalists have been attracted to this 'ordered vision' they could not remain insensitive to the ripostes of the economic historians (who, in their turn, have been quick to point out the many shortcomings of much of this work – especially that of Rostow and Frank),[244] and began to relentlessly expose some of the gross methodological and empirical misrepresentations which they contained. This criticism from the specialists has implied that however suggestive theorising at such levels may be, unless the work is finally anchored to the known historical record – and not some highly selective appropriation of it – there is bound to be an inference of unreliability. However, because the combination of theoretical insight and thorough historical research has rarely been found, those developmentalists who have felt the need to invoke some general sort of historical dimension have been faced with an unpalatable choice. If they wish to avoid taking on an examination of the detailed 'nuts and bolts' of history they can either continue to accept the utility of the grand designs (albeit with reservation) or, short of undertaking the task of synthesis themselves, somehow persuade the historians to do the job for them.

This dilemma leads us to consider the particular reasons why the Liberal-Orthodox school has eschewed historical work. As I see it, there seem to be two major forces at work. In the first place, the evolutionary path taken by Development Economics and Development Studies has failed to generate a significant effective 'demand' for the specific subject matter of history; and second, the perceived nature and scope of economic and social history as practised in the English-speaking world has not appeared to offer a very worthwhile 'supply' of intellectual capital to developmentalists. Let us discuss these forces in turn. On the 'demand' side I would pinpoint three factors. First, the emphasis given to policy formulation alluded to in Section I has almost inevitably orientated developmentalists towards short-run analysis. Governments and planners in the Third World are primarily interested in the problems of today and perhaps tomorrow, and the major development preoccupations such as the removal of mass rural poverty and of burgeoning populations have an obvious immediacy. In order to meet these challenges and at the same time become involved with the aid programmes sponsored by the Western powers, the Liberal-Orthodox academics had to ensure that their contribution was 'relevant'. Now the early writers (usually doubling as consultants of one sort or another) were well aware of the partiality of this approach and certainly did not subscribe to the view that the past was somehow 'redundant'. But, due to the inexorable presence of events, this insight seems to have been deflected and very soon the hypothetico-deductive mode of analysis appeared to offer far more practical value. And when the technologists were invited to join in the development effort in a project designing planning sense, this trend accelerated since they themselves had no reason to regard history as being operationally useful.

Second, many of the pioneering Liberal-Orthodox school tended to perceive the basic development problem in the rapidly decolonising world to be essentially that of how to copy or replicate the Western experience (albeit within a much telescoped time horizon). This was understandable. They observed the characteristics of the handful of countries that had passed the development 'bar', noted the desire on the part of the LDC political leadership to follow suit, and set about generalising the patterns or typologies that held for given periods of time. In other words the standard of development had been set and what was next required was a purposeful investigation of how to overcome the barriers that stood in the way of its effective and most rapid realisation. This overall perspective was then translated into a whole set of particular, but inter-locking, ideas and strategies. Thus, to take one obvious example, the centrality of capital in the development thinking of the late 1940s and 1950s derived partly from a reading of what Karl Polanyi called the 'Great Transformation' of Western economic history (especially that of the UK) over the eighteenth and nineteenth centuries.[245] This suggested that a gearing-up of the savings and investment rates was a crucial significance in the achievement of any sustained breakthrough to a higher growth level; that the phenomenal amount of capital exported over 1870–1914 had been a vital prerequisite for the development of the White Settler states outside Europe; and that a 'deepening' of the industrial base was a core component of economic advance. These perceptions – now theoretically propped up by the emerging neo-Keynesian growth models – had their analogues in a development strategy which emphasised the need for LDCs to make every effort to raise the domestic rates of saving and investment (typically from around 5 to 10–12 per cent of GNP); to ensure that they acquired sufficient amounts of loan or aid capital from the West to break the chain of 'vicious circles'; and to advise governments to direct investment towards the capital − rather than the consumer − goods industries. These in turn had important implications for the general management of the economy and hence dovetailed into a package of complementary actions. Now when this whole approach began to be undermined as a result of the combination of disappointing economic and political experience on the one hand, and the chipping-away of the historical premises on the other,[246] this opened the flood-gates for an avalanche of criticism to descend upon the heads of those who advised aping and replication, and who had taken the Western model as the norm. Michael Todaro goes as far as to argue that one of the 'principal failures' of development economics in the 1950s and 1960s was 'its inability to recognize and take into account the limited value of the historical experience of economic growth in the West for charting the development path of contemporary Third World nations'.[247] This then provided a justification for simply sidestepping or ignoring history but, as I hope to argue, it was tantamount to throwing out the proverbial baby together with all the water.

Finally, the one tradition which has consciously adopted a coherent historical dimension into their work − the Marxists and neo-Marxists − are regarded by many in the Liberal-Orthodox development establishment as being unacceptably deterministic. This may well have led some developmentalists to equate the use of history with Marxism and has therefore been politically and academically unacceptable.

4. *The Makers of History*

We next turn our attention to the 'supply' side. Here the argument is based upon the proposition that in their normal course of business (economic and social) historians have somehow 'failed' to provide the kind of work that is deemed appropriate for the needs of the Liberal-Orthodox developmentalists. Of course, by this I do not intend to suggest that the development economists look upon their historian colleagues as mere cyphers whose task in academic life is to input data and ideas! Rather, it is my judgement that many present-day developmentalists, to the extent that they have actually considered this matter (either explicitly or implicitly), do not appear to believe that historians have much to offer. Since this point of view is rarely committed to print − Professor Eugene Staley's observation that after 'a fair amount of historical reading and study' he found that 'the economic historians in general, have for the most part not made their studies and written their reports in ways that answer the questions to which I needed answers'[248] is an exception − it is not easy to tie down and authenticate. However, on the basis of an admittedly subjective round of private and seminar discussions, and an impression of what the popular profile of economic history may be,[249] in what follows I shall attempt to sketch a picture of four presumed, and two unambiguously real, supply constraints.

In the first place, it might be held that most historians are interested in the past for its own sake and that they do not see the product of their craft as providing a ready basis for understanding – let alone actually grappling with – contemporary development issues. Further, any notion that history could provide effective 'guidance' to policy-makers might well be shrugged off with disdain. Second, because historians are thought to have been keen on emphasising the significance of unique factors and forces in both national and individual destiny, this stands in the way of the derivation of more general patterns and processes. Third, it has been a widely held belief that the majority of historians, especially those based in Britain, have had a distaste for explicit theorising and have preferred to persist with what might best be termed a 'traditional' inductive approach to their particular field of specialism. By this of course I mean the strong desire to follow the logic of the primary sources, and only then perhaps engage in an essentially pragmatic search for a framework in order to examine 'the facts'.[250] This has yielded a vast body of mainly descriptive work, and it is therefore difficult for anyone with limited time to disentangle any unambiguous explanatory threads. Fourth, until relatively recently, economic historians are thought to have regarded the nation state as the most normal unit of study, and hence this might have stood in the way of those seeking to draw out comparisons. Staley was certainly moved to comment on this: 'what has been done is on a country-by-country basis and is not in a form that lends itself readily to cross-country comparisons', and without such comparisons 'one is generalizing from single cases'.[251]

If it should be objected that the argument so far rests on little more than a combination of conjecture (how the 'typical' developmentalist might 'see' history) and caricature (of the 'public face' of the discipline), and that well-informed development professionals have by now realised that many economic historians – especially the younger generation – have long since abandoned these traditional biases and approaches (though this is surely something of a heroic assumption), then there are still two further 'supply' impediments that cannot be so readily impugned. Indeed the first of them comes directly out of the last point. That is, over the last two decades the practice and preoccupations of historians in general, and of economic and social history in particular, have undergone such far-reaching and radical change that it is by no means easy for anyone within – let alone formally outside – the discipline to be aware and kept abreast of all that has happened. The scope of the discipline has been immeasurably extended; governments, dynasties and ruling classes have been relegated to the sidelines, and in their stead the history of 'ordinary people' – families, women, children, the working classes and their institutions, and ethnic minorities – has emerged in full flower; the history of ideas and technology has acquired a new professionalism and carved out a separate sub-branch for itself; a new battery of techniques – as we have already indicated – has been introduced; entirely fresh source materials have been tapped; and now specialist journals have been established.[252] All of this has naturally brought in its wake new schools or traditions of historical study.[253] Such diversity and dynamism makes the task of 'dipping into' the subject – with the view to 'appropriation' – exceedingly difficult and time-consuming. The temptation to leave well alone and accept the logic of this new division of labour must be strong.

The second impediment I would like to discuss follows from the first – but in a rather paradoxical way. In line with what I have said about the evolution of the discipline, prior to about the mid-1960s the study of history and economic history was overwhelmingly focused upon the West. To the extent that the Third World was examined at all, it was either viewed in relation to the events in the 'centre', i.e., the metropolitan powers, or as part of what Tony Hopkins refers to as 'the flourishing and prestigious'[254] pursuit of Imperial studies – which, for the most part, was an unhappy amalgam of the history of pro-nationalist political movements and opinion, and of the coming of the 'age of improvement'[255] heralded by the arrival of European influence. Now although there has been a pronounced improvement in both the quality and quantity of Third World economic and social history since those days the subject is still a very long way from being properly established either in the Third World itself or in the West,[256] and in my view not only are its roots extremely shallowly implanted, but are in constant danger of being swept away. There seem to be two main reasons for this low status and precarious state.[257] First, vis-à-vis other areas of historical enquiry, resources are more than usually scarce. Both LDCs and the Western countries have other – apparently more pressing – claims to meet. Furthermore, depending upon whether they are located in the Third or First Worlds, it is my impression that the patrons appear to prefer to finance studies and research proposals which promise – or suggest – an outcome which favours the justification of nationalist rhetoric and moral indignation (directed against colonialism), or 'neutral' and 'scientific' accounts which play down the colonial and imperial impact, to those which simply seek to provide edification.[258] Second, and not unrelated to the above, the subject does not appear attractive enough to ensure a high and consistent level of recruitment. Apart from the problems of securing sufficient and no-string funding, and the rather ambivalent and lonely position many Third World specialists encounter within University departments, the subject lacks the standing and publicity that come with following more mainstream areas of enquiry. Moreover the would-be Third Worldist has to surmount a number of specific intellectual hurdles and get on top of a whole series of unique practical problems – and this applies to many Third World nationals (especially if they have been educated and trained in the West or in the Western manner at home) to only a marginally less degree.[259] These include, *inter alia*, the paucity of written records, the scarcity of statistics, linguistic problems, the whole question of cultural differences and, not least, the need to construct a distinctive theoretical framework capable of handling the stories of 'limited' growth and development, as well as 'arrest' or 'failure'. Thus, all-in-all, Third World economic historians have had neither the means nor the incentive to supply the sort of data and ideas that the developmentalists might wish for.

5. *The Sins of Omission*

The consequences of this unfortunate state of affairs have been far-reaching and deleterious. In my view, Development Studies and Development Economics have been seriously weakened and their viability damaged; and, by extension, I believe that if somehow a greater degree of historical awareness could be infused, it would help rehabilitate both. One result of the rift that has opened up between history and the Liberal-Orthodox developmentalists is that there has been a notable failure by the latter to seek fundamental causal explanations for a whole range of pressing contemporary problems. Without an awareness of the long-run and deep-seated value of many of these, it is patently impossible to understand their true nature – let alone devise a solution for their eradication. History has the ability to tell us how long-standing a particular phenomenon is, and therefore affects our perception of possible solutions. Thus the meeting of 'Basic Needs' is unlikely to be achievable unless and until we can begin to understand why so many people are in this dismal position. Similarly, the thinking behind a great many of the re-distributive land reforms which were undertaken in the 1960s and 1970s tended to underestimate the system of power relationships within the rural areas that had evolved over many years or even centuries.[260]

Second, the absence of a historical dimension has restricted vision and has narrowed − rather than widened − the range of alternatives. It seems to me that a knowledge of history would have cautioned the adoption of those rather simplistic hypotheses and even policy strategies that were the stuff of development economics for many years: industry 'or' agriculture; balanced 'versus' unbalanced growth; a capital-intensive 'rather than' a labour-intensive choice of technique; small-scale 'as opposed to' large scale units of ownership or managment; centralised 'or' decentralised structures of decision-making − these sorts of dichotomies which have pervaded the literature generally fail to capture the large number of potential options.

Third, the purging of history has been instrumental in paving the way for a kind of technological determinism to gain ground. The reasoning here is that if an entirely new method, technique, or whole technology is brought in to help solve a problem − say for example the high yielding variety of seeds package, or the IUD and the Pill − there seems little obvious need to consider the past since the start is defined as 'year one'. An acquaintanceship with the intractabilities of Third World agricultural and demographic history would surely have been a healthy antidote to all the hopes so unrealistically pinned upon the Green Revolution's potential to transform traditional agriculture, and the power of mass-produced contraceptive devices to change the time-honoured traditions of child-bearing.

Fourth, the divorce from history has permitted some developmentalists to go down a road which may be best signposted as leading to the economics of the *tabula rasa*. By this I mean that by something akin to a sleight of hand, the less developed countries are presented *en masse* and distinguished only by a set of common characteristics. This process, which began with the lumping together and homogenisation of Third World countries, was taken a step further by the work of the Structuralist wing of the Liberal-Orthodox tradition, especially those interested in deriving information from whole LDC clusters − thus Hollis Chenery and Moises Syrquin deliberately chose to omit the development effects arising from the 'individual history' of their sample 101 nations;[261] and has found ultimate expression in the creation of entirely fictitious backward countries such as Michael Roemer and Joseph Stern's 'Beracia'[262] − a book now widely used as a teaching aid to American and British graduate students. This last work must indeed be history's *reductio ad absurdum* since, by using this method, the authors are not only compelled to deny any real history to the Third World, but then add insult to injury by inventing what they must regard as a typical 'history' − which, incidentally, only starts in 1956 − and contains imaginary dates, coups d'état, a full run of statistics, 'representative' politicians and even a detailed map![263] To be fair, this sort of exercise has only limited aims and one would expect that those recommending such a book would also point out other more balancing studies: but without reading too much into it I would suggest that it is at least indicative of this entire approach. Finally, the fact that neo-Marxism uses history means that a further wedge has been driven between the two traditions, thus making some sort of 'reconciliation' between them all the more remote.

6. *The Argument for a Historical Perspective*

(*a*) *Initial Observations*

If we wish to help turn the intellectual tide of Development Studies and Development Economics, then we need to put up a convincing case for the re-introduction of a historical dimension and justify its presence in a positive way. In addition, we will have to suggest how this aim might be practically accomplished. In view of what we have argued so far, however, these are by no means straightforward tasks. For obvious reasons we cannot hide behind the sort of vague generalities that go along the lines that history 'broadens the perception', 'widens the focus', 'uncovers the roots', or even imparts 'a greater understanding of the human condition'.[264] Such assertions are unlikely to cut much ice with academics, let alone today's dispensers of funds. Nor, for equally obvious reasons, can we simply point to the achievements of the Marxian Tradition – since not only are many of these denied or hotly disputed (not least, to repeat myself, because of the failure to forward a consistent line of approach), but the ideological underpinnings and the preferred route out of under-development (a total disengagement or a gradual de-linking from the capitalist world economy) are hardly in keeping with prevailing orthodoxy. Furthermore, many historians of the Third World – a key target group in our design – may not see their subject in this light, and could well argue that it is absurd to think in terms of a utilitarian type of 'justification' – even if it could be shown that such a role may not be in conflict with other objectives of scholarly pursuit.[265] After all, with the exception of those who are passionate believers in the 'lessons of history' – be they Rostovians or latter-day Stalinists – it is seldom that one comes across an argument justifying history on the grounds of either à priori reasoning or its potential 'use-value' and 'track record'. Nor is it easy to see quite how an explicit historical dimension can be slotted into either Development Economics or Development Studies. Since it would be foolish to advocate anything that might smack of intellectual polymathy, and given that the former is now heavily burdened with technical preoccupations, and that the interdisciplinary makeup of the latter has been under sharp attack for many years, the presence of history in an educational capacity is far from the current scheme of things. We should also bear in mind the danger of peddling an easily accessible but altogether superficial kind of history; as John Toye points out in the context of outlining an ideal (post-graduate) development education: 'it is most important for students to grasp the variety and specificity of development in history'.[266] And, as we have already pointed out, because historians do not possess the metaphorical 'box of tools', they are generally not to be found scurrying along the corridors of the planning ministries.

(b) *An aid to definition and conceptualisation*

Despite these difficulties and objections I think that it is possible to develop a persuasive case. In making it, I do not propose to invoke the much wider set of arguments about the general value of historical study (although some of them will necessarily be at the back of what I have to say), but instead concentrate upon the development brief. The first plank must surely be that a study of economic and social history can better help classify – and hopefully clarify – the competing definitions and conceptualisations of economic growth and economic development/underdevelopment. Out of the current state of confusion on this – discussed above – we may identify two very broad divisions. One maintains that growth and development are processes which have happened in a number of countries and have a definite set of properties or characteristics; thus LDCs need to try to follow suit. On this basis the role of economic history is self-evidently clear and important. The second view is that for various reasons this is not a practicable option and therefore something entirely 'new' is required. Now at first sight this appears to make history an irrelevance. But upon closer examination history cannot be so easily banished from the scene. This is because of three important considerations. First, one needs to have a fair idea of what the 'old' consists of (primarily Western and Soviet history) before the slate is, so to speak, 'wiped clean'. Second, although it is a mere truism to say that 'nothing is really new under the sun', it is likely that 'newness' will involve at least some grafting on of the 'old' – albeit in a different form and in a different set of permutations: so once more one cannot entirely escape from the past. Finally, in our particular context, it would be difficult to interpret the meaning of 'new' in a way other than by envisaging the growth and development of the indigenous or traditional sectors. What I have in mind here is Henry Bruton's 'bottom-up' 'alternative approach' which he discusses in the following (highly idealistic) terms:

> the development objective would be to so modify the traditional sector that it becomes a dynamic, flexible sector, responding to the wants and ambitions emerging from within that traditional environment. One would seek an indigenous dynamic that moves this traditional sector in ways chosen by it. The developing nation would then seek to find its own way, rather than to follow along after the currently rich countries.[267]

In my view this particular variant of the rather trendy 'Another Development' idea clearly posits an important place for the historical study of the nature of these indigenous or traditional sectors, and the value system underlying them. Thus, if nothing else, history provides the reference points that are required to successfully define the processes involved.

(c) The long-run nature of the problem

The second plank of our justification directly follows from the first. If economic growth and development/underdevelopment are thought to fundamentally revolve around the long-run production potential and the mechanisms of distribution of the economy in question, then we must necessarily be looking at long time horizons. As Douglass North reminded us, the current preoccupations with variables such as the rate of investment, capital–output ratios, the pace of innovation, enhancements to the quality of the labour force, and even 'X efficiency' may be misleading.[268] These factors are not the 'causes' of growth and development; they *are* growth and development. The 'ultimate' or 'real' causes are to be found through an examination of much deeper phenomena such as the social, judicial and political structures, as well as of the 'ground rules' underlying economic behaviour. Since such structures and rules have a long and complex pedigree, it clearly follows that only a detailed study of the past will yield the kind of insight that is required to understand and help explain the nature of change.

(d) Improving Theory

My third plank – history's role in informing theory – has already been mentioned in passing, but is now in need of a little further elaboration. Although we all know that theories are derived from many different – and often quite unexpected – sources, in view of what we have argued about growth and development being long-run entities, it would be surprising if theories directed towards their elucidation were not potentially enrichable by a historical perspective.

History may help in four sorts of ways. First, it can identify what needs to be explained. Second, it can suggest a set of intelligent questions and hypotheses. Third, it can help comment upon the assumptions that are deployed. Finally, it can (sometimes) provide the material on data which can be used for the testing procedure. Now even if it were feasible to examine the many general, and the even more numerous range of partial, theories that have been put forward over the last two decades or so in order to try to ascertain the extent to which history − either explicitly or implicitly − was used in such ways, this is clearly not the appropriate place to do so. However, it is my strong impression that relatively few modern theorists have consciously turned to history: I say this partly because when such a clear-cut case does emerge − such as A. K. Sen's work in famines[269] − it really does stand out. But the validity of this argument does not really rest upon a mere listing of such instances and a disparaging of the remainder. Rather it turns upon whether we can demonstrate either the advantages of looking at history and/or the disadvantages of not doing so. Now it seems to me that one of the clearest points that could be made here concerns the nature of the basic assumptions underlying economic activity. Just as the Social Anthropologists and Sociologists have shown that the standard neo-Classical assumption of individualism, rationality (whether 'restrictive' or 'bounded')[270] and utility maximisation, may not have been the most useful as far as modelling the behaviour of a great many of the (especially rural) inhabitants of Third World states is concerned, many historians have produced plenty of evidence to suggest that a quest for individual gain on the basis of everyday actions has been relatively unusual and at odds with the historical experience of large numbers of people living in both the North as well as the South.[271] Thus, a knowledge of history would not only have been useful in adding greater depth to the findings of the social scientists concerned with the present and hence acting as an additional guardian against the fashioning of unwarranted assumptions, but could well have improved upon them. Moreover, beleaguered Development Economists now under attack from their neo-Classical critics for countenancing 'perversions of standard economic principles'[272] might have found ready support from the historians on this score − had they but looked for it.

(e) *As a contextual marker*

In addition to its role in helping to inform and perhaps improve theory, history may be useful in its capacity as a contextual 'marker' of the succession of competing theories, and indeed theoretical traditions. This fourth plank in our justification takes us directly to the second of the two types of historical dimension that I mentioned earlier, in that it is centred upon ideas rather than events. Under this head I see history performing two main functions. First, the very discipline of identifying relevant theoretical contributions, examining them with care and a critical eye, and then tracing their influence through time and space, in itself ensures exposure to the breadth, depth and richness of the subject matter. This sort of call – which echoes our previous general plea for more priority to be afforded to history of economic thought courses – must surely yield important educational dividends in as much as it inculcates a healthy respect for the weight and longevity of intellectual opinion that has been given to development problems. Moreover, both informal as well as more purposive (Ph.D. orientated) investigations can lead to the re-discovery of interesting and perhaps important insights. Thus we should all now be more fully aware of the prescient studies of luminaries such as Lenin (*The Development of Capitalism in Russia*), Chayanov (*On the Theory of Peasant Economy*) and even the Malthus of 1820 (*Principles of Political Economy Considered with a View to their Practical Application*) rather than of the famous and evergreen 1798 *Essay* (on population), and also of specific theories contributed by more than one author (such as the evaluation by the Classical economists of the costs and benefits of emigration and immigration and of capital export and import); but mindful of the great stock of ideas that has been built up over the centuries, it is surely not fanciful to suggest that recent research is likely to throw up many more. In fact, even in these ahistorical times, it is possible to point to promising areas of work such as Anthony Winston's analysis of the 'Prussian Road' of agrarian development[273] and J. Plattanaau's study of the two Mills's notions of agrarian reform.[274] Unfortunately, the great majority of today's developmentalists seem to take a very blinkered view of these antecedents, and on those few occasions when they do bother to look back it would be difficult to disagree with John Toye's comment that 'When teachers of development studies contemplate their own history, they rarely look further than to 1945', and that their history is the history of 'the post-1945 international organisations ... of the adoption of Keynesianism ... and of a few alternative development strategies – Soviet planning, the Cuban experience and Maoism'.[275] Now whilst there is un-doubtedly a great deal which can be learned from even 'such a grossly foreshortened perspective'[276] – especially if it is done with imagin-ation (how many present-day students are introduced to the apposite work of Michael Kalecki?),[277] thoroughness (how many are led through the labyrinth channels of neo-Keynesianism, Dualism or even Structuralism?)[278] and with due regard to changes in midstream (sometimes rather euphemistically referred to as intellectual development!)[279] – there are inevitably considerable limitations. Thus to quote Professor Toye again:

> It is difficult to accept that the only history relevant to develop-
> ment studies has occurred within the life-time of the average
> Development Studies teacher. Development studies did not
> spring fully-armed from the contemporary mind. On the
> contrary, the underlying assumptions and methods of con-
> temporary development theorists have been fashioned in debates
> about socio-economic development which have been actively
> prosecuted over at least the last two hundred years.[280]

Second, I believe that history can help impose some logical order upon the multiplicity and diversity of development theories. As we have seen, at the present time there are three main umbrella traditions: but lurking beneath them on rather less Olympian heights are a large number of formulations which manage to find some degree of shelter and compatibility – though often with great discomfort. Of the three, what I have elected to call the Liberal Orthodox tradition is probably the untidiest collection, and is composed of a whole host of disparate elements.[281] History, by forcing us to consider how such differences and similarities arose, and why they were not resolved, enables us to grasp them all the better, and perhaps even permits us to make a more informed choice between and within the traditions than we might otherwise have been able to do. But I hasten to add that we would then need to re-integrate material factors into the picture since the derivation and popularity of ideas – particularly those on and around economics – have obviously been deeply influenced by the play of real world events. The search for the reasons why a theory or group of theories appear when they do, and as the case may be, take hold of general opinion and even effect the making of policy, is not only important in its own right (it allows us a better glimpse of how the world works), but edges us a bit closer towards explaining the causes of theoretical 'bunching' at certain points of time.

(f) The design of appropriate development strategies

Having discussed justification in terms of history promoting a clearer comprehension of the meaning of 'development' and then helping us to make more sense of the range of theories and traditions that have been 'on offer' over the years, we next need to consider how an appreciation of the origins of present-day underdevelopment may be of use to all of those interested parties who seek to effect change. Let us begin with the general – and hopefully uncontentious – proposition that it is quite impossible to understand the present without a knowledge of the formative past.[282] A special sort of dialogue exists between the 'dead' past and the 'living' present, and indeed the stuff of the present is no more than a working out of long-run tendencies and forces juxtaposed with those arising from more immediate sources. I would therefore argue that it is more appropriate to conceive of development as being a continuum rather than a series of independent discrete temporal changes. It is possible to think of any number of both intangible as well as tangible examples to drive this point home. Constitutional forms, legal and educational systems, displaced ethnic minorities, the ubiquity of the English language and balkanised frontiers come readily to mind. Thus, to take only the most topical of illustrations, the states of sub-Saharan Africa and South Asia are, respectively, still grappling with the legacy of the Berlin Conference (1885) and the disastrous Partition of the Indian sub-continent (1947); and Sri Lanka is today embroiled in what amounts to a chaotic civil-war situation because of the continuing failure to deal with her Tamil problem. History then helps us to grasp the character of many aspects of contemporary underdevelopment and, as Keith Griffin puts it, 'Economic history, and theories firmly based upon historical knowledge, would appear to be essential in understanding the nature of underdevelopment'.[283]

Two further points follow from this. First, the study of history may reveal not only the fact of LDC heterogeneity but also its cause and very possibly aid in estimating its extent. Thus neither the incidence nor (what Oscar Lewis once called) the 'culture of poverty'[284] is remotely the same in all poor Third World settings; and its variation is best explained in historical terms. This perception has materially reduced the credibility of the once popular 'vicious circles of poverty' notions because they usually took a blanket sort of uniformity of poverty for granted;[285] hopefully, such a perspective will sooner or later be brought to bear upon the work of those now engaged in mechanically preparing cross-sectional 'Quality of Life' indices. Second, if the Marxian insight that underdevelopment is not a natural condition but, on the contrary, is a product of definite historical forces associated with the growth of capitalism in Europe and the overseas expansion of the major colonising powers from the end of the fifteenth century is a reasonable one, then this must cast a long and corrective shadow over those types of argument which begin with (some variation of) the assumption that the main distinguishing feature of Third World countries is the dreaded 'low-level equilibrium trap'.[286]

From the focus upon origins and nature we turn to examine how history may enlighten the thinking behind the design of development strategies. We have already mentioned how history can be of service to theorising; but neither theory nor particular techniques of analysis are the only elements that academics bring to bear upon this task. They, and the politicians and their top civil servant advisors who are at the cutting edge of strategy formulations, frequently use analogy, invoke past parallels, and refer to important precedents. History acts as an organised collective record or memory that can be 'freely' (and often illegitimately) drawn upon to serve such ends. Standards from which to judge the feasibility of proposed actions can be derived; positive and negative (in the sense of what to avoid) guidelines may be obtained; the desire to achieve continuity − or the wish to radically depart from a given state or condition − can only be based upon the knowledge of a specific historical situation; and a calculation of trade-offs between conflicting goals and interest-groups may well be informed by an appeal to history. What all this amounts to is that the past offers an extraordinarily rich tapestry of development and underdevelopment (in the Marxian sense) experience; and let us be clear that this experience is not simply restricted to the part of those 'advanced' countries − be they located in the West or East − that have succeeded in achieving 'development': it also holds for the past of the Third World itself − though since many poor countries seek to mimic the pace-setters in some way, this has not been given as much prominence as the record of the former category.

Many of the most urgent development problems have a definite parallel in history. Demographic pressure on limited resources (especially land), poverty, the growth of pauperisation, famines, unemployment, urban crises, impediments to the inter-sectoral flow of factors, the nature of international economic relations, indebtedness and the transmission of depressions are but a small sample of issues of great contemporary significance which can surely be more fully understood and appreciated by an acquaintanceship with history.[287] Obviously the more detailed and profound the knowledge of these antecedents the better the comprehension of the problems of the moment. Further − and here we do single out the history of the developed countries, since there are over two centuries of experience to go by, even in the narrow sense of Kuznets' 'modern economic growth' − whatever the strategy chosen by today's Third World there is bound to be some sort of historical precedent,[288] however oblique it might turn out to be. Here it is only possible to give a limited number of examples of what I have in mind. Differences in economic systems and hence differences in values (from the market to the collectivist routes); the time period of development (centuries to decades); resource endowments (of human as well as of a natural kind); the size of nations (cf. the USSR and Denmark); changes in the relative importance of the major economic sectors in the development process (cf. Australasia and Japan); the size and form of the social overheads (canals and canal irrigation systems, roads, railways, harbours, docks and airports); the role of capital and money markets in providing short- and long-term loans (cf. Scottish banking networks, the English 'country' banks, the Japanese Hypothec Bank, and the famous French Crédit mobilier and Crédit foncier); the origins and values of private entrepreneurs (the influence of specifically religious factors); the emergence of a stable and 'committed' labour force in the modern factories, mines and plantations (varying methods of recruitment and disciplining); issues of distributional tolerance (high to low inequalities); radically different land tenure structures (estate farming to peasant proprietorship); currency and foreign exchange management (gold to paper-backed: fixed to floating); the size and structure of industrial and commercial units (partnerships, joint-stock enterprise); long-run elasticities of demand for a broad category of outputs (consumption behaviour); and the choice of technique (the degree of labour- and capital-intensity) – all these and many more[289] can provide, and indeed must have actually helped to provide, meaningful pointers to the present.

Naturally the qualities of caution and sensitivity – both in about equal measure – are required in order to relate such past experience to the problems of the present. In particular, we must guard against the temptation to rip a specific element from its overall context and this is what was probably in McCloskey's mind when he recently observed that

> The fascination in poor countries now with industrialization on the British pattern, complete with exports of manufactures (in an age of ubiquitous skill in making them), puffing railways (in an age of cheap road transport), and centralised factories (in an age of electric power) would seem odd without the historical example in mind. The ghosts of grasping capitalists, expropriated small farmers, and exploited factory workers still haunt economics and politics.[290]

Now although this is obviously a very dated disclaimer, the basic point is well taken and neatly illustrates the danger of our being led down the determinist 'lessons of history' road. Indeed the difficulties of abstracting from the past in this way are not to be underestimated, and when we take into account the general absence of suitable interpretative histories it is perhaps not altogether surprising that only a tiny number of even rich country 'case-studies' – including the 'very special' case of the pioneering industries of the UK[291] – are thought to possess a 'usable' past. This itself has dangers since it is necessary to avoid giving the impression that national experience can be somehow considered in isolation. Thus students of the history of technology and its diffusion (partly via the forerunners of today's trans-national corporations) need no reminding of the fact that 'the process of technological change has for many years been the means by which global inequalities in wealth and power have been continuously recreated'.[292]

Let me wind up this point by first quoting Seymour Mandlebaum's injunction to historians, made in a different but related context (that of social policy), and then duly qualifying it. In a recent paper entitled 'The Past in Service to the Future', Professor Mandlebaum writes that 'Without abandoning the precious values of detachment and freedom from narrow partisanship, I believe it is possible for historians to enrich their own sense of purpose and their practice by directly and responsibly meeting the intellectual demands of policy formulation'.[293] It should now be clear that I would interpret the word 'directly' ('responsibly' goes without saying!) in a rather more restrictive way than the author intends. Thus I am not for one moment advocating that historians should shy away from their usual intellectual platform — especially if it is more inclined towards offering an explanation of past experiences and not simply a description of them. Though policy advisory work is undoubtedly far more glamorous and certainly much better financially rewarded, most historians are either not interested or not equipped to become involved. Also if they are to start filling in some of the gaps we have earlier identified, and if they are to tackle the analysis of the deep-seated structural problems of long-run development and underdevelopment in any real depth,[294] then there simply is not sufficient time to spare. This sort of work can make an important contribution to the thinking behind strategy design. But of course whether any notice will be taken of it is quite another matter, and that is not really in the hands of the historians — though by gradually extending the scope of their studies it will be increasingly difficult for the developmentalists to ignore.

(g) *A better understanding of the barriers to successful implementation*

The final plank in our justification exercise concerns history's role in shedding light on the many barriers to the implementation of development policies and strategies. As is widely recognised, this aspect of the development problem is at least as important as the design of a sound strategy — indeed for some developmentalists (especially those concerned with the creation of policy, of course) it is more important than that. What does history have to offer here? It is my contention that historians, particularly those specialising in social and political history, are in a unique position to prise open that complex of factors that make up the institutional structure of country – which is clearly at the core of the implementation issue. Douglass North, no doubt following the seminal study by John Commons,[295] defines institutions as

> (1) a set of constraints on behaviour in the form of rules and regulations; (2) a set of procedures designed to detect deviations from and enforce compliance with the rules and regulations and (3) an existing framework of moral and ethical behavioural norms that influence the way the rules are specified and the costs of compliance.[296]

Now it is through this institutional structure that development necessarily proceeds. If a market (which is itself, of course, a particular type of social institution) route is chosen, then due recognition must be given to those other institutions which constrain the way in which it may operate. Neo-Classical economists and some of the latter-day development economists usually assume that the wider environment within which the market functions has no important influence upon economic behaviour; thus the economic system works in an identical manner in both a developed Western country and in those Third World states which are nominally pledged to the free market. But this is patently at odds with real world experience. Social anthropologists, social psychologists, political scientists and sociologists have clearly demonstrated how a whole panoply of institutions 'affects the way economic agents respond to conventional economic incentives, to the acceptance of new ideas and new opportunities, to search [sic] and the idea of progress, to the kind of social and economic justice that is acceptable, and to the idea of the "good life"'.[297] Such non-market institutions include the practice of sharing within extended families, formal kinship duties, an array of non-financial entitlements, a web of extra market transactions, tribal loyalties, religious 'taboos' and obligations, the culture of the bazaar and its distinctive system of time-keeping, huge areas of altruistic behaviour, tied labour services, and those extra payments for services rendered which are often called 'corrupt practices' by those who hold to a different code of ethics. On the other hand, those countries which have opted for a more planned and authoritarian route (whether of the Right or the Left) out of development must sooner or later face up to the fact that it is one thing to pass a law to give effect to some desired economic reform or act of management, but quite another to ensure that it is carried out. The same set of institutions which may thwart the price mechanism, may well delay, alter, or even altogether prevent the implementation of any edict which seriously threatens the particular vested interest under attack. Now although I would not go as far as Professor Hayek who has recently argued that there are certain categories of 'rules' which can never be altered by decree,[298] it seems clear enough that development by order can encounter just as much stiff resistance as the other 'ideal type' strategy. In fact, of course, few Third World – or, if it comes to that, Western and increasingly Socialist – countries voluntarily choose either the first or the second for any appreciable length of time, but in practice elect for some sort of mix, and I suspect that this may well be connected – in a fundamental way – to this very issue.

History makes an entrance here because the institutional structure has evolved over many centuries and – in the case of those countries boasting a 'Great Civilisation' – even millennia. Now without going into the debate between those who believe that the most enduring institutions are the most syncretic in character, and those who incline towards the opposite view, it seems clear to me that many development strategies have foundered and sometimes sunk on the rocks of these structures. Whether such strategies have been about doing entirely different things or doing the same things differently (or even some combination of the two), the common denominator is the 'hurry' and speed with which they are encouraged or urged on. The dilemma is often that time-honoured habits and values (the preference for sons, for example) generally have an important and sensible rationale in relation to a given environment; development strategies which are geared towards changing this environment, however, need to enlist the help of the population in order to do just that – but those trying to implement development can scarcely hope to change these habits and values without first changing the environment. Attempts to bulldoze a way through this sort of conundrum (the Emergency Period in India) create social tensions and occasionally revolution. Historians can help the developmentalists to more fully understand the reasons why certain institutions are more impervious to change than others;[299] and they can also help identify those values, methods of work, ways of doing things, mental habits and traditions which, for all practical purposes, may well have to be considered as being sacrosanct since any attempt to violate their integrity, even through indirect means, can bring the whole development strategy tumbling down with a spectacular crash (witness Iran).

7. *A Programme of Work*

We are now in a position to pull the main threads of our preceding arguments together and to suggest the most promising shape for a historical dimension. Let us begin at the most mechanistic level. Even if it were thought to be desirable to somehow reverse the current division of academic labour and imagine a fusion between developmentalists and historians (the rationale being that the 'best' type of inter-disciplinary work is done within one's own head), it would not be realistic. Specialisation is here to stay, and even in the world of Marxian scholarship − for all its emphasis upon holism − this is now accepted *de facto*. What can be done however is to open up better channels of communication. This could proceed in three steps. First, historians would need to design and provide relevant courses for (mainly, I suspect, post-graduate) students which I would then make compulsory parts of the curriculum.[300] This didactic role could be explored during regular meetings between the two constituencies. At present economic historians belong to one professional association (in Britain the Economic History Society) and developmentalists to another (the Development Studies Association), and despite the efforts of bridging groups[301] the division remains strong. If a means could be found to establish routine exchanges − and that is surely not beyond our collective wisdom − then this might also lead to the instigation of particular joint research initiatives and perhaps ultimately might foster a commitment to joint work in general. If those − like me − who believe that the only real way to even begin to understand the central causes of mass poverty is by a process of active scholarly co-operation which encourages − or even compels − the frequent crossing of disciplinary boundaries are correct, then such steps are long overdue. Clearly this is not the best place either to specify the content of such courses or to anticipate any research initiatives, but it might be useful to briefly set down some general suggestions. As I have already argued I think there is an overwhelming case for highlighting the history of development/underdevelopment ideas, concepts and theories. Little more needs to be added to what we have already said, save perhaps the reiteration that 1945 is not the optimal starting date!

Second, as far as material history is concerned, if it is accepted that the primary contemporary development problem is the need to reduce the tragically high levels of world poverty, then the role of the academic must surely be the contemplation of such issues with the aim of arriving at an understanding of the major forces at work. Without at the outset attacking such basic deprivation and starvation, it is impossible to conceive of achieving any of the wider aspects of 'development'. Of course, even if it were possible to envisage the end of mass absolute poverty, this would not obviate the importance of historical enquiry − it would only involve a refocusing exercise. I am thus advocating a positive development orientation to historical courses and perhaps research work, and as such, this represents something of a break with the conventional approach of those historians who are generally concerned with the past for its own sake. But this is not necessarily as revolutionary a position as it may seem at first sight. From the late 1950s many Economic Historians consciously set out to examine the past – invariably the Western past – from the perspective of long-run economic growth and development.[302] Those historians have borrowed certain ideas and techniques of analysis from Development Studies; for example, the notion that Great Britain in the eighteenth century could be usefully viewed as a 'developing economy'.[303] This represented a somewhat novel way of re-examining a longstanding question *viz.* the origins of the first Industrial Revolution, and undoubtedly re-invigorated the general study of British[304] and then subsequently European economic history.[305] As David Cannadine has shown, this 'bringing together' of economic history and economic development produced (in the 1960s) a 'new generation of textbooks' which 'spoke little of the social consequences of industrialisation' or the 'influence of the trade cycle' – hitherto the dominant preoccupations of the historiographer.[306] In their stead the bibliographies of these texts 'included the works of development economists', and furthermore:

> They made extended references to contemporary underdeveloped countries (especially Nigeria and India) when describing pre-industrial England. They all adopted sectoral analysis, and spoke of a shift of productive resources away from agriculture and towards industries and services. They saw Britain as blazing the trail which the Continent, the United States and the rest of the world were ultimately to follow.[307]

But this honeymoon came to an abrupt end in the mid-1970s. According to Cannadine, 'at the same time that economic growth in the West became more uncertain and/or more unacceptable, economic development became less confident as a discipline and less credible as a policy'.[308] Economic historians moved on to other themes, developed new methods and, with a few lingering exceptions,[309] parted company with developmentalists. Whether a renewed period of economic growth will cause the historians to seek a reconciliation is a moot point, but in any event since the main object of the exercise – a reconsideration of the Western experience – is only of indirect significance for our purpose here, we need not harbour too many regrets. Further, the quality of the contributions has been sufficiently high for many of them to be still of use and, whatever the intellectual fashion may be today or tomorrow, it is unlikely that the relevant insights developed over c. 1958–1974 will be entirely discredited.

But our main concern must surely be to thoroughly investigate and eventually put on courses which centre upon the history of the material conditions of life and labour experienced by the great mass of men, women and children that make up the population of the Third World. To the extent that the daily struggle for existence is affected by parliaments, political parties, presidents, viceroys, monarchs, civil servants, other elites, and powerful vested economic interests, it is obvious that these groups require detailed study; however, in my view, they should not – as has often been the case – be considered important purely in their own right. Instead, what I have in mind here is an extension of the idea of a 'People's History' – which has recently been re-formalised by the radical History Workshop Group primarily for use in British history,[310] but has now started to spread out to the Third World[311] – especially South Asia – where it appears now as 'Subaltern Studies',[312] and parts of Africa.[313] Now although many scholars acknowledge the importance of this initiative (perhaps starting with Albert Memmi's book written in the early 1960s)[314] there are many practical difficulties since the greater part of the extant archival resources available to scholars were kept by the literate, articulate, and invariably non-indigenous (colonial) minority. Some of these holdings do refer to certain aspects of the routine of day-to-day existence, but generally seen through the somewhat blinkered eyes of reporting officialdom. In any case, the 'great events' feature more prominently and hence open a distorted window on reality. To the best of my knowledge a Third World 'equivalent' of E. P. Thompson's seminal study, *The Making of the English Working Class*, has yet to emerge;[315] but there is some evidence, particularly in relation to Southern Africa and India, of recent interest in just such an approach.[316] And of course the excellent *Journal of Peasant Studies* (Frank Cass and Co.) has been in the forefront of research as regards the rural sector of Third World populations. An imaginative use of the available written sources combined with the relatively new and still somewhat controversial (at least for historians) technique of Oral History and the utilisation of other cultural media such as archaeology, art, sculpture, drama, songs and folklore have been deployed to compensate for archival bias and lacunas.[317] Moreover, in recent years there has been an increasing commitment to a consideration of the more 'commonplace' dimensions of human existence (for example, people's apparel, diet, and the patterns of disease) and this, in my view, represents a useful complementary line of inquiry and must be welcomed in that it seems to deepen our understanding of basic socio-economic structures.[318]

A second potentially exciting task for researchers and teachers might be to identify and explore the many interesting comparisons of the historical experience of the Third World. There have been relatively few research or teaching initiatives in this direction, and with the exception, almost by definition, of the 'World System' theorists, the unit of analysis has been the nation state.[319] Whilst there have obviously been good practical reasons for this choice (international comparisons of levels of per capita income growth have, after all, yielded suggestive historical insights) the deployment of different units of analysis can be equally useful – if not more so. What is in fact the most appropriate unit is clearly dependent upon the underlying themes that we select for close scrutiny. The family, the village, the city – including the company town – the mine, the plantation, the railway, and the institutional organisation of business all *inter alia* represent new comparative frontiers. I realise that the intellectual investment that this work implies is considerable. In fact the trend to area specialisation presents institutional problems of the first order, and it is becoming increasingly difficult for the 'Indianist' or the 'Africanist' or the 'Latin-Americanist' to transcend his or her chosen field of study. I would not want to deprecate this in any way but surely there is also a need to draw together the mushrooming number of case studies. This suggests either a commitment to team research or, less controversially, regular academic interchanges with comparative themes forming a central part of the agenda.[320] Clearly there are significant inter-continental differences in the working out of historical processes – but this in itself may often stimulate fresh research initiatives. A good example of how fruitful traditional comparative work may be is the work on business organisation and banking institutions in Europe, America and Japan over the last century associated with the pioneering studies of Alfred Chandler, Rondo Cameron and Charles Kindleberger.[321] For the Third World (once again the methodological follower) there is considerable scope for similar exercises which might, for example, compare and contrast the Managing Agency System (India), the Agency System (South America) and the *Zaibatsu* (Japan).[322]

It is also necessary to be as clear as possible about the appropriate time period to be adopted for the explanation of the relevant historical phenomena. The 'past' is of course continuous, and any arbitrary partitioning of it is inevitably somewhat artificial. However, no one can simply research 'the past' in its entirety; the selection of time-periods and within these the choice of problems and the range of issues to be studied will be dependent upon both the theoretical approach and the historian's subjective bias.[323] For Marxist historians, historical time is differentiated in terms of the existence of distinct modes of production and the transitory phases between them.

Consequently, traditional chronology and the significance of specific dates is secondary to the understanding of the working out of the class struggle and the processes of material reproduction. For their part, non-Marxists demarcate particular historical phases – within precise chronological boundaries – on the basis of the empirical phenomena they seek to explain. I would argue that there is a need to clearly posit a consistent method of dividing up the past which, in the context of this paper, would incorporate the following considerations. First, the need to study the Third World prior to both colonisation and integration into the international economy.[324] Contrary to many Eurocentric interpretations the 'real' history of the Third World commenced neither with capitalism nor colonisation, and myths of 'golden ages' or 'primitive savagery' (in however sophisticated a form they may appear) are no longer tenable in the light of recent research findings, as we have seen earlier in the case of India. Second, I believe it is necessary to consider the longish sweep of European history rather than to focus only upon the most modern epoch.[325] An examination of Western pre-capitalist society has offered many interesting insights that are relevant for our purposes, as the work of historians such as Braudel and, to a lesser extent, Coleman, Supple and Cameron demonstrates.[326] Third, the nature of the interaction between the Third World and the West has undergone many fundamental changes over time; and these relationships have had a profound effect upon the internal structure of Third World economies and societies. We therefore need to carefully break down blanket terms like 'colonialism' and 'imperialism' with a view to more finely drawing out the distinction between the rulers and the ruled over a specific span of time.

Given the rather elastic contours of this proposed shape to our historical dimension, it should be possible to accommodate within its boundaries many of the different types of economic and social history that are currently being taught and researched. Historians of economic thought should face no inherent difficulty in isolating the development/underdevelopment aspects of past work. Traditional historians are still needed to carefully peruse the available documentation and put it in some sort of usable order: indeed in view of the lamentable gaps in our knowledge of the Third World this is certainly going to be a key task. As long as there are markets – in however 'imperfect' a form they may be – historians inspired by the neo-Classical outlook and method will be required. Since there will always be a quantitative element about economic change, the New Economic Historians will be in demand, and their expertise at conducting counterfactual analysis will no doubt continue to excite curiosity as well as opprobrium. Social historians, including those in the *Annales* tradition, will be called upon to penetrate the 'structures of everyday life' and highlight the experiential lot of the mass of the Third World populations. The catholicity of the Institutional historians will be particularly valued by those who seek to understand the nature of the underlying environment. And of course the Marxist and neo-Marxist historians bring a distinctive methodology, an alternative set of insights, and a good track record in initiating new perspectives (especially in labour history in general and peasant studies in particular) and powerfully criticising many long-standing interpretations. Such eclecticism should not be taken to mean that I regard all of these approaches as being somehow equally useful: rather it is meant to encourage the enlistment of all those with a possible contribution to make.[327]

IV CONCLUSION

In this essay I have tried to show that over the last decade the Liberal-Orthodox formulations on Development Economics and Development Studies have lost a great deal of their earlier authority and conviction. In contrast to the optimism, self-confidence, and rapid growth that characterised both subjects during the period from around the end of the Second World War to the early 1970s, we have recently been witnessing a mounting series of attacks upon most of the central intellectual positions from Left and Right. In the wider world the credibility of the developmentalists' policy prescriptions has suffered badly and there has been a palpable decline in their prestige. Now although I believe the Tradition is resilient enough to survive – and that all talk of terminal illness and even 'death' is premature – it would be foolish to deny the existence of a widespread feeling of malaise. Indeed the fact that so many academics are now questioning the state of the art is indicative of a general lack of confidence as well as the very real threat to its receipt of public funding. It is my contention that one of the reasons for this condition is that both subjects cut themselves off from a key point of mooring – a historical dimension – as a result of the social science 'revolution' of the 1960s. In order to return to a relevant and clearly defined course I believe it is necessary to re-incorporate such a dimension as far as research and teaching is concerned. Clearly this 'line' cannot be the same as the earlier Eurocentric one – primarily because many of the underdeveloped countries are no longer interested in slavishly aping Western norms. But there are a number of very promising alternatives which I have here tried to identify and briefly sketch out. By proceeding in this general direction it will also be possible to include the work of the Marxists and some of those committed to neo-Classicism. It seems to me that at a time of deep anxiety over the plight of countless millions of starving people, any initiative which can potentially bring scholars together into meaningful dialogue, and perhaps even co-operation, is a step forward.

NOTES

This essay has grown out of two conference discussion papers. The first, entitled 'Economic History and Economic Development: A Plea for the Integration of a Historical Dimension into Development Studies' (mimeo, Autumn, 1981), co-authored with Robert Kirk, was written for a special workshop session of the Historical Dimensions of Development Studies Group convened at the University of Salford on 30 March 1982. It was then delivered at the Third World Economic History Society Conference at the University of Liverpool, 17–19 September 1982, and subsequently presented at seminars at the University of Manchester and at North Staffordshire Polytechnic. Unfortunately, professional commitments prevented Dr. Kirk from further involvement, and so I would like to take this opportunity to place on record my gratitude for his valuable contribution. The second paper, 'Development Economics in the late 1980's: Charting a Course for a Rudderless Vessel' (mimeo, November 1984) was prepared for the first – and hopefully not the last – formally instituted session of the Annual Economic History Society Conference specifically devoted to Third World issues (University of York, 29–31 March 1985). Immediately prior to that occasion I had the benefit of airing the paper at seminars held at Sunderland Polytechnic and the University College of Swansea. In view of this long process of deliberation and scholarly interchange, I am indebted to a number of people who have been kind enough to tender gracious advice and judicious criticism. In particular, I owe special thanks to my colleagues Barbara Ingham, Robert Millward and Barrie Gleave. In addition Clive Dewey, Phil Leeson, Tony Hopkins, David Fieldhouse and John Toye have also offered several pertinent suggestions and have given me much friendly encouragement. But having acknowledged this help, the usual disclaimer applies absolving all the groups and individuals mentioned above from any responsibilty for the views herein expressed.

1. For a stimulating modern account of the leading Classical formulations (on both 'growth' *and* 'development') see W. Eltis, *The Classical Theory of Economic Growth* (London, 1984). Interest in what the Classical Political Economists had to say about the causes and course of long-run economic change has, of course, been greatly stimulated in recent years as a result of Pierro Sraffa's work on David Ricardo. Indeed, there is now a thriving neo-Ricardian perspective on the underdeveloped economies, much of it appearing in the *Cambridge Journal of Economics*.

2. For an informed discussion of the significance of the *Tableau Economique* see Eltis, ibid., Chapter 1, and Ronald Meeks' impressive general study of the Physiocrats in his early book *The Economics of Physiocracy* (London, 1962). A somewhat more speculative case has been made by Percy Selwyn for including Samuel Johnson as a relevant ancestor; see his 'Johnson's Hebrides: Thoughts on a Dying Social Order', *Development and Change*, 10 (3), 1979.

3. For some brief comparative considerations of both Marx and Schumpeter in this light, see H. W. Arndt, 'Economic Development: a Semantic History', *Economic Development and Cultural Change*, 29 (3), 1981, pp. 458ff; the essay by J. E. Elliott, 'Marx and Schumpeter on Capitalism's Creative Destruction' in the *Quarterly Journal of Economics*, 95, Aug. 1980, and the follow-up controversy between him and J. B. Foster, 'Schumpeter and Marx on Capitalist Transformation' in the same Journal, 98, May 1983; and the relevant sections in P. Deane, *The Evolution of Economic Ideas* (Cambridge, 1978), and A. Maddison, *Phases of Capitalist Development* (London, 1982). For slightly more detailed treatment, see the essays by Tsuru, Harris, Meek and Heertje in M. C. Howard and J. E. King (eds.), *The Economics of Marx* (London, 1976), and J. E. Elliott, 'Joseph A. Schumpeter at 100 and the Theory of Economic Development at 72', mimeograph,

Economics Research Paper No. 8302, Dept. of Economics, University of Southern California (July 1983).

4. Some interesting observations on colonial development are contained in Arndt, op. cit., pp. 460 ff; A. G. Hopkins, 'Imperial Connections' pp. 1–19 in A. G. Hopkins and C. Dewey (eds.), *The Imperial Impact: Studies in the Economic History of Africa and India* (London, 1978), and his 'Africa's Age of Improvement', *History in Africa*, 7, 1980; and C. Dewey, 'The Government of India's "New Industrial Policy" 1900–1925: Formation and Failure' in K. N. Chaudhuri and C. Dewey (eds.), *Economy and Society: Essays in Indian Economic and Social History* (New Delhi, 1979).

5. See D. Rimmer, 'Some Origins of Development Economics', *Development and Change*, 10 (3), 1979, for consideration of the work of the League of Nations and the ILO.

6. P. N. Rosenstein-Rodan, 'Problems of the Industrialization of Eastern and South-Eastern Europe', *Economic Journal*, 53, 1943, and 'The International Development of Economically Backward Areas', *International Affairs*, XX, 1944. For a discussion of Rosenstein-Rodan's contribution see C. Chakeravarty, 'Paul Rosenstein-Rodan: An Appreciation', *World Development*, 11 (1), 1983.

7. For India under Nehru, see Government of India (Ministry of Information), *Jawaharlal Nehru's Speeches, 1949–53* (Calcutta, 1954), Chapter 2; J. N. Bhagwati and P. Desai, *India, Planning for Industrialisation* (London, 1970); G. Shankar, 'Socialist Ideas of J. Nehru', *Journal of Indian History*, LVII (1–2), 1979; and B. H. Farmer, *An Introduction to South Asia* (London, 1983), Chapter 6. For Nkrumah's Ghana, see K. Nkrumah, *Neo-Colonialism: The Last Stage of Imperialism* (London, 1965); B. Davidson, *Black Star: a View of the Life and Times of Kwame Nkrumah* (London, 1973), Chapter 4; and T. Killick, *Development Economics in Action: a Study of Economic Policies in Ghana* (London, 1978).

8. The institutional aspects of the early history of the discipline have not as yet been adequately explored since those writers interested in tracing the evolution of the subject have concentrated (not unnaturally) upon theoretical developments. As far as the UK is concerned and relating only to academic issues, see K. Martin and J. Knapp (eds.), *The Teaching of Development Economics* (London, Cass, 1967), and D. Seers (ed.), 'Teaching Development at Graduate Level in Britain', *I.D.S. Bulletin* (Sussex, 1980).

9. See Alan Milward's *The Reconstruction of Western Europe, 1945–51* (London, 1984) for a revisionary account of the importance of Marshall Aid.

10. This popular – but highly contentious and essentially misleading – shorthand term will only be advisedly deployed in the rest of this paper in accordance with general usage. For some interesting observations on the derivation and utility of the term see L. Wolf-Phillips, 'Why Third World?'; P. Worsley, 'How Many Worlds?'; S. D. Mundi, 'The Third World: Concept and Controversy'; and A. B. Mountjoy, 'Worlds Without End' – all in the *Third World Quarterly* respectively 1 (1), 1979; 1 (2), 1979; 1 (3), 1979; and 2 (4), 1980.

11. For a standard account of the Soviet position see V. L. Tyagunenko, V. M. Kollantai, V. V. Rymalov, Y. A. Bragina and A. I. Chekhutov, *Industrialisation of Developing Countries* (Moscow, 1973); and V. F. Stanis *et al.*, *The Role of the State in Socio-economic Reforms in Developing Countries* (Moscow, 1976). Much of the work on developing countries was conducted by Faculty members of the Patrice Lumumba Friendship Society.

12. See S. Clarkson, *The Soviet Theory of Development* (London, 1979), especially Chapters 1 and 4, V. B. Singh (ed.), *Patterns of Economic Development* (Bombay, 1970), and W. A. Beling and G. Totten, *Developing Nations: Quest for a Model* (New York, 1970), especially Chapters 5 and 6. By way of contrast, see Jack Gray's now obviously dated essay 'The Chinese Model' in A. Nove and G. Nuti (eds.), *Socialist Economics* (London, 1978). For more recent cases see C. K. Wilbur and K. P. Jameson (eds.), *Socialist Models of Development* (Oxford, 1981), P. Wiles (ed.), *The New Communist Third World: an Essay in Political Economy* (London, 1981), and G. White, 'Developmental States and Socialist Industrialisation in the Third World', *Journal of Development Studies* 21 (1), 1984. For an illuminating discussion of the objective basis jof comparing development between the Western and Soviet economies over recent decades see P. Weidemann, 'Comparing the Process of Socio-Economic Development in Market and non-Market Economies: the EEC and the CMEA', *Cambridge Journal of Economics* 8 (4), 1984.

13. An interesting discussion of self-interest (in marked contrast to the 'mutuality-of-interests' view propounded by the two Brandt Commission Reports) may be found in the collection of essays edited by R. Cassen et al, *Rich Country Interests and Third World Development* (London, 1982).

14. For the experience of the most important agencies see The World Bank, *I.D.A. in Retrospect: the First Two Decades of the International Development Association* (Oxford, 1983); for the IMF see 'The Institutional Evolution of the International Monetary Fund' contributed by the editorial staff of *Finance and Development* 21 (3), 1984; and for the World Bank itself see the articles by D. Sommers, 'An Institution Emerges' and R. Chaufournier, 'The Coming of Age', both in *Finance and Development* 21 (2), 1984; and S. Please *The Hobbled Giant: Essays on the World Bank* (Westview, 1984).

15. A helpful and thought-provoking discussion of the changing meaning of economic liberalism may be found in Keith Tribe's translation of R. Walther's 'Economic Liberalism', *Economy and Society* 13 (2), 1984. As far as the label 'Orthodoxy' is concerned it is my contention that the vast majority of Western developmentalists had a sufficient number of shared beliefs so as to constitute a definite tradition of thinking and writing. This tradition soon captured centre-ground, and in this sense can be considered to be the Orthodoxy. Thus the argument of writers such as Deepak Lal – who consider neo-Classical theory to be the standard from which all must be judged, and therefore view any departure from it 'unorthodox' – is irrelevant in the present context.

16. See D. Seers's well-known and oft-quoted article 'The Limitations of the Special Case', *Bulletin of the Oxford Institute of Economics and Statistics*, 25 (2), 1963. The basic idea had, of course, been in circulation for some time prior to Seers's statement, and Gunnar Myrdal in particular had been striving to make the same sort of point from at least the mid-1950s – see his *Economic Theory and Underdeveloped Regions* (London, 1957), and this was later to form the theoretical core of his ambitious empirical study *Asian Drama: An Inquiry into the Poverty of Nations* (London, 1968), see esp. Part 1, Vol. 1. This work stimulated a stout defence of the relevance of the Classical (but not at that stage neo-Classical) position, and Hla Myint is perhaps the best-known exponent of what may be called 'Classical Resurrectionism', see in particular his 'Economic Theory and the Underdeveloped Countries', *Journal of Political Economy*, 73 (5), 1965.

17. For a brief history of planning see H. B. Chenery, 'The Evolution of Development Planning', Development Discussion Paper No. 158, Harvard Institute for International Development, mimeo (Dec. 1983), and D. T. Healey, 'Development Policy: New Thinking about an Interpretation', *Journal of Economic Literature*, 10, Sept. 1972, for a more critical evaluation.

18. See N. Leff's survey article 'Entrepreneurship and Economic Development: The Problem Revisited', *Journal of Economic Literature*, 17, March 1979.

19. As far as 'envy' is concerned see A. O. Hirschman, 'The Rise and Decline of Development Economics' in his *Essays in Trespassing: Economics to Politics and Beyond* (Cambridge, 1981). For the economist as a dispenser of advice cf. H. W. Singer and W. A. Joehr, *The Role of the Economist as Adviser to Governments* (London, 1955); L. Currie, *The Role of Economic Advisers in Developing Countries* (Westport, 1981); and Singer's and I. Livingstone's reviews of Currie in, respectively, the *Journal of Development Studies*, 19 (3), 1983, and the *Economic Journal*, 94, June 1984. On a more anecdotal level, at a Development Studies Association Workshop held in Dublin in 1979, the late Professor Seers casually informed me that he had just returned from a short 'advice-giving' trip to Colombia during which he had twice been to see the President – and that worthy had not only owned to having 'read with pleasure' a recent article penned by Professor Seers, but had actually instructed the top brass of his Treasury to 'take it to heart'. This should not, of course, be taken to mean that Third World governments slavishly followed either the theoretical writings of the academics or the reports and advice tendered by the visiting experts: obviously there were, and still are, entirely autonomous local factors at work which affected the take-up and implementation of general development strategy. For an early discussion of these factors see Seers's own article 'Why Visiting Economists Fail', *Journal of Political Economy*, 70, Aug. 1962, and for a later discussion see D. Goulet, 'Development Experts: the One-Eyed Giants', *World Development*, 8 (7–8), 1980.

20.   As far as I am aware no one has yet tried to systematically measure either the quantity or (much more nebulously) the quality of this stream of literature. In some disciplines, especially those with a long pedigree – such as economic theory and economic and social history – those academics with a strong interest in classifying, codifying and quantifying the available stock of literature (especially those articles appearing in the prestigious journals) have been beavering away at this hard-grind task for some time now. By the sorts of standards set by these efforts, my procedure for appraising the flow of material has been distinctly impressionistic and has involved no more than a perusal of library shelves, catalogues and indexes, and has in the main been confined to English language sources. Even so, for the period 1950–75 I would guess that in terms of scope and ambition, the surge of publications in the development area was comparable – at the very least – to the rate of expansion elsewhere in the social sciences.

21.   D. Lehmann, 'The Rise of the Jet-Set Proletariat', *Times Higher Education Supplement*, 27 Sept. 1984.

22.   As we shall see, over the last five years or so, a clutch of publications have appeared which attempt (usually in passing) some sort of appraisal of the history of the subject. For the most part the treatment is highly selective, generally biased towards justifying or condemning a particular viewpoint, and quite superficial. The most notable exception is Phil Leeson's unpublished paper 'Development Economics and its Companions', *Manchester Discussion Papers in Development Studies*, No. 8304, 1983.

23.   Paul Baran's early article 'On the Political Economy of Backwardness', which appeared in *The Manchester School*, January 1952, pp. 66–84, contained the basic gist of the argument he was to develop in *The Political Economy of Growth* (New York, 1957).

24.   For a useful discussion of some of the problems see D. J. Casley and D. A. Lury, *Data Collection in Developing Countries* (Oxford, 1982). With regards to the intractability of much historical data see S. Kuznets, *Modern Economic Growth: Rate, Structure, Spread* (New Haven, 1966), and his *Economic Growth of Nations: Total Output and Production Structures* (Cambridge, Mass., 1971); P. Bairoch, *The Economic Development of the Third World Since 1900* (London, 1975), and his 'International Industrialization Levels from 1750 to 1980', *Journal of European Economic History*, 11 (2), 1982; and L. G. Reynolds, 'The Spread of Economic Growth to the Third World', *Journal of Economic Literature*, 21 (3), 1983.

25.   For some of the early work in this area see M. Gilbert et al, *Comparative National Products and Price Levels* (Paris, 1958), W. Beckerman, *International Comparisons of Real Incomes* (Paris 1966), and R. Bacon and W. Beckerman, 'International Comparisons of Income Levels: A Suggested New Measure', *Economic Journal* 76, Sept. 1966.

26.   The basic study on PPPs (purchasing power parities) has been carried out by members of the Statistical Office of the UN and the World Bank. A large team of researchers, led by Irving B. Kravis, has now completed a three phase study of the subject – the International Comparison Project – published in three volumes by the Johns Hopkins Press (Baltimore), viz. *Phase I: A System of International Comparisons of Gross Product and Purchasing Power* (1975); *Phase II: International Comparisons of Real Product and Purchasing Power* (1978); and *Phase III: World Product and Income: International Comparisons of Real GDP* (1982). A more digestible account of their findings may be found in I. B. Kravis, A. Heston and R. Summers, 'Real GDP Per Capita for More than One Hundred Countries', *Economic Journal*, 88, June 1978. This work is not without its critics, and for some recent discussion see E. B. Maciejewski, 'Real Effective Exchange Rate Indices: A Re-examination', International Monetary Fund, *Staff Papers* 30 (3), 1983; L. H. Officer, *Purchasing Power Parity and Exchange Rates: Theory, Evidence and Relevance* (Michigan, 1983); the respective studies by M. Keren and J. Weinblatt, and S. Swamy and P. Samuelson, on 'International Real Income Measures' in the *Economic Journal*, 94, June 1984; and the exchange between Professor Kravis and Robin Marris, 'Comparing the Incomes of Nations' in the *Journal of Economic Literature*, 22 (1), 1984.

27.   Partly on account of the popularity of the 'Basic Needs' approach to development, a large and expanding literature on the 'Quality of Life' criteria of development has sprung up, and for the connection between the approach and the measure see N. Hicks and P. Streeten, 'Indicators of Development: the Search for a Basic Needs Yardstick' in

P. Streeten and R. Jolly (eds.), *Recent Issues in World Development: A Collection of Survey Articles* (Oxford, 1981). Over the last seven years or so most of the specialist journals have carried articles on various aspects of the subject – with *World Development* well to the fore. One of the most useful surveys is M. D. Morris' *Measuring the Conditions of the World's Poor: the Physical Quality of Life Index* (New York, 1979). For some criticism of the PQLI see D. A. Brodsky and D. Rodrik, 'Indicators of Development and Data Availability: The Case of the PQLI', *World Development*, 9 (7), 1981; and for a recent alternative procedure in the same underlying spirit see J. Silber, 'ELL (The Equivalent Length of Life) or Another Attempt at Measuring Development', *World Development*, 11 (1), 1983.

28. The best sources for national accounts are to be found in the *Yearbook(s) of National Accounts Statistics* put out by the UN Department of International Economic and Social Affairs (New York), the *Statistical Yearbook(s)* (New York) produced by the same agency, and the various *World Development Report(s)* (New York, 1977–). These, of course, need to be used in conjunction with the reports of the International Comparison Project alluded to in note 26 above. For a rather more interpretative treatment of trends see S. Kuznets, *Modern Economic Growth: Rate, Structure and Spread,* op. cit., *Economic Growth of Nations: Total Output and Production Structures*, op. cit., and his Nobel lecture, 'Modern Economic Growth: Findings and Reflections', *American Economic Review* 63 (3), 1973; and Angus Maddison's *Phases of Captialist Development*, op. cit., 1982; and D. Morawetz, *Twenty-five Years of Economic Development 1950–75* (Washington, 1977).

29. See W. Warren, 'Imperialism and Capitalist Industrialization', *New Left Review* 81, Sept. 1973; 'The post-war economic experience of the Third World' in K. Q. Hill (ed.), *Towards a New Strategy for Development: A Rothko Chapel Colloquium* (New York, 1979), and *Imperialism: Pioneer of Capitalism* (London, 1980). Since Bill Warren's untimely death, his ideas on this have been defended and further developed by J. Schiffer in 'The changing post-war pattern of development: the accumulated wisdom of Samir Amin', *World Development*, 9 (6), 1981.

30. A. O. Hirschman, 1981, op. cit.

31. P. Streeten, 'Development Ideas in Historical Perspective', in his *Development Perspectives* (London, 1981).

32. D. Seers, 'The Birth, Life and Death of Development Economics', *Development and Change*, 10 (4), 1979.

33. Ibid.

34. W. A. Lewis, 'The State of Development Theory', *American Economic Review*, 74 (1), 1984.

35. Although the following list of works written in this vein may seem long, it is illustrative rather than exhaustive and, as a convenient shorthand, surveys and readings have been used as a surrogate for further citative referencing. Works marked with a * are particularly relevant for our purpose here, and those with a + are Radical or neo-Marxian in perspective.

1985 E. de Kadt, 'Of Markets, Might and Mullahs: a Case for Equity, Pluralism and Tolerance in Development', *World Development*, 13 (4); F. Stewart, 'The Fragile Foundations of the Neo-classical Approach to Development', *Journal of Development Studies*, 21 (2); M. Todaro, *Economic Development in the Third World*, 3rd ed. London; J. Toye, 'Dirigisme and Development Economics', *Cambridge Journal of Economics*, 9 (1). J. Galtung, 'Development Theory: Notes for an Alternative Approach', *International Institute for Environment and Society*, preprint 85–11. K. Griffin and J. Gurley*, 'Radical Analyses of Imperialism, The Third World, and the Transition to Socialism: A Survey Article', *Journal of Economic Literature*, 23, Sept. H. Bruton*, 'The Search for a Development Economics', *World Development*, 13 (10 and 11). H. W. Arndt, 'The Origins of Structuralism', *World Development*, 13 (2). L. G. Reynolds, *Economic Growth in the Third World, 1850–1980*, Yale University Press.

1984 K. Basu, *The Less Developed Economy: a Critique of Contemporary Theory*, Oxford; C. Suriyakumaran, *The Wealth of Poor Nations*, London; G. M. Meier, *Emerging from Poverty**, Oxford; G. M. Meier and D. Seers (eds.) *Pioneers in*

Development, Oxford; A. G. Frank +, *Critique and Anti-Critique: Essays on Dependence and Reformism,* London; S. Roy, *Pricing, Planning and Politics: a Study of Economic Distortions,* London; W. A. Lewis*, *A.E.R.,* op. cit.; R. H. Chilcote, *Theories of Development and Underdevelopment* + (Westview); P. Worsley +, *The Three Worlds: Culture and World Development,* London; the 'Symposium on Reassessing Development Experience'* in *World Development,* 12 (9), especially the essays by Adelman, Singer, Scitovsky and Fishlow; *Capital and Class* +, 22, Spring, especially the articles by A. Lipietz, W. Andreff and R. Jenkins, all on the New International Division of Labour Debate. S. N. H. Naqvi*, 'Development Economists in "Emperor's Clothes"?', *Pakistan Development Review,* 23 (2 and 3). M. Syrquin, L. Taylor and L. E. Westphal (eds.), *Economic Structure and Performance: Essays in Honor of H. B. Chenery;* Orlando. L. Donaldson, *Economic Development: Analysis and Policy,* St. Paul. B. Hettne*, 'Approaches to the Study of Peace and Development', European Association of Development Research and Training Institute Working Paper No. 6, August.

1983 D. Lal, *The Poverty of Development Economics,* London; J. Toye*, 'Commentary: the Disparaging of Development Economics', *Journal of Development Studies,* 20 (1); R. M. Sundrum*, *Development Economics: a Framework for Analysis and Policy,* London; A. K. Sen*, 'Development: Which Way Now?', *Economic Journal,* 93, December; F. Perroux, *A New Concept of Development: Basic Tenets,* London; P. Leeson*, op. cit., P. Hall, *Growth and Development: An Economic Analysis,* Oxford; P. Limqueco and B. Macfarlane + (eds.), *Neo-Marxist Theories of Development,* London; C. Furtado +, *Accumulation and Development,* Oxford; C. A. Barone +, 'Dependency and Marxist Theory', *Review of Radical Political Economy,* 15 (1); F. Tökei +, 'On the Historical Basis of Problems of Development of the Third World', *Journal of Contemporary Asia,* 13 (3); K. Choi, *Theories of Comparative Economic Growth,* Iowa; K. Cole*, 'Economic Theory and Development Studies', *Jurnal Ekonomi Malaysia,* 7, June; J. N. Bhagwati*, 'Development Economics: What Have we Learned?' Discussion Paper No. 36, International Economic Research Center, University of Columbia, Oct. 1983; H. J. Bruton*, 'The Search for a Development Economics', Research Memorandum Series RM−87, Center for Development Economics, Williams College, Mass., Nov. 1983; R. H. Chilcote and D. L. Johnson (eds.) +, *Theories of Development: Mode of Production or Dependency?,* Beverley Hills; 'Economic Development and the Development of Economics'*, *World Development,* 11 (10), especially the essays by Rosen, Streeten, Solow, Weisskopf and S. Roy; R. Higgott*, *Political Development Theory: The Contemporary Debate,* London.

1982 A. M. Hoogvelt +, *The Third World in Global Development,* London; A. K. Bagchi +, *The Political Economy of Underdevelopment,* Cambridge; H. Alavi *et al* +, *Capitalism and Colonial Production,* London; I. M. D. Little*, *Economic Development: Theory, Policy and International Relations,* London; F. I. Nixson*, 'Beyond Economic Development', *Manchester Discussion Papers in Development Studies,* No. 8203 (which appears as Chapter 2 in the present volume); I. Livingstone (ed.), *Approaches to Development Studies: Essays in Honour of A. Mackintosh,* London, especially Livingstone's* 'The Development of Development Economics'; M. Bienefeld and M. Godfrey (eds.), *The Struggle for Development,* London; P. T. Bauer, *Equality, the Third World and Economic Delusion,* London; P. W. Preston*, *Theories of Development,* London; H. Alavi and T. Shanin (eds.) +, *Introduction to the Sociology of 'Developing' Societies,* London; G. Kitchin*, *Development and Underdevelopment in Historical Perspective: Populism, Nationalism and Industrialisation,* London. Olson, *The Rise and Decline of Nations: Economic Growth, Stagflation and Social Rigidities,* Yale University Press.

1981 H. W. Arndt*, op. cit.; A. O. Hirschman*, op. cit.; M. P. Todaro, *Economic Development in the Third World,* London, 2nd ed.; M. Gersovitz (ed.), *The Theory and Experience of Economic Development: Essays in Honour of Sir W. A. Lewis,* London; P. Fourie*, 'The Illusive Concept of Development', *Development Studies on Southern Africa* 4, (1); P. Streeten and R. Jolly (eds.), *Recent Issues in World Development: a Collection of Survey Articles,* especially the essay by G. Palma +, Oxford; D. Goodman and M. Redclift +, *From Peasant to Proletarian,* Oxford; R. J. Holton +,

'Marxist Theories of Social Change', *Theory and Society*, 10 (6); H. G. Mannur*, 'Development Economics and Economic Development – Old Theories and New Perspectives', *Indian Journal of Economics*, 62 (2–4), July; special issue of *Latin American Perspectives*+, 'Dependency and Marxism', 7, Summer and Fall; R. Bahro, *The Alternative in Eastern Europe*, London.

1980 W. Warren+, op. cit.; I. Sachs, *Studies in the Political Economy of Development*, Oxford; I. Abdulla, 'What Development?', *International Development Review*, 22 (2–3); K. P. Clements*, *From Right to Left in Development Theory*, Singapore; A. Brewer+, *Marxist Theories of Imperialism*, London; J. de Bandt, P. Mardi and D. Seers, *European Studies in Development: New Trends in European Development Studies*, London; N. Mouzelis+, 'Prospects for a Theory of Third World Formations', *Journal of Peasant Studies*, 7 (3); J. Love, 'Prebisch and the Doctrine of Unequal Exchange', *Latin American Research Review*, 15 (3); V. V. Bhatt*, *Development Perspectives: Problem, Strategy and Policies*, Oxford; F. Fröbel, J. Heinrichs and O. Kreye+, *The New International Division of Labour*, Cambridge; *I.D.S. Bulletin**, 11 (3) essays by J. Toye, 'Does Development Studies Have a Core?', and C. Leys, 'Challenging Development Concepts'; J. Friedmann, T. Wheelwright and J. Connell, *Development Strategies in the Eighties*, Sydney.

1979 D. Lehmann (ed.)*, *Development Theory: Four Critical Studies*, especially the essays by Bernstein, Seers and Nafziger, Frank Cass, London; D. Seers*, op. cit., *Development and Change*; K. Q. Hill (ed.)*, *Towards a New Strategy for Development: a Rothko Chapel Colloquium*, New York, especially the essays by Hirschman, Seers, Streeten, Warren, Minhas and Ohlin; J. Robinson+, *Aspects of Development and Underdevelopment*, Cambridge; D. A. Nugent and J. B. Yotopoulis*, 'What Has Orthodox Development Economics learnt from Recent Experience?', *World Development*, 7 (6); H. W. Singer*, 'Poverty, Income Distribution and levels of living: Thirty Years of Changing Thought on Development Problems' in C. H. Rao and D. C. Joshi (eds.), *Reflections on Economic Development and Social Change: Essay in Honour of Professor V. K. V. R. Rao*, Bombay; I. Roxborough*, *Theories of Underdevelopment*, London; J. K. Galbraith, *The Nature of Mass Poverty*, Cambridge, Mass.; J. Taylor+, *From Modernisation to Modes of Production*, London; C. K. Wilbur (ed.)*, *The Political Economy of Development and Underdevelopment*, New York, 2nd ed., especially parts 1, 2, 6 and 8; F. H. Cardoso and E. Falleto+, *Dependency and Development in Latin America*, Berkeley; I. Wallerstein+, *The Capitalist World-Economy*, Cambridge; R. Flammang, 'Economic Growth and Economic Development: Counterparts or Competitors?', *Economic Development and Cultural Change* 28, (1), 1979; C. A. O. Nieuwenhuize, 'Balance Carried Forward: a review of twenty-five years of development studies at the Institute of Social Studies' in the Proceedings of the ISS 25th Anniversary Conference, *Development of Societies: the next twenty-five years* (The Hague, 1977); S. Smith and J. Toye, 'Three stories about trade and poor economies', *Journal of Development Studies*, 15 (3); K. Mohri, 'Marx and Underdevelopment', *Monthly Review*, 30, April.

1978 P. Deane*, op. cit.; A. Foster-Carter+, 'The Modes of Production Controversy', *New Left Review*, 107; G. Williams+, 'Imperialism and Development: a Critique', *World Development* 6 (6 and 7); B. Higgins*, 'Development Economics in the USA: a Comment', *Journal of Development Studies* 15 (2); L. Currie, 'The Objectives of Development', *World Development*, 6 (1); B. Hettne and P. Wallenstein (eds.), *Emerging Trends in Development Theory*, Swedish Agency for Research Co-operation with Developing Countries, May.

1977 A. Phillips+, 'The Concept of Development', *Review of African Political Economy*, 8, Jan.–April; M. Nash (ed.)*, *Economic Development and Cultural Change: Essays in Honour of B. F. Hoselitz* (Supplement to E.D.C.C. 25), Chicago, especially the essays by G. V. Papanek, 'Economic Development Theory: The Earnest Search for a Mirage', G. Ranis, 'Development Theory at Three Quarters Century', and S. Kuznets, 'Notes on the Study of the Economic Growth of Nations'; C. J. Reynolds, *Image and Reality in Economic Development* (New Haven); Pugwash Symposium on 'The Role of Self-Reliance in Alternative Strategies for Development', *World Development*, 5 (3);

R. Brenner +, 'The Origins of Capitalist Development: a Critique of neo-Smithian Marxism', *New Left Review*, 104; F. Cardoso*, 'The Originality of Copy: ECLA and Development', *CEPAL Review*, 4; O. Sunkel*, 'The Development of Development Thinking', *I.D.S. Bulletin* 8 (3); D. Morawetz*, *Twenty-five Years of Economic Development: 1950–1975*, Washington; F. H. Cardoso, 'The Consumption of Dependency Theory in the USA' *Latin American Research Review*, 12 (3); E. Laclau +, *Politics and Ideology in Marxist Theory*, London; J. Nyilas (ed.) +, *Theory and Practice of Development in the Third World*, Budapest.

1976   I. Livingstone*, 'After Divorce: the Re-marriage of Economic Theory and Development Economics?', *Eastern African Economic Review* 8 (1); T. Szentes +, *The Political Economy of Underdevelopment*, 2nd ed., Budapest; J. W. Mellor*, *The New Economics of Growth: a Strategy for India and the Developing World*, Cornell; W. Nafziger +, 'A Critique of Development Economics in the US', *Journal of Development Studies*, 13 (1); M. Wolfe*, 'Approaches to Development: Who is Approaching What?', *CEPAL Review*, 1976; S. Lall, 'Conflicts and Concepts: Welfare Economics and Developing Countries', *World Development*, 4 (3).

1975   W. A. Lewis*, 'The Diffusion of Development' in T. Wilson and A. S. Skinner (eds.), *The Market and the State: Essays in Honour of Adam Smith*, Oxford; G. Kay +, *Development and Underdevelopment: a Marxist Analysis*, London; H. Brookfield*, *Interdependent Development*, London; H. W. Singer (ed.), *The Strategy of International Development: Essays in the Economics of Backwardness*, New York; 'A Re-assessment of Development Economics'*, *American Economic Review*, 65 (2), especially the essays by I. Adelman, 'Development Economics – a Re-assessment of Goals' and S. A. Resnick, 'State of Development Economics'; I. Oxaal *et al* (eds.)* *Beyond the Sociology of Development*, London; C. Leys +, *Underdevelopment in Kenya: the political economy of neo-colonialism 1964–1971*, London.

36. The most recent being 'The State of Development Theory', ESRC Development Economics Group, University of Warwick, Nov. 1984; the Speical Issue on 'Third World Industrialisation in the 1980s: Open Economies in a Closing World', *Journal of Development Studies*, 21 (1), Oct. 1984; the 'Symposium on Technological Change and Industrial Development', *Journal of Development Economics*, 16 (1–2), Sept.–Oct. 1984; the 'Symposium on Reassessing Development Experience', *World Development*, 12 (9), Sept. 1984; and 'Economic Development and the Development of Economics', *World Development*, 11 (10), Oct. 1983. A similar acceleration in the tempo of discussion on 'what is development?' has occurred during the regular meetings of the Development Studies Association of the UK and Ireland, and its respective Study Groups, over the last five years.

37. Such as Professors H. W. Singer, E. E. Hagen, G. Myrdal and, of course, R. Prebisch. They all emphasised the 'formidable obstacles' such as the 'agricultural bottlenecks', the 'foreign exchange constraints' and the 'vicious circle' syndromes that stood in the way of development. Indeed Professor Singer opined that 'the complexity of the real world makes a mockery of any preconceived universal optimism or pessimism. There is a lot of good as well as a lot of bad. The better approach seems to be pragmatic'. See his *International Development: Growth and Change* (New York, 1964) p. 16.

38. After a brief flirtation with Thomas Kuhn's 'paradigms' (*The Structure of Scientific Revolutions*, Chicago, 1962) in the 1970s cf. L. Lefeber, 'On the Paradigm for Economic Development', *World Development*, 2 (1), 1974, and A. Foster-Carter, 'From Rostow to Gunder Frank: Conflicting Paradigms in the Analysis of Underdevelopment', *World Development*, 4 (3), 1976, the word had been all but dropped from the development vocabulary.

39. For obvious reasons there has been a tremendous surge in the number of publications addressed to defining, measuring and examining the incidence of poverty, hunger and malnutrition in the last few years. For a selection of work from different perspectives see S. Reutlinger and M. Selowsky, *Malnutrition and Poverty: Magnitude and Policy Options* (Johns Hopkins University Press, 1978); S. A. R. Shastry, 'Poverty: Concepts and Measurement', *Indian Journal of Economics*, 61, Sept. 1980, and his 'A Survey of the Literature on Poverty', *Artha Vijnana*, 21 (1), 1980; A. K. Sen, *Poverty and*

Famines: An Essay on Entitlement and Deprivation (Oxford, 1981); A. Berg, *Malnourished People: a Policy View* (World Bank, 1981); P. Isenman, *et al., Poverty and Human Development* (Oxford, 1982), and G. M. Meier, *Emerging from Poverty*, op. cit., 1984. For a longer-run view see D. Grigg, 'Counting the Hungry: World Patterns of Undernutrition', *Tijdschrift voor Econ. en Soc. Geografie*, 73 (2), 1982.

40. Much of the pioneering work on analysing and measuring inequality and distribution was done by Simon Kuznets, see especially his 'Economic Growth and Income Inequality', *American Economic Review*, 45, March 1955, and 'Quantitative Aspects of Economic Growth of Nations: III, Distribution of Income by Size', *Economic Development and Cultural Change*, 11 (1), 1963. For later work see I. Adelman and C. Taft Morris, *Economic Growth and Social Equity in Developing Countries* (Stanford, 1973); A. K. Sen, *On Economic Inequality* (New York, 1973); W. R. Cline 'Distribution and Development: a Survey of the Literature', *Journal of Development Economics*, 2 (3), 1975; M. S. Ahluwalia. 'Inequality, Poverty and Development', *Journal of Development Economics*, (3), 1976; C. R. Frank and R. C. Webb (eds.), *Income Distribution and Growth in the Less Developed Countries* (Washington, 1977); G. S. Fields, *Poverty, Inequality and Development* (Cambridge, 1980), and A. Bigsten, *Income Distribution and Development: Theory, Evidence and Policy* (London, 1983).

41. See H. W. Singer's essay 'Recent Trends in Economic Thought on Underdeveloped Countries' in his *International Development: Growth and Change*, op. cit., 1964, for a discussion of 'pendulum shifts' over the very long run.

42. Especially J. D. Gould, *Economic Growth in History: Survey and Analysis* (London, 1972) especially Ch. 1; R. A. Flammang, 'Economic Growth and Economic Development: Counterparts or Competitors?', op. cit., 1979; and H. W. Arndt, 1981, op. cit.

43. J. D. Gould, op. cit., p. 4.

44. Ibid., pp. 4f. Thus the French tend to use *croissance* and *développement* interchangeably; the Germans use *Wachstum* (growth) to refer to both — few choosing to follow Schumpeter's term *Entwicklung*; and the Italians depend upon *sviluppo* (development).

45. Ibid., p. 4, and Arndt, op. cit., p. 465.

46. R. A. Flammang, op. cit., p. 61.

47. J. A. Schumpeter's *The Theory of Economic Development: an Enquiry into Profits, Capital, Credit, Interest and the Business Cycle* originally appeared in German in 1911 and was only translated into English in 1934; the most recent edition appears in 1983 with a helpful Introduction by J. E. Elliott (Transaction Books, New Brunswick). Elliott illuminates the distinction between *Entwicklung* and Growth (a discussion of the latter appears in Schumpeter's later two volume study of Business Cycles). For Marx see K. Mohri, op. cit.

48. Cf. J. D. Gould, op. cit., p. 4, H. W. Arndt, op. cit., p. 458, and R. Flammang, op. cit., p. 55.

49. See Chapter 2.

50. *Growth without Development — an Economic Survey of Liberia* by R. W. Clower, G. Dalton, M. Harwitz and A. A. Walters, with R. P. Armstrong, J. Cole, R. E. Cole and G. Lamsom (Evanston, Northwestern University Press, 1966). The team, which consisted of an unusual (to say the least) combination of academics, originally prepared a report for the Liberian Government (presented in 1962), but because this was highly critical of the existing regime, it was never publicly released.

51. J. H. Boeke, the founder of the Leiden School of 'Tropical Economics', was the father of dualism; see his two studies *The Evolution of the Netherlands Indies Economy* (New York, 1946), and *Economics and Economic Policy in Dual Societies as Exemplified by Indonesia* (Haarlem, 1953). For an early critical assessment see Benjamin Higgins, 'The "dualistic theory" of underdeveloped areas' in *Ekonomic dan Kenangan Indonesia*, Feb. 1955, and for a rather later evaluation of dualism see H. W. Singer, 'Dualism Revisited: a New Approach to the Problem of Dual Society in Developing Economies', *Journal of Development Studies*, 7 (1), 1979. Although Boeke's ideas were genuinely original, he did owe something to J. S. Furnivall's earlier studies based upon India and Burma, cf. his 'The Organisation of Consumption', *Economic Journal*, 20, 1910, and *Colonial Theory and Practice: a comparative study of Burma and the Netherlands Indies* (Cambridge, 1948).

52. H. Myint, 'An Interpretation of Economic Backwardness', *Oxford Economic Papers*, 6, June 1954, and his *The Economics of the Developing Countries* (London, 1964), especially Ch. 4; and J. V. Levin, *The Export Economies* (Cambridge, Mass., 1960). These theoretical antecedents are partly acknowledged on p. 4 of *Growth without Development*.

53. *Growth without Development*, op. cit., p. vi.

54. A perusal of the *Journal of Economic Abstracts* (the precursor of the *Journal of Economic Literature*) over 1966–68 reveals that the book seems to have been all but completely ignored by the reviewing editors of the principal journals. Certainly the two main development outlets, *Economic Development and Cultural Change* (in America) and the *Journal of Development Studies* (the UK) never gave the book any notice, and the *Economic Journal* also let it slip through. The only review I have been able to trace is the short – and hostile – piece by P. B. Huber in the *American Economic Review*, 62 (3), 1967, pp. 617f.

55. See George Dalton's (independent) article 'History, Politics, and Economic Development in Liberia', *Journal of Economic History*, 25 (4), 1965.

56. One of the earliest studies outlining the persistence of mass poverty within a growing economy was that of V. M. Dandekar and N. Rath, *Poverty in India* (Bombay, 1971); for later general work see note 39 above. The 'gap' between 'Rich' and 'Poor' countries became an increasingly dominant theme of the development literature during the period: for a very recent discussion see M. A. Seligson (ed.), *The Gap Between Rich and Poor: Contending Perspectives on the Political Economy of Development* (Westview, 1984).

57. Credit – if that is the right word – for opening up the concept of 'development' must go to Denis Goulet, see his book, *The Cruel Choice: a New Concept on the Theory of Development* (New York, 1971) and article 'Development ... or Liberation', *International Development Review*, 13 (3), 1971. Dudley Seers has also been influential, see his 'The Meaning of Development' in N. Baster (ed.), *Measuring Development* (London, Cass, 1972), and 'The Meaning of Development, with a Postscript' in D. Lehmann (ed.), op. cit. Readers familiar with the literature will immdiately recognise the source of derivation of these criteria of what constitutes 'development'. Two useful surveys may be found in the series of articles included in the Institute for Social Studies, *Development of Societies: the next twenty-five years* (The Hague, 1977), and P. C. Fourie, op. cit. See also E. de Kadt, op. cit., 1985.

58. Cf. the most popular modern textbooks, especially M. Todaro, op. cit., Ch. 3; A. P. Thirlwall, *Growth and Development: With Special Reference to Developing Economies* (3rd ed., London, 1983), Ch. 1; E. W. Nafziger, *The Economics of Developing Countries* (Belmont, Calif. 1984), Chs. 2, 4 and 5; and M. Gillis, D. W. Perkins, M. Roemar and D. R. Snodgrass, *Economics of Development* (New York, 1983), Chs. 2 and 4.

59. Human Geographers, Ecologists, Social Anthropologists, Historians, Political Scientists, Social Planners, Sociologists, Social Administrators and even Social Psychologists (especially David McClelland) have all made respective contributions to the meaning of 'development'. One of the most lucid yet wide-ranging discusssions appears in L. Mair's *Anthropology and Development* (London, 1984), Ch. 1.

60. International Labour Organisation, *Employment, Incomes and Equality, a Strategy for Increasing Productive Employment in Kenya* (Geneva, 1972).

61. H. B. Chenery, M. S. Ahluwalia, C. I. G. Bell, J. H. Duloy and R. Jolly, *Redistribution with Growth: policies to improve income distribution in developing countries in the context of economic growth* (Oxford, 1974).

62. The literature on the 'Basic Needs' approach – closely associated with the recent work of Paul Streeten – is now quite large; for a selection see ILO, *Employment, Growth and Basic Needs: a One-World Problem* (New York, 1977); N. Hicks and P. Streeten, 'Indicators of Development: the Search for a Basic Needs Yardstick', *World Development*, 7 (6), 1979; N. Hicks, 'Growth vs. Basic Needs: Is there a Trade-off?', *World Development*, 7 (11–12), 1979; P. Streeten, 'Basic Needs and Human Rights', *World Development*, 8 (2), 1980; P. Streeten, *et al.*, *First Things First: Meeting Basic Human Needs in the Developing Countries* (London, 1981); P. Streeten, 'Basic Needs: Some Unsettled Questions', *World Development*, 12 (9), 1984. For the link between RWG and Basic Needs see H. W. Singer, 'Poverty, Income Distribution and levels of Living ...', op. cit., pp. 33–8, and A. R. Jolly, 'The World Employment Conference: The Enthronement of Basic Needs', *ODI Review*, 2, 1976.

63. For an excellent discussion of the deleterious consequences of such tendencies see Chapter 2.
64. P. Streeten, 'Basic Needs: Some Unsettled Questions', op. cit., which also appears in *The Kashmir Economic Review*, 1 (1), 1984.
65. See G. H. Jensen, *Afro-Asia and Non-alignment* (London, 1966) and P. Worsley, *The Three Worlds*, op. cit., especially Ch. 5.
66. For an inside account of this Conference and the subsequent developments that led to the formation of the OAU see K. Nkrumah, *I Speak of Freedom* (London, 1961), especially Ch. 21. See also A. Sesay, O. Ojo and O. Fasehun, *The OAU After Twenty Years* (Westview, 1985).
67. See the special issue of the *I.D.S. Bulletin* devoted to 'Britain on Brandt', 12 (2), 1981, for one such European reaction. The fate of the Brandt Report in the UK cannot, of course, be reduced to the antipathy between Edward Heath – a prominent member of the Commission – and Margaret Thatcher!
68. Three useful sources of reference for these summits and also for the more numerous low-level technical meetings are the Editorials in the *Third World Quarterly* 1979–   , and the journals *Development Dialogue* 1981– and *South*. For a critical overview of the whole New International Economic Order discussion see W. Loehr and J. R. Powelson, *Threat to Development: Pitfalls of the NIEO* (Boulder, Colorado, 1983), and R. A. Mortimer, *The Third World Coalition in International Politics* (Westview, 1984); and for UNCTAD see the Special Number of the *Foreign Trade Review*, 19 (2) July–Sept. 1984, especially the essays by J. C. Baker and E. R. Brunswick, G. Sundarama and W. N. Talwar.
69. See C. Hamilton, 'Capitalist Industrialization in the Four Little Tigers of East Asia', *Journal of Contemporary Asia*, 13 (1), 1983.
70. These categories appear in the Appendices of the *World Development Report 1984*.
71. This is not to underestimate the significant contribution being made by the New Classical Economics inspired by Pierro Sraffa and alluded to in fn. 1 above. The work of writers such as Krishna Bharadwaj, Simon Hollander, P. Garegnani, John Eatwell and Terry Peach has undoubtedly been extremely significant. But I think that it is fair to say that (with the obvious exception of Prof. Bharadwaj) their principal preoccupation to date has been with pure economic theory (especially related to capital and wages) rather than its application to underdeveloped countries – see A. Klamer, *Conversations with Economists: New Classical Economists and Opponents Speak Out* (New Jersey, 1983) for an interesting presentation of respective positions. This new Cambridge School is, of course, quite distinct from the earlier formulations of Professor H. Myint, notes 18 and 52 above.
72. See note 23 above.
73. In P. T. Bauer and B. S. Yamey, *The Economics of Underdeveloped Countries* (Cambridge, 1957) and P. T. Bauer, *Some Economic Aspects and Problems of Under-Developed Countries* (Forum of Free Enterprise, Bombay 1959).
74. D. Lal, *The Poverty of Development Economics,* op. cit., Preface, p. xi.
75. Ibid.
76. See his 'Foreign Economic Aid: Means and Objectives' in J. A. Pincus (ed.), *Reshaping the World Economy* (New York, 1968) and most recently his book, co-written with Rose Friedman, *Free to Choose: A Personal Statement* (London, 1980).
77. See A. C. Harberger and D. Wall, 'Harry G. Johnson as a Development Economist', *Journal of Political Economy*, 92 (4), 1984.
78. P. T. Bauer, *Dissent on Development* (London, 1972), *Equality, the Third World and Economic Delusion* (London, 1981) and *Reality and Rhetoric: Studies in the Economics of Development* (London, 1984).
79. Aspects of this theme were debated at the conferences held in Manchester in 1964, see J. Knapp and K. Martin (eds.), op. cit., and at Dar-es-Salaam in 1972, see I. Livingstone *et al.* (eds.), *The Teaching of Economics in Africa* (London, 1973).
80. Opinion on the actual number of countries that fall within the category of 'NICs' varies from less than a dozen (cf. OECD, *The Impact of the Newly Industrializing Countries on Trade and Manufactures*, Paris 1979) to two dozen (Foreign and Commonwealth Office, *The Newly Industrializing Countries and the Adjustment Problem*, London, 1979).

81. Cf. I.M.D. Little, T. Scitovsky and M. Scott, *Industry and Trade in Some Developing Countries* (Oxford, 1970).
82. J. Bhagwati and P. Desai, *India: Planning for Industrialisation*, op. cit.
83. B. Belassa, *The Newly Industrializing Countries in the World Economy* (Oxford, 1981).
84. L. Turner and N. McMullan, *The Newly Industrialising Countries: Trade and Adjustment* (London, 1982).
85. I.M.D. Little, *Economic Development: Theory, Policy and International Relations*, op. cit., especially Chs.4, 9 and 10.
86. T.W. Schultz, *Transforming Traditional Agriculture* (New Haven, 1964).
87. Associated with the work of economists such as Herbert Stein, Martin Feldstein, Robert Barro, James Buchanan, Gordon Tullock and Robert Lucas. For a short review of this stream of writing see B. Bartlett, 'Supply-side Economics: Theory and Evidence', *National Westminster Bank Quarterly Review*, Feb. 1985.
88. K. Marsden, 'Links Between Taxes and Economic Growth: Some Empirical Evidence', *World Bank Staff Paper* No.605, Aug. 1983.
89. IMF, *Tax Systems and Policy Objectives in Developing Countries: General Principles and Diagnostic Tests*, DM/83/78, Nov. 1983.
90. W. Elkan's review appears in *The Economic Journal*, 94, Dec. 1984, pp.1006f.
91. Convenient surveys of the neo-Marxian – and Marxian – formulations appear in A. Brewer, op. cit.; P. Worsley, *The Three Worlds*, op. cit.; R.M. Sundrum, op. cit.; P. Leeson, op. cit.; P. Limqueco and B. Macfarlane, op. cit.; R.H. Chilcote and D.L. Johnson, op. cit.; A.M. Hoogvelt, op. cit.; D. Goodman and M. Redclift, op. cit.; and, most recently, R.H. Chilcote, *Theories of Development and Underdevelopment* (Westview, 1984).
92. For this see F. Cardoso, 'The Originality of Copy ...', op. cit., and G. Pama, 1981, op. cit.
93. Frank has undergone something of a change of mind in recent years in as much as he has come to recognise some of the limitations of his original conception of capitalism (little more than exchange relations) and has now accorded a greater emphasis to the play of internal Third World factors arising out of production relations, see particularly his *World Accumulation 1492–1789* (London, 1978) and *Dependent Accumulation and Underdevelopment* (London, 1979). It is interesting that this 'Mark II' Frank has not sold nearly as well or generated quite as much controversy as the earlier work; and the downward spiral has continued with respect to his latest clutch of publications.
94. The references for the last two authors are P. Khvoinik, *Trade Among Capitalist Countries* (Moscow, 1982), and C. Palloix, 'The Internationalisation of Capital and the Circuit of Social Capital' in H. Radice (ed.), *International Firms and Modern Imperialism* (London, 1975).
95. The debate, which originally appeared in *Science and Society* (republished as R.H. Hilton (ed.), *The Transition from Feudalism to Capitalism*, London, 1979), is now spilling over into underdevelopment theory, see Leeson, op. cit., p.30; R.S. Gottlieb, 'Feudalism and Historical Materialism: A Critique and a Synthesis', *Science and Society*, 48 (1), 1984; D. Laibman, 'Modes of Production and Theories of Transition', *Science and Society*, 48 (3), 1984; H.J. Kaye, *The British Marxist Historians* (Oxford, 1984) especially Chs.2 and 3; and A. Sen, 'The Transition from Feudalism to Capitalism', *Economic and Political Weekly*, 28 July 1984.
96. Cf. A. Brewer, op. cit., C. Leys, 'Underdevelopment and Dependency: Critical Notes', *Journal of Contemporary Asia*, 7 (1), 1977, and his 'Kenya: What Does "Dependency" Explain?', *Review of African Political Economy*, 17, 1980; N. Mouzelis, 'Prospects for a Theory of Third World Formations', op. cit., and his 'Review Article' in the *Journal of Development Studies*, 19 (4), 1983; P. Leeson, op. cit., p.34; and H. Bernstein, 'Sociology and Underdevelopment ...', op. cit. Also see note 208 below. P. Worsley, op. cit., pp.41, 189f.
97. H. Bernstein, ibid., p.94.
98. See M. Hollis and E.J. Nell, *Rational Economic Man: A Philosophical Critique of Neo-Classical Economics* (Cambridge, 1975) for a more generalised attack, and at a more popular level see A. Lindbeck, *The Political Economy of the New Left* (New York, 1977).
99. P. Leeson, op. cit., p.36. However, he doesn't feel that this is justified – the fears

of co-optation, infiltration and a loss of conviction he believes are exaggerated, and he goes on to opine that 'a fruitful interaction is now more possible'. I am not so sanguine.

100. D. Seers, 'The Congruence of Marxism and Other neo-Classical Doctrines' in K. G. Hill (ed.), op. cit. Less extreme notions running in the same direction have been forwarded by Ian Livingstone, 'The Development of Development Economics', op. cit., and Paul Streeten, 'Development Ideas in Historical Perspective' in P. Streeten, *Development Perspectives*, op. cit.

101. Over the last decade this has certainly been my own personal experience in teaching Development Economics to both undergraduate and postgraduate students.

102. For an appreciation of Hoselitz's work see the Festschrift volume of essays by Manning Nash, op. cit.

103. Cf. M. Lipton, 'Interdisciplinary Studies in Less Developed Countries', *Journal of Development Studies*, 7 (1), 1970; C. Leys, 'Challenging Development Concepts' in the *I.D.S. Bulletin* 11 (3), 1980, devoted to 'teaching development at graduate level in Britain'. See also M. P. Moore, 'The Logic of Interdisciplinary Studies' in the *Journal of Development Studies*, 11 (1), 1974, and Sir John Hicks's remarks in the Introduction to his classic study *Capital and Growth* (London, 1965).

104. See, for instance, John Taylor's stricture that A. Foster-Carter's long review article on neo-Marxism (a version of which appeared in the *Jnl. Contemp. Asia*, 3 (1), 1973) 'is, above all else, a sociological discourse' in his 'Neo-Marxism and Underdevelopment – A Sociological Phantasy', *Journal of Contemporary Asia*, 4 (1), 1974. Foster-Carter managed to return some of the medicine in his review of Taylor's book on the *Modes of Production*, see the *Journal of Development Studies*, 17 (2), 1981.

This is not a problem, of course, for the neo-Classicals: they argue for academic specialisation anyway. Presumably, whenever it was deemed necessary – say in a project evaluation study – they would be perfectly happy to 'buy-in' expertise.

105. It is well known that Britain's record on overseas aid and development assistance over the last decade has been extremely poor – even by the modest (and now reduced) standards set by the other OECD countries. For a recent statistical survey see H. M. Treasury, *The Expenditure Plans 1984–85 to 1986–87*, Cmnd. 9143–II; ODI Briefing Paper, 'Facts and Figures on Aid', Dec. 1984; and *Help Yourself: The Politics of Aid* put out by *LINKS 20*' (London, Sept. 1984). For an attack on the whole aid programme – but from two very different quarters – cf. P. T. Bauer, *Reality and Rhetoric*, op. cit., and T. Hayter and C. Watson, *Aid: Rhetoric and Reality* (London, 1985): note the identical use of words ('reality', 'rhetoric') – but the change in their order!

106. In order to avert the threat of closure the IDS was recently forced to mount a 'save-us' lobbying campaign: though now 'reprieved' the enforced retrenchment is clearly a serious matter.

107. As far as this country is concerned, witness the joint ESRC–DSA Workshop on 'The Relevance of Development Studies to the Study of Change in Contemporary Britain', 14–15 May 1985. This is symptomatic of a much more general trend.

108. The supply of new academic recruits (postgraduate students) has dwindled alarmingly in the last few years: thus the membership of the DSA has fallen dramatically since the late 1970s.

109. See esp. G. M. Meier, *Emerging from Poverty*, op. cit.; G. M. Meier and D. Seers (eds.), *Pioneers in Development,* op. cit.; R. M. Sundrum, op. cit.; J. N. Bhagwati, 1983, op. cit.; H. J. Bruton, 1983, op. cit.; R. Higgott, op. cit.; I. M. D. Little, 1982, op. cit.; I. Livingstone, 1982, op. cit.; H. W. Arndt, 1981, op. cit.; A. O. Hirschman, 1981, op. cit.; P. Streeten, *Development Perspectives*, op. cit.; H. G. Mannur, 1981, op. cit.; J. Toye, 1980, op. cit.; D. Morawetz, 1977, op. cit.; O. Sunkel, 1977, op. cit.

110. See D. Seers, 'Back to the Ivory Tower? The Professionalisation of Development Studies and their extension to Europe', *IDS Bulletin*, 9 (2), 1977; D. Seers, B. Schaffer and M. L. Kiljunen, *Underdeveloped Europe: Studies in Core–Periphery Relations* (Brighton, 1979); D. Seers and C. Vaitsos (eds.), *Integration and Unequal Development* (London, 1980); J. de Bandt, P. Mani and D. Seers (eds.), *European Studies in Development: New Trends in European Development Studies* (London, 1980); D. Seers, 'The Second Enlargement of the EEC in Historical Perspective', *IDS Discussion Paper*, 158, 1981; and D. Seers

and C. Vaitsos (eds.), *The Second Enlargement of the EEC: The Integration of Unequal Partners*. One wonders whether Iberia and Greece still fall within the 'peripheral' category since their recent accession to the Common Market.

111. A. Lewis, 'The State of Development Theory', op. cit.; I. Livingstone, 'The Development of Development Economics', op. cit.; P. Streeten, 'Development Ideas in Historical Perspective', op. cit.; and S. Lall, 'Conflicts and Concepts: Welfare Economics and Developing Countries', *World Development*, 4 (3), 1976.

112. See L. Taylor *et al., Models of Growth and Distribution for Brazil* (New York, 1981), and L. Taylor, *Structuralist Macroeconomics: Applicable Models for the Third World* (New York, 1983). As Editor of the *Journal of Development Economics* Professor Taylor is in a good position to influence the future direction of the subject.

113. This arose from his earlier work on famines and is now collected together in *Poverty and Famines: An Essay on Entitlement and Deprivation* (Oxford, 1981). Despite the analytical rigour and the derivation of new terminology at least one critic has denied that Sen's 'exchange entitlements' amounts to anything genuinely novel — see M. D. Morris' review in the *Journal of Economic History*, 42 (4), 1982, pp. 889–91. For Professor Sen's attempt to generalise the approach see his 'Development: Which Way Now?', op. cit., especially Part IV, pp. 758–60.

114. See her paper 'Beyond Export-Led Growth' together with the commentaries upon it by Hans Singer, Tibor Scitovsky and Albert Fishlow, all in *World Development*, 12 (9), 1984.

115. In a previous paper (' "Arrested Development" in India — Worthwhile Epithet, Hostage to Fortune or Plain Utopianism?', *Salford Papers in Economics*, 84–3, 1984, and shortly to be published in a volume of essays edited by C. Dewey, *Arrested Development in India: The Historical Dimension* (forthcoming). I have tried to explore the nature of these elements in the specific context of the long run growth of the Indian economy.

116. This, of course, refers to the title of E. H. Carr's famous book which was first published exactly a quarter of a century ago (1961). For a reassessment of the value of the work see Arthur Marwick's 'In Pursuit of the Past', *Times Higher Educational Supplement*, 16 Nov. 1984. For a more recent — but equally popularistic — review of the whole question see J. Tosh, *The Pursuit of History* (London, 1984); and for rather more formal discussion see P. Gardiner, *The Nature of Historical Explanation* (Oxford, 1978), Part II, and M. Oakeshott, *On History and Other Essays* (Oxford, 1983). Jonathan Steinberg's important review of a whole clutch of new books on and around the subject, ' "Real Authentic History" or What Philosophers of History Can Teach Us', *The Historical Journal*, 24 (2), 1981, is also of use in this context.

117. For a formal but conveniently short definition of Idealism and Materialism see J. Speak (ed.), *A Dictionary of Philosophy* (London, 1979), p. 149 and pp. 205f.

118. For an appreciation of the complexity of these issues and restricting the field of vision to the Marxists cf. E. P. Thompson, *The Poverty of Theory and Other Essays* (London, 1978), especially pp. 193–397; K. Nield and J. Seed, 'Theoretical Poverty or the Poverty of Theory: British Marxist Historiography and the Althusserians', *Economy and Society*, 8 (4), 1979; H. R. Bernstein, 'Marxist Historiography and the Methodology of Research Programs', *History and Theory*, 30 (4), 1981; G. A. Cohen, *Karl Marx's Theory of History* (Oxford, 1980); G. McLennan, *Marxism and the Methodologies of History* (London, 1982), and E. Hobsbawn, 'Marx and History', *New Left Review*, No. 143, Jan.–Feb. 1984 — which was the opening paper of the important UNESCO-sponsored conference marking the 100th anniversary of Marx's death, held in Linz, Austria, in October 1983. For a revisionist tilt at 'orthodox' Marxism in so far as it specifically relates to economic history, see S. Resnick and M. Wolff, 'A Reformulation of Marxian Theory and Historical Analysis', *Journal of Economic History*, 42 (1), 1982.

119. Such as the more extreme of the neo-Classical writers like Peter Bauer and Deepak Lal. Both hold that the causes of 'less' development are simple to identify and that the solutions are staring governments in the face — if only they would divest themselves of the 'heresies' propounded by the Liberal-Orthodox school. One suspects that the very simplicity of this viewpoint was a factor in (*a*) the ennoblement of the former; (*b*) the Elkan review of the latter (as referred to above in note 90); and (*c*) the 'counter-revolution' that *The Times* pronounced was underway as a result of Lal's booklet (22 Aug. 1983; 9 Sept. 1983). Presumably, this 'editorially independent' organ of the press, having 'lost out' to

The Guardian in terms of Third World coverage (the 'Third World Review' section has been a standard feature of the newspaper for several years now) saw the appearance of this IEA-sponsored attack on the Liberal position as a golden opportunity to swipe at its main newspaper rival. For an exposure of the shallowness of Bauer's work see M. Lipton's piece on aid in the *Financial Times*, 1 Aug. 1981; M. Desai, 'Homilies of a Victorian Sage: A Review of Peter Bauer', *Third World Quarterly*, 4 (2), 1982; A.K. Sen, 'Just Deserts', *New York Review of Books*, 4 March 1982; A.P. Thirlwall's 'review', *Journal of Development Studies*, 21 (3), 1985; and John Toye's excellent paper 'The Disparaging of Development Economics', op. cit.; and for Lal, see J. Toye, 'Dirigisme and Development Economics', *Cambridge Journal of Economics*, 9 (1) 1985, and F. Stewart, 'The Fragile Foundations of the Neo-Classical Approach to Development', *Journal of Development Studies*, 21 (2), 1985.

120. Deepak Lal's contention, op. cit., that the problems of the LDCs over the last three decades or so have been caused by the 'dirigiste dogma' propounded by the development economists accords a somewhat greater influence to this school of thought than almost anyone else – including its most fervent apologists – would accept.

121. Cf. P.C. Pitt (ed.), *Development from Below: Anthropologists and Development Situations* (Manchester, 1985) and L. Mair, op. cit., especially pp. 10–14. Professor Mair writes that 'only rarely and recently have anthropologists been invited to contribute to projects for development, and when they are invited they are seldom allowed the time that they would consider necessary to enable them to speak with real authority. Indeed one cost-benefit analysis has calculated that the advantages of the anthropologist's contribution is not worth the delay to the project that it entails'! (p. 11).

122. D.N. McCloskey, 'Does the Past Have Useful Economics?', *Journal of Economic Literature*, 14 (2), 1976.

123. Thus there is an extremely large and disparate literature on the subject of the 'lessons' of the post-Meiji Japanese experience for the developing world – much of it appearing in the *Journal of Developing Economies* – the major English langauge outlet for the Japanese scholars. See also L. Klein and K. Ohkawa (eds.), *Economic Growth: The Japanese Experience Since the Meiji Era* (New York, 1968); I. Inkster, *Japan as a Development Model? Relative Backwardness and Technological Transfer* (New York, 1971), and H. Rosovsky, 'What are the "lessons" of Japanese Economic History?' in A.J. Youngson (ed.), *Economic Development in the Long-Run* (London, 1972). Some of the – many – difficulties of this approach have been identified by B.R. Tomlinson in his cogently argued essay 'Writing History Sideways: Lessons for Indian Economic History from Meiji Japan', paper presented to the Annual Economic History Society Conference, University of York, March 1985.

124. This point has been forcefully made by R.M. Hartwell over many years, cf. his 'The Causes of the Industrial Revolution: An essay in Methodology', *Economic History Review*, 18 (2), 1965; *The Industrial Revolution and Economic Growth* (London, 1971) especially Ch. 1; and 'Progress and Dissimilarity in Historical Perspective', in C.P. Kindleberger and G. di Tella (eds.), *Economics in the Long View: Essays in Honour of W.W. Rostow, Vol. 1, Models and Methodology* (London, 1982).

125. E. Hobsbawn, 'The Social Function of the Past', *Past and Present*, 50, May 1972. See also the excellent collection of essays edited by Profs. Hobsbawn and T. Ranger, *The Invention of Tradition* (Cambridge, 1983), and the Festschrift volume in Hobsbawn's honour, *The Power of the Past: Essays for Eric Hobsbawn* edited by P. Thane, G. Crossick and R. Floud (Cambridge, 1984); and at a more popular level, David Lowenthal's entertaining *The Past is a Foreign Country* (Cambridge, 1985).

126. Rather quaintly entitled *Poverty and un-British Rule in India* (London, 1871). This remarkable Parsi went on, in 1892, to become the first Indian member of the House of Commons (as a Liberal).

127. For a survey of the economic thinking of the Nationalists and the INC see B. Chandra, *The Rise and Growth of Economic Nationalism in India* (New Delhi, 1966); N.V. Sovani, 'Indian Economics and Indian Economists', *Indian Economic Journal*, 21 (1), 1974; B.N. Ganguli, *Indian Economic Thought: Nineteenth Century Perspectives* (New Delhi, 1978); and B. Datta, *Indian Economic Thought: Twentieth Century Perspectives* (New Delhi, 1978). For more biographical (but not hagiographical) work see the useful

'The Builders of Modern India' series published by the Ministry of Information and Broadcasting of the Government of India over 1962–1974.

128. For details, see J.M. Brown, *Gandhi's Rise to Power: Indian Politics 1915–1922* (Cambridge, 1972).

129. In the famous debate on the Indian Budget for 1901–2 (see A.K. Bagchi, *Private Investment in India, 1900–1939*, Cambridge, 1972, Introduction). Other apologists, including many members of the ICS (who were extraordinarily interested in history), the 'unofficial' business and commercial community, empire-minded journalists and academics, rallied to the cause and sought to spotlight the beneficent nature of British rule – the most well-known exemplifiers being Sir W.W. Hunter, Sir P. Griffiths, Sir J. Strachey, T. Morisson and Professors L.C.A. Knowles, F.J. Atkinson and V. Anstey.

130. With the partial exception of Rosa Luxemburg's brief allusions to India (in Section 3 of her *The Accumulation of Capital*, London ed., 1963) written in 1913, there was little follow-up to Marx's observations on the subcontinent made in the mid-19th century before the inter-war period (see S. Avineri (ed.), *Karl Marx on Colonialism and Modernization*, New York, 1969; V. Kiernan, *Marxism and Imperialism*, London, 1974; and U. Melotti, *Marx and the Third World*, London, 1977). The work of the Communist Party of India, and in particular that of M.N. Roy and R.P. Dutt, are best presented in: CPI, *Historical Development of the Communist Movement in India* (Calcutta, 1944); G. Adhikari (ed.), *Documents of the History of the C.P.I.*, vol. 1, 1923–25, and IIIa, 1926 (New Delhi, 1971–78); S.D. Gupta, *Comintern, India and the Colonial Question* (Calcutta, 1980); M.N. Roy, *India in Transition* (Geneva, 1922); and R.P. Dutt, *India Today* (London, 1940). For more interpretative accounts see the articles by G. Omvedt, 'Marxism and the Analysis of South Asia' and B. Chandra, 'Marxism in India' – both in the *Journal of Contemporary Asia*, 4 (4), 1974; S.C. Jha, *Studies in the Development of Capitalism in India* (Calcutta, 1963), I. Habib's two pieces 'Problems of Marxist Historical Analysis', *Enquiry* (new series), Monsoon, Vol. 3 (2), 1968, and 'Colonialization and the Indian Economy' *Social Scientist* 32, March 1975, B. Davey, *The Economic Development of India* (Nottingham, 1975), and A. Sen, *The State, Industrialization and Class Formation in India* (London, 1982).

131. With one short break after the 'Emergency' period when the Janata coalition formed the central government, the INC – in its various *avatars* – has enjoyed power from 1947 to the present day. The Nehrus have also all but dominated the leadership, see T. Ali's *The Nehrus and the Gandhis: An Indian Dynasty* (London, 1985) for a readable (but not always reliable) account of this close-knit family. Of the important family members – Motilal, Jawaharlal, Indira, Sanjay and Rajiv – it was Jawaharlal, of course, who was the most knowledgeable about Indian (and probably world) history, see especially his *The Discovery of India* (London, 1945) and *Glimpses of World History* (Delhi, 1951). This interest has also been discussed by his main biographers M. Brecher, *Nehru: A Political Biography* (Oxford, 1969) and S. Gopal, *Jawaharlal Nehru 1947–56* (London, 1979).

132. R.C. Dutt, *The Economic History of India – vol. 1, Under Early British Rule 1757–1837* (1st Indian edition, New Delhi, 1976), p.xxv.

133. R.S. Sharma, 'Cottage Industries, 1857–1947' in V.B. Singh (ed.), *Economic History of India* (Bombay, 1975), p.281.

134. The most notable exception was, of course, the continued existence of the downtrodden Untouchables or *Harijans*.

135. Largely out of deference to Gandhi's views on such matters (and given the sheer number of people involved) the INC leadership has always been keen on promoting and protecting the interests of the rural handicraft workers – especially the producers of the (symbolic) khadi-gram cloth. Indeed, an interesting sub-theme of India's post-Independence development strategy has been the struggle between the 'hell-for-leather' modernisers and the heirs of the Gandhian perspective.

136. See note 171 below for a full list of references relating to this issue, and my article 'Indistrialisation, De-industrialisation and the Indian Economy', op. cit., for a discussion of its longstanding nature.

137. Refer to C. Dewey, note 4 above.

138. The East India Company only lost its monopoly of trade with India (but not China)

in 1813, and it was not until 1833 that it was no longer permitted to undertake any trading activity. This, of course, was part and parcel of the general attack on Mercantilism – a policy which had had very serious implications for India's trade in the crucial 18th century.

139. The phrase comes from K. Chaudhuri – who can hardly be considered as being a person generally sympathetic to the Nationalist School – 'India's Foreign Trade and the Cessation of the East India Company's Trading Activities, 1828–40', *Economic History Review*, 1, 9 (2), 1966.

140. There is a large literature on the subject of the 'drain' of wealth. For a short review of the major issue see B. N. Ganguli, *Naoriji and the Drain Theory* (Calcutta, 1965), T. Mukherjee, 'The Theory of Economic Drain: The Impact of British Rule on the Indian Economy 1840–1900' in K. E. Boudling and T. Mukherjee (eds.), *Economic Imperialism: A Book of Readings* (Ann Arbor, 1972); K. N. Chaudhuri's 'India's International Economy in the Nineteenth Century: An Historical Survey', *Modern Asian Studies*, 2 (1), 1968, and his 'Foreign Trade and Balance of Payments 1757–1947' in D. Kumar and M. Desai (eds.), *The Cambridge Economic History of India vol. 2: c. 1757–1970* (Cambridge, 1983).

141. The best short discussion of this is still to be found in S. B. Saul's *Studies in British Overseas Trade* (Liverpool, 1960) and his earlier article 'Britain and World Trade, 1870–1914', *Economic History Review*, 7, 1955, pp. 64f.

142. For details see C. Dewey, 'The End of the Imperialism of Free Trade: The Eclipse of the Lancashire Lobby and the Concession of Fiscal Autonomy to India' in C. Dewey and A. G. Hopkins (eds.), *The Imperial Impact*, op. cit.

143. Thus, according to Bipan Chandra, the Nationalists 'made full use of contemporary economic theories ... and they tried to utilise the experience of contemporary developing countries': see his 'Re-interpretation of Nineteenth Century Indian Economic History' in M. D. Morris *et al.*, *Indian Economics in the Nineteenth and Twentieth Centuries* (Delhi, 1969), p. 39.

144. The following references all contain an outline of these principles and policies: D. R. Gadgil, *Planning and Economic Policy in India* (Poona, 1961); A. H. Hanson, *The Process of Planning: A Study of India's Five-Year Plans 1950–1964* (Oxford, 1966); P. Streeten and M. Lipton (eds.), *The Crisis of India's Planning: Economic Planning in the 1960's* (London, 1968); Bhagwati and Desai, op. cit.; G. Myrdal, *Asian Drama*, op. cit., Vol. II, Part 4; and C. D. Wadhva (ed.), *Some Problems of India's Economic Policy* (New Delhi, 1977), especially Part One. For more recent overviews see P. Chaudhuri, *The Indian Economy* (London, 1978), F. Frankel, *India's Political Economy* (Princeton, 1979), and P. Bardhan, *The Political Economy of Development in India* (Oxford, 1984).

145. With reference to Nos. 1 and 3, many Third World politicians – not just those from the subcontinent – have found it convenient to blame colonial rule and neo-colonialism for a whole range of development failures.

146. As with Nos. 1 and 3, No. 2 – with suitable amendments – has also been frequently trotted out by Third World leaders to justify action aimed at restoring those values and institutions that purportedly existed in the pristine pre-colonial past (e.g. certain aspects of African 'socialism').

147. This was the basis of the famous Second Five-Year Plan. This Plan, which was mainly drawn up by Professor P. C. Mahalonobis, has received a great deal of attention and for an outline discussion of the debate see A. Vaidyanathan, 'The Indian Economy since Independence' in the *Cambridge Economic History of India vol. 2,* op. cit., pp. 954–7.

148. Apologists and Marxists have also been fair game, of course.

149. Such as the *South Asian Studies* series published by Cambridge University Press, which now has over 30 titles to its credit.

150. The most notable (in English) being the *Indian Economic and Social History Review* (begun in 1963), *Bengal Past and Present, South Asia, Artha Vijnana, Modern Asian Studies*, the *Journal of Asian Studies*, and the *Journal of Imperial and Commonwealth History*.

151. Thus cf. W. H. Moreland's 'Recent Work in Indian Economic History', *Economic History Review*, 2, (OS), 1929–30, and even M. D. Morris' and B. Stein's 'The Economic History

of India: A Bibliographical Essay', *Journal of Economic History*, 21 (2), 1961, with R. J. Moore, 'Recent Historical Writing on the Modern British Empire', *Journal of Imperial and Commonwealth History*, Jan. 1975, S. Cornish, 'Recent Writing in Indian Economic History', *Journal of Economic History*, 37 (3), 1977, and especially V. D. Divekar (Chief Editor), *An Annotated Bibliography on the Economic History of India 1500 A.D.–1947* (Bombay, 1977–8) in 4 vols.

152. Cf. M. H. Case, *South Asian History 1750–1950: A Guide to Periodicals, Dissertations and Newspapers* (Princeton, 1968), D. A. Low *et al.* (eds.), *Government Archives in South Asia: A Guide to National and State Archives in Ceylon, India and Pakistan* (Cambridge, 1969), M. D. Morris, 'Quantitative Resources for the Study of Indian History' in V. R. Lorwin and J. M. Price (eds.), *The Dimensions of the Past* (Yale, 1972) and M. D. Morris and C. B. Dudley, 'Selected Railway Statistics for the Indian Subcontinent, 1853–1946/47', *Artha Vijnana*, 17 (3), 1975.

153. Such as the symposium on Indian Economic and Social History at St. John's College, Cambridge in July 1975 (which yielded the valuable volume edited by C. Dewey and K. N. Chaudhuri, op. cit.), and the biennial European Conference on South Asian Studies (No. 9 planned for Heidelberg in 1986).

154. *The Cambridge Economic History of India*, vol. 1 c. 1200–c. 1750, edited by T. Raychaudhuri and I. Habib (Cambridge, 1982) and vol. 2, op. cit.

155. The process of reassessment has focused upon such topics as the dynamics of demographic change, agricultural and industrial growth rates, the causes of famine, the true nature of regional, district and even village-level agrarian structures, occupational characteristics, the career of particular industries and handicrafts, the forms of both European and indigenous entrepreneurship, the character of labour and capital markets, the working of the monetary system, the performance of the international trade sector, the coming of trade unionism and the regional consequences of certain economic policies.

156. M. D. Morris, 'Towards a Re-interpretation of 19th Century Indian Economic History', *Journal of Economic History*, 23 (4), 1963.

157. See the volume by M. D. Morris, *et al.*, op. cit., 1969.

158. See, for example, P. Robb, 'British Rule and Indian Improvement', *Economic History Review*, 34 (4), 1981.

159. The most recent – and readable – of which is N. Charlesworth's *British Rule and the Indian Economy* (London, 1982).

160. According to many contemporary Delhi-watchers Rajiv's eyes are set firmly on the future – not the past – and he is said to have expressed the desire to 'drag India into the twenty-first century come what may'. For two contrasting views of Rajiv's political leanings and the legacy of Mrs. Gandhi's long premiership cf. T. Ali, op. cit., pp. 263–300, and W. H. Morris Jones, 'India after Indira: A Tale of Two Legacies', *Third World Quarterly*, 7 (2), 1985.

161. Sir John Hicks, *A Theory of Economic History* (London, 1969). For an interesting review of this work by Peter Bauer see 'Economic History as Theory', *Economica*, 38 (2), 1971, pp. 163–79.

162. D. C. North and R. P. Thomas, *The Rise of the Western World: A New Economic History* (Cambridge, 1973) and 'The First Economic Revolution', *Economic History Review*, 30 (2), 1977.

163. D. Lal, 'The Poverty of Development Economics', op. cit., Ch. 4, Part 7.

164. I. M. D. Little, 'Indian Industrialization Before 1945' in M. Gersovitz (ed.), op. cit.

165. D. Lal, op. cit., p. 83.

166. Ibid., p. 86.

167. Loc. cit.

168. Loc. cit.

169. Such as the dated essay by R. Lidman and R. J. Domerese, 'India' in W. A. Lewis (ed.), *Tropical Development 1880–1913: Studies in Economic Progress* (London, 1970), and, not surprisingly, Little's own piece on Indian industrialisation is also quoted, op. cit.

170. Draft mimeo, University College, London, 1981. This paper which purports to cover no less than 2480 years of Indian history must be an extraordinary document. Few modern historians would undertake such a venture; but clearly the task has not daunted Deepak Lal – despite the apparently busy professional life he leads which not only takes

in academic work but involves much globe-trotting as an 'Economic Advisor' – see the notes about 'The Author' on p. xiii of the Hobart Paper, op. cit.

171. Leaving aside the discussion of de-industrialisation contained in the work of the Nationalist writers, for a modern consideration of the issues cf. D. Thorner, 'De-industrialisation in India 1881–1931' in D. and A. Thorner, *Land and Labour in India* (Bombay, 1962); M. D. Morris, 'Towards a Re-interpretation ...' op. cit., *Indian Economy in the Nineteenth Century*, op. cit., and M. D. Morris, 'The Growth of Large-Scale Industry' in the *Cambridge Economic History of India vol. 2*, op. cit., especially pp. 668–76; R. Chattopadhyay, 'De-industrialisation in India Reconsidered', *Economic and Political Weekly*, 10 (12), March 1975; M. Desai, 'Demand for Cotton Textiles in Nineteenth Century India', *Indian Economic and Social History Review*, 10 (4), 1971; A. K. Bagchi, 'De-industrialisation in Gangetic Bihar' in B. De (ed.), *Essays in Honour of Professor S. C. Sarkar* (New Delhi, 1976), 'De-industrialization in India in the Nineteenth Century: Some Theoretical Implications', *Journal of Development Studies*, 12 (2), 1976; M. Vicziany, 'The De-industrialization of India in the Nineteenth Century: A Methodological Critique of Amiya Kumar Bagchi', and A. K. Bagchi, 'A Reply', both in the *Indian Economic and Social History Review*, 16 (2), 1979; A. Orr, 'De-industrial-isation in India – A Note', *Journal of Development Studies*, 16 (1), 1980; W. J. Macpherson, 'Economic Development in India Under the British Crown, 1858–1947' in A. J. Youngson (ed.), *Economic Development in the Long-Run* (London, 1972), pp. 138–43; P. Robb, op. cit., M. J. Twomey, 'Employment in Nineteenth Century Indian Textiles', *Explorations in Economic History*, 20 (1), 1983; N. Charlesworth, op. cit., Ch. 3; F. Perlin, 'Proto-industrialization and Pre-Colonial South Asia', *Past and Present*, No. 98, 1983, especially pp. 34, 53; J. Krishnamurthy, 'Changes in the Composition of the Working Force in Manufacturing 1901–51: A Theoretical and Empirical Analysis', *Indian Economic and Social History Review*, 4 (1), 1967, 'De-industrialisation Revisited', *Economic and Political Weekly*, 11 (26), June 1976, 'The Distribution of the Indian Working Force 1901–1951' in K. N. Chaudhuri and C. Dewey (eds.), op. cit., pp. 258–75, 'Changing Concepts of Work in the Indian Censuses: 1901–61', *Indian Economic and Social History Review*, 14 (3), 1977, and his essay on 'The Occupational Structure' in the *Cambridge Economic History of India vol. 2*, op. cit., pp. 533–50; K. Specker, 'De-industrialisation in 19th Century India?: The Textile Industry in Madras Presidency', paper presented to the Anglo-German Workshop on 'Arrested Development in India', University of Heidelberg, July 1984, *Weber im Wettbewerb: Das Schicksal des Südingischen Textilhandwerks im 19 Jahrhundert* (Wiesbaden, 1984); and G. Pandey, 'Economic Dislocation in Nineteenth-Century Eastern Uttar Pradesh: Some Implications of the Decline of Artisanal Industry in Colonial India' in P. Robb (ed.), *Rural South Asia: Linkages, Development and Change* (London, 1983), pp. 89–129.

172. For the tariff see C. Dewey, 'The End of the Imperialism of Free Trade ...', op. cit., and 'The Government of India's New Industrial Policy ...', op. cit.; I. Drummond, 'Indian Tariffs, Cottons and Japanese Competition, 1919–39', Ch. 4 of his *British Economic Policy and the Empire 1919–1939* (London, 1972), M. D. Morris, 'The Growth of Large Scale Industry', op. cit., pp. 607–40 and B. Chatterji, 'The Political Economy of "discriminating protection": the case of textiles in the 1920s', *Indian Economic and Social History Review*, 20 (3), 1983.

   For the question of labour conditions, see M. D. Morris, *The Emergence of an Industrial Labour Force in India: A Study of the Bombay Cotton Mills* (Berkeley, 1965), R. Newman, *Workers and Unions in Bombay 1918–29: A Study of Organisation in the Cotton Mills* (Canberra, 1981), and his 'Social Factors in the Recruitment of the Bombay Mill Hands' in K. N. Chaudhuri and C. Dewey (eds.), op. cit., R. Chandavarkar, 'Workers' Politics and the Mill Districts in Bombay between the Wars', *Modern Asian Studies*, 15 (3), 1981, D. Kooiman, 'Jobbers and the Emergence of Trade Unions in Bombay City', *International Review of Social History*, 22 (3), 1977, R. Kumar, 'Family and Factory: Women in the Bombay Cotton Textile Industry, 1919–1939', *Indian Economic and Social History Review*, 20 (1) 1983), and S. Bhattacharya, 'Capital and Labour in Bombay City', *Economic and Political Weekly*, 14 (42–3), Oct. 1981.

173. In fact both contributions are unlikely to be acceptable even to those professional historians who incline towards their basic ideological position. So far as I am aware,

to date both these essays have not even been acknowledged by the Indianists as meriting consideration – let alone serious rebuttal.

174. T. Schultz, *Transforming Traditional Agriculture*, op. cit., especially Ch. 4.
175. Cf. A. Lewis, *Manchester School*, op. cit.; J. C. H. Fei and G. Ranis, *Development of the Labour Surplus Economy* (Homewood, Ill., 1964), and their 'A Model of Growth and Employment in the Open Dualistic Economy', *Journal of Development Studies*, 11, Jan. 1975.
176. A. K. Sen, 'Surplus Labour in India: A Critique of Schultz's Statistical Test', *Economic Journal*, March 1967, M. Harwitz, 'The Significance of an Epidemic', *Journal of Political Economy*, 73 (4), 1965, S. Mehra, 'Surplus Labour in Indian Agriculture', *Indian Economic Review*, 1 (1), 1966, and also T. Balogh's review article in the *Economic Journal*, Dec. 1964, pp. 996–9.
177. A. K. Sen, loc. cit., p. 154. Sen's rebuttal prompted Prof. Schultz to offer a response, 'Significance of India's 1918–19 Losses of Agricultural Labour – A Reply', pp. 161–3, which in turn was neatly answered in Sen's 'Surplus Labour in India: A Rejoinder', both in the *Economic Journal*, March 1967, pp. 163–5.
178. T. W. Schultz, 'Nobel Lecture: The Economics of Being Poor', *Journal of Political Economy*, 88 (4), 1980 and his essay 'On Economic History in Extending Economics' in M. Nash (ed.), op. cit., pp. 245–53.
179. 'Nobel Lecture', ibid., p. 641.
180. Loc. cit.
181. See E. H. Phelps-Brown, 'The Underdevelopment of Economics', *Economic Journal*, March 1972; D. C. North, 'Structure and Performance: The Task of Economic History', *Journal of Economic Literature*, 16, Sept. 1978; D. N. McCloskey, 'Does the Past Have Useful Economics?', op. cit.
182. D. N. McCloskey, loc. cit.
183. To start with the Indian case cf. P. Harnatty, 'Cotton Exports and Indian Agriculture', *Economic History Review*, 24 (3), 1971; D. Narain, *The Impact of Price Movements on Areas Under Federated Crops in India, 1900–1939* (Cambridge, 1965); B. M. McAlpin, 'Railroads, Prices and Rationality: India 1860–1900', *Journal of Economic History*, 34 (3), 1974; and M. M. Islam, *Bengal Agriculture 1920–46: A Quantitative Study* (Cambridge, 1978). Another related example would be the neo-Classical assault on that hoary old concept of the 'backward-bending' supply curve of labour.
184. For an informed modern account of the vital early 20th century period see the collection of essays in R. M. Myers and M. R. Deattie (eds.), *The Japanese Colonial Empire 1895–1945* (Princeton, 1984) and especially the essays by Peter Duus (Ch. 3); Patricia Tsurumi (Ch. 7); Samuel Ho (Ch. 9); M. Toshiyuki and Y. Yuzo (Ch. 10); Ronald Myers and Y. Saburo (Ch. 11) and Bruce Cummings (Ch. 13). For some discussion of the latter period see the ESRC *Newsletter 54*, March 1985, on 'Some Pacific Economies: The Far East', pp. 7–31 especially the articles by R. Wade on Taiwan and A. Michell on South Korea.
185. And which severely limits the possible range of topics and the time period to the last 20 years or so.
186. T. W. Schultz, 'Nobel Lecture', loc. cit.
187. The best of the recent works on this immense subject are by Professor Geoffrey A. Cohen, *Karl Marx's Theory of History*, op. cit., and by Gregor McLennan, *Marxism and the Methodologies of History*, op. cit. Of course I discount the hostility towards history enunciated by Barry Hindess and Paul Hirst in their *Pre-Capitalist Modes of Production* (London 1975) especially pp. 309–23 – not least because they themselves seem to have disowned their earlier views, *vide Mode of Production and Social Formation: An Auto-critique of Pre-Capitalist Modes of Production* (London, 1977).
188. See note 35 above for a list of appropriate references (marked +). Especially useful are the studies by Peter Worsley (1984); R. M. Sundrum (1983); P. Limqueco and B. Macfarlane (1983); R. H. Chilcote and Dale Johnson (1983); Ankie Hoogveldt (1982); Amiya Bagchi (1982); Hamza Alavai *et al.* (1982); David Goodman and Michael Redclift (1981); Bill Warren (1980); Antony Brewer (1980); Nicos Mouzelis (1980); K. Mohri (1979); Ian Roxborough (1979); Gavin Williams (1978); Anne Phillips (1977); and Robert Brenner (1977). The matter is also discussed with insight in S. Avineri (ed.), *Karl Marx*

on *Colonialism and Modernisation*, op. cit., especially the Introduction; U. Melotti, *Marx and the Third World*, op. cit.; Victor Kiernan, *Marxism and Imperialism*, op. cit., especially Ch. 1; R. J. Owen and R. B. Sutcliffe (eds.), *Studies in the Theory of Imperialism* (London, 1972) especially the essay by Bob Sutcliffe; M. B. Brown, *The Economics of Imperialism* (London, 1974) especially Ch. 3; M. C. Howard and J. E. King, *The Political Economy of Marx* (2nd ed., London, 1985), especially Ch. 14.

189. Cf. A. Foster-Carter, 1978, op. cit., J. Taylor, 1979, op. cit., and A. Brewer, op. cit., Ch. 11.

190. The major protagonists in this debate have included Ashok Rudra, Hamza Alavi, Kathleen Gough, Utsa Patnaik, Jairus Banaji, Pranab Bardhan, Amiya Bagchi, Joan Mencher, Gail Omvedt, Paresh Chattopadhyay, André G. Frank, Doug McEachern, Bipan Chandra, Ranajit Sau, and Nirmal Chandra. Most of the contributions have appeared in the pages of the *Economic and Political Weekly* over the 1970s and early 1980s.

191. Cf. the surveys by A. Brewer, op. cit., Ch. 11; Doug McEachern's articles, 'The Mode of Production in India', *Journal of Contemporary Asia*, 6 (4) 1976, and 'Capitalism and Colonial Production: An Introduction' in H. Alavi *et. al.*, op. cit., pp. 1–21; A. Thorner, 'Semi-Feudalism or Capitalism: Contemporary Debate on Classes and Modes of Production in India', *Economic and Political Weekly*, in three parts: 4.12.82, 11.12.82 and 18.12.82; John Harriss, 'The Mode of Production Controversy: theories and problems of the debate' in I. Livingstone (ed.), *Approaches to Development Studies*, op. cit.; Bipan Chandra, 'Karl Marx, His Theories of Asian Societies, and Colonial Rule', *Review*, 5 (1) 1981.

192. Having been unceremoniously shunted into an obscure siding for many decades (see M. Sawer's 'The Politics of Historiography: Russian Socialism and the Question of the Asiatic Mode of Production, 1906–1931', *Critique* 10–11, Winter/Spring 1978–9) the concept of an AMP was revived following the appearance of Karl Wittfogel's *Oriental Despotism: A Comparative Study of Total Power* (New Haven, 1957) for which see Irfan Habib's review 'An Examination of Wittfogel's Theory of "Oriental Despotism"', *Enquiry*, n.s. 6, 1962. Since then a veritable flood of literature has emerged. For a selection of the more general studies see Eric Hobsbawn's 'Introduction' to his edited version of Karl Marx, *Pre-Capitalist Economic Formations* (London, 1964); L. Krader, *The Asiatic Mode of Production: Sources, Development and Critique* (Assen, 1975); U. Melotti, op. cit.; B. Hindess and P. Q. Hirst, *Pre-Capitalist Modes of Production* op. cit.; F. Tokei, *Essays on the Asiatic Mode of Production* (Budapest, 1979); P. Anderson, *Lineages of the Absolutist State* (London, 1974) especially Note B, pp. 462–549; F. L. Pryor, 'The Asian Mode of Production as an Economic System', *Journal of Comparative Economics*, 4 (4) 1980; J. Taylor, *From Modernization ...*, op. cit., especially pp. 172–85; A. M. Bailey and J. K. Llobera, *The Asiatic Mode of Production: Science and Politics* (London, 1981); and H. Lubasz, 'Marx's Concept of the AMP: A Genetic Analysis', *Economy and Society*, 13 (4) 1984.

As far as particular application to India is concerned, see D. Thorner, 'Marx on India and the Asiatic Mode of Production', *Contributions to Indian Sociology*, 9, Dec. 1960, S. Avineri, op. cit., S. Naqvi, 'Marx on Pre-British Indian Society and Economy', *Indian Economic and Social History Review*, 9 (4) 1972, K. C. Roychowdhury, 'Marx's Asiatic Mode of Production and the Evolution of the Indian Economy', *Indian Economic Journal*, 22, July–Sept. 1974; B. Davey, *The Economic Development of India* (London, 1975), Ch. 2; B. Chandra, 'Karl Marx, His Theories of Asian Societies', op. cit.; R. A. C. H. Gunawardana, 'The Analysis of Pre-Colonial Social Formations in Asia in the Writings of Karl Marx', *Indian Historical Review*, 11 (2) 1976. For references to the related research on 'Indian Feudalism' cf. D. Thorner, 'Feudalism in India' in his posthumous *The Shaping of Modern India* (New Delhi, 1980); H. Mukhia, 'Was There Feudalism in Indian History?', *Journal of Peasant Studies*, 8 (3) 1981; A. Rudra, 'Against Feudalism', *Economic and Political Weekly*, 26 Dec. 1981; S. Baru, 'Karl Marx and Analysis of Indian Society', *E.P.W.* 10 Dec. 1983; and A. Sen, 'The Transition from Feudalism to Capitalism', *E.P.W.*, 28 July 1984.

There has also been a considerable volume of work (much of it in French) on the application of the AMP to the African continent. For the views of one of the most influential writers, Samir Amin (who prefers to speak of a Tribute Paying rather than an Asiatic mode) see his *Accumulation on a World Scale* (London, 1974) vol. 1, Ch. 2, Part 1, and *Unequal Development: An Essay on the Social Formations of Peripheral Capitalism* (London, 1976) especially Chs. 1 and 6.

193. For a discussion of Kautsky's work prior to his 'ultraimperialism' stage (for which he was branded by Lenin as little better than a recidivist) see V. Kiernan, *Marxism and Imperialism*, op. cit., Ch. 1, pp. 9–17, G. Steenson, *K. Kautsky, 1858–1938: Marxism in its Classic Years* (Pittsburgh, 1978), M. Salvadori, *K. Kautsky and the Socialist Revolution* (London, 1979), and the two articles by L. Meldolesi, 'The Debate on Imperialism Just before Lenin', *Economic and Political Weekly*, 19 (42 and 43), 20–7 Oct. 1984.

194. R. Luxemburg, *The Accumulation of Capital*, op. cit.

195. N. Bukharin, *Imperialism and World Economy* (London, 1972).

196. V. I. Lenin, *Imperialism, the Highest Stage of Capitalism* (Moscow, 1964).

197. P. M. Sweezy, *The Theory of Capitalist Development* (Oxford, 1942).

198. See E. Stokes, 'Late Nineteenth Century Colonial Expansion and the Attack on the Theory of Economic Imperialism: A Case of Mistaken Identity?', *Historical Journal*, 12, 1969, and N. Etherington's article 'Reconsidering Theories of Imperialism', *History and Theory*, 21 (1), 1982 and his book *Theories of Imperialism* (London, 1984).

199. For a short enunciation of this idea see R. H. Chilcote, *Theories of Development ...*, op. cit., 1984, pp. 18–21, and for more extended treatment refer to the relevant sections of Trotsky's own *The Russian Revolution* (New York, 1962), I. Deutscher (ed.), *The Age of Permanent Revolution: A Trotsky Anthology* (New York, 1964), B. Knei-Paz, *The Social and Political Thought of Leon Trotsky* (Oxford, 1978), and G. Novack, *Uneven and Combined Development in History* (New York, 1966).

200. See U. Melotti, op. cit., S. Avineri, op. cit., and especially K. Mohri, 'Marx and "Underdevelopment"', op. cit.

201. Cf. A. Foster Carter, 'Neo-Marxist Approaches ...', op. cit., A. Hoogveldt, op. cit., Ch. 5, A. Brewer, op. cit., Ch. 2, and R. H. Chilcote, op. cit., 1984.

202. A. Brewer, op. cit., p. 155.

203. R. H. Chilcote, op. cit., 1984, p. 131.

204. See R. H. Chilcote, op. cit., 1984, especially Ch. 4 for a convenient general survey. For the internationalisation of capital variant the standard source is C. Palloix, 'The Self Expansion of Capital on a World Scale', *Review of Radical Political Economy* 9, Summer 1977, and also refer to note 94 above.

205. The best all-round survey of the various strands of thinking that make up the Dependency approach is in G. Palma, op. cit., 1978. For a more up-to-date account see R. H. Chilcote, op. cit., 1984, and the special number devoted to 'Dependency and Marxism' in *Latin American Perspectives*, 7, Summer and Fall, 1981.

206. See for example Alain Lipietz's critique of Warren in 'Marx or Rostow?', *New Left Review* 132, March-April, 1982; Peter Worsley's attack on Wallerstein, 'One World or Three? A Critique of the World-System Theory' in R. Miliband and J. Saville (eds.), *The Socialist Register 1980* (London, 1980), Robert Brenner's attack on Frank, 'The Origins of Capitalist Development', op. cit., 1977, and Charles Bettleheim's attack on Emmanuel in the latter's *Unequal Exchange: A Study of the Imperialism of Trade* (New York, 1972) together with K. Bharadwaj's 'A Note on Emmanuel's "Unequal Exchange"', *Economic and Political Weekly*, 28 July 1984. This is only a very small – but nevertheless fairly representative – sample of the debate within the Marxist tradition ... For further references see A. Brewer, op. cit., R. H. Chilcote and D. L. Johnson, op. cit., 1983, R. H. Chilcote, op. cit., 1984.

207. Such as Haldan Gulalp, op. cit., 1984.

208. J. S. Saul, 'Development Studies for Social change in Southern Africa', *Review* 8 (2), 1984, p. 179. Terry Byres also notes that Marxism is now not only 'a house of many mansions', but 'a house of so many mansions that those approaching it for the first time are likely to be bewildered, whilst even those who have become familiar with one or two of the locations may be quite unsure as to the others, and quite what they are about' – see his review article 'Eurocentric Marxism and the Third World! View from the Academy in the Anglophone Metropolis', *Economic and Political Weekly*, 28 July 1984,

p. 1199. See also Peter Worsley's pithy remarks on the divisions in *The Three Worlds*, op. cit., Prolegomena, p. 41.

209. See for example E. Mandel's *Marxist Economic Theory* (London, 3rd impression, 1974), and his *Late Capitalism* (London, Verso ed., 1978). In both these sizeable texts only a very limited amount of space is given to the Third World, refer to Chapters 13 and 11 of the respective texts.

210. See G. Hardach, D. Karras and B. Fine, *A Short History of Socialist Economic Thought* (London, 1978). Ian Steedman's work is a particualarly good example of what I have in mind.

211. Cf. E. P. Thompson, *The Poverty of Theory ...*, op. cit., G. A. Cohen, op. cit., G. McLennan, op. cit., and especially B. Hindess and P. Q. Hirst, op. cit., 1975.

212. P. Worsley, op. cit., pp. 189f. The nub of his charge is that: 'What is striking about all this theorizing is its disconnection from any examination of the now-voluminous data accumulated from numerous field-studies. Research of that kind was categorized, not as *empirical* work, but as mere empiri*cism*. Theory, on the other hand, was something constructed in the study, by assiduous re-reading of Marx's writings of one hundred years ago. The search, often, is for some hitherto overlooked passage, usually in the *Grundrisse* on Volume 3 of *Capital*, which might provide the required revelation. Out of this reading, a model is constructed and then applied ... The dialectical conception of a continuing interplay between concept formation and the observation of reality is notable by its absence. One hunts in vain through such texts for anything so mundane as a fact – or even a datum' (p. 189).

213. Rather than attempt to list these achievements in a simplistic way let me refer to the Marxist-inspired work on areas such as Latin America, the Caribbean, southern and eastern Africa, and South Asia which has revolutionised our knowledge and perception of long-run change.

214. The criticisms of Frank's historical work are legion and include Marxist as well as more orthodox historians. See for example G. P. C. Thompson's review of Mexian agriculture in the *Economic History Review*, 23 (4), 1980; the essays by R. Miller and Bill Albert and P. Henderson in *World Development* 9 (8), 1981, and R. Brenner, 'The Origins of Capitalist Development', loc. cit.

215. G. Hardach, D. Karras and B. Fine, op. cit., 1978, p. 80.

216. G. M. Meier and R. E. Baldwin, *Economic Development: Theory, History, Policy* (New York, 1957). The claim of being first in the field was made in the Preface to the 1976 Reprint, p. v. See Part 2, 'Historical Outline of Economic Development', Chapters 7–12.

217. B. Higgins, *Economic Development: Principles, Problems and Policies* (New York, 1959). See Part 3, Chapters 9 and 10.

218. W. W. Rostow, *The Stages of Economic Growth*, op. cit.

219. See Axel Leijonhufvud's article 'Life among the Econ.' in his *Information and Co-ordination: Essays in Macroeconomic Theory* (New York, 1981) for an amusing – but sharply penetrating – disquisition on the subject of the contemporary education given to economists in North American universities. Although the trend has not gone quite so far on this side of the Atlantic, all the indications are that we seem destined to follow suit.

220. For example, see the list of publications of Sir Arthur Lewis in M. Gersovitz (ed.), op. cit., pp. 391–4, for an indication of his contributions to economic history. It is also interesting to note that both Lewis and Kuznets were awarded their Nobel Prizes for their work in economic history as well as development economics. See A. Lindbeck, 'The Prize in Economic Science in Memory of Alfred Nobel', *Journal of Economic Literature* 22, March 1985, pp. 50f.

221. S. Kuznets, *Modern Economic Growth ...*, op. cit., *Economic Growth of Nations ...*, op. cit., and the Nobel Lecture, op. cit.

222. G. Myrdal, *Asian Drama*, op. cit., Chapter 14, pp. 673–705.

223. See the relevant sections of A. W. Lewis, *The Theory of Economic Growth*, op. cit., and *Development Planning: The Essentials of Economic Policy* (London, 1966).

224. W. W. Rostow, *The Stages of Economic Growth*, op. cit., especially Chapters 1–6.

225. R. Nurkse, *Problems of Capital Formation in Under-developed Countries* (Oxford, 1953), *Patterns of Trade and Development* (Oxford, 1961), and his 'International Investment

To-Day in the Light of Nineteenth Century Experience', *Economic Journal* 64, Dec. 1954.

226. B. F. Hoselitz, 'Social Structure and Economic Growth', *Economia Internazionale*, 6 (3), 1953, 'The City, the Factory, and Economic Growth', *American Economic Review*, 45 (2), 1955, and 'Small Industry in Underdeveloped Countries', *Journal of Economic History* 19, 1959.

227. The examples I have in mind here are the studies by Dean and Cole and later Charles Feinstein on the rather modest build-up of capital investment during the British Industrial Revolution, cf. P. Deane and W. H. Cole, *British Economic Growth 1688–1959* (Cambridge, 1967 2nd ed.), Chapter VIII, P. Deane, 'The role of capital in the industrial revolution', *Explorations in Economic History* 10, 1973, pp. 349–64, and C. H. Feinstein, 'Capital Formation in Great Britain' in P. Mathias and M. M. Poston (eds.), *The Cambridge Economic History of Europe*, vol. 7, Part 1, pp. 28–96; Nathaniel Leff's work of entrepreneurship, op. cit.; the empirically-based criticism of Rostow contained in W. W. Rostow (ed.), *The Economics of Take-Off into Sustained Growth* (New York, 1965); and A. K. Dasgupta's critique of the 'differences in initial conditions' literature in his two articles 'Underdevelopment, Past and Present – Some Comparisons of pre-Industrial Levels of Living', both in the *Indian Economic and Social History Review*, 15 (1), 1978 and 16 (1), 1979.

228. By this I mean that Europe and Japan were considered the benchmarks from which to assess the experience of the LDCs.

229. For an appreciation of Lord Balogh's all-round contributions to economics see Paul Streeten's 'In Memory of Thomas Balogh', *World Development*, 13 (4), 1985.

230. For a lively account of this process see Lawrence Stone's *The Past and Present* (London, 1981), especially the chapter on 'History and the Social Sciences in the Twentieth Century'.

231. A. Bullock, 'Breaking the Tyranny of the Present', *The Times Higher Education Supplement*, 24 May 1985, p. 19. For a rather more extended treatment see P. McClelland, *Causal Explanation and Model Building in History, Economics, and the New Economic History* (New York, 1975).

232. Because this trend has excited so much critical attention and since this is hardly the most appropriate place to refer to the specialist disciplinary literature, I see little point in attempting to cite references. Readers familiar with journals such as *Comparative Studies in Society and History, History and Theory, Past and Present* and *Science and Society* will be aware of just how wide-ranging the controversies have been, and for a limited discussion of the debate in one subject cf. T. Azad (ed.), *Anthropology and the Colonial Encounter* (London, 1973), B. S. Cohn, 'History and Anthropology: The State of Play', *C.S.S.H.*, 22 (2), 1980, and J. Comaroff, 'Dialectical Systems, History and Anthropology: Units of Study and Questions of Theory', *Journal of Southern African Studies*, 8 (2), 1982.

233. In order to try to ascertain the extent and nature of (economic) history in the development economics literature, Robert Kirk and I sampled a wide variety of English language sources, especially bibliographies, journal contents, abstracts, research registers, conference proceedings, and university course prospectuses. The difficulties which we encountered – particularly the problem of isolating the indirect influence of history in theorising; the question of how to separate the specific and purposive study of history from the many general references to 'the past'; how to judge quality; and deciding upon a convention for determining just when history begins or ends – have meant that our survey is of only impressionistic value. Nevertheless, despite our inability to 'prove' the point we both remain convinced that there is substance to the basic contention.

234. Meier goes on to say that 'economic history was to be revitalized from the perspective of development' in order for the pioneers to 'conceptualize, deduce principles, build models, and establish empirical relationships', G. M. Meier and D. Seers (eds.), *Pioneers in Development*, op. cit., p. 19. It is clear that Meier himself not only took these preoccupations seriously, but continued to adhere to them in his own writing – see his edited book of readings *Leading Issues in Economic Development*, 4th ed., op. cit., where, in his introduction to section II.A, Historical Perspectives, he notes that 'If we are to appreciate fully the variety, complexity, and pervasiveness of development problems, we must be aware of their historical dimension. Historical perspective is one of the best safeguards against a superficial view of these problems' (p. 90).

235. See, for example, M. Gillis, *et al, Economics of Development*, op. cit., 1983, pp. 16f. and A. P. Thirwall, op. cit., p. 10.
236. E.g. W. Nafziger, op. cit., 1984, Chapter 7, and M. Todaro, op. cit., 1985, Chapter 3.
237. E.g. M. Todaro, ibid., W. Nafziger, ibid., M. Gillis, *et al*, op. cit., Chapter 2, and G. M. Meier, *Leading Issues ...*, op. cit., Chapter IIA.
238. E.g. W. Nafziger, ibid., Chapter 4, M. Todaro, ibid., Chapter 4, and A. P. Thirlwall, op. cit., Chapter 1.
239. See for example W. Nafziger, ibid., Chapter 6, p. 118, Chapter 7, pp. 194f. Chapter 12, pp. 275–9, and Chapter 13, pp. 309–11.
240. This is discussed more fully further on in the chapter.
241. A. K. Sen, *Poverty and Famines*, op. cit., and I. Adelman and C. T. Morris, 'A Typology of Poverty in 1850' in M. Nash (ed.), op. cit., 1977, pp. 314–43, 'Growth and Impoverishment in the Middle of the Nineteenth Century', *World Development*, 6 (3), 1978, and 'An Inquiry into the Course of Poverty in the Nineteenth and early Twentieth Centuries' in R. C. O. Mathews (ed.), *Economic Growth and Resources* (London, 1980).
242. W. W. Rostow, op. cit., 1960; A. G. Frank especially 'The Development of Underdevelopment', *Monthly Review*, 18 (4), 1966, and *On Capitalist Underdevelopment* (Oxford, 1975); A. Gerschenkron, *Economic Backwardness in Historical Perspective* (Cambridge, Mass., 1962); Barrington Moore Jr., *Social Origins of Dictatorship and Democracy* (London, 1967); E. L. Jones, *The European Miracle* (Oxford, 1981); G. Kitching, op. cit., 1982; R. G. Wilkinson, *Poverty and Progress* (London, 1973); P. Maitra, *Economic Development With or Without Industrial Revolution* (London, 1978); A. S. Guha, *An Evolutionary View of Economic Growth* (London, 1981) and M. Olson, *The Rise and Decline of Nations: Economic Growth, Stagflation, and Social Rigidities* (London, 1982).
243. See M. Gillis, *et al*, op. cit., Chapter 2; G. M. Meier (ed.), *Leading Issues ...*, op. cit., Chapter II; A. P. Thirwall, op. cit., Chapter 1; M. Todaro, 1985, op. cit., Chapter 3, and his edited book of readings, *The Struggle for Economic Development* (London, 1983), Chapter 2; and W. Nafziger, op. cit., Chapter 4.
244. Refer to note 214 for Frank, and note 227 for Rostow, together with the early reviews by Robert Fogel, 'Empty Economic Stages?', *Economic Journal*, 75, March 1965, and H. Rosovsky, 'The Take-off into Sustained Controversy', *Journal of Economic History*, 25 (2), 1965.
245. K. Polanyi, *The Great Transformation: The Political and Economic Origins of Our Time* (Boston, 1957; orig. pub. by Rinehart and Co. in 1944).
246. In point of fact the chipping-away had begun as early as the late 1940s with the publication of T. S. Ashton's little classic *The Industrial Revolution, 1760–1830* (Oxford, 1948), in which he gave only qualified support to the idea that the fall in the rate of interest in the UK from the mid-eighteenth century had been the key to the Industrial Revolution (p. 11). For non-British experience cf. M. Abromavitz, 'Resources and Output Trends in the United States since 1870', *American Economic Review, Papers and Proceedings*, 46, 1956; J. D. Gould, op. cit., Chapter 2; and C. M. Cipolla's 'Introduction' to the *Fontana Economic History of Europe: The Twentieth Century, Part I* (London, 1976).
247. M. Todaro, 1985, op. cit., p. 119. Arguing against 'stages' theory, he goes on to say that 'the fact is that the growth position of these countries today is in many important ways significantly different from that of the currently developed countries as they embarked on their era of modern economic growth', p. 120. This argument, of course, derives from Myrdal's work of the 1960s.
248. E. Staley, *The Future of Underdeveloped Countries: Political Implications of Economic Development* (2nd ed., New York, 1961), pp. 79f.
249. Say as represented in works such as N. B. Harte (ed.), *The Study of Economic History: Collected Inaugural Lectures 1893–1970* (London, Cass, 1971).
250. See B. C. Hurst's essay 'The Myth of Historical Evidence' in *History and Theory*, 20 (3), 1981, for an informed discussion of this procedure.
251. E. Staley, op. cit., pp. 80f.
252. See A. Bullock, op. cit., for a fuller sketch.
253. Cf. the three surveys of articles on the cliometric, *Annales* and neo-Marxist schools written by D. McCloskey, Robert Forster and J. S. Cohen, respectively, in the *Journal of*

Economic History, 38 (1), 1978. For an outline of what looks fair to become a new school of tradition – that of Transactions Costs – see D. C. North, 'Transactions Costs in History', *Journal of European Economic History*, 14 (3), 1985.

254. A. G. Hopkins, 'Imperial Connections', C. J. Dewey and A. G. Hopkins (eds.), *The Imperial Impact ...*, op. cit., p. 1.

255. I refer once more to Professor Hopkins' observations – this time in his essay 'Africa's Age of Improvement', Inaugural Lecture delivered at the University of Birmingham, 9 May 1978, and published in *History in Africa*, 7, 1980. See also R. Constantino, 'Notes on Historical Writing for the Third World', *Journal of Contemporary Asia*, 10 (4), 1980, pp. 233–40.

256. This impression is based upon my involvement with the 'Third World Economic History and Development' and the 'Historical Dimensions of Development Studies' groups since 1978; the fact that the main-line journals and conferences of the Economic History Society of the UK and its US equivalent have allocated relatively little space and time for Third World topics; that in relation to the historiography of the Western and Japanese cases there are enormous and basic lacunas relating to the Third World; that there are few suitable general textbooks available; and finally, that there have been few methodological breakthroughs stemming from Third World economic history.

257. A discussion of this 'sociology of knowledge' issue in the particular context of India can be found in my 'Industralisation, De-Industrialisation and the Indian Economy ...', op. cit., Part II.

258. I gratefully acknowledge Clive Dewey's advice on this point.

259. For a suggestive – but ultimately disappointingly restricted – discussion of these issues see H. L. Wesseling and P. C. Emmer, 'What is Overseas History? Some Reflections on a Colloquium and a Problem', in their edited book *Re-appraisals in Overseas History: Essays on Post-War Historiography about European Expansion* (Leiden, 1979).

260. I have found *The Selected Papers of Wolf Ladejinsky: Agrarian Reform as Unfinished Business*, edited by C. J. Walinsky for the World Bank (Oxford, 1977), especially instructive on this issue.

261. H. Chenery and M. Syrquin, *Patterns of Development*, op. cit., p. 5.

262. M. Roemer and J. J. Stern, *Cases in Economic Development: Projects, Policies and Strategies* (London, 1981). I also recall coming across a reference to another such study with 'Freedonia' as the country in question.

263. Ibid., Report I, pp. 30–42.

264. The first of these phrases comes from D. N. Stearn, 'Applied History and Social History', *Journal of Social History*, 14 (4), 1981, p. 534, and the last from A. Bullock, op. cit., p. 19. It would not take the interested reader long to come across the intervening phrases – and many more written in the same general spirit, see for example D. Lowenthal, op. cit. 1985, especially pp. 16–52.

265. For one attempt to argue along these lines see S. Mandelbaum, 'The Past in Service to the Future', *Journal of Social History*, 11, (1), 1977.

266. J. Toye, 'Does Development Studies Have a Core?', op. cit., p. 18.

267. H. Bruton, 'The Search for a Development Economics', op.cit., 1983, pp. 16f.

268. D. North, *Structure and Performance*, op. cit. I am indebted to Robert Millward for pointing me in this direction.

269. A. K. Sen, *Poverty and Famines*, op. cit.

270. For a modern discussion of the different variations of rationality see H. Simon, *Reason in Human Affairs* (Oxford, 1983).

271. For a convenient bibliography of references see H. Bruton, op. cit., 1983, pp. 87–94.

272. See J. Toye, 'Dirigisme and Development Economics', op. cit., Part I.

273. A. Winston, 'The "Prussian road" of Agrarian Development: a reconsideration', *Economy and Society*, 11 (4), 1982.

274. J. P. Plattanaau, 'Classical Economics and Agrarian Reform in Underdeveloped Areas: The Radical Views of the Two Mills', *Journal of Development Studies*, 19 (4), 1983.

275. J. Toye, 'Does Development Studies Have a Core?', op. cit., p. 16. This characterisation is true of most of the references cited in note 109 above.

276. Ibid.

277. Cf. M. Kalecki, *Essays on Developing Economics* (London, 1976), and the M. Kalecki's

65th Birthday Anniversary Committee, *Problems of Economic Dynamics and Planning: Essays in Honor of M. Kalecki* (Oxford, 1966).

278. For the influence of Keynesian ideas on development see J. Knapp, 'A Keynesian Analysis of Underdevelopment and Growth Points', *Tiers Monde*, Jan.–March 1969, and his 'Economics or Political Economy?', *Lloyds Bank Review*, 107, Jan. 1973; M. Barratt Brown, *The Economics of Imperialism* (London, 1974), Chapter 2; and the essays by K. N. Raj, 'Keynesian Economics and Agrarian Economics' and Sukhamoy Chakravarty, 'Keynes, "Classics", and the Developing Economies' which appear as Chapters 8 and 6 respectively in C. H. Hanumantha Rao and P. C. Joshi (eds.), *Reflections on Economic Development and Social Change*, op. cit. For Dualism see note 51 above. As for Structuralism, this takes in Prebisch's pioneering work with the ECLA in the 1940s and 1950s, the early Hollis Chenery and Lance Taylor formulations, and the later 1970s versions which primarily focus upon distributional questions. In my view, few of the modern textbooks even attempt to trace these ideas through and are all the poorer for that.

279. Here I have in mind not only the work of avowed 'changers of mind' such as A. G. Frank and Colin Leys, but also the less spectacular acknowledgement of past errors of judgement or even misconceptions – cf. A. C. Harberger and D. Wall's essay on the late Harry Johnson, *J.P.E.*, 1984, op. cit.; John Adams' study of J. K. Galbraith, 'Galbraith as a Development Economist', *Journal of Post-Keynesian Economics*, 7 (1), 1984; Hans Singer, 'Poverty, Income Distribution and levels of living ...', op. cit.; and the retrospective reflections of the so-called 'pioneering fathers' in G. M. Meier and D. Seers (eds.), *Pioneers in Development*, op. cit.

280. J. Toye, 'Does Development Studies Have a Core?', op. cit., p. 16.

281. This rarely comes through in the modern textbooks on development economics; like the writers of the more mainstream branches, many of our authors seem to prefer to enunciate what they call the 'principles' of the subject even though there is probably far less 'internal' agreement about what these consist of.

282. But note that in a stimulating essay on the subject of 'Anthropology and History' written in 1961, the late Professor E. E. Evans-Pritchard neatly inverted this proposition by arguing that it was not possible to 'properly' study the past without first having a firm understanding of the present; the main point of the essay, however, was an appeal to Social Anthropologists to take up historical study and, to that extent, is not inconsistent with my general argument – see his *Essays in Social Anthropology* (London, 1962).

283. K. Griffin, 'Underdevelopment in History' in C. K. Wilbur (ed.), *The Political Economy of Development and Underdevelopment*, op. cit., p. 77.

284. I refer of course to Oscar Lewis' path-breaking study *The Children of Sanchez* (London, 1961).

285. Ragnar Nurkse was one of the first to articulate this notion in his *Problems of Capital Formation in Underdeveloped Countries*, op. cit.

286. Like the 'vicious circles of poverty' phrase this has now passed out of common development parlance, but there are many modern instances where the idea appears albeit in a slightly altered guise.

287. Cf. G. D. N. Worswick, 'Two Great Recessions: The 1980's and the 1930's', *Scottish Journal of Political Economy*, 31 (3), 1984; M. de Cecco, 'The International Debt Problem of the Inter-War Period', European University Institute Working Paper No. 84/103, Florence, April 1984 (mimeo); and C. Saint-Etienne, *The Great Depression 1929–1938: Lessons for the 1980's* (New York, 1984).

288. For an early discussion of this view see G. Ohlin, 'Remarks on the Relevance of Western Experience in Economic Growth to Former Colonial Areas', *Journal of World History*, 9, 1965.

289. Those interested in pursuing this line of thought should turn first to the work of the new growth-minded economic historians published in the mid-1960s, cf. B. Supple, 'Has the Early History of Developed Countries any Current Relevance?' and R. Easterlin, 'Is There a Need for Historical Research of Underdevelopment?', both in the *American Economic Review*, 55, Supplement, 1965, and R. Cameron, 'Some Lessons of History for Developing Nations', *American Economic Review*, 57, 1967. Four other books which appeared at around the same time and with undoubtedly the same intellectual stimulus were A. J. Youngson (ed.), *Economic Development in the Long Run*, op. cit., and his

Possibilities of Economic Progress (Cambridge, 1959); B. Supple (ed.), *The Experience of Economic Growth: Case Studies in Economic History* (New York, 1963); and M. Falkus (ed.), *Readings in the History of Economic Growth* (Nairobi, 1968). I hasten to add that all of these authors, editors and essay contributors acknowledged the dangers of drawing out simplistic 'lessons' from history.

290. D. N. McCloskey, 'The Industrial Revolution 1780–1860: A Survey' in R. Floud and D. N. McCloskey (eds.), *The Economic History of Britain Since 1700, Vol. 1, 1700–1860* (Cambridge, 1981), p. 104.

291. Though the uniqueness of the British case – especially, of course, the Industrial Revolution period – has been accepted for generations, because the literature on it is so plentiful, accessible and of a generally high standard, it is often used as the main point of reference. In fact, in many university libraries in the English-speaking parts of the Third World, the stock of material on Britain's economic history comfortably exceeds that of all others – including that of the country itself – put together.

292. J. Toye, 'Dirigisme and Development Economics', op. cit.

293. S. Mandelbaum, op. cit., p. 193.

294. I discuss these points in a little more depth further on in the chapter.

295. J. R. Commons, *Institutional Economics* (New York, 1934).

296. D. North, 'Transactions Costs in History', op. cit., p. 559.

297. H. J. Bruton, 'The Search for a Development Economics', op. cit. 1983, p. 35.

298. These are 'rules that are merely observed in fact, but have been stated in words ...', and 'rules that, though they have been stated in words, still merely express approximately what has long been observed in action'. See F. A. Hayek, *New Studies in Philosophy, Politics, Economics and the History of Ideas* (Chicago, 1978), pp. 8f. It is interesting to compare these theoretical strictures with actual experience, and for one possible area of application see A. Fforde, 'Reflections on the Vietnamese Socialist Revolution: the problem of plan non-implementability and the difficulties involved in realising Social Construction in a low-income Social Developing Country', Discussion Papers in Economics, Birkbeck College, no. 168, April 1985.

299. It is heartening to learn that American Institutionalists are now starting to investigate the long-run aspects of their subject with special reference to the underdeveloped countries, see M. Bolin, 'An Institutionalist Perspective on Economic Development', *Journal of Economic Issues*, 18 (2), 1984.

300. Which since 1983/4 we have attempted to do at Salford as part of our M.Sc. degree programme in Economic Development. Our two relevant courses 'The Economics of Imperialism' and 'The Historical Aspects of Development' not only take in but also go well beyond John Toye's suggested ingredients ('Does Development Studies have a Core?', op. cit.) of 'the changing structure of world commerce, colonialism and neo-colonialism, the history of capitalist monetary arrangements and the internationalisation of production, including the multinational firm, movements of capital and international labour migration', pp. 18f.

301. Such as the 'Third World Economic History and Development Society' and the 'Historical Dimensions of Economic Development' group.

302. The focus on economic growth and development represented a major innovation in the practice of economic history. For a discussion of the early impact of growth considerations see C. Goodrich, 'Economic History: One Field Or Two?', *Journal of Economic History*, 20 (4), 1960, where he writes that economic historians would 'gain greater vigor in their own work by giving more conscious attention to the problem of economic development. By so doing they will be able to take a more effective part in the common task which, in its application to the aspirations of the less developed countries, seems to be the most intellectually challenging and the most generously-directed concern of the economists of our day'. For a later and therefore much more fully articulated discussion see David Cannadine's excellent article 'The Present and the Past in the English Industrial Revolution 1880–1980', *Past and Present*, 103, May 1984, especially Section III, pp. 149–58.

303. See R. M. Hartwell (ed.), *The Causes of the Industrial Revolution* (London, 1967); *idem, The Industrial Revolution and Economic Growth* (London, 1971); and H. J. Habakkuk, 'The Historical Experience on the Basic Conditions of Economic Progress' in M. Falkus (ed.), op. cit.

304. Cf. P. Mathias, *The First Industrial Nation* (1st ed., London, 1969), especially Chapter 1; E. L. Jones (ed.), *Agriculture and Economic Growth in England, 1650–1815* (London, 1967), Introduction; E. L. Jones and S. Woolf (eds.), *Agrarian Change and Economic Development* (London, 1970), Introduction; a number of contributions in R. Floud and D. N. McCloskey (eds.), op. cit., e.g. N. C. R. Crafts, 'The Eighteenth Century: A Survey', pp. 1–16; and G. R. Hawke and J. P. P. Higgins, 'Transport and Social Overhead Capital', pp. 227–52; J. G. Williamson, 'Why Was British Growth so Slow During the Industrial Revolution?', *Journal of Economic History* 44 (3), 1984, and C. H. Lee, 'Regional Growth and Structural Change in Victorian Britain', *Economic History Review*, 34 (3), 1981.

305. Cf. W. Ashworth, 'Typologies and Evidence: Has Nineteenth Century Europe a Guide to Economic Growth?', *Economic History Review*, 30 (1), 1977; and N. F. R. Crafts, 'Patterns of Development in Nineteenth Century Europe', *Oxford Economic Papers*, 36 (4), 1984.

306. D. Cannadine, 'The Present and the Past ...', op. cit., p. 155.

307. Ibid.

308. Ibid., p. 160.

309. See the references to the work of Williamson and Lee (note 32 above); and Ashworth (which is really a 'one-off' article anyway) and Crafts (note 33 above).

310. See particularly *History Workshop* Nos. 6–8, and R. Samuel (ed.), *People's History and Socialist Theory* (London, 1981) especially pp. xv–xxxiii, where the development of this History is considered and a number of definitions are offered.

311. See the Editorial 'Towards a People's History: Re-writing Asian History', *Journal of Contemporary Asia*, 10 (3), 1980, and R. Constantino, 'Notes on Historical Writing for the Third World' in the same issue.

312. To date three volumes under this title have appeared (1982, 1984 and 1985), all edited by Ranajit Guha and published by OUP, Delhi. See especially Chapter 1 of Vol. 1, 'On Some Aspects of the Historiography of Colonial India', pp. 1–8, contributed by the editor.

313. See the four essays on African History by A. Triulzi, Shula Marks, R. Rathbone and R. Law in R. Samuel (ed.), op. cit., pp. 285–320. I confess to having little knowledge about any relevant Latin American developments, and indeed as readers will realise, this is a general weakness of this chapter as a whole.

314. A. Memmi, *The Colonizer and the Colonized* (New York, 1965). Compare this to the view from 'the other side' as discussed by Victor Kiernan in his *The Lords of Human Kind: European Attitudes to the Outside World in the Imperial Age* (London, 1969).

315. By this I do not mean to infer that a classical working class has in fact emerged in the Third World. The study of the formation of a labour force, its conditions of life and work, and its mode of reproduction has only got underway in the last two decades – and this, of course, is in marked contrast to the long tradition in Britain that antecedes Edward Thompson's work – especially the studies by the Hammonds, the Webbs and Cole and Postgate.

316. For southern Africa see the bibliography provided by Shula Marks (note 41 above); for India see my 'De-Industrialisation, Industrialisation and the Indian Economy', op. cit.

317. These techniques are indubitably becoming more acceptable in both British and pre-colonial African History. As far as Oral History is concerned, the technique suggested in J. Vansina, *Oral Tradition: A Study in Historical Methodology* (London, 1965); P. Thompson, *The Voice of the Past: Oral History* (Oxford, 1978); the journal *Oral History*; J. White, *Rothschild Buildings* (London, 1980); R. Samuel, *East End Underworld* (London, 1980); R. Samuel (ed.), 1981, op. cit., pp. 49–77; and *Social Analysis*, 'Special Issue on Using Oral Sources', 4 Sept. 1980.

318. For an interesting contrast in this context see E. Le Roy Ladurie, *Montaillou* (London, 1978), and K. Ballhatchet, *Race, Sex and Class Under the Raj* (London, 1980).

319. The comparative literature on the history of the Third World is small relative to that for Western Europe. For a selection of the former see R. Palmer and N. Parsons (eds.), *The Roots of Rural Poverty in Central and Southern Africa* (London, 1977); the review of this work by T. Ranger, 'Growing from the Roots: Reflections on Peasant Research in Central and Southern Africa', *Journal of Southern African Studies*, 5 (1), 1978; T. J. Byres and P. Nolan, *Inequality: India and China Compared 1950–1970* (Open University

Press, 1976); S. Swamy, 'The Response to Economic Challenge: A Comparative Economic History of China and India, 1870–1952', *Quarterly Journal of Economics*, 43 (1), 1979; I-Kuan Chen and J. S. Uppal, *Comparative Economic Development of India and China* (New York, 1971); P. Bairoch, *The Economic Development of the Third World since 1900* (London, 1975); A. J. H. Latham, *The International Economy and the Underdeveloped World, 1865–1914* (London, 1978); and his *The Depression and the Developing World* (London, 1981); T. Kemp, *Industrialization in the non-Western World* (London, 1983); P. Bairoch and M. Levy-Leboyer (eds.), op. cit.; and L. G. Reynolds, 'The Spread of Economic Growth to the Third World 1850–1980', op. cit.

320. The advantages – and limitations – of such interchange may be observed from C. Dewey and A. G. Hopkins, op. cit. This volume which set out to be genuinely comparative unfortunately lapsed into traditional area-based specialist work. This also happened in D. L. Johnson (ed.), *Middle Classes in Dependent Countries* (Beverley Hills, 1985).

321. Cf. A. D. Chandler and H. Dalms (eds.), *Managerial Hierarchies: Comparative Perspectives on the Rise of Modern Industrial Enterprise* (Cambridge, Mass., 1980); and R. Cameron (ed.), *Banking in the Early Stages of Industrialization: A Study in Comparative Economic History* (London, 1967); and C. P. Kindleberger, 'Financial Institutions and Economic Development: A Comparison of Great Britain and France in the 18th and 19th Centuries', *Explorations in Economic History*, 21 (2), 1984.

322. For a bibliographical starting point see Sidney Chapman's essay 'British-based Investment Groups before 1914', *Economic History Review*, 38 (2), 1985.

323. Incidentally, I would strongly deny that 'following the logic of the primary sources'; 'common sense'; an 'open-minded' and supposedly 'value-free' starting point; and even a tendency towards a weakly articulated form of eclecticism, lead to the writing of a more 'objective' type of history than that which is provided by those historians who are explicit in stating their methodological and theoretical perspectives.

324. There is a growing interest in this period and many fine studies on Africa and South Asia have been published within the last ten years. For a useful lead-in see the essays in Part 1 of *The Roots of Rural Poverty*; A. G. Hopkins, *An Economic History of West Africa*, Chapters 1–3; and J. Forbes Munro, *Africa and the International Economy* (London, 1976), Chapters 1, 2. For South Asia see T. Raychaudhuri and I. Habib (eds.), *The Cambridge Economic History of India, Vol. 1: c. 1200–1730* (Cambridge, 1982), and F. Perlin, 'Proto-industrialization and Pre-colonial South Asia', *Past and Present*, 98, 1983.

325. But I am not suggesting we go back as far as the Ancient period – excellent though G. E. M. de Saint Croix's book *The Class Struggle in the Ancient Greek World* (London, 1981), is!

326. See F. Braudel, *Capitalism and Material Life 1400–1800* (London, 1974); D. C. Coleman, *The Economy of England 1450–1750* (London, 1977); B. Supple, 'Economic History and Economic Growth', *Journal of Economic History*, 20 (4), 1960; 'Economic History and Economic Underdevelopment', *Canadian Journal of Economics and Political Science*, 27 (4), 1961, Introduction to 1963, op. cit., and 1965, op. cit.; and R. Cameron, 1967, op. cit., and 'Economic History, Pure and Applied', *Journal of Economic History*, 36 61), 1976.

327. Surely we can all agree with John Toye that 'As scholars we must set an example of curiosity, open-mindedness and willingness to learn from colleagues trained in unfamiliar ways of thinking. This may also help us as citizens to learn to co-operate with our fellows in the discharge of our deeper human obligations, to feed the hungry, to heal the sick and to make a just peace between enemies.' See the last two sentences of his paper 'Dirigisme and Development Economics', op. cit.

2

'Economic Development': A Suitable Case for Treatment?

FREDERICK NIXSON

INTRODUCTION

The origins of this paper lie in the increasing dissatisfaction felt by the author over the past few years with the way in which the concept of 'economic development' has evolved and with the manner in which the concept has been employed by the development profession. It presents a critique of the concept(s) of economic development currently fashionable in the literature and it argues that much of the pessimism currently expressed about the 'state' or 'status' of development economics can in fact be seen as a consequence of the abstract and unrealistic character of the notion of 'economic development' itself.

The starting point of our discussion is the distinction that is commonly made between economic growth and economic development. The development profession has been virtually unanimous in its insistence on the necessity of clearly distinguishing between economic growth and structural change on the one hand, and economic growth and economic development on the other hand, with structural change itself often being equated with 'development'. Dissenting voices have been heard recently (for example, Palma, 1978; Bernstein, 1979; Warren, 1980), but across the spectrum of development economics — neo-classical, structuralist, dependency and neo-Marxist — the assumption remains that it is both valid and useful to make the distinction.

Indeed, the concern of development economics with policy (political) issues, which essentially underlies the variety of normative concepts of development propounded, is seen by many in the profession as a source of strength. For example, Lehmann (1979, p. 2), in his Introduction to the collection of essays by four well-known authors, notes the 'deep dissatisfaction with patterns of development' observed and the wish 'to discover a more egalitarian and autonomous pattern for the future' which has motivated their writing.

He continues:

> This concern and involvement which lie so close to the surface of writing on development problems are not a defect but a virtue, and are one (but only one) element which makes the subject so potentially creative. (Lehmann, 1979, p. 2)[1]

This paper argues, however, that although the distinction between economic growth and economic development has served a valuable purpose, the current hopeless confusion of explanation (or what Leeson (1983) refers to as the 'historical-analytic') with policy prescription is such as to obscure, rather than illuminate, what is happening in the less developed parts of the world. It is further argued that the recognition of the need to keep separate historical-analytic and policy issues should lead to a greater preoccupation with explanation and understanding and with the attempt to identify and comprehend underlying trends in the development of the world economy on the part of those not directly concerned with policy-making or consultancy.[2]

THE DEVELOPMENT OF THE CONCEPT OF 'ECONOMIC DEVELOPMENT'

Arndt (1981) has traced the emergence and evolution of what is now referred to as 'economic development' from Adam Smith onwards.[3] It is not our intention to repeat that exercise. Our more limited objective is to examine some of the salient features of the concept of 'economic development' as it has evolved in the more recent past and, more specifically, to highlight the divorce of economic development from economic growth. No attempt is made to present a comprehensive survey.

Arndt (1981, p. 460) highlights the important distinction that can and should be made between (*i*) economic development as an 'historical process that happened without being consciously willed by anyone'; and (*ii*) economic development as an activity, consciously engaged in, mainly but not solely by governments, with the intention of reaching or approaching specific goals or objectives. We will discuss briefly each of these concepts.

The discussion of the concept of economic development as an historical process is to be found in the work of Karl Marx and Joseph Schumpeter.

For Marx, development was the major preoccupation, and in Deane's words (Deane, 1978, p. 130), 'Marx ... saw the task of the political economist as being primarily an investigation into the long-term development of modern economic society'. His economic analysis was distinguished by its historical setting (Dobb, 1970, p.6) and his historical interpretation was derived from Hegelian philosophy which envisaged progress as the product of continuous conflict (Dean, 1978, p.127). Marx, however, rejected Hegel's idealistic philosophy and applied dialectics to material reality:

> the dialect of development started from Nature, and from Man as initially an integral part of Nature. But while part of Nature and subject to the determinism of its laws, Man as a conscious being was at the same time capable of struggling with and against Nature — of subordinating it and ultimately transforming it for his own purposes. (Dobb, 1970, p. 7)

For Marx, the analysis of society had to start with the examination of the structure of social relations specific to any particular mode of production:

> In the social production of their existence, men inevitably enter into definite relations, which are independent of their will, namely relations of production appropriate to a given stage in the development of their material forces of production. The totality of these relations of production constitutes the economic structure of society, the real foundation, on which arises a legal and political super-structure and to which correspond definite forms of social consciousness. The mode of production of material life conditions the general process of social, political and intellectual life. (Marx, 1970, pp.20–1)

Each mode of production, however, contains within it the seeds of its own destruction:

> At a certain stage of development, the material productive forces of society come into conflict with the existing relations of production ... From forms of development of the productive forces these relations turn into their fetters. Then begins an era of social revolution. The changes in the economic foundation lead sooner or later to the transformation of the whole immense superstructure ... In broad outline, the Asiatic, ancient, feudal and modern bourgeois modes of production may be designated as epochs marking progress in the economic development of society. (Marx, 1970, p.21).

Society, according to Marx, thus evolves through a series of stages or modes of production, although as Brewer (1980, p.13) has pointed out, what is of greater importance is the 'analytical primacy of the mode of production, not the inevitability of a certain succession of stages'.

The concept of economic development as an historical process is also to be found in the work of Joseph Schumpeter (an economist familiar with, but critical of, the work of Marx).

In his *Theory of Economic Development* (1934; 1961),[4] Schumpeter clearly distinguished between growth and development (or evolution). He began with the concept of a 'stationary state' or 'circular flow', 'running on in channels essentially the same year after year – similar to the circulation of the blood in an animal organism' (Schumpeter, 1961 ed., p. 61). Deane (1978, p. 192) has described this state as the 'quasi-equilibrium starting point', characterised by the fact that 'labour, capital and output are all growing at the same rate and just enough capital is being annually accumulated to equip additions to the labour force at a constant capital–labour ratio'. Schumpeter continues:

> Economic life changes; it changes partly because of changes in the data, [changes in market conditions, consumer tastes, natural conditions, changes in social, commercial or economic policy] to which it tends to adapt itself. But this is not the only kind of economic change; there is another which is not accounted for by inflence on the data from without, but which arises from within the system, and this kind of change is the cause of so many important economic phenomena that it seems worthwhile to build a theory for it, and, in order to do so, to isolate it from all the other factors of change ... what we are about to consider is that kind of change arising from within the system *which so displaces its equilibrium point that the new one cannot be reached from the old one by infinitesimal steps.* (Schumpeter, 1961 ed., p. 64, footnote 1, emphasis in original)

The 'mere growth of the economy', as shown by the growth of population and wealth, is not designated as development, for 'it calls forth no qualitatively new phenomena, but only processes of adaptation of the same kind as the changes in the natural data' (Schumpeter, 1961, ed., p. 63). Thus:

> Development in our sense is a distinct phenomenon, entirely foreign to what may be observed in the circular flow or in the tendency towards equilibrium. It is spontaneous and discontinuous change in the channels of the flow, disturbance of equilibrium, which forever alters and displaces the equilibrium state previously existing ... (Schumpeter, 1961 ed., p. 64)

Schumpeter further argued that 'Development in our sense is ... defined by the carrying out of new combinations' (p. 66), that is, the introduction of a new good or new quality of good, the introduction of a new method of production, the opening of a new market, the conquest of a new source of supply of raw materials and the carrying out of new organisation of any industry (for example, the creation, or the breaking down of a monopoly position). The carrying out of these new combinations is called 'enterprise' and the individuals whose function it is to carry them out are 'entrepreneurs' (Schumpeter, 1961 ed., p. 74).

In his *Business Cycles* (Vol. 1, 1939), Schumpeter focuses more specifically on the importance of innovation in the process of what he now terms 'Economic Evolution'. Innovation ('the setting up of a new production function' (p. 87)) is the basis of the model of the process of economic change:

> The changes in the economic process brought about by innovation, together with all their effects, and the response to them by the economic system, we shall designate by the term Economic Evolution. (Schumpeter, 1939, p. 86)

Of significance to our argument below is Schumpeter's assertion that

> evolution is lopsided, discontinous, disharmonious by nature − that the disharmony is inherent in the very modus operandi of the factors of progress ... the history of capitalism is studded with violent bursts and catastrophes ... evolution is a disturbance of existing structures and more like a series of explosions than a gentle, though incessant, transformation. (Schumpeter, 1939, p. 102)

The second concept of economic development referred to above, emerged in the 1920s through the writings of those to whom Arndt (1981, p. 480) refers as the 'British historians of empire', and now dominates main-stream development economics.

Although it was in general the case that, in the immediate post-war period, economic growth and economic development were seen as being synonymous (Arndt, 1981, p. 465), the position was perhaps less clear-cut than this statement would suggest. The authors of a leading textbook of the 1950s and 1960s (Meier and Baldwin, 1957) argued that:

> No single definition of 'economic development' is entirely satisfactory. There is a tendency to use the terms economic development, economic growth and secular change interchangeably. Although it is possible to draw some fine distinctions among these terms, they are in essence synonymous. (Meier and Baldwin, 1957, p. 2)

They went on, however, to qualify the above statement:

> Although an increase in output per head is in itself a significant achievement, nevertheless we cannot equate this with an increase in economic welfare, let alone social welfare, without additional considerations. To specify an optimum rate of development we must make value judgements regarding income distribution, composition of output, tastes, real costs, and other particular changes that are associated with the overall increase in real income. (p. 8)

In this statement, development is clearly distinguished from growth and there appears to be some conflict with the first quotation. We find what is perhaps the clearest distinction between growth and development in the work of Clower et al (1966) on Liberia:

> The title of our book, 'Growth Without Development', is intended to emphasise a central feature of Liberian economy, namely, that enormous growth in primary commodities produced by foreign concessions for export has been unaccompanied either by structural changes to induce complementary growth or by institutional changes to diffuse gains in real income among all sectors of the population. Our principal conclusion is that the rapid growth in production between 1950 and 1960 has had little developmental impact on Liberia or Liberians. (Clower et al, 1966, p. vi)

Again,

> Liberia's economic progress has consisted more of growth than of development. Major changes have occurred in the volume of primary commodities produced for export and the quantity of manufactured goods purchased from abroad. Development involves much more than this. It involves structural change in lines of production undertaken by Liberians moving from subsistence production in the tribal sector to production for sale; the adoption of more efficient techniques; a continuous decline in the proportion of unskilled labor in the labor force; and new social achievements and aspirations. Specifically, it involves the acquisition of social overhead capital (such as roads, power facilities and schools) and institutional improvements (more and better government services, higher levels of education and skill, and the transformation of tribal agriculture). (Clower et al, 1966, p. 31)

Clower et al appear to be making two distinct points in the above quotations:

1. economic growth does not necessarily lead to changes in economic structure, whereas structural change is an essential part of economic development;[5]
2. economic development involves the move towards certain normative goals and objectives, which economic growth on its own may not achieve.

The first proposition is not, in our opinion, a tenable one. A conceptual distinction can be made between economic growth and structural change if it is explicitly assumed that all sectors in the economy grow at equal rates so as to leave the proportions of the national economy that they represent unchanged. In reality, however, it is highly unlikely that all sectors of the economy will grow at equal rates and thus the concept of economic growth as consisting of continuous increases in total or per capita incomes, within unchanged structures, cannot be defended. Szentes (1971) has convincingly argued that

> Any distinction between the theories of 'development' and 'growth' can at best only be accepted for practical reasons, ... however, by no means, as a scientific distinction.
> The terminological distinction on a semantic basis is unacceptable, because development always and everywhere involves and presupposes the dialectic of quantitative and qualitative changes, of evolution and revolution. And even if a purely quantitative 'growth' can be observed in a given place and at a given time within the framework of the existing structures or system, it is not only the consequences of a previous qualitative change but it also inevitably paves the way for a new one. (Szentes, 1971, p. 14)[6]

For a large number of less developed countries (LDCs), economic growth has been rapid and sustained in the post-World War II period. World Bank data show that between 1960 and 1973, the GDP of the LDCs grew on average by 6.0% per annum. The average fell to 5.1% per annum over the period 1973−79, and there was a further fall during the 1980−82 recession (World Bank, 1983, p. 7). Average figures, of course, conceal significant variations between different groups of LDCs, but overall, the growth experience of the LDCs in the post-war period has been impressive.

The LDCs have also experienced significant structural change during this period, as Table 1 clearly shows. As we would expect, the share of agriculture in GDP has fallen and the shares of industry and services have risen. Clearly, the LDCs have experienced both growth and structural change and indeed, as we have already noted above, it would be very surprising if this was not found to be the case in reality.[7]

The emergence of a variety of 'structuralist' schools of thought, ranging from radical, neo-Marxist approaches in Latin America to the more orthodox 'structuralism' of Chenery and the World Bank, has been an important feature of the 'development' of development economics in the post-war period. Chenery (1975, p. 310) conceives of the structuralist approach as an attempt to 'identify specific rigidities, lags and other characteristics of the structure of developing economies that affect economic adjustments and the choice of development policy'. The 'imperfections' of the real world will never be 'fully overcome' (it will never be possible to achieve perfect knowledge or instantaneous adjustment to market signals) and thus such 'imperfections' are incorporated into the economic model of the LDC in order that more realistic economic policies may be devised to cope with them.

'Development', for Chenery and Syrquin, is a 'multidimensional transition from one relatively constant structure to another' (Chenery and Syrquin, 1975, p. 8) and, in describing the processes

TABLE 1

LESS DEVELOPED COUNTRIES: STRUCTURE OF PRODUCTION, 1960 AND 1981 DISTRIBUTION OF GROSS DOMESTIC PRODUCT (%)
(weighted average)

	Agriculture		Industry		Manufacturing (a)		Services	
	1960	1981	1960	1981	1960	1981	1960	1981
Low Income Economies (b)	48	37	25	34	11	16	27	29
Middle Income Economies	24	14	30	38	20	22	46	48
Oil Exporters	27	13	26	40	15	17	47	47
Oil Importers	23	14	33	36	22	25	44	50
Lower Middle Income	36	22	25	35	15	17	39	43
Upper Middle Income	18	10	33	39	23	24	49	51

Notes: (a) Manufacturing is part of the industrial sector, but its share of GDP is shown separately because it typically is the most dynamic part of the industrial sector.
(b) Economies are classified as follows: 34 low-income LDCs with GNP per capita of less than $410; 60 middle-income LDCs with GNP per capita greater than $410.
Source: World Bank (1983), Annex Table 3.

of development, they try 'to replace the notion of a dichotomy between less developed and developed countries with the concept of a transition from one state to another. This transition is defined by a set of structural changes that have almost always accompanied the growth of per capita income in recent decades' (Chenery and Syrquin, 1975, p. 135).

The identification and analysis of 'patterns' of development is, of course, an important exercise that yields many insights and one does not lose sight of the need for the analysis of the 'real world'.[8] But its normative underpinnings and policy prescriptions are often implicit rather than explicit and its search for an abstract pattern of development, outside of, or separate from, specific historical, political and social structures has led to a tendency to elaborate and recommend optimistic (some might say naïve) policy prescriptions which are often divorced from political reality.

With respect to the second proposition listed above, it is in the work of Dudley Seers (1972; 1979A) that we find the most influential and widely reproduced arguments for distinguishing between economic growth and economic development. For Seers,

> 'Development' is inevitably a normative concept, almost a synonym for improvement. To pretend otherwise is just to hide one's value judgements. (Seers, 1972, p. 22)

Posing the question 'where are these values to come from?', Seers replies:

> Surely the values we need are staring us in the face, as soon as we ask ourselves: what are the necessary conditions for a universally acceptable aim, the realization of the potential of human personality? (Seers, 1972, p. 22)

As is well known, the criteria that Seers suggests to judge whether or not development is taking place relate to poverty, inequality and unemployment.[9] Other indicators relate to the educational and political dimensions of development and in the Post Script to the republished article in Lehmann (ed.) (1979), Seers adds a further dimension – 'development now implies, inter alia, reducing cultural dependence on one or more of the great powers' (pp. 27–8). Self-reliance thus becomes a crucial element in the contemporary concept of development.[10]

The criteria that Seers advances relating to poverty, inequality and unemployment appear eminently reasonable, sensible and acceptable and it seems unlikely that development economists, at least, would argue about the desirability of eliminating such problems (what they would argue about would relate to definitional and conceptual issues, the time period over which specific objectives were to be achieved and the strategies/policies implemented to achieve agreed objectives). Although arguably utopian, Seers' economic criteria are at least rooted in reality and have an appeal that is both understandable and sympathetic.

It is our contention that these qualities are lost in the definitions of development advanced in two recently published, widely discussed and influential books – Todaro's *Economic Development in the Third World* (2nd ed., 1981) and the Brandt Commission Report (1980).

Todaro builds on Seers' definition and then goes way beyond it:

> Development must, therefore, be conceived of as a multidimensional process involving major changes in social structures, popular attitudes, and national institutions, as well as the acceleration of economic growth, the reduction of inequality, and the eradication of absolute poverty.
>
> ... at least three basic components or core values should serve as a conceptual basis and practical guideline for understanding the 'inner' meaning of development. These core values are life-sustenance, self-esteem and freedom, representing common goals sought by all individuals and societies. (Todaro, 1981 ed., p. 70)[11]

Likewise, the Brandt Commissioners have their eyes fixed on somewhat extravagant and utopian goals:

> One must avoid the persistent confusion of growth with development, and we strongly emphasise that the prime objective of development is to lead to self-fulfilment and creative partnership in the use of a nation's productive forces and its full human potential. (Brandt Commission Report, 1980, p. 23)[12]

It is not immediately obvious what purposes the idealised conceptions of economic development of Seers, Todaro, Brandt, etc. serve. Presumably, few would wish to argue that such conditions actually exist in the developed economies, capitalist or socialist. Furthermore, although it is not our intention to deny that economic progress has been made by these economies, there is no unambiguous evidence that would lead us to believe that they are moving, in some simple and straightforward manner, in the direction of fulfilling these objectives.[13] In the LDCs themselves, although political leaders and development plans pay lip service to the achievement of various political and economic goals (national development, democracy, socialism, equality, etc.), again there is little evidence to suggest that such goals are, in reality, being pursued, apart perhaps from the efforts of a small group of countries which have experienced revolutionary changes.

Before speculating on why such idealised definitions of development have become so widespread and popular, it is important to acknowledge the historical significance of the distinction that was first made in the 1960s between growth and development. With hindsight, the naïvety of those who expected economic growth to solve all problems is striking. To assume that the benefits of economic growth would be evenly spread between all sectors and classes ('trickle down') and that poverty and unemployment would be eradicated, irrespective of the economic, political and social structures within which such growth was occurring, was tantamount to closing one's eyes both to the lessons that could be drawn from the study of the history of the developed capitalist economies and to the salient features of contemporary development.[14] The recognition that economic growth did not automatically lead to the wider, normatively defined goals of development was thus an important step in the evolution of the study of economic development in the post-war period. Having served its purpose, however, as we argued above, the utopian concept of development is an obstacle to the further evolution of development economics.[15]

WHY DO WE NEED TO GO BEYOND THE CONCEPT OF ECONOMIC DEVELOPMENT?

We have argued above that the popular concept of development refers to an ideal world or state of affairs that is both ahistorical and apolitical — ahistorical because it postulates an idealised structure that does not and never has existed, and apolitical because development is defined in an abstract sense and is not related to any particular political/social/economic structure. The type of economic development espoused by Seers, Todaro, Brandt, etc. does not, in reality, exist and there is no evidence of significant movements in that direction.

It is the argument of this paper that this abstract conceptualisation of economic development has four significant but undesirable consequences.

First, it is in part a cause of the pessimism currently expressed over the 'condition' and 'life expectancy' of development economics as a discipline. Seers (1978B) laments the fact that development economics has not proved as useful as expected and doubts whether it can survive as a subject. Streeten (1979, p. 23) refers to the 'present atmosphere of gloom, boredom and indifference surrounding discussions of development problems', compared to the 'exciting time of ferment' of the early years. Hirschman (1981, p. 1) argues that in the early years of the development of the discipline, 'development economics did much better than the object of its study, the economic development of the poorer regions of the world', but more recenlty, 'this particular gap has been narrowing, not so much unfortunately because of a sudden spurt in economic development, but rather because the forward movement of our subdiscipline has notably slowed down'. (For a further discussion and critique, see Leeson, 1983.)

Underlying this pessimism is the notion that the discipline of development economics has 'failed' or is doomed to extinction because of its own supposed failure to, in some way, change the world, presumably in the direction of idealised 'economic development'. But development economics as such can hardly be blamed for present conditions in LDCs, however misguided its early analyses and policy pronouncements may have been (for a contrary view, from a neo-classical perspective, see Lal, 1983; Little, 1982). Development theory may well have 'failed' in the sense that it gave a false or misleading explanation of the problems of underdevelopment and development, but it is not a cause of those problems. Our argument, therefore, is that part of the current pessimism in the profession is related to its own concept of economic development, and its own inflated expectations of what economists as policy-makers or advisers could be expected to achieve in LDCs.

This point is closely related to the second consequence of the conceptualisation of development in an abstract and utopian form − the confusion between explanation (the historical-analytic) and policy prescription.

Without wishing to descend to parody, the present situation in much writing about development problems is as follows: it is recognised that economic growth and structural change are occurring, often to a widespread and significant extent, but because the economic, political and social consequences of these specific patterns of growth and change[16] are not consistent with the analyst's normative concept of development, the typical reaction is to seek for policies which will change the situation, rather than to attempt to understand and explain why that situation had developed in the first place.

As far as development economics is concerned, much writing masquerading as analysis is in reality far more concerned with policy prescription, a conflation found in both the neo-classical and structuralist/dependency paradigms.

In the neo-classical critique of import-substituting industrialisation, for example, government intervention in product and factor markets, leading to so-called 'policy-induced distortions', is variously condemned as excessive, misguided and/or irrational (see the classic study of Little et al, 1970, and the more recent attack of Lal, 1983). The logical policy prescription is that government intervention should be reduced and/or made more selective (the promotion rather than the protection of industry, for example).

As we have argued elsewhere, however (Nixson, 1981), it cannot simply be asserted that all government intervention not consistent with neo-classical percepts is 'unreasonable, illogical, absurd, not endowed with reason' (the dictionary definition of 'irrational') or that government policies are motivated purely by ignorance, perversity, corruption or sheer stupidity. The attempt must be made to understand why governments behave as they do in the economic sphere, recognising that, of course, they make mistakes and that some intervention is undoubtedly irrational, but emphasising nevertheless that most government policies serve specific interests or are directed at the achievement of certain objectives (even though those interests or objectives may not be acknowledged or made public).

With respect to Latin American structuralism and dependency theory, we find a similar situation. As Warren (1980, pp. 157–8) has argued:

> the inadequacy of existing theory and the propriety of formulating a new approach were grounded above all in the desire to elaborate adequate policies for national development. Analysis was secondary. In itself this need not have adversely affected analysis, had the theorists either controlled policy or represented a class or group realistically capable of doing so; or, for that matter, had they been able to probe the politics of economic policy. But since none of these conditions pertained, the policy orientation rendered analysis prey to nationalist utopias; actuality, potentiality, and desirability became hopelessly confused. The dynamics of Latin American capitalist development were approached on the basis of subjective-moralistic criteria, which not only produced conclusions widely at variance with reality, but even prevented the posing of the relevant questions, whether analytical or practical. (Warren, 1980, pp. 157–8)[17]

Our general point, therefore, is that the policy orientation of much work in the field of development studies has undoubtedly weakened the analytical grasp and value of that work. Again, to avoid misunderstanding, it is not the intention of this paper to argue against policy prescription per se. As Leeson (1983, p. 24) argues, 'Certainly most development economists would reject the notion that policy advice is not a proper sphere for the involvement of the profession'. Rather, we are criticising the blurring of the distinction between the historical-analytic and the policy-prescriptive, the intermingling of ought with is (Lall, 1976, p. 182), the confusion of the desire for a better world with the fuller understanding of the very imperfect reality.

The third undesirable consequence of utilising an abstract concept of economic development is that the concept itself is devoid of political content and the problem of development is effectively, for want of a better term, depoliticised. Again, without wishing to parody the situation, in much writing we see a failure or a refusal to recognise that the undesirable features of growth and structural change are not the inevitable consequence of these forces as such, but are, rather, the characteristic features of the specific process of capitalist development as it is unfolding in contemporary LDCs. What should be condemned, therefore, if it is felt necessary or desirable to pass judgement, is capitalism itself, rather than some (unspecified) economic system that does not produce results consistent with the normative definition of development. Very rarely in the mainstream of development literature do we find capitalism itself condemned and alternative economic and social systems proposed. Rather, the attempt is made, via redistribution with growth, basic needs strategies, etc. to promote policies that will produce more acceptable results within unchanged political and economic structures.[18]

Our general point, therefore, is that the introduction of the normative concept of development denies the specificity of the processes of growth and change that are occurring in contemporary LDCs. Attention is diverted from the characteristics of capitalist development within these countries and instead it is usually concluded that development is not taking place.

The fact that the consequences of capitalist development in these countries are not similar to the normative concept of development of Seers et al, that is, that 'development' is not leading to an equitable distribution of the benefits of material progress and is not 'solving' the problems of poverty and deprivation, should come as no surprise to those familiar with the history of the now developed capitalist economies. One of the striking features of capitalist development is its unevenness, both between countries and between groups, classes, regions, etc. within individual countries. The greater material benefits enjoyed by the mass of the population in the developed capitalist economies, particularly in the post-war period, have resulted not merely from the interplay of impersonal market forces or 'benevolent' state intervention (that is, not merely as the result of some abstract concept of 'development'), but also (and perhaps largely) as a result of the interplay between specific economic, political and social forces (including the state) within those countries, forces which will not necessarily manifest themselves with equal intensity in other countries or at other times.

The final consequence of the utilisation of an abstract concept of development partly arises from what has been said above. Development economics all too often assumes that structural problems have somehow been 'solved' in the developed capitalist economies and that their problem is 'merely' one of ensuring self-sustaining and continuous growth, a process which is essentially non-problematic.[19]

This is, of course, not the case. Problems of unemployment, inequality, poverty and deprivation and various kinds of structural disequilibria (balance of payments problems, problems relating to 'de-industrialisation', etc.) exist in many of the developed capitalist economies (for example, the USA, UK, Italy). These are problems rooted in the very structure and fabric of society that have not been 'solved' by capitalist development within these countries. Indeed, they are, in some instances, problems that arise as a consequence of both the specific forms of capitalist development within those countries and of changes within the international capitalist economy. In this sense, these countries 'need' structural and other kinds of change as much as many LDCs.

This point is now being increasingly recognised. Seers (1979 A, pp. 28–9) refers to the 'geographical extension of development studies' to cover all countries and argues that 'development' now 'involves our all working on common worldwide problems, while paradoxically, keeping national interests (long-term, of course) firmly in mind'. The Brandt Commission Report, too, emphasises the global nature of many problems (energy, the environment), and recognises that 'development' has not come to an end in the 'North' (see note 13). However, the full implications of this shifting perspective have not yet been fully worked out. Clearly, the poorer countries do have problems, both structural and otherwise, that are not found in the developed capitalist economies and it is too early to pronounce (conventionally defined) 'development economics' dead. Nevertheless, the recognition that structural problems exist in all countries and that the very process of development continually solves and yet at the same time generates new problems, is an important advance on the previously uncritical acceptance of the normative definition of 'development'.

SOME CONCLUSIONS

The first point that we wish to emphasise, following on from the above, is that economic development is not smooth, undirectional and non-problematic, but is, to borrow Schumpeter's words (quoted above), 'lopsided, discontinuous, disharmonious'.[20] In contemporary LDCs, we see the solution of one set of problems leading to the creation of new ones. Enterprises may be nationalised, 'solving' problems relating to ownership but creating new problems relating to control. Gains achieved by one group or class during one period are dissipated or eliminated with a change of regime and policy (perhaps the latter are even brought about by those previous gains) and the direction that development is taking can be effectively reversed (for example, with respect to the role of foreign capital). Many other examples could be given of the point that is being made.

In this respect Arndt (1981, p. 466) is surely wrong when he argues that, in order to get away from the identification of 'economic development' with 'economic growth', economists have breathed 'into "development" some of the Hegelian connotations that had got lost on the way'. The divorce of 'development' from 'growth' has indeed been virtually complete for over 20 years, but more to the point, as this paper has tried to argue, it is precisely the 'Hegelian connotations' that have been deliberately eliminated in the increasingly utopian definitions of 'development' adopted. The recognition of the dialectical nature of the development process should, therefore, lead to the abandonment of abstract definitions of development.

The use of the term 'dialectical' to describe the development process requires clarification. We are using the term in a general sense to argue that every new development brings with it new problems and adjustments, which, in turn, may either reinforce or oppose the initial development. This is not meant to imply that development happens by chance, nor is it meant to deny the possibility of directing or exercising some 'control' over 'development'. It is meant to emphasise, however, the complex and often contradictory character of the development process, a process which, in Leeson's words, involves

> growth of output, of luxuries and necessities, sectoral change, new tastes, new technologies, new distribution of income, new classes and pressure groups, new forces pressing on the state, new vested interests inside the state, new policies. (Leeson, 1983, p. 36)

It is the argument of this paper that the dialectical nature of the development process is best captured in the concept of development as an historical process. We should, therefore, move away from the position where we see 'development' as an activity, or as a set of objectives, and return to the Marxian/Schumpeterian concept of development as an historical process which unfolds itself in a dialectical manner. Such a perspective will also inevitably highlight the unevenness of the development process, to which we have already referred, and to which we must now briefly return.

Given the unevenness of economic growth and structural change within the less developed parts of the world, and the general heterogeneity of LDC societies, the question must be raised as to whether it is still, in Warren's words, 'appropriate to treat these societies in aggregate' and whether 'the related conceptual division of the world into developed and underdeveloped countries is at all accurate' (Warren, 1980, pp. 189–90).

Warren's answer to his own question is that

> The present situation could more appropriately be conceptualized as a spectrum of varying levels, rates and structures of national development, one in which the positions of individual countries are constantly shifting. Nevertheless, the Third World countries do retain sufficient common features to justify aggregate treatment, provided the elements of change qualifying such treatment are duly taken into account ... (Warren, 1980, p. 190)

This is remarkably similar to the argument of Chenery and Syrquin quoted on p. 107 above, and is clearly not a completely satisfactory answer to the question posed. Increasingly in the future, it will become necessary to elaborate alternative classificatory schemes which, while recognising that LDCs are part of a single global economic system and that they possess characteristics common to all capitalist societies, nevertheless will acknowledge and accommodate the diversity of LDC experience. We should also add the qualification that the similarity of certain structural problems in both developed capitalist economies and LDCs should be recognised, and that the categorisation of some countries as 'developed' should not be taken as implying that specific normative objectives have, in practice, been realised in those countries.

Another aspect of the uncritical acceptance of an ahistorical and idealised concept of development has been the characterisation of the contemporary development experience as being either different from that which previously occurred elsewhere and/or different from that which should be occurring now.[21] Various terms have been used to describe contemporary development patterns (with the authors usually referring to industrial development) – 'distorted' (Seidman, 1974); 'perverse' (Rweyemamu, 1973; Sachs, 1980); 'dependent capitalist development' (Cardoso, 1972, and a large number of other dependency theorists). For Rweyemamu, for example, 'perverse capitalist industrial development' is perverse because, in its given institutional setting, it is unlikely to lead to self-generating and self-sustaining development as was the case with classical industrial capitalism. However, at the same time, Rweyemamu thinks it impossible that classical industrial growth could repeat itself in contemporary LDCs (Rweyemamu, 1973, p. 90).

Clearly, both non-Marxist and Neo-Marxist/Marxist writers have in their minds some ideal model or pattern against which the actual experience of contemporary LDCs can be judged.[22] Moreover, it is implied by many authors that, in the words of Warren (1980, pp. 166–7), there is a 'latent, suppressed historical alternative to the development that actually took place'. Furthermore, it is argued, the failure of this alternative to materialise was the result of external forces (colonialism), yet if that alternative had been achieved, economic growth and development would have been more rapid and in some sense superior to that actually achieved.

There is little to be gained from this sort of speculation ('what would have happened if ...?'). Obviously, what are now referred to as the LDCs would have developed along different lines in the absence of colonialism and, in that somewhat limited sense, alternative courses of development were 'open' to them. But we cannot simply assert that any particular alternative would have been superior to that which actually occurred, and again to quote Warren, it cannot be assumed that 'social forces capable of embodying the allegedly suppressed (and superior) alternative actually exist' (Warren, 1980, p. 167). To argue that there existed, in the past, some suppressed, superior pattern or model of development, the achievement of which was prevented solely by external forces, is as misleading as arguing for the utopian, idealised concept of development that we have criticised in this paper.

It goes without saying that it is logically impossible for contemporary LDCs to replicate the development experience of the developed capitalist economies.[23] It is thus necessary to recognise the specificity or uniqueness of the development experience of the former countries and to refrain from making comparisons with often idealised and ahistorical alternatives.

Once we abandon our search for an all-embracing and utopian definition of economic development and focus our attention instead on what is actually happening in the LDCs, the specificity, unevenness and dialectical nature of the process of growth and structural change in these countries becomes apparent. The processes of change that we observe occur within specific political and social structures and if we wish to criticise the consequences of particular changes, we need also to recognise that the political and social structures themselves cannot escape criticism. Equally, if it is our intention to promote particular forms or objectives of development, we must acknowledge the political content or implications of such proposals and begin to ask: what political and economic system is going to permit the realisation of full employment, low levels of inequality, 'participation in the productive use of the nation's resources', etc.? Paradoxically, even though we are arguing in this paper for the primacy of the historical-analytic over the policy-prescriptive, policy issues, far from being ignored by this approach, come to the very forefront of the discussion.

We appreciate that this paper raises a number of questions that it either does not answer, or answers only imperfectly or partially. Nevertheless, we remain convinced that once development economists begin to go beyond the mere espousal of abstract ideals and begin to pose, and attempt to answer, such questions, both explanation and policy prescription will begin to acquire qualities of conviction and perception that they all too frequently lack at present.

NOTES

This paper is a revised version of 'Beyond Economic Development?', Manchester Discussion Papers in Development Studies, 8203, 1982. I would like to thank Philip Leeson, Mohammad Yamin, Michael Tribe, Theodore Morgan, Ian Steedman, Robert Millward and Colin Simmons for their comments on earlier drafts. It has not been possible to incorporate all their suggestions into this version, and no doubt they will disagree with some of the arguments presented. All errors of fact and interpretation remain my responsibility.

1. Lehmann does subsequently observe, however, that 'The drawback of concern with policy is that it may attract attention away from wider theoretical issues insofar as it encourages research to concentrate on problems defined by national or international bureaucracies in terms of their definitions of situations or their ideological or propagandistic requirements' (Lehmann, 1979, p. 3).
2. This is not meant to imply that policy prescription is not important nor that moral judgements should not be made about current political and economic developments (nor indeed, that attempts should not be made to change the world). It simply means that such judgements should not be confused with, or take the place of, explanation. It is also recognised that 'explanation' as such can never be wholly objective but will in part be a reflection of the ideological position of the person advancing that particular explanation.
3. Flammang (1979) too identifies and discusses various definitions of economic development, but he does not confront the problem to which this paper is addressed and the conclusions that he reaches are somewhat idiosyncratic.
4. This book was first published in German in 1911 and was entitled *Theorie der wirtschaftlichen Entwicklung*. It was not translated into English until 1934.
5. See also Meier (1976 ed.): 'economic development involves something more than economic growth. Development is taken to mean growth plus change' (p. 6).
6. Cf. Schumpeter (1961, p. 64): 'Every concrete process of development finally rests upon preceding development ... Every process of development creates the prerequisites for the following.'
7. As with economic growth, it is necessary to point out the diversity of experience among LDCs, with respect to structural change. The data in Table 1 must be treated with great caution and, at the very most, they only illustrate one aspect of the complex changes

taking place in many LDCs. We recognise also that in particular cases what appears as 'structural change' may be a statistical rather than a substantial phenomenon, but there are no reasons for believing this is the case for all LDCs. On the other hand, however, structural change may be occurring in LDCs but the 'results' of that change have yet to manifest themselves in various economic or socio-political indicators.

8. The various statistical exercises concerned with identifying 'normal' patterns of development have not, of course, escaped criticism. See Sutcliffe (1971, Chapter 2); Jameson (1982).

9. 'The questions to ask about a country's development are therefore: What has been happening to poverty? What has been happening to unemployment? What has been happening to inequality? If all three of these have become less severe, then beyond doubt this has been a period of development for the country concerned. If one or two of these central problems have been growing worse, especially if all three have, it would be strange to call the result "development", even if per capita income had soared. This applies, of course, to the future too. A "plan" which conveys no targets for reducing poverty, unemployment and inequality can hardly be considered a "development plan"' (Seers, 1972, p. 24).

10. A large amount of ingenuity and resources have gone into the design of 'better' measures of development, including modifications of GNP, social indicators and composite indicators of development. For a recent survey, see Hicks and Streeten (1979).

11. Life sustenance: the ability to provide for basic needs; self-esteem: to be a person; freedom: to be able to choose. Todaro's statement that such goals are sought by all individuals and societies is clearly contentious but a critique of it is beyond the scope of this paper.

12. In another widely used and influential textbook (Kindleberger and Herrick, 3rd ed., 1977), the authors, after listing the usual all-embracing economic and political dimensions of development, admit without embarrassment that 'This characterization of economic development implies lofty goals. Because the human condition is our foremost concern, we feel strongly that anything less would not do' (Kindleberger and Herrick, 1977, p. 2).

13. The Brandt Commission Report (1980, p. 24) recognises that the process of technological and economic development has not yet come to an end in the 'North'. Seers too (Seers, 1979A, p. 28) in spelling out the implications of his extended definition of development, makes an important point that we shall return to below: 'if "development" is now not primarily about per capita income, but also about distribution, and even more about the national capacity to negotiate with transnational corporations, and to cope with their technological innovations and their cultural impact, then it is not just needed in "developing" countries, but in all countries'.

14. We do not wish to imply that all theories or models of economic development assumed the immediate achievement of all desirable goals. In the so-called 'Lewis Model' (Lewis, 1954), increased inequality in the distribution of income will, under certain assumptions, accompany the process of economic growth.

15. To avoid any possible confusion, it should be emphasised that it is not being argued that self-reliance, freedom, self-fulfilment, etc., are not of importance. Our purpose is to argue that merely because such objectives have not been achieved in reality, it should not be concluded that 'development' has not taken place.

16. Structuralist and dependency theorists would be mainly concerned with the problems of greater inequality, marginalisation, military dictatorships, etc.; neo-classical theorists might be more concerned with excessive government intervention in the economy, bureaucracy, inefficiency, etc.

17. See also Palma (1978, p. 908).

18. It is also necessary and desirable to highlight, analyse and criticise the undesirable features of the various models of 'socialist' development.

19. At its simplest level, the 'developed' economies must have, by definition, solved the problems of 'development'.

20. From a different analytical perspective, a similar point is made by Nugent and Yotopouolos, 1979, p. 543.

21. That early theorising about economic development assumed the model of the developed capitalist economy as the archetypal developed economy, towards which all others were moving, is now well known and generally accepted. A similar criticism could perhaps

be made of many of the arguments put forward by Warren (Warren, 1980). Chenery's work is certainly open to the charge that it views development as a single 'path' along which all countries are moving in the same direction, towards the same goal, with some countries merely being 'in front' of the others. In his later published work (Chenery, 1983), he argues, inter alia, that further empirical work will make possible the formulation of computable models in which the distinction between developed economies and LDCs will be reduced 'to observable differences in certain statistical parameters: initial conditions, price and income elasticities, and adjustment lags' (p. 853). Chenery also makes the somewhat surprising observation that the economic transformation of the more advanced economies is 'near completion'.

22. Phillips (1977, p. 11) argues: 'The "development" against which "underdevelopment" is conceptualised has tended to become an amalgam of different concepts, such that the theories are partly drawing a contrast between the process of development in the advanced capitalist countries and in the underdeveloped countries, but partly a contrast between development in the UDCs and an idealised process of development which would ensure "maximum utilisation of resources" or the "most rational allocation of surplus".' See also Bernstein (1979, pp. 91–4) for an elaboration of this point and further examples of the left's pre-occupation with 'misdevelopment', 'deformed development' etc.

23. This is not to deny the many similarities between countries at different levels of economic development, in terms of the goods that they produce, the technologies that they utilise, the life-styles and consumption patterns enjoyed by the middle and upper income groups of different countries, and so on. But to note the similarities only is like looking at a snapshot of these countries – a moment frozen in time – and to ignore how they have got where they are and where they are going after the photograph has been taken.

BIBLIOGRAPHY

Arndt, H. W. (1981), 'Economic Development: A Semantic History', *Economic Development and Cultural Change*, 29 (3), April.

Bernstein, H. (1979), 'Sociology of Underdevelopment vs. Sociology of Development?' in Lehmann, D. (ed.) (1979).

Brandt Commission Report (1980), *North–South: A Programme for Survival*, London, Pan Books.

Brewer, A. (1980), *Marxist Theories of Imperialism*, London, Routledge & Kegan Paul.

Brookfield, H. (1975), *Interdependent Development*, London, Methuen.

Cardoso, F. H. (1972), 'Dependency and Development in Latin America', *New Left Review*, No. 74, July–August.

Chenery, H. B. (1975), 'The Structuralist Approach to Development Policy', *American Economic Review Papers and Proceedings*, 65 (2).

Chenery, H. B. (1983), 'Interaction between Theory and Observation on Development', *World Development*, 11 (10), October.

Chenery, H. B. and Syrquin, M. (1975), *Patterns of Development 1950–70*, Oxford University Press for World Bank.

Clower, R., Dalton, M., Harvitz, M. and Walters, A. A. (1966), *Growth Without Development: An Economic Survey of Liberia*, Evanston, Northwestern University Press.

Deane, Phyllis (1978), *The Evolution of Economics Ideas*, Cambridge, CUP.

Dobb, M. (1970), 'Introduction' to Marx, K., *A Contribution to the Critique of Political Economy*, Progress Publishers, Moscow and Lawrence and Wishart, London; first published in German, 1859.

Flammang, R. A., (1979), 'Economic Growth and Economic Development: Counterparts or Competitors?', *Economic Development and Cultural Change*, 28 (1), October, 47–61.

Hicks, N. and Streeten, P. (1979), 'Indicators of Development: The Search for a Basic Needs Yardstick', *World Development*, 7 (6), June.

Hirschman, A. O. (1981), 'The Rise and Decline of Development Economics', in *Essays in Trespassing: Economics to Politics and Beyond*, Cambridge, CUP.

Jameson, K. P. (1982), 'A Critical Examination of "The Patterns of Development"', *Journal of Development Studies*, 18 (4) July, 431–46.

Kindleberger, C. P. and Herrick, B. (1977), *Economic Development*, 3rd ed., McGraw-Hill.

Lal, D. (1983), *The Poverty of 'Development Economics'*, London, Institute of Economic Affairs.

Lall, S. (1976), 'Conflicts of Concepts: Welfare Economics and Developing Countries', World Development, 4 (3), March.

Leeson, P. F. (1983), 'Development Economics and its Companies', *Manchester Discussion Papers in Development Studies 8304*, mimeo.

Lehmann, D. (ed.) (1979), *Development Theory: Four Critical Studies*, London, Frank Cass.

Lewis, A. (1954), 'Economic Development with Unlimited Supplies of Labour', *Manchester School*, May.

Little, I. M. D. et al (1970), *Industry and Trade in Some Developing Countries: A Comparative Study*, London, OUP.

Little, I. M. D. (1982), *Economic Development: Theory, Policy and International Relations*, New York, Basic Books Inc.

Livingstone, I. (1976), 'After Divorce: The Remarriage of Economic Theory and Development Economics?', *Eastern Africa Economic Review*, 8 (1), December, 35–50.

Livingstone, I. (1981), 'The Development of Development Economics', *ODI Review*, 2, 1–20.

Marx, K. (1970), *A Contribution to the Critique of Political Economy*, Progress Publishers, Moscow and Lawrence and Wishart, London; first published in German, 1859; introduction by Maurice Dobb.

Meier, G. M. (1976), *Leading Issues in Economic Development*, 3rd Ed., New York, OUP.

Meier, G. M. and Baldwin, R. E. (1957), *Economic Development: Theory, History, Policy*, New York, John Wiley & Sons, Inc.

Nixson, F. I. (1981), 'State Intervention, Economic Planning and Import-Substituting Industrialisation: The Experience of the Less Developed Countries', *METU Studies in Development* (Ankara, Turkey), Special Issues, pp. 55–76.

Nugent, J. B. and Yotopoulos, P. A. (1979), 'What Has Orthodox Development Economics Learned from Recent Experience?', *World Development*, 7 (6), June.

Palma, G. (1978), 'Dependency: A Formal Theory of Underdevelopment or a Methodology for the Analysis of Concrete Situations of Underdevelopment?', *World Development*, 6 (7/8).

Phillips, A. (1977), 'The Concept of ''Development'' ', *Review of African Political Economy*, No. 8, January–April.

Rweyemamu, J. (1973), *Underdevelopment and Industrialisation in Tanzania: A Study of Perverse Capitalist Industrial Development*, Nairobi, OUP.

Sachs, I. (1980), *Studies in Political Economy of Development*, Pergamon Press, Oxford.

Schumpeter, J. A. (1934; 1961), *The Theory of Economic Development*, New York, OUP.

Schumpeter, J. A. (1939), *Business Cycles*, Vol. I, New York, McGraw-Hill.

Seidman, A. (1974), 'The Distorted Growth of Import Substitution Industry: the Zambian Case', *The Journal of Modern African Studies*, 12 (4).

Seers, D. (1972; 1979A), 'What are we trying to measure?' in Baster, N., ed., *Measuring Development*, London, Frank Cass, and in Lehmann (ed.) (1979).

Seers, D. (1979B), 'The Birth, Life and Death of Development Economics (Revisiting a Manchester Conference)', *Development and Change*, Vol. 10, 707–19.

Streeten, P. (1979), 'Development Ideas in Historical Perspective', in Kim Q. Hill (ed.), *Toward a New Strategy for Development: A Rothko Chapel Colloquium*, Pergamon Press.

Streeten, P. (1981), 'Programmes and Prognoses', in *Development Perspectives*, London, Macmillan.

Sutcliffe, R. B. (1971), *Industry and Underdevelopment*, Addison-Wesley Publishing Co.

Szentes, T. (1971), *The Political Economy of Underdevelopment*, Budapest, Akademiai Kiado.

Todaro, M. P. (1981), *Economic Development in the Third World*, 2nd ed., New York & London, Longman.

Warren, Bill (1980), *Imperialism: Pioneer of Capitalism*, London, Verso.

World Bank (1983), *World Development Report 1983*, published for the World Bank by OUP.

PART TWO

3

Colonialism and Peripheral Development

BARBARA INGHAM

The contributions in Part II of this volume are concerned with British colonialism, taking us from the victory at Plassey which began Britain's long and discontinuous process of colonial acquisition in India, through to the decolonisation movement in British West Africa before and after World War II.

No one now doubts the significance of this era of British overseas expansion. During the two centuries which followed Plassey, Britain and other states in Europe established and maintained formal and informal control over peripheral countries. Braudel tells us that what was involved here was nothing less than a clash of civilisations, and when civilisations clash,

> the consequences are dramatic. Today's world is still embroiled in them. One civilisation can get the better of another; this was the case with India following the British victory at Plassey, which marked the beginning of a new era for Britain and the whole world ... Plassey had immense consequences, which is how great events are recognized: they have a sequel.[1]

The material consequences of European imperialism was that today's Third World countries became locked into a colonial system of trade, payments and resource transfers. The most important aspect of this was the periphery as a net importer of capital from the centre. Exports of rural origin exchanged for manufactured goods. Skilled labour migrated from Europe, and unskilled labour moved from one to another part of the tropical world. This colonial pattern of trade, investment and migration continues to have implications for present-day divisions in the world economy.

The broad theme of the different case studies presented in Part II is the impact of colonialism on the 'development potential' of the periphery – a debate which is now backed by a large literature from a variety of theoretical standpoints. At this juncture it is useful to remind ourselves of the key points in the debate. There are two possibly interrelated questions to which the literature addresses itself, viz. what were the causes of European overseas expansion and the associated rise in colonial trade during the eighteenth and nineteenth centuries? And, what were the consequences for peripheral areas, of the spread of colonialism?

Research from a radical perspective has long regarded colonies and imperial expansion as functioning as part of the contradictions of capitalism. Colonial exploitation was listed by Marx as one of the counteracting tendencies to the falling rate of profit. For the Marxists, imperialism has to do with capitalist firms striving for surpluses and seeking to use their surpluses wherever they can by incorporating new areas of the world economy into the system of accumulation. This answers to the fundamental causes of imperial expansion, with dependency analyses (as a general field of study) contributing to the question of the impact of imperialism on the economic development of dependent peripheral areas. Dependency theorists have strongly identified colonialism with 'underdevelopment' (Frank) and more latterly with political weakness, social instability and constrained economic choices in the Third World.[2]

In the alternative mainstream literature, there are two theoretical perspectives on colonialism which may usefully be distinguished. First there is the liberal or neo-classical school, with economic historians classified as an important sub-group within this tradition. Hicks is a respected modern exponent of the classical liberal view, distinguishing 'colonisation', an entirely welcome widening of the market by peaceful trading, from 'colonialism', which involved attempts to regulate trade in the national interest as part of the wider process of territorial annexation.[3] For this process many economic historians reject purely economic forces as a motivation, political, strategic and ideological explanations being invoked to explain the acquisition of colonies by modern states.[4]

As far as the economic development of the colonies is concerned, the neo-classical view is generally a favourable one. Trade it is true may be subjected to protectionist pressures, and alien rule may unleash unwelcome authoritarian and nationalist tendencies (Lewis). But against this must be balanced the 'opening up' of previously isolated economies to market forces, the liberation of enterprise, acquisition of superior physical capital and human skills from abroad. On balance it is likely that material progress was enhanced rather than retarded by the colonial relationship.[5]

A less sanguine view is taken by the second mainstream tradition, viz. the neo-Keynesian or structuralist school, which has a view of imperialism distinct in a number of respects from the classical liberal perspective. For the Keynesians colonisation is an expression of national policy, in which military and economic forces interact and reinforce each other. Colonialism is one of the ways in which capitalism can be 'managed', to provide a favourable balance of trade, to secure investment opportunities for domestic capital at home and abroad, and to maintain high levels of domestic employment.

Those who argue in these terms stress that it is necessary to place overseas expansion within its proper historical context. Special geo-political circumstances may be invoked to explain the 'vast secular boom' of the nineteenth century, associated with the opening up of new lands, overseas investment and the growth of foreign trade. Colonisation may then be seen as a struggle for power between mercantilist states. There is no reason to expect this struggle to be peaceable. Instead of the mutual benefit, harmony and co-operation which is implicit in liberal free trade doctrine, colonisation implies protectionism, rivalry and restriction.[6]

In a stimulating interpretation of British imperialism between 1715 and 1950, Cain and Hopkins have argued that an understanding of the changing face of British overseas expansion requires analysis of the structure and performance of the British economy. Describing their work as being undertaken from the standpoint of political economy, they invoke 'the management of the national economy, and strategies devised to secure state revenues, domestic employment and public order' to explain changes through time in the British presence abroad.[7]

There are two propositions associated with this argument, which have a bearing on some of the research themes pursued in this volume. First, there is Cain and Hopkins' claim that the northern manufacturing interest did not always enjoy economic and political dominance in Britain between 1750 and 1914. Competing groups, particularly southern landed interests and the City, had a significant influence on imperial expansion. Although colonial trade began to play a major part in the demand for British exports during the eighteenth century, traders were not 'the advance guard of a new industrial order' (op. cit. p.471). 'Accommodation was made not with the factory but with the City.' After 1780 the expansion of industry meant greater power for industrial interests, especially after 1815, when with rising population, Britain moved to free trade. Declining trade prospects in the 1870s brought an aggressive search for new markets. It also seems that financial interests had come to dominate industrial capital by this time, an assertion which we can also find in Keynes. From the last quarter of the nineteenth century the strongest possible ties obtained between imperial expansion, overseas investment and City interests.

The second proposition advanced by Cain and Hopkins is that

throughout their period, geographical shifts in Britain's overseas presence linked up to the policies of major trading rivals:

> The motive, timing and extent of Britain's expansion into the non-European world were determined very largely by her varying ability either to penetrate the markets of other major powers or to command imports independently of them ... the extension of Britain's presence overseas can be seen as an expression of her failure to dominate her chief competitors, and especially to prevent their industrialisation. (op. cit. p.466)

Dr. Webster's contribution, Chapter 4 in this volume, supports the proposition that Asian markets in the eighteenth century provided Britain with some compensation for loss of markets elsewhere, particularly the loss of markets in Europe to France. After the acquisition of Bengal, the defence of British interests in India proved extremely costly. South-east Asia subsequently assumed major importance in the light of Anglo-Dutch military and economic rivalry. The Anglo-Dutch treaty of 1824 not only established British interests in South-east Asia on a permanent basis, it also marked the decline of the Dutch as a major commercial power and the rise of Britain to pre-eminence in Europe. Dr. Webster supports additionally the proposition that the export interests of Bengal developed as part of the old commercial structure, in which financial rather than manufacturing interests dominated. In the course of the nineteenth century, however, agency houses and private merchants found themselves unable to cope with the flood of cotton textiles into India. 'Mercantilist monopoly' was ultimately to collapse in the face of new market pressures generated from the metropolis.

Though both Marxist and Keynesian traditions strongly support economic interpretations of imperialism, among historians there is still a body of opinion which rejects economic factors as principal motivations for European imperialism. One of the contributions in the present volume, Chapter 5, reflects this view. Christensen argues that British interests on the North-West Frontier, dating from the annexation of the Punjab in 1849, were entirely military and strategic in character. Economic matters did not come to the fore until the 1940s and, even then, not in the context of British well-being, but rather in terms of the economic development of the frontier peoples as a preliminary to decolonisation. British policy on the North-West Frontier can be understood only in political terms, he claims. The region was of strategic value as a buffer separating India from Afghanistan. It is a case which has no significance for an economic interpretation of overseas expansion.

By the end of the 1930s, if we are to accept a hypothesis put forward by Flint, policies of decolonisation were under active consideration for British West Africa. Two centuries of informal influence and formal control were coming to an end. Britain, the first industrial nation and the strongest of the European colonial powers, was also the first to decolonise. No other colonial power contemplated such action, at least before the mid-1950s.[8]

According to Flint, the reality of events in Britain and West Africa at this time contrasts with the views of both the liberal/nationalist and dependency schools. Liberals and nationalists see decolonisation as the outcome of a long struggle between imperialist pressures and nationalist ideologies, with World War II finally ending an era of European economic and political domination. The triumph of nationalism was thus the inevitable result of weakened colonial authority in the face of rapidly developing nationalist aspirations. Not so, argues Flint. Policies of decolonisation were entirely British in inspiration and ante-dated the outbreak of war. They were not the reaction of an exhausted imperial power realising its own weakness, but were actively contemplated from the mid-1930s onwards as a means of strengthening Britain's economic and international influence in the changed circumstances of the world economy.

Flint claims that the dependency school comes closer to the reality of decolonisation, but argues that it is wrong to suggest that the planned purpose of decolonisation was the creation of a comprador bourgeoisie which would perpetuate colonial relationships. Britain had always been hostile to the emergence of an African capitalist class, and especially opposed to the creation of an African landlord class. There was no wish to create compradors or to transfer power to them. The nationalist parties were led by a new educated elite, which ultimately was encouraged to demonstrate that it enjoyed the mass support of peasants and urban working classes. In this sense 'the emergence of nationalist political parties was the result of decisions to decolonize and a creation of imperial policy' (op. cit. p. 390).

There are two contributions in this volume which deal with West Africa between the wars and during World War II, the period directly relevant to the decolonisation debates. Both of these studies relate to British West Africa and attempt to show the enormous gulf which existed during the 1930s and early 1940s between the political strategy of decolonisation and the policy of social and economic development which it demanded. Treasury calls for retrenchment dominated colonial policy during the 1930s and World War II, as West Africa was managed in accordance with the requirements of the British economy. In the Dependent Empire primary production was still to be the mainstay of the economy. There was some increase in spending on health, education and the infrastructure, but from a very low base. Colonies had to pay their own way. The position of sterling and the requirements of the UK budget, together with British employment levels, were of paramount importance. West Africa nevertheless does offer some evidence of increasing prosperity during this period, largely involving those urban and professional classes who would ultimately play a key role in the process of decolonisation.[9]

Turning specifically to the question of the impact of colonialism on peripheral areas, the literature, from different theoretical standpoints, is diverse, extensive and frequently controversial. There are, in addition, a number of new perspectives which owe not a little to the advances in recent years in the study of Third World history. In this category we can place Laitin, who claims to share a common theoretical base with Cain and Hopkins.[10] The underlying argument is that Britain, a hegemony after 1815, pursued a specific set of economic policies, managing the international economy, to enhance its power and wealth. Laitin parts company with some writers who adopt a similar approach (Hobsbawm, Polanyi, Cohen, Kindleberger) by claiming that Britain still had a mercantilist perspective after 1815. Free trade was supported only when it suited Britain's interest. 'Openness', if it did exist, concerned primarily trade among the core states of the international economy since 'free trade is the mercantilist policy of the competitive'. It frequently did not apply to centre−periphery trade. Pax Britannica exemplified *mercantilism* and not liberalism.

Laitin argues that after the fall of Napoleon, Britain pursued an aggressive mercantilist trade policy which involved closing up peripheral trade channels to European and North American competitors. Towards the periphery Britain adopted a trade policy which, although it may have been perceived at the time as laissez-faire, was in fact the management of peripheral trade to serve British interests, through a combination of ideology and coercion. Slaves were not crucial to the continued capitalisation of the British economy in the nineteenth century, therefore free trade in slaves was abandoned in favour of legitimate commerce in palm oil and other raw materials from the periphery, items which played a vital role in Britain's industrialisation. Military action on the West African coast supported the suppression of the slave trade, ensuring that European rivals would not benefit from abolition by taking advantage of a trade which Britain had already relinquished. Legitimate commerce was similarly supported by force.

> The British navy bombarded (1851) and finally colonized (1861) Lagos, a main port of entry for the Oyo Empire, not because

its king was against trade but rather because his interest in the slave trade made him an enemy of Britain.[11]

The case which Laitin makes is argued from a West African perspective. There are some interesting points of comparison, however, with Webster's account of imperialist expansion in South-east Asia in the nineteenth century, which centres on the foundation of Singapore in 1819. In the case of South-east Asia, economic rivalry between the British and Dutch after 1815 is of key importance in analysing British overseas expansion. But according to Webster it was not the British government but T.S. Raffles, representing established commercial interests in Bengal, who led British resistance to Dutch ambition. His aim was to defend exports of Bengal commodities, newly directed to South-east Asia, rather than to provide a market for exports of manufactures from Britain. The simple alliance between metropolitan government and British-based export interests is brought into question for this early phase of imperialist expansion. Greater weight is given to British commercial interests operating within the periphery itself, and particularly to the alleged precipitating effects of an economic crisis in the Bengal economy itself.

For a much later epoch in British colonialism, Westcott's contribution in Chapter 7 of this volume makes a similar point. In East Africa during the inter-war period, the European sisal growers, many of whom were small independent producers, used their local political power to lobby successfully for improved returns on their export activities. To a large degree they were independent both of the colonial government and of the large merchant firms. Thus in other parts of the periphery too, research indicates that there was no straightforward identity of interest between the metropolitan government and metropolitan capital. Reality was far more complex.

The complexity of metropolitan peripheral relationships is underlined in the study of Third World history, which has proceeded at a fast rate during the past 25 years. To the analysis of colonialism it has brought a number of new perspectives. There has been increased emphasis on the periphery itself, as generating certain pressures which may have been instrumental in European imperialist expansion. Hopkins argued to this effect for the partition of West Africa, citing the decline in the terms of trade for West African produce in the last quarter of the nineteenth century, and the resultant pressure from European merchants on their respective metropolitan governments to establish formal empire.[12] At a later stage Hopkins developed his argument to take account of the revolutionary changes in property rights in West Africa which accompanied the growth of legitimate commerce.[13] Formal empire then swung Britain's political weight behind the institutional changes needed to uphold the new export trade, and gave decisive impetus to the creation of individual rights in land. The shift from informal presence to informal rule was an unanticipated but logical development validated by the civilizing mission and aimed at pulling the region into line with British interests. (op. cit. p.795)

Again for the periphery, other writers have stressed political developments in Africa as precipitating factors in the European scramble. In answer to the question as to why Europeans could no longer rely on influence alone to secure their interests, Robinson and Gallagher argued that new forces within Africa itself, particularly nationalist movements in Egypt and South Africa, drove Britain step by step to a strategy of occupation in order to protect traditional interests.[14] By minimising the importance of economic factors in favour of strategic and defensive motivations, Robinson and Gallagher opened up a new era of debate on African partition. They also provoked much closer investigation of the local factors, the particular African circumstances, which may have played an important role in partition.

Another way in which the substantial research effort of Third World history has been brought to bear on analysis of colonialism, is by studying the impact of overseas expansion on the periphery. In this respect, improving knowledge of what actually happened on the periphery may require radical reappraisal of the accepted wisdoms. Outside of the Marxist and liberal traditions, the outcome of the relationship between centre and periphery is uncertain, in both economic and political aspects. The periphery is subject to a variety of pressures operating in the interests of the centre. In economic terms these are likely to include, at the very least, some exploitation in the form of manipulation of commodity or factor markets, in order to create employment in the metropolis and to generate privately profitable investment opportunities for metropolitan capital. Against this may be set the possibility that colonialism could indeed create new market outlets for the periphery, vents for surplus, and be the source of many new and important wealth-creating activities there. Thus for Yorubaland, Laitin argues, a century of slave-trading brought great prosperity. Profits were high, and imports of salt, manufactured goods, guns and cowries rose.

> Dependency itself did not preclude the Yorubas effectively exploiting opportunities for material advantage in the international economy ... dependency for the Yorubas did not lead to economic stagnation and restricted choice, but to opportunities to exploit new markets in the world economy. (op. cit.)

Nor did the slave trade weaken the state politically. If anything the trade in slaves strengthened the Oyo state. Peripheralisation led not to a weakened, rather to a strengthened state. But there is nothing automatic about this: 'in West Africa capitalist incorporation was associated with a strong state which collapsed (Oyo), a strong state that remained stable (Asante) and congeries of weak states that persisted (the Igbo areas).'[15] His conclusion is that we can no longer accept general propositions that Africa or the periphery as a whole lost out from colonialism. What we require is an analysis of who lost and who won, which social groups, which states and regions, were able to capture markets and take advantage of economic opportunities, and what that implied for state creation.

Issues involving differential responses to market opportunities, and associated aspects of social and political differentiation, are not tackled directly in the contributions to this volume, though what is said, for instance, about Malay society in Martin Rudner's paper, or about income distribution between rural and urban groups in West Africa, has implications for questions of this kind. Clearly this represents an important aspect of the study of the impact of colonialism on the periphery, one to which Third World history can be expected to make a real contribution. Pioneering work of this nature is represented by Polly Hill's work on the Gold Coast cocoa farmers, perceived as a readily identifiable group of 'rural capitalists', migrant farmers from the south-east of modern-day Ghana, who moved northwards, purchasing land for cocoa-growing from the chiefs of the local Akin peoples. Polly Hill's work indicates that such studies benefit from a strong injection of interdisciplinearity, to cope with factors on the supply side (land tenure systems; attitudes towards thrift, enterprise, and the employment of hired labour; the availability of family labour; command over finance) as well as factors from the side of demand.[16]

The study of development under colonialism often identifies official policies with directives and pressures emanating from metropolitan governments. The essays in Part II of this volume provide a useful reminder that this may be an oversimplification. It was not until World War II that the initiative in colonial policy-making moved unambiguously from the colonies to London, under the twin pressures of wartime exigencies and the burgeoning decolonisation movement. The message of the various contributions is that before World War II what happened on the ground, as it were, in British colonial policy sometimes bore little relationship to what was being said and done in London. Possibly the clearest example of this is in the career of Guggisberg, the development-minded Governor of the Gold Coast in the 1920s, whose policies so outraged colonial office circles that even in the expansive and interventionist mood of the 1940s his name was a byword for incompetence and extravagance. Guggisberg was not, however, liberal and far-sighted in political matters. Though observers such as Hailey might argue in the 1930s for a strong association between economic development and decolonisation, such ideas were far removed from Guggisberg's political scenario. Thus a further way in which Third World economic history may influence our perceptions of the impact of colonialism on peripheral development, is in the light it throws on the official mind of the colonial administrator, and his attitudes towards development.

With his emphasis on capital expenditure and development of the infrastructure, Guggisberg was quite exceptional as British colonial governors went before World War II. In a critique of British policy in Tropical Africa from partition to independence, Cyril Ehrlich has perceptively described the common attitudes and beliefs of the local administrators of those days and the institutions through which they worked: anti-modernisation, anti-urban, and anti-development. Regulations and barriers against innovation proliferated. The economic theory which was utilised had little relevance to African problems. Official policy did nothing to encourage the emergence of a commercial middle class. Its effect instead was to establish a highly formidable machinery of bureaucratic control.[17] Similar ideas can be found in Lewis. The most damaging effect of colonial policy on the ground was the way in which it hindered the emergence of a 'native modernizing cadre', one result of which 'was to divert into long and bitter anti-colonial struggles much brilliant talent which could have been used creatively in development sectors'.[18]

Local officials were often hostile to industrial interests and to educated elites.[19] Education was a particularly difficult area for colonial policy at the local level. Official statements stressed the need for relevance. But the bureaucracy demanded a European curriculum, buttressed by exclusivity and privilege. 'Relevance', where it obtained, too frequently meant agricultural rather than vocational technical education. Much of this is echoed in Rudner's contribution, Chapter 6 in this volume, dealing with colonial education policy in Malaya. Before World War II the bulk of government spending went to a tiny minority of pupils educated in English-style schools. The aim was to create a cadre of government officers and clerks educated in accordance with Western principles. An enormous cultural gap existed between this elitist Anglophone caste and the vernacular masses. The rural bias of mass education was evident in Malaya as in other parts of the Dependent Empire, and reflected to a very large degree an anti-development ethos, and a desire to maintain the existing social structure. Although the 1930s brought increased spending on education in Malaya as elsewhere, the process of transformation was a slow one. Lack of skills represented a major weakness at Independence.

Dr Rudner's essay on Malaya, as all the contributions in Part II of this volume, sets the colonial experience within the context of peripheral development. Implicitly or explicitly, all the authors recognise that some quarter of a century after independence, the countries covered by the case studies are relatively poor by the standards of industrialised metropolitan economies, and relatively underprivileged in terms of a broad range of social indicators: literacy rates, nutrition, life expectancy and employment opportunities. But the various contributions also demonstrate that the political economy of colonialism is a complex subject. Though all the countries share the common experience of colonialism, Part II does not lend itself to generalised statements about the relationship between colonialism and material progress in the periphery. There is a great deal which does not fit satisfactorily into popular theories. Undoubtedly some peripheral regions, groups, and classes gained from the colonial contact. Others, quite unambiguously, lost out. Our perception of the ways in which differential economic opportunities were generated and acted upon affects our interpretation of peripheral development under colonialism. As these case studies demonstrate, that perception probably requires not only the special insight of the historian, but also that offered by the economists and other social scientists. In particular, the essays indicate that a significant contribution to development studies can be made by historical perspectives which offer a deep research commitment to Third World history, in combination with new approaches to the economic history of the metropolis. From this point of view the period 1750–1950 is of crucial significance to the present-day divisions in the world economy, with the changing basis of economic and political authority in the metropolis linked into market relationships and productive systems at the periphery.

NOTES

1. Braudel F., *Capitalism and Material Life* (London, 1967, 1973), p. 64.
2. Leys C., *Underdevelopment in Kenya, the Political Economy of Neo-Colonialism* (London, 1975).
3. Hicks, J., *A Theory of Economic History* (Oxford, 1969), Chapter IV.
4. Robinson R. and J. Gallagher, *Africa and the Victorians: The Official Mind of Imperialism* (London, 1961).
5. Because the orthodox approach is very much a matter of balancing out costs and benefits there is of course, room for a very wide spectrum of views. Even Bauer, one of the

strongest apologists for colonial rule, concludes that 'all we can do is set down some pertinent observations and considerations, recognizing that there is scope for wide and legitimate difference of opinion in this discourse'. Although Bauer recognises that colonial rule had major social and political as well as material consequences, it is only the material consequences on which as an economist he feels impelled to comment. On economic progress he says: 'Whether colonial rule promoted or retarded progress cannot be shown conclusively because one cannot say for certain what would have happened without it. But I think it may be said confidently that colonial rule promoted rather than obstructed progress, and was even necessary to it.' Economic change, according to Bauer, had its roots in external contact. Colonialism was the means whereby skills, capital, new commodities and new markets came to Africa. Basic transport facilities and public security were the important legacies of colonial rule. And though colonialism also brought force and coercion, 'the hardships inflicted, though by no means negligible, were nevertheless modest in view of the conditions of pre-colonial Africa and of the extent of the changes'. P. Bauer, 'Economic Retrospect and Aftermath' in P. Duignan, and L. H. Gann, *Colonialism in Africa*, Vol. 4: *The Economics of Colonialism* (Cambridge, 1975). See also, in the same vein, H. Frankel, 'Economic Change in Africa in Historical Perspective', in A. J. Youngson (ed.), *Economic Development in the Long-Run* (London, 1972).

6. See the characterisation of 'Keynesian' views of imperialism in M. Barrett-Brown, *The Economics of Imperialism* (London, 1974); J. Robinson, *The New Mercantilism* (Cambridge, 1966); E. Durbin and J. Knapp, *Economics* (London, 1949).

7. P. J. Cain and A. Hopkins, 'The Political Economy of British Expansion Overseas', *Economic History Review*, 33, 1980.

8. J. Flint, 'Planned Decolonisation and its Failure in British Africa', *African Affairs*, 82, (328), July 1983.

9. The numbers of skilled urban and educated professional people were still very low. The Gold Coast was better off in this respect than other African colonies but still had only 1,000 children in secondary education, and 30 in the higher education college at Achimota. Flint argues that discussions in the 1930s had 'merely identified a *future* class to which power could *eventually* be transferred'.

10. D. Laitin, 'Capitalism and hegemony: Yorubaland and the international economy', *International Organization*, Autumn 1982.

11. Laitin, op. cit., p. 706.

12. A. G. Hopkins, 'Economic Imperialism in West Africa: Lagos 1880–1892', *Economic History Review*, 21, 1968. See also J. F. A. Ajayi and R. A. Austen, 'Hopkins on Economic Imperialism in West Africa', *Economic History Review*, 25, 1972, and Rejoinder by Hopkins in the same volume.

13. A. G. Hopkins, 'Property Rights and Empire Building: Britain's Annexation of Lagos, 1861', *Journal of Economic History*, 40 (4), Dec. 1980.

14. By general agreement, the idea (Lenin, Hobson) that imperialism was the necessary stimulus to a depressed and over-capitalised home economy (conveniently linking the onset of the 1870s depression in Europe to the partition of Africa) has not come out particularly well from empirical studies.

> It has been repeatedly demonstrated that 'investors' and 'bankers' were far less influential in policy making than Lenin or even Hobson supposed; that in the relevant period capital exports to tropical Africa were insignificant; that some very active imperialist powers (Italy, Portugal) had no chronic shortage, and that throughout the later nineteenth and early twentieth centuries the markets and the raw materials of tropical Africa were alike of almost negligible importance to the European economy (G. N. Sanderson, 'The European Partition of Africa: Coincidence or Conjecture', in E. F. Penrose (ed.), *European Imperialism and the Partition of Africa* (London, Cass, 1975)).

In their study Robinson and Gallagher argued against any strong political or commercial movements in Britain in the late nineteenth century, favouring imperial acquisitions in Africa. One consideration alone influenced official policy on the annexation of African territories. This was the need to secure the route to the East. The safety of the route to India dictated the decision to uphold British supremacy in South Africa, impelled the occupation of Egypt, forced Britain to go into East Africa and the Upper Nile, and to yield parts of West Africa to other European powers: 'If the papers left by the policymakers are to be believed, they moved into Africa not to build a new African empire, but to protect the old empire in India ...' (Robinson and Gallagher, op. cit.).

15. Laitin, op. cit., p. 711. His claims concerning the political diversity, and conflicting fortunes, of West African states are borne out by the literature. See, for instance, P. Curtin, *African History* (London, 1978), D. Northrup, *Trade Without Rulers* (Oxford 1978), K. Arhin, *West African Traders in the Nineteenth and Twentieth Centuries* (London, 1979). C. Newbury, 'Trade and Authority in West Africa, 1850–1880', in Duignan and Gann (eds.), *Colonialism in Africa*, Vol. 1, *History and Politics of Colonialism*, (Cambridge, 1969).

16. P. Hill, *The Migrant Cocoa Farmers of Southern Ghana* (Cambridge, 1963). See also questions of differential response as discussed in S. Berry, *Cocoa, Custom and Socio-economic Change in Rural Western Nigeria* (Oxford, 1975). J. Hogendorn, 'Economic Initiative and African Cash Farming: Pre-Colonial Origins and Early Colonial Developments' in Duignan and Gann, *The Economics of Colonialism*, op. cit., p. 284.

17. C. Ehrlich, 'Building and Caretaking: Economic Policy in British Tropical Africa, 1890–1960', *Economic History Review*, 26, 1973, pp. 649–67.

18. W. A. Lewis, *Growth and Fluctuations, 1870–1913* (London, 1976), p. 214.

19. In part this was a reflection of the ethos of the British colonial service, which Hancock described as an alliance between Wilberforce and Adam Smith. In the British colonial service, 'the industrial and mercantile bourgeoisie, in whose interest the empire was supposedly being expanded, was little represented. The service instead had a church and professional flavour, with a heavy scent of the parsonage. It consisted of men with a mission in life, men who regarded colonialism as a venture in applied philanthropy – not as an enterprise designed to maximise metropolitan profits' L. H. Gann and P. Duignan, *The Rulers of British Africa* (London, 1978), pp. 50–1.

In British West Africa colonial administrators were characterised by caution and restraint, the result of which has been argued to be an overall 'sluggishness' in economic policy and, quite possibly, according to Kay, a reduction in the overall rate of growth in British West Africa during the period of formal empire (G. B. Kay, *The Political Economy of Colonialism in Ghana* (Cambridge, 1972), p. 11).

4

British Export Interests in Bengal and Imperial Expansion into South-east Asia, 1780 to 1824: The Origins of the Straits Settlements

ANTHONY WEBSTER

INTRODUCTION

The meteoric rise of the British East India Company, from its position as a struggling mercantile interest in the early 1700s to that of the most powerful political entity on the Indian sub-continent by the end of the century, has already received detailed analysis. For most of the second half of the eighteenth century, the new British rulers of Bengal were beset by many economic difficulties, the most pressing of which was the search for export commodities, and an effective commercial structure which could furnish a satisfactory profit for the Company in its trading relationship with Britain and Europe.

This chapter is concerned with the evolution of British commercial organisation in Bengal, as it strove to meet these objectives. It provides an insight into the role played by private commercial interests in both the development of the colonial export economy, and the shaping of British imperial policy in the East. We examine the changing role of private export interests in the complex commercial system upon which the Company's Bengal administration came to depend, and their importance in influencing British policy in South-east Asia during the early nineteenth century, a crucial phase which culminated in the foundation of Singapore in 1819.

Particular attention has been paid by some historians to the evolution of the system of colonial administration and economic management, which was the most striking feature of British rule in Bengal by the end of the 1830s, when Company rule was coming to an end. Historians have written on the development of the Company's colonial system of commerce and government in Bengal, from Clive's victory at Plassey in 1757 to the collapse of that system in the early 1830s, a collapse largely caused by economic difficulties.[1]

It will be seen that the colonial system rested upon the creation of an intricate network of financial and trading relationships between the EIC and independent mercantile organisations (agency houses) which operated within the terms of the Company's monopoly of trade with the UK and Europe. These relationships operated to the mutual benefit of both the Company and the independent agency houses, providing financial support and a supply of export commodities for the Company and lucrative profits for merchants involved in the houses. The nature of this relationship between Company and private interests is a central theme of this chapter. Its role in Bengal's economic development and the further expansion of British rule in South-east Asia will be explored.

Most historians examining the eighteenth century British colonial system in Bengal have directed their attention to its evolution and eventual collapse. The impact of the system on domestic agricultural productivity and economic activity in general have also been explored.[2] In the latter case, a great deal of work has been done on the development of the land revenue system up to, and after, the Permanent Settlement of 1793.[3] Other aspects of colonial rule have received less attention. The activities of the agency houses have been examined by only a few historians, who have been concerned principally with their role in the survival of the colonial economic system.[4] There has been little analysis of the impact of the agency system upon the long-term development of the Bengal economy. Although this chapter provides only limited assessment of that question, its aim is to stimulate further research and debate.

The present work is concerned with another neglected feature of agency house activity: their importance as a political pressure group in Bengal, which in defence of its interests played a major part in stimulating imperial expansion into South-east Asia. The conclusion is that the British port of Singapore was primarily a result of their efforts.

The agency houses came to occupy a central position in the colonial economy. While the EIC controlled all trade with Europe, it was the agency houses who provided the finance essential for the production of export commodities. As a result of this, they exercised a considerable degree of control over the export sector. There was little concern with production to serve the domestic Bengal market. Production for export to China, Europe and South-east Asia was the principal objective and activity. While individuals involved in the houses prospered and expanded their interests and influence, Bengal continued a long process of economic stagnation which had begun even before the advent of British rule. As Tripathi says:

> Bengal did not begin to go downhill from a certain date in 1757. The causes of disintegration had begun to operate in her political, economic and social system before the British assumed the sovereignty of Bengal.[5]

There were few linkages between the domestic and export sectors of the economy which could promote long-term growth and development. While the Bengali population was extensively involved in export production as labourers and middlemen, a combination of heavy taxation, low wages and rising population all served to restrict any advantages for long-term development. These problems were not exclusive to British rule. Habib has shown that the internal power structure of Mughal society, with its many layers of authority and power, tended to stifle internal economic development from as early as the mid-seventeenth century.[6]

The Mughal system of provincial administration, based as it was upon non-hereditary local rule by powerful Mansabdars, effectively drained the Indian peasantry and mercantile classes of the surplus capital necessary for advanced economic development. The maintenance of a substantial bureaucracy and military support, and also the personal aggrandisement of senior officials, all served to escalate the financial drain of the agricultural and merchant classes. This process was intensified by the disintegration of the Mughal empire at the end of the eighteenth century. The rivalries, fears and wars generated by the decay of the old Mughal source of authority prompted local rulers and administrators to increase their demands on their local economic bases. Armies had to be paid for, to defend or expand territorial possessions. In the wake of their conquest of Bengal, the British faced similar problems to those of any localised power in India.[7] Warfare to preserve their territory from hostile powers necessitated high levels of taxation on land and trade. As a consequence, domestic economic development in Bengal in the first century of British rule was restricted mainly to the export sector. High taxation, and the British preoccupation with developing external commerce with Europe and China, ensured that for 60 years after Plassey the Bengal economy would experience substantial growth and development only in the various export-oriented activities cultivated by the EIC and the agency houses.

Other indigenous factors had contributed to this trend. Chaudhuri has shown that for much of the seventeenth and eighteenth centuries Bengal's domestic economic development had been oriented towards the export trade in textiles.[8] Cheap labour in yarn production and weaving, good river transport to the coast, and a sophisticated system of capital support for textile production from a flourishing indigenous merchant class, all contributed to the advance of textile exports. The European East India Companies were the principal beneficiaries of these developments, particularly the British from the mid-seventeenth century onwards.[9] From this time, the British successfully utilised links with Bengali merchant middlemen to secure a regular supply of Bengal piece goods which brought high and much needed profits in the British market.

Prakash has shown that the rise of the textile export industry in Bengal did bring some benefits for the Bengal economy.[10] Prakash estimates that in the early eighteenth century between 8% and 12% of the Bengal workforce were provided with employment by textile production, and he argues that during this period the export trade generated widespread growth throughout Bengal society. He argues that textiles did contribute significantly to long-term economic development. Other historians have been more sceptical. Gupta's interpretation of the reasons for the imposition of British rule shows that external threats and pressures brought about by the disintegration of the Mughal empire tended to undermine any long-term benefits from textiles.[11] In order to resist the warlike ambitions of the Marathas, successive Nawabs of Bengal were forced to increase their revenue demands on the Bengal economy. Gupta shows that these demands were a major factor in the severe and prolonged economic depression between 1748 and 1756, a depression which itself contributed significantly to the internal instability which precipitated the crisis of 1756/57, and the imposition of British rule. Plainly forces were at work in Bengal society which, while stimulating export-based economic growth, also prevented the benefits of that growth from generating long-term domestic economic development. Thus, the advanced development of export activities in the stagnant Bengal economy was a consequence not only of the nature of British colonialism after 1757, but also of a much older and more complex system of indigenous economic relations in Bengal.

EUROPEAN EXPORT INTERESTS AND THE EVOLUTION OF
THE COLONIAL ECONOMIC SYSTEM 1757–1813

After the acquisition of Bengal by the British, a number of serious economic problems confronted successive British administrations. While the establishment of British rule had been a military success, the new administrative and governmental role adopted by the EIC brought many difficulties, which in the long run threatened to undermine the economic basis of Company rule.

First, the cost of political control and defence of Bengal proved to be a severe drain on Company resources throughout the latter part of the eighteenth century. The British found that in order to defend their interests in India an almost constant policy of imperial expansion and warfare had to be sustained and financed. These costs could be only partly offset by continually increasing domestic taxation in Bengal.

This problem was further complicated by a second major difficulty. In spite of the apparent fertility and potential wealth of the province, Bengal did not readily furnish the British with exports which could find a ready market in Europe. Only textiles, particularly cotton piece goods, initially provided substantial returns for the Company's trade between India and Europe. For a period of nearly 30 years, the Company struggled from economic crisis to crisis, before a satisfactory colonial system emerged which provided an answer to this problem.[12] The solution which eventually emerged involved a complex network of trading relationships between Calcutta, Canton and ports in South-east Asia. In China, the British found not only a market for certain Indian commodities, particularly piece goods and opium, but also a source of exports which could find the profitable European markets which the British so desperately needed. The teas and silks of China were heavily in demand in Britain and Europe, and proffered a channel through which the EIC could translate the output and revenues of Bengal into a profitable commerce with Britain. By exporting Indian commodities to China, and exchanging them for teas and silks, the British could earn the profits necessary to sustain their growing political commitment in India.[13]

The China trade was a slow, difficult, expensive and complicated avenue of commerce to develop. Trade, though beginning in the 1760s, took several decades to become established. There were various reasons for this slow development. First, the capital requirements of the trade were heavy. Heavy investment in shipping was necessary to facilitate trade with the Far East. The Company, already burdened with heavy commitments in shipping for the Europe–India trade, and the spiralling expenses of its territorial acquisitions, were hard-pressed to finance this new branch of commerce. Eventually, the Company was to strike up a special relationship with 'free merchants' based on the Indian presidencies, private entrepreneurs who traded in the 'country trade' of the Eastern seas in pursuit of private profit. By the end of the eighteenth century, these merchants were trading throughout the Far East, though they were carefully kept away from the Company's monopoly of European trade. By the 1780s, arrangements were developing between these free merchants and the EIC, to the mutual benefit of both interests, which facilitated the rapid growth of the China trade. The free merchants undertook the often

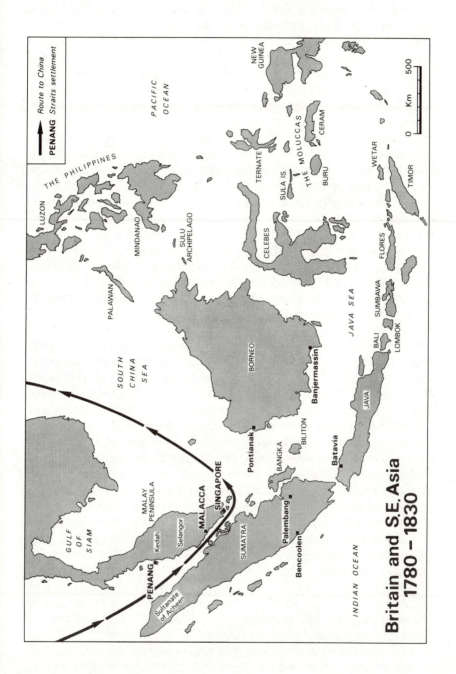

Britain and S.E. Asia
1780 – 1830

Route to China
PENANG Straits settlement

THE PHILIPPINES

LUZON

MINDANAO

PALAWAN

SULU
ARCHIPELAGO

PACIFIC
OCEAN

NEW
GUINEA

TERNATE

SULA IS.

CERAM

BURU

THE MOLUCCAS

WETAR

TIMOR

CELEBES

BORNEO

JAVA SEA

BALI

SUMBAWA

LOMBOK

FLORES

Banjermassin

Pontianak

BILITON

BANGKA

JAVA

Batavia

SOUTH
CHINA
SEA

GULF
OF
SIAM

MALAY
PENINSULA

Kedah

Selangor

PENANG

MALACCA

SINGAPORE

SUMATRA

Palembang

Bencoolen

Sultanate
of Acheen

INDIAN OCEAN

0   Km   500

perilous and expensive risks involved in the export of Bengal commodities to the East, tempted by the large profits to be made in the China market.

Upon sale of their exports in China, the special relationship between the free merchants and the Company came into operation. The returns in currency received by the free merchants were paid into the coffers of the Company's headquarters in Canton, in return for bills of exchange payable in London. This provided the Company with the specie requirements to finance their purchases of tea and silks, which were then shipped to Europe on the Company's East Indiamen. In return, the free merchants were granted a means of remittance of their wealth to London in the bills of exchange. Transferring wealth made in the East to Britain was a major problem for private entrepreneurs. The Company's monopoly prevented remittance of wealth through trade, and generations of free merchants experienced deep frustration at the problem of transmitting their gains home. Tripathi describes the considerable problem this was to cause the Company by the end of the century, as the desire to remit wealth to London led many merchants into illicit channels such as the clandestine trade between Calcutta and Europe conducted by rival European companies.[14]

While this elaborate, complex and vulnerable network of trade was ultimately to provide a significant contribution to the economic security of British India, it was only after the 1790s that this trade flourished to its full potential. There were many problems. Free merchants, operating on limited capital resources in an uncertain and volatile commercial climate, could only develop their trade links with the East slowly and tentatively. In years of recession, bankruptcy and ruin were ever present dangers for many of these entrepreneurs. Neither was the trade exempt from the perils of war and piracy along the turbulent route to China through the Malay archipelago. Native pirates and hostile foreign powers, particularly the French and Dutch, were formidable obstacles. Those traders who were too daunted by these problems often restricted their trading activities to the islands of the Malay archipelago, which provided a valuable market for Bengal commodities seeking an outlet. Although later the Malay archipelago was to be valued by the British as a useful source of commodities in demand in China, initial interest was prompted by the need to find markets for Bengal produce. In the 20 years which followed the establishment of British rule, this was a significant problem, as the output of Bengal increased dramatically in response to the expansion of economic activities by private entrepreneurs and company servants in the province. Marshall shows that markets were not readily available for this sudden increase of production, and that for two decades the British in Bengal struggled to achieve commercial viability for their new colonial possession.[15]

In this environment of economic difficulty, the Company stumbled from crisis to crisis from 1757 until the end of the century. In order to finance its export trade from China to Europe, the Company initially had to export exorbitant quantities of silver from Bengal to China. This drain of resources on Bengal helped to cause severe economic crises in 1772 and 1784. On both occasions the Company had to turn to the British Government for help.[16] In 1784, in the wake of the second major crisis, the British Government asserted strict conditions on their aid to the struggling EIC. A special Board of Control, under the Government's authority, was established to supervise Company affairs and the administration of its Eastern possessions. This development was rightly perceived by many Company directors and servants as an intrusion into the Company's right to conduct its own affairs. Indeed, it marked the beginning of a long process of absorption of the Company into the British state, a process which was eventually completed by the middle of the nineteenth century.

The prolonged period of economic difficulty experienced by the Company only began to be relieved in the last decade of the eighteenth century, and the early decades of the nineteenth. During this period, several major changes in the structure and organisation of British commerce brought about a substantial strengthening of the Bengal – China trade, and with it a general improvement of the Company's position.

One of the most important of these changes was the dramatic expansion of opium production which began to occur after the late 1790s. Up till 1797, the control of opium production had been in the hands of first Indian merchants, and later Company servants acting as private contractors in an independent capacity. Neither system had proved satisfactory, when the EIC decided in 1797 to impose direct Company control over the production of opium. The new official monopoly was intended to eliminate the inefficient and corrupt practices of the contract system which had undermined both the productive capacity of peasant cultivators and the quality of the opium output. The improvements in production by the opium monopoly proved most beneficial for British colonialism in Bengal. From 1797 onwards there was a dramatic expansion in both the production and export of opium. The Company's monopoly was able to ensure a steady supply of high quality opium at realistic prices. Shrewdly, the Company left the export of opium to the private traders and agency houses, who purchased the commodity at the Company warehouses in Calcutta. The policy proved to be most successful.

The value of opium exports grew dramatically in the first two decades of the nineteenth century: from 13,31,255 rupees in 1796/97 to Rs. 47,12,611 in 1806/1807.[17] By 1814/1815, the value of the opium export trade had risen to Rs. 91,76,506, an increase of over 700% since 1797. The benefits accruing to the Company from this expansion were incalculable. The China trade, which for so long in the late eighteenth century had proved difficult to maintain, provided the main market for Bengal opium, absorbing approximately 70–75% of annual opium exports by 1810. In opium the British had at last found a commodity which could furnish a regular exchange for the teas and silks of China, without resorting to the disruptive practice of exporting silver from Bengal, which had caused so many problems in the late eighteenth century.

Second, the 1780s saw reforms in Bengal which at once removed much of the corruption and inefficiency of the Company's administration in Bengal, and also provided a dramatic impetus for private commercial enterprise outside the Company's monopoly. In the wake of the financial crisis of the early 1780s a new Governor-General, Lord Cornwallis, was appointed in 1785 to deal with Bengal's economic problems. Cornwallis' reforms were dramatic in their impact.[18] Company servants were excluded from private involvement in commerce and enterprise. For Cornwallis, corruption in the service of the Company was at the root of the Bengal administration's problems. He firmly believed that Company servants who were more concerned with private fortune-hunting rather than their public duties were a principal cause of the Company's financial ills. By excluding Company servants from private enterprise and increasing their salaries, Cornwallis hoped to establish new and impeccable standards of loyalty, integrity and competence. This would provide a solid foundation upon which to build future prosperity in Bengal. While Cornwallis certainly believed that private enterprise had a place in the structure of British rule, he felt strongly that there should be clear demarcation between private and Company interests.

The effect of Cornwallis' administrative reforms was to accelerate changes in European private enterprise in Bengal which were already under way by the early 1780s. By this time, private merchants and the 'free traders' had begun to initiate fundamental changes in the organisation of their enterprises. Many found that the old problem of capital shortage could be dealt with by pooling their resources with those of other merchants, and also by expanding the range of their commercial activities. Banking and insurance proved to be key areas of expansion which helped these free merchants to establish a system of agency houses, which was to become so important for early British rule in Bengal.

By the early 1780s, the problems involved in private enterprise had persuaded many Europeans to seek safer and more reliable returns for their investments, and the agency houses seemed to offer an attractive alternative to the risks of private commercial activity on an individual basis. The attractions of investment in an agency house through its banking, insurance or other activities were very potent; an investor was assured of a reliable rate of interest on his capital, which involved no effort or trouble on his own part. By the 1780s the agency houses were already building up a strong reputation for reliability and commercial good sense. This reputation relied upon several important features of their organisation. First, the scope of their activities was very wide indeed. They were extensively involved in the country trade, shipbuilding, indigo, opium-contracting, construction, insurance, banking and finance, and silk production. This diversity reassured many investors, who perceived greater safety and less vulnerability in a wide distribution of agency house funds throughout a number of profitable enterprises. Few individual investors held sufficient capital to replicate this diversity, and usually commercial activity on an individual's own account meant a perilous committment of the bulk of his resources into one field of commerce.

Second, by the mid-1780s, the value of the agency houses to the Company was becoming apparent to the European community. Not only did the agency houses finance the increasingly important China trade, they also provided a significant source of finance for the Company's administration in Bengal. Faced with the heavy costs of its Indian wars, the Company increasingly turned to the agency houses for loans and financial support.[19] This help was particularly important to the Company during the Mysore wars of the 1780s and 1790s. Shrewd Europeans came to realise that the Company had a vested interest in supporting the agency houses during times of economic difficulty, and that consequently the houses were a peculiarly safe channel of investment.

Cornwallis' reforms added to the momentum of these developments. Excluded from private involvement in commerce, the Company's 1,300 servants turned to the agency houses to invest their substantially increased salaries. Almost overnight, in 1758 Cornwallis had effectively channelled the private wealth of Company employees in Bengal into the agency house system.

By 1790, 15 leading agency houses had come to dominate private commercial activity in Bengal. The most prominent of these were the houses of Fairlie, Fergusson and Co.; Paxton, Cockerell and Delisle; Lambert and Ross; Colvins and Bazett; and Joseph Barretto. The leading houses financed the production of silk, indigo, sugar and opium; and provided the Bengal administration with a useful source of loan capital in times of crisis. They were at the centre of the financial structure of the Bengal economy, running three banks and four insurance companies. The houses were constantly involved in speculation in public securities and bills. With their massively enhanced capital resources, the agency houses were able to finance that expansion of the country trade which was so necessary for the economic success of the Company, and which had proved so difficult to achieve in the 1760s and 1770s. In this sense the Bengal administration came to depend upon the houses for economic survival. As Tripathi says:

> The Company could not draw upon the income of its own servants without the co-operation of the agency houses, or send funds to Madras, Bombay or Canton unless the agency houses speculated in opium or salt. In other words, the Company always felt the agency houses' hands at its throat in any political or financial crisis.[20]

At the core of any analysis of colonial export interests in Bengal under the EIC, must be a clear understanding of the relationship between the Company's administration and the agency houses. The houses marshalled and channelled private capital resources in Bengal into activities which directly benefited the Company and reinforced its authority. Their emergence was at the root of the substantial improvement in the Company's commercial position after the 1790s into the first two decades of the nineteenth century. The houses were responsible for a dramatic expansion of the country trade with China and South-east Asia, and the fortunes of Bengal's export sector. Successive administrations strove to understand Bengal's complex economic system, and through necessity paid close attention to the needs and requirements of the agency houses. Pressure upon these organisations could have the most severe repercussions for the Company itself, and the defence of these private interests became an increasingly significant priority for Bengal administrations. As a consequence of this, certain prominent agency house entrepreneurs came to exercise considerable political influence in Bengal. Perhaps the most significant of these was John Palmer, who established a reputation as the wealthiest merchant in Bengal during the first 20 years of the nineteenth century.[21] Palmer built up his reputation in the house of Paxton, Cockerell and Delisle, of which he was eventually to become a senior partner. This increasingly important source of private influence was not restricted to India. It was the ultimate aim of most private merchants in India to remit their wealth to Britain, and establish themselves in the home country. Many returning merchants established new firms in Britain, which maintained commercial and personal links with their former agency houses in India. A number of these 'sister' houses acquired substantial shareholdings in the EIC, and by the early 1820s came to exercise an important influence in the Company directorate.[22] In this respect, the political influence of the agency houses was deeply entrenched in the structure of the Company.

The extent to which private interests shaped the actions of Bengal administrations remains a major question arising from the period of Company rule in India. It is unclear how far decisions such as those concerning territorial expansion involved the protection of vital private interests; and to what extent domestic policy in the territories under British rule was determined by the Company's relationship with the agency houses. Plainly such questions have an important bearing upon any assessment of the long-term implications of early British colonial rule for the development of the Indian economy, as they illuminate the circumstances which generated British colonial policy.

There is insufficient space for detailed discussion of all aspects of colonial policy, but examination of one particular area of policy provides a useful insight into the potency of private commercial influence. The Bengal administration's policy in South-east Asia from the 1780s until the early 1820s displayed just how powerful private interests could be in pursuit of success. The agency houses played a vital role in the expansion of British commerce into the Malay archipelago, and they were to become increasingly active in shaping British intentions and actions. Particularly, the British decision to establish Singapore in 1819 was a response to the pressures upon the agency houses and the commercial structure of the Bengal economy, which threatened to undermine the economic base upon which the Company rule depended.

BENGAL EXPORT INTERESTS AND THE FOUNDATION OF SINGAPORE

British interest in South-east Asia began early in the years which followed the acquisition of Bengal. Marshall shows that, following the establishment of British rule, there was a commercial boom in Bengal, increasing the production of Indian commodities such as cotton piece goods and opium, which needed new markets. The decline in the 1740s of the older trade between India and the Arabian markets of the Gulf and Red Sea presented serious problems for British private traders based in Bengal, particularly in the late 1750s and 1760s.[23] In the last decades of the eighteenth century the China market emerged as a replacement for the Arabian markets, but in the intervening period, in the 1760s and 1770s, South-east Asia itself became an important outlet for Indian commodities. While this area could not absorb all Bengal exports, it became important as a marginal market which offered at least some opportunity for traders desperate for markets. Indeed this marginal market function was to remain important, even after the China trade became firmly established.

After the China market became the main outlet for the Bengal economy, the Malay archipelago acquired importance as a means of exchanging Bengal commodities which could not readily find a market in China, such as Indian cotton goods, for Malay commodities which were more acceptable. The Malay archipelago also had a crucial strategic significance for the China trade. The major trade routes to China passed through the archipelago, an area in which the Dutch enjoyed territorial supremacy for over 200 years. The British recognised that passage through the Straits of Malacca and Sunda could be made very difficult by the Dutch with whom diplomatic relations were strained to the point of hostility throughout the second half of the eighteenth century. The British therefore maintained a constant vigil over Dutch activity in South-east Asia, and the safety of trade routes to China.

By the 1770s, these considerations prompted bolder measures by the British. In that decade, a series of expeditions was sanctioned by the Bengal and Madras authorities to explore the possibility of establishing a British outpost in the archipelago.[24] Private traders such as Francis Light and Thomas Forrest were sent to the courts of Malay princes in Sumatra and the Malay peninsula to investigate and negotiate for the establishment of a new British settlement. These early attempts were unsuccessful, but war in the East with the French and the Dutch in the early 1780s persuaded the British to redouble their efforts.[25] In 1786 the free merchant Francis Light used his influence with the Sultan of Kedah to secure a British military and commercial settlement on the island of Penang. The EIC hoped that Penang would develop to become both the defender of British access to the Straits and the major centre of commerce in the archipelago. These aspirations dominated British policy towards Penang and the archipelago for over 20 years.[26]

British efforts to consolidate Penang's position and expand the commerce of the port met with only limited success in the first ten years of the port's existence. There were various reasons for this. The Bengal administration was reluctant to aggravate relations with the Dutch, and so refused to sanction diplomatic efforts by the Penang administration to establish commercial and political treaties with the Malay states. Also, Penang itself was too far north to fulfil

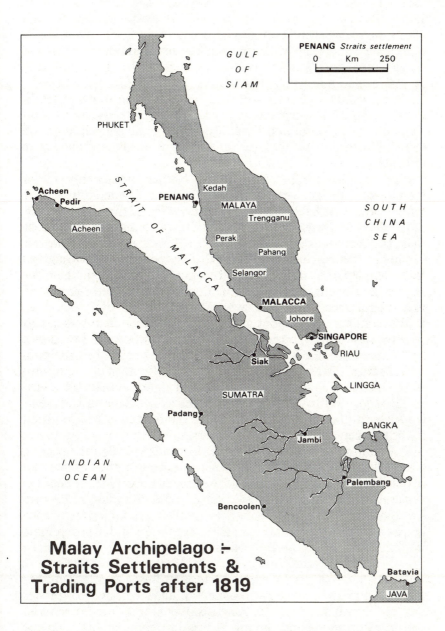

GULF
OF
SIAM

PENANG *Straits settlement*

0   Km   250

PHUKET

Acheen
Pedir

Acheen

STRAIT OF MALACCA

PENANG

Kedah

MALAYA

Trengganu

Perak

Pahang

Selangor

MALACCA

Johore

SINGAPORE

RIAU

Siak

LINGGA

SUMATRA

Padang

BANGKA

Jambi

INDIAN
OCEAN

Palembang

Bencoolen

SOUTH
CHINA
SEA

Batavia

JAVA

Malay Archipelago :-
Straits Settlements &
Trading Ports after 1819

some of the optimistic predictions made by Light and other enthusiasts for the new settlement.[27] Light had originally convinced the Bengal authorities that Penang could successfully attract the indigenous trade of the archipelago, and establish itself as an emporium which would supply the China trade with essential Malay commodities. By 1795, it was plain from reports by visitors to the new settlement that these objectives had not been achieved.[28] At that time, future prospects for Penang and the expansion of British commerce in South-east Asia seemed doubtful. Subsequent developments dramatically transformed this situation, and paved the way for the consolidation of British imperial influence over the Malay peninsula and the Strait of Malacca.

First, the French invasion of the Netherlands in 1793/1794 presented the British with the threat of seizure of Dutch possessions in South-east Asia by the French. The British feared that, if the French controlled the strategically important Dutch colonies in South-east Asia, they could sever the vital trade link between British India and China. To prevent this, in 1795, the British took pre-emptive action, and occupied the major Dutch colonies at Malacca and in the Moluccas. For the duration of the European wars these remained in British hands. Under the favourable conditions of British rule, British commerce and economic interests in South-east Asia found little resistance to expansion. In 1811, British control was extended by the invasion of Java, the nerve centre of the Dutch Eastern empire. T.S. Raffles, later to become famous as the founder of Singapore, established his reputation as a prominent figure in British Eastern policy from 1811 to 1816 during his time as Lt. Governor of Java. Under his authority, British commerce established a firm foothold in the markets of the Malay archipelago.[29]

The temporary establishment of British rule over South-east Asia after 1795 coincided with the transformation of the commercial structure of Bengal and the rise of the agency houses. These changes had crucial implications for the expansion of British trade into South-east Asia. By utilising their enhanced financial resources, the agency houses were able to promote a dramatic expansion of trade from India into the archipelago, an expansion which was closely linked to the rise of the China trade. During the later 1790s and early 1800s there was an upsurge of Bengal exports into South-east Asia, an upsurge facilitated by the growing willingness of agency houses to finance this trade. Two main exports benefited from these developments — cotton piece goods and opium. It was in opium exports that the greatest benefits were felt from the expansion of trade with the archipelago. Richards has shown that total opium exports from Bengal increased significantly in both volume and value between 1797 and 1815, and that this made a vital contribution to the revenues of the EIC.[30] Richards also shows that the price of opium rose continuously from the end of the eighteenth century until 1815, after which time the price remained steady.

Two additional points should be made here. First, the high profits made by the agency houses on the export of opium was a vital factor in their success. Both Tripathi and Singh acknowledge that opium was a crucial source of profit for the houses. Second, the Malay archipelago played a very important part in ensuring the rising price of opium and the increasing profits which the commodity brought to both the Company and the agency houses. Appendix I shows that in the period a significant proportion of the exports of opium from Bengal was absorbed by the archipelago, ranging over the whole period between 15% and 45%.

In the period 1796–1802, the archipelago provided a very important market for Bengal, and this appears to have been an important factor in the overall growth of the opium trade, ensuring high prices and secure markets at a crucial period in the development of this branch of commerce. In the years which followed, the China market flourished, but the archipelago remained important. Throughout the following 20 years the Malay archipelago fulfilled a vitally important marginal market function, providing a much needed outlet for Bengal opium when the China market was depressed. This helped maintain the high price of opium and high profits of the agency houses and the Company, providing a secure and stable economic base for the colonial economy of Bengal. The importance of the archipelago as a marginal market varied from time to time, being viewed principally as a secondary market of lesser importance than China. However, in times of recession and difficulty in the China trade, or in the Bengal economy generally, the markets of the archipelago took on a new significance, and efforts were made both to protect and to expand trade with the region.

The marginal market function of the Malay archipelago has been largely ignored by both historians working on the development of the Bengal colonial economy in the period, and by those concerned with the expansion of British imperial influence into South-east Asia. The general consensus on the value of the archipelago to the Bengal economy in the first 15 years of the nineteenth century is that the region was initially of strategic importance to the British. The role of supplying Malay exports to China was an additional, secondary attraction. According to the consensus, the archipelago came to be of paramount importance in an economic sense, only with the expansion of British industrial exports to the Far East after the Charter Act of 1813.[31] This Act opened India and South-east Asia to British cotton textile manufacturers desperate for markets in the perilous climate of depression which beset British industrialism in the post-war period. British economic interest in the archipelago is thus seen as originating principally from Britain itself, and the eventual acquisition of Singapore is regarded as a response to the needs of industrial economic interests at the metropole. Not only does this view overlook the important marginal market function of the archipelago, it also, because of its Eurocentric emphasis, misses an opportunity to explore and analyse the domestic pressures and interests. In Bengal, these pressures prompted the colonial administration to despatch Raffles on his fateful mission in November 1818. It was these interests, committed to Bengal's export economy, which were to play a crucial role in establishing British supremacy over the Malay peninsula.

The expansion of British trade in the archipelago brought increased agency house involvement in commercial activities in the ports of the region. Prominent agency house merchants such as John Palmer established a network of commercial contacts throughout the archipelago. On Penang, Palmer's contacts included David Brown, a respected and prosperous entrepreneur whose interests included trade and pepper planting.[32] Another contact was Syed Hussein, an Achenese merchant who became deeply embroiled in the succession dispute in Acheen after 1814.[33] Palmer displayed a keen interest in the outcome of this dispute, as he had an interest in trade with Acheen, and he felt that a sympathetic ruler in Acheen would further his interests considerably. Other merchants also developed commercial links with the Straits Settlements. Fairlie, Fergusson and Co. of Calcutta had close contact with Carnegy and Co. at Penang, probably the most successful merchant house on the island, and Clark and Hare at Malacca.[34] Palmer had also developed substantial commercial interests in the southern archipelago. He had a close commercial relationship with the Sultan of Pontianak.[35] He also owned several plantations at Tjikandi, on Java.[36] At one stage in 1820, he even showed a keen interest in the idea of raising a loan in Calcutta for the Dutch administration of the East Indies, although nothing came of the deal in the end.[37] There is also evidence that Joseph Barretto traded extensively in gold dust with Malacca.[38] Other evidence suggests that Fairlie, Fergusson and Co. were becoming increasingly involved in the export trade with Borneo.[39]

The expansion of Bengal's trade into the Malay archipelago thus played an important part in the continuing success of the agency houses and the export trade of Bengal. However, by 1815 several developments threatened to curtail this successful branch of commerce, just at a time when the commercial structure of the province began to come under new pressures which threatened to throw the Bengal economy into chaos.

The initial problem stemmed from the fact that with the end of the European war in 1814 an independent Dutch state was re-established. This became of paramount importance in British foreign policy as a buffer against future French ambitions in northern Europe. In order to facilitate Dutch economic recovery, the British agreed at the Convention of 1814 to hand back those Dutch possessions in South-east Asia which had been seized during the course of the war. It was believed that these would provide a secure economic base for the Dutch, strengthening them in the face of hostile powers. Under this policy Java and the Moluccas were returned to Dutch control in 1816, and Malacca followed in 1818. Thus European political affairs were given priority over EIC and colonial interests in the Malay archipelago. Indeed, there was no consultation with these interests.

The return of the Dutch colonies came at a most inopportune time for the Bengal colonial economy, the agency houses and the EIC. It became apparent very quickly that the Dutch intended to re-assert their protectionist policy in South-east Asia to the exclusion of British commerce.[40] In the years following the return of Java, Bengal's export trade to that island came under increasing pressure, much to the alarm of the Bengal administration and the private traders.

Moreover, new Dutch restrictions on trade were not the only problem. Fundamental changes were being forced on the Bengal economy and the very fabric upon which British rule was based. Political and economic pressure from cotton manufacturers and merchants in Britain had persuaded the British government to open the India market to British industrial exports. The British cotton industry had suffered considerably from the closure of continental markets during the war, and the colonial markets of India and the Far East were perceived as a source of some relief from economic difficulties. Fearful of the social and political consequences of industrial depression, the British government succumbed to the industrialists' demands, and the Act of renewal of the Company's Charter in 1813, opened India to free commerce with Britain.[41]

The Charter Act of 1813 ended the Company's India monopoly, opening trade with India and the archipelago to private traders in Britain. The impact of this development on the commercial organisation of Bengal is described by Tripathi and Singh.[42] Under the India monopoly, the Company and the agency houses had sustained an economic relationship which suited the needs of both parties. The agency houses facilitated the operation of the China trade, through their country trading activities and their arrangements with the

Company's post at Canton. They also provided an important source of loan capital for the Bengal administration. Through their banking and investment activities the houses were able to utilise the untapped capital resources of the Company servants, and on occasion the Bengal administration relied upon loans from the houses to provide the 'Investment', the stock of Indian goods which were sold in Britain to offset the expenses of the Company and pay the dividend.[43] In turn, the agency houses enjoyed 'a monopoly of commerce' within the Company's trading empire. The country trade and other economic activities carried on in Bengal such as banking, ship-building, indigo planting and insurance, fell into the hands of the six leading firms. These firms also dominated the distribution of British manufactures imported by the Company. The leading houses owed much of their dominance to the restriction of competition brought about by the Company's monopoly. Under the auspices of the monopoly, overstocking of British goods in the Bengal market was prevented, together with the competition and falling prices which that would have involved. Since the Company issued the licences which permitted involvement in the China trade, it was also able to control commercial competition within that trade. Plainly, a certain degree of competition between the houses was beneficial to the Company, a fact illustrated by the high returns which resulted for the Company from the auction of opium to private traders. However, it was feared that the existence of too many houses would bring instability and bankruptcies, from which the Company would ultimately suffer.

Even within this framework of mutual monopoly, fluctuations of fortune for both the houses and the Company were not unknown. The return to England of many mercantile partners caused not only a drain of capital from the Bengal houses to Britain, it also created room for a growth in the number of houses, in spite of the controlled economic environment of the Company monopoly. The break up of old partnerships often led to the spawning of new mercantile houses, as old partners went their separate ways. The number of houses increased from 16 in 1803 to 25 in 1812 and the number of insurance companies increased from six to 11 in the same period.[44] Withdrawals by departing partners exacerbated the problems of capital shortage in Bengal brought about by the war. The heavy military and administrative expenditure of the Minto regime, and the cessation of bullion exports from Europe and America to India, caused severe contraction of economic activity by 1813. By this time the Bengal administration more than ever depended upon the financial assistance of the agency houses.

Free trade and the Charter Act plunged the Bengal administration into an even deeper crisis by upsetting the symbiotic relationship between the Company and the agency houses. The sudden opening of the Bengal market to British exports brought by private traders in 1813/1814 had crucial consequences for the commercial organisation of Bengal. Hectic speculation in Bengal goods for the British market forced up the value of the rupee against sterling. This was alarming for the Bengal administration, since in 1813 it needed to borrow substantial sums from the agency houses for the Investment. The Company bills and securities normally issued to raise funds for the administration offered a far lower exchange for the rupee than that to be obtained in private transactions.[45] Furthermore, the sudden rise in demand for Bengal commodities stimulated the agency houses to invest their already scarce resources in production of those commodities in demand. The relationship between the administration and the agency houses was becoming increasingly strained.

From 1813 to 1817, the financial problems precipitated by the opening of the Indian trade, combined with wars with the Nepalese and the Marathas, placed the Bengal administration under continual financial pressure.[46] In these years, high military expenditure exacerbated the serious economic difficulties just described, to pose serious problems for the Bengal administration. The value of the annual Investment fell almost continually during these years, and only rapid victory over the Marathas in December 1817 prevented the most severe crisis for the administration. The Marquis of Hastings has been described as a man who followed Wellesley's great imperial ambition, and it seems that but for his success against the Marathas, this quality would have proved his undoing.[47]

In the event, Hastings' imperial instincts were to stand him in good stead. The instability brought to the Bengal economy by free trade began to change in nature. Those Bengal commodities which had proved so popular in the British market after 1813 began to decline in popularity by 1817/18. Bengal piece goods rapidly lost favour and were soon followed by raw cotton, when peace with the US reopened supplies from that area.[48] Other commodities such as silk and indigo also declined, and the outlook was bleak for those Bengal houses which had invested heavily in these commodities. Falling demand for Bengal commodities in Britain was associated with a new phenomenon – the rapid increase of British-made cotton goods into Bengal, particularly after 1816.[49] This created a new problem – how to remit to Britain the returns from these rapidly expanding imports. Since demand for Bengal goods was falling in Britain, private traders found it increasingly difficult to remit money to Europe through the medium of Bengal exports. This was exactly the reverse of the situation of 1813 when Bengal goods were so much in demand. The rupee fell drastically against sterling, and money was plentiful. A situation arose where large quantities of capital accumulated in Bengal and could find no productive outlet which might furnish a means of remittance.[50]

The situation was made even more difficult by the effect upon the agency houses of this revolutionary reversal of the balance of trade. With the increased imports of British manufactures, the number of mercantile houses dealing with the distribution of these commodities increased dramatically. In 1815 there were about 20 major British firms in Calcutta, dominated by the six powerful houses. By 1829 there were 32 firms, many having connections with outports in Britain. This reflected their main concern with the export of British manufactures. The six dominant houses faced unwelcome competition not only in the distribution of British manufactures, but also in their traditional country trading activities. The new houses became involved in the country trade and tried to break into other activities hitherto dominated by the old houses. The disastrous result of their venture into the China trade has been summarised by Greenberg as 'increased competition, overabundant stocks, falling prices and general depression'.[51]

In August 1818 the need for new markets was brought to Hastings' attention by a report from the import warehousekeeper of Calcutta who attributed the collapse of several mercantile houses to the need for new markets and the glut of British manufactures. Increased competition among the Bengal agency houses in both the distribution of British imports and the old commercial enterprises of Bengal was exacerbated by the fall in British demand for Bengal goods, and by the saturation of the Bengal market by British cotton goods. Falling prices and overstocking in both these spheres created a growing demand in Bengal for new markets for both Indian and British manufactures.

The glut of unremitted capital in Bengal and the lack of suitable outlets for sound investment combined with intensified competition to create other problems. Many of the older houses depended upon their function as investors of capital. The collapse of demand for Bengal commodities forced these houses to seek new investment opportunities, many of which proved to be unreliable. This development further undermined the commercial structure of Bengal, and a contemporary correspondent, John Crawford, regarded it as a major factor contributing to the eventual demise of many of the older houses in 1831.[53] In this extract Crawford comprehensively described the effect of the post-1813 competition:

> The competition of the more prudent and cautious commercial traders of Europe, which followed the change of 1814, enabled

the latter to engross a considerable share of the export trade, heretofore nearly monopolised by the six firms. It was then that deprived to a considerable extent of the ordinary mode of employing the large amount of deposits which still continued to flow in upon them, they felt obliged to resort to other and more precarious means.

These 'precarious means' included housing in Calcutta, shipbuilding, tanneries, cotton mills, coffee and spice plantations and rice mills. When the collapse of 1831 came, the funds of the Calcutta firms were trapped in these often only marginally profitable activities. As Crawford says:

> Such funds were, consequently, unavailable to meet their obligations. To these imprudent speculations is to be ascribed the immense amount of nominal balances which appeared on the books at the credit of partners of the concerns, at the time of their failure.

It is important to grasp that the old firms' need for outlets for investment, and for markets for Bengal produce, changed their attitudes to the role of the Malay archipelago in the Eastern economy. The archipelago, which had long been developing into an important market for Indian cotton and opium, came to be seen as a safety valve for the increased pressure on the Bengal economy after 1813. This urgency for new markets and investment outlets, and its direction towards South-east Asia, has not been clearly isolated as a factor promoting British resistance to the Dutch after 1815. Indeed, the nature and expansion of Bengal-based commerce into South-east Asia after that date has not been fully analysed within the context of the debate surrounding the foundation of Singapore.

Certainly the Bengal administration and leading private merchants such as Palmer were deeply concerned about the advancing Dutch threat. Following the return of Java to Dutch authority, Hastings was notified in both 1817 and 1818 of increasing difficulties involved in pursuing trade with the island. The Bengal Commercial Reports for both years indicated an appreciation of the importance of the Bengal trade with Java.[54] There was also alarm at the prospect of the trade being severely curtailed. In 1818 the Board of Trade advised Hastings that

> The valuable and extensive productions of Java have justly rendered the island a place of first importance in a commercial point of view, and the disadvantages which may eventually be sustained by the mother country by the restoration of Java to his Netherlands Majesty are almost incalculable.[55]

They also pointed out to Hastings the value of Bengal's export trade to the island:

> the place became under our government a mart for the numerous products of the rich surrounding islands, conveyed there by native coasting vessels, and in return opium, piece goods of various kinds, tobacco, salt and other commodities, the manufacture and produce of India were taken away, tending greatly to promote the interests of British India.

In the following year these warnings became even more urgent:

> The advantages which flowed to Great Britain from the conquest and possession of Java were so obvious, that the restoration of the island to the Netherlands Government has been very generally condemned as one of the greatest errors against sound policy that ever was committed.[56]

The Board argued that trade with other parts of the archipelago had also suffered as a result of Dutch efforts to re-assert their authority. Particularly it was felt that Bengal's commerce with Sumatra was under threat, following a decrease in the value of Bengal's exports to the island in 1818/19:

> With respect to this decrease it may be fairly ascribed, we are of the opinion, to the restoration to the Netherlands authorities of their settlement at Padang which has given the Dutch an influence on this coast which is prejudicial to our trade.

For Bengal's commercial community, John Palmer made plain his support for a policy of resistance against Dutch revival in the archipelago. He strongly advocated British retention of Malacca, in defiance of the 1814 Convention, and was a vocal supporter of the establishment of a new British port in the archipelago. Such a port, argued Palmer, could become an emporium for the commerce of the region, and dramatically strengthen the position of British trade. In the end, his views on the siting of such a port proved prophetic.

> The Dutch will not suffer factories or even intercourse where they are established; and unless we choose to relinquish the trade we must struggle for a possession somewhere in the straits of Singapore, Dryon or Bangka.[57]

Palmer expressed his views most strongly to private merchants such as David Brown at Penang, and to company officials such as W. Farquhar at Malacca. Palmer also used his considerable influence in Calcutta to fuel the Bengal administration's alarm at developments in the archipelago.

Tensions between the British and the Dutch began to build up after 1816, when the Dutch had re-established their authority over Java. In the following two years they set about restoring their authority over the Malay states, to return their monopoly to its former strength. This policy involved persuading and coercing Malay rulers to trade only with the Dutch, excluding all commercial intercourse with other Europeans. With this objective in mind, the Dutch sent agents to Pontianak in Borneo, to the Lampongs area in southern Sumatra, and to the south of the Malay peninsula, with instructions to impress the Malay rulers with Dutch determination and strength.

British officials and merchants were alarmed by these moves. At Penang anxiety grew at the extension of Dutch influence, and the impending return of Malacca. The mercantile community of Penang feared that the Dutch would remove all duties at Malacca, and establish the port as a formidable competitor. It was widely feared that the Dutch could exploit Malacca's greater proximity to the islands of the southern archipelago to undermine Penang's position. William Farquhar, Commandant at Malacca, saw that the surrender of Malacca would effectively deliver the southern archipelago into Dutch hands. However it was T.S. Raffles who led British resistance to Dutch ambitions, initially with only cautious support from Bengal, but later with much more positive encouragement.

After the return of Java to the Dutch in 1816, Raffles returned to Britain temporarily out of favour with the Company. His policy of retaining Java and expanding British political and commercial influence throughout South-east Asia had been rejected by the British even before the Convention of 1814. However Raffles did not remain idle after his return to England. He used his energies to further his opinions among the highest ranks of the EIC and government.[58] Raffles expressed his views in person, and in minutes drafted to Company Directors and government ministers. In a long paper to George Canning, President of the Board of Control, entitled 'Our interests in the eastern archipelago', he set out his basic strategy to curtail Dutch expansion.

In this, Raffles argued that the British treaties with the native states which he had concluded as Lt. Governor of Java morally and legally obliged the Dutch to protect British trade in the archipelago. However the crux of his plan involved the acquisition of a new station at the centre of the southern archipelago, either at Bangka or Riau. This central settlement would form, with the old settlements of Penang and Bencoolen, a chain of ports confronting the Dutch and preserving the Straits of Malacca and the Straits of Sunda for British commerce. A clear line of demarcation would be established against future Dutch expansion. The central port would also function as an entrepot to attract the trade and produce of the southern archipelago and provide an outlet for British and Indian exports. While this central port was crucial to his strategy, Raffles did not restrict his attention to that objective. Total exclusion of Dutch influence from Sumatra required a strong British presence, and so he advocated a British settlement in Acheen to protect the northern entrance to the Straits. Bencoolen and its satellite settlements on the western coast of Sumatra were to be maintained, a strategy which Raffles advocated particularly strongly after his appointment as Resident at Bencoolen in March 1818. Settlements in Borneo such as the one at Sambas would not only keep the island free of Dutch control, they could also open up markets in the Eastern territories of South-east Asia, particularly Celebes and the Moluccas. Combined with British domination of the Straits of Malacca, a settlement on the Sunda straits would not only deliver control of the archipelago almost entirely into British hands, it would also encourage native smuggling to the new port and away from Java. This would be particularly beneficial to Bengal traders who were increasingly anxious at the prospect of a return to Dutch protectionism. Raffles must have felt his views on this to be fully justified by the Dutch tariff increase in Java in 1818.

Historians such as Wright, Marks and SarDesai have interpreted Raffles' interest in the archipelago as a desire to find new markets for British industrial exports, principally textiles. This interpretation of Raffles' intentions has been a crucial element in the view that the foundation of Singapore was precipitated by the defence of British-based industrial export interests. As there is little evidence of direct lobbying in Britain by export or manufacturing interests for the establishment of a new port in the Malay archipelago, historians have tended to rest their case on Raffles' own statements which indicate that he appreciated the market potential of South-east Asia for British textile exports. Although Raffles clearly did recognise the opportunities for British export expansion, his concern for Eastern economic interests has been underestimated. Insufficient attention has been given to his fear of economic crisis within the Bengal economy. Raffles expressed this fear clearly in his writings. For example, when discussing the need to find new markets in South-east Asia for Indian piece goods, he argued that

> To ensure a market for the manufactures of India, and thus promote its industry and prosperity, and give an advantage beneficial to the energy of its people becomes an object of great and increasing importance. The extraordinary advance of British manufactures having in a great measure excluded those of India from the European market, it is to the populous and

less civilised countries of the further east that we can alone look for a permanent demand ... The consequences which would attend the loss of this trade, limited as it now is, are too obvious to require explanation, and the security and improvement of it are in consequence most intimately connected with the prosperity of our Indian empire.[60]

Raffles was given an opportunity to carry out his policies when he was appointed to take command of the Company's station at Bencoolen, on the west coast of Sumatra, in March 1818. Almost immediately after taking up the appointment, Raffles began to energetically harass the Dutch, and pursue a policy of consolidating the British position in the archipelago. This involved the pursuit in March in 1818 of a scheme to establish a port at Semangka bay at the southern tip of Sumatra, followed by an energetic policy of resistance to the Dutch at Palembang and the Sumatran interior in July. Although later in the year the Governor-General, Hastings, was to reject virtually all of Raffles' moves in Sumatra, Raffles had established a reputation with the British and the Dutch as the leading Company official in the resistance against Dutch recovery. In November, he was to develop this even further, when Hastings called him to Calcutta, and sent him on a mission which involved the establishment of a new British port in the southern archipelago. Raffles enthusiastically took up Hastings' orders and established a British settlement at Singapore in January 1819.

Certainly of all the Company officials and merchants interested in the question of South-east Asia, Raffles was the most energetic, far-sighted and formidable. While others hesitated, he acted swiftly and decisively. Interest in the efforts of this remarkable individual has tended however to lead historians away from recognition of the importance of the efforts of others. Nowhere is this more clearly illustrated than in the case of Hastings.

Hastings has not received adequate attention from historians. His role in the foundation of Singapore has been reduced almost to passive acquiescence. Marks for example writes of Raffles' 'indoctrination' of the Governor-General to the idea of a new station.[61] In SarDesai's account Hastings gave Raffles 'cautious approval' for his plan.[62] Raffles, who went to Calcutta in November 1818 to convince Hastings of the validity of his strategy, has been credited as almost the sole architect of a southern port. This view has obscured the role of the important Bengal firms and Hastings' own concern for the welfare of the Bengal economy. In fact, Hastings did not accept Raffles' views uncritically, as has been implied by SarDesai and Marks.[63] Indeed, Hastings dismissed most of Raffles' proposals as a political impediment to an acceptable settlement with the Dutch, and he seems to have been irritated by Raffles' apparent lack of political finesse.[64] Hastings was coming to the view that Bencoolen, Raffles' own command, should be exchanged for Malacca. In this Hastings showed his interest in the Straits of Malacca and the depth of his understanding of the needs of British commerce in the archipelago.

Hastings was concerned with the welfare of British India, contrary to SarDesai's view that the establishment of Singapore was a measure calculated to open South-east Asia to British manufactures. Hastings perceived that South-east Asia was an expanding market for Indian commodities, and this was a development of considerable importance given the decline of demand for those same commodities in Britain. From his Minute of November 1818, it is clear that Hastings' primary motivation for a new port was the defence of the established trade to South-east Asia in Bengal commodities, rather than the opening of the region to British manufactures.[65] And it is evident that Raffles shared Hastings' concern for the welfare of the Bengal interests involved in the production of these goods.[66]

It seems likely that the idea of a new port was the work of interests and officials in Bengal, as well as of Raffles and the Straits officials. Hastings' own judgement has been underestimated. Far from being a Governor-General led by his subordinates, Hastings displayed an ability to distinguish crucial British interests from the diverse and often conflicting aims of officials and traders. He grasped that the welfare of the China trade and the markets of the archipelago were central to British interests in India and throughout Asia.

After their meeting in November 1818, Hastings despatched Raffles and another official to Penang to deal with the question of the succession to the Achenese throne. Raffles was also ordered to establish a new port in the southern archipelago. After reaching Penang in December, Raffles learnt that Riau and Johore had been taken under Dutch control. Hastings had ordered Raffles to withdraw in the event of confrontation with the Dutch, but Raffles had now come too far to give up his objective. On his own initiative he set out for the south, and reached Singapore on 19 January 1819. Raffles now used his intimate knowledge of Malay politics to advantage. The Dutch had obtained control of Riau by treaty with the Sultan of Johore, Abdul Rahman, but Raffles discovered that Abdul's brother, Tunku Hussein, also claimed the throne of Johore. One of the principal officers of the Johore empire, the Temmengong, supported Tunku Hussein's claim. Raffles offered his support to Tunku Hussein in return for the cession of the island of Singapore to the British. This agreement was consolidated and Singapore was founded. Raffles had achieved his great goal, with the help of William Farquhar, who had accompanied him.[67]

Initially Hastings was uncertain of the legality of the settlement. On 20 February 1819, Hastings had written to Bannerman, Governor of Penang, warning him that Raffles should not press his objectives to the point of forcing a confrontation with the Dutch. Upon hearing that the Dutch were becoming suspicious of Raffles' activities, Hastings strongly advised abandonment of the mission, if its objective had not yet been achieved.[68]

The Dutch expected Hastings to repudiate Raffles' venture. However, upon learning of the establishment of Singapore, Hastings pledged his full support for the settlement in the face of protests from Van der Capellen, the Dutch Governor-General. As Marks shows, in spite of his uncertainty about the legality of Raffles' actions and concern over their consequences for Anglo-Dutch relations in the future, Hastings was sufficiently convinced of the potential of the settlement to wish to maintain control over it for as long as possible.[69] Significantly, Hastings received the full support of the Bengal commercial community. In March 1819, the *Calcutta Journal*, one of a number of mercantile organs in Calcutta, welcomed Singapore 'as a fulcrum for the support of our commercial views and speculations'.[70]

The years which followed the events of January 1819 saw Singapore grow into an indispensible component of Britain's Eastern empire. As an entrepot, Singapore was ideal for the distribution of British and Indian manufactures throughout South-east Asia, and these markets were important both to the turbulent Bengal economy and Britain's rapidly growing industrial export economy. By 1825, 20% of Singapore's total trade was with India, mainly Bengal.[71] The Bengal firms rushed to establish commercial agents at the new settlement, an indication of their great enthusiasm for the port. While Raffles, Farquhar and others had debated, schemed and squabbled over the question of a new port, ultimately it was the defence of Bengal's commercial interests which was the decisive factor. Their importance to the Indian empire had prompted Hastings to disobey London's directive to avoid conflict with the Dutch. In this sense, the Bengal interests were the true founders of the Lion's City.

CONCLUSION

At first, news of the foundation of Singapore was not universally welcomed in Britain. While commercial interests involved in trade with India and the East Indies greeted the acquisition with enthusiasm, the British government was initially embarrassed. The Dutch made their anger known at what they considered to be a blatant disregard for their territorial rights in South-east Asia. It took nearly five years of painful negotiation before a treaty could be signed which met the needs of both the Dutch and the British. The Anglo-Dutch treaty of 1824 established a new order of European power in South-east Asia. The British were firmly established as the paramount power over the Malay Peninsula and the straits of Malacca, while the Dutch retained their supremacy over Java, the paramount power over the Malay Peninsula and the Straits of Malacca, while the Dutch retained their supremacy over Java, the Moluccas and the area to the south of the Straits of Malacca. The British foreswore all ambitions and influence in Sumatra and transferred the settlement of Bencoolen to Dutch authority. In return, the Dutch accepted the British right to Singapore, surrendered Malacca to the British and renounced their former interests in the states of the Malay Peninsula. Not only did the terms of the treaty establish British influence in South-east Asia on a permanent basis, and entrench British commercial infiltration into the area, it also represented a fundamental shift of power within Europe, signifying the decline of the Netherlands as a colonial and European power to a subordinate position in relation to Britain. In this respect, the efforts of Bengal's export interests had precipitated events in South-east Asia which made plain the new supremacy of the British in Europe and the colonial world.

In the late eighteenth century, Bengal's export interests had developed within the context of mercantilist monopoly, with very strong restrictions on commerce between Britain and the Indian empire. The Bengal economy had been developed to meet the needs of this commercial monopoly, and this resulted in the orientation of export production to serve the China trade and South-east Asian markets. The EIC and private merchants had evolved an elaborate and complex financial system which was necessary for this monopolistic form of colonial organisation to survive. In this respect, Bengal's export interests, principally the agency houses, were a product of a particular phase of imperialist economic development.

The end of this phase, marked by the disintegration of the Company's India monopoly in the Charter Act of 1813, necessitated dramatic adjustments and changes in the Bengal economy to meet the new international economic environment. Given the entrenchment of private commercial interests in the old monopoly, and the interdependence and complexity inherent in the old system, it was inevitable that change would be painful, and for some, disastrous. With the flood of cotton textiles to India came new markets and entrepreneurs who competed fiercely with the establishment agency houses and private trade. Ultimately this increased competition brought about the collapse of the old colonial commercial structure in the 1830s, when several of the leading agency houses collapsed. However, for a period of almost 20 years, the Bengal administration and the leading agency houses struggled on, trying to adjust to the new, difficult circumstances. Resistance to Dutch revival and the founding of Singapore were both of them attempts to secure markets for opium and Bengal textiles, thereby strengthening the agency houses in the face of the pressures and destabilisation brought about by the 1813 Charter Act. In this respect, imperial expansion was employed in 1819 to resist unwelcome changes generated from the metropole of empire.

The agency houses and private merchants who financed and controlled Bengal's key export commodities, such as opium, cotton piece goods and indigo, played a crucial role in persuading and influencing Hastings' decision in 1818, and in this respect Singapore was the child of Bengal's export interests. Ultimately, Singapore and South-east Asia could not insure the Bengal agency houses and commercial structure against collapse. In the early 1830s, the inevitable happened, and by 1834 all six major agency houses had collapsed, including the house of John Palmer. It was left to the British government and the Bengal administration to establish the basis of a new organisation for British commercial enterprise in the Charter Act of 1833. Imperial expansion into South-east Asia had failed to save the old colonial export interests.

However, Singapore and the Malay archipelago remained valuable to the British, not only as a commercial and strategic support for trade with China, but also eventually as a valuable channel for British textiles and other manufactures in the markets of South-east Asia. Thus in the long run, Singapore and the Straits Settlements, essentially the product of attempts to bolster the Bengal export economy, served to draw South-east Asia into the rapidly expanding world industrial economy. It was the beginning of a long process of absorption of the Malay peninsula into the British Empire, with all the consequences that entailed for indigenous political and economic development.[72] Britain's industrial interests were to benefit considerably from the Straits Settlements and the later expansion of British rule into the Malay peninsula. Ironically, Singapore, which had come about in an attempt to protect Bengal export interests which had flourished as a monopoly, eventually was to operate to the advantage of British-based export interests who were advocates of free trade.

NOTES

Abbreviations

I.O.L.   India Office Library
J.S.E.A.H.   Journal of South-East Asian History
J.M.B.R.A.S.   Journal of the Malaysian Branch of the Royal Asiatic Society
J.S.E.A.S.   Journal of South-East Asian Studies
S.S.R.   Straits Settlements Records
Eur. Mss.   European Manuscripts

 1. Tripathi, A., *Trade and Finance in the Bengal Presidency 1793–1833* (OUP, 1979, 2nd edn.); Marshall, P. J., *East Indian Fortunes* (OUP, 1976); Singh, S. B., *European Agency Houses in Bengal* (Calcutta 1966).
 2. Tripathi's account is probably the most thorough, although Phillips, C. H., *The East India Company* (Manchester 1940), is also useful.
 3. See Tripathi, ibid.
 4. Tripathi, ibid.
 5. Tripathi, ibid, p. 215.
 6. Habib, I., 'Potentialities of Capitalist Development in the Economy of Mughal India' in *Journal of Economic History*, 29 (1969), 32–79.
 7. Stokes, E., 'The First Century of British rule in India: Social Revolution or Social Stagnation?' Stokes argues that the British adopted a similar position in Indian society to that of previous conquerors, i.e. an elite which sustained its rule by the maintenance of a cumbersome and expensive administrative machine. In this way the British merely continued a process of economic and social stagnation which had first been implemented under the old order.
 8. Chaudhuri, K. N., 'The Structure of the Indian Textile Industry in the 17th and 18th centuries' in *The Indian Economic and Social History Review*, 2, 2/3, (1974).
 9. A particularly useful account of these developments is to be found in the early chapters of Gupta, B. K., *Sirajudaullah and the E.I.C. 1756–1757* (Leiden 1962).
10. Prakash, O., 'Bullion for goods: International Trade and the Economy of early eighteenth century Bengal' in *The Indian Econ. and Soc. Hist. Rev.*, 13, 2 (April/June 1976).
11. See note 9.
12. Marshall, P. J., *East Indian Fortunes*. Marshall charts the decline of the older trade links with Western Asia (particularly the Persian Gulf) in the early 19th century, and shows that it was nearly 50 years before Bengal's trade with China and South-east Asia emerged as an effective replacement for this Western trade. Marshall refutes Furber's earlier thesis that the rise of the China trade coincided with the decline of the Western trade. Furber had argued that the gradual emergence of the China trade prevented any major crisis which might have resulted from the decline of the Western Asia trade. Marshall shows that such a crisis actually did occur between the 1750s and 1780s. See Furber, H., *John Company at Work* (Harvard 1948).
13. Two of the best explanations of the China trade are to be found in Tan Chung, 'The Britain–China–India Trade Triangle 1771–1840' in *The Indian Econ. and Soc. Hist. Rev.*, 2, 4 (Dec. 1974), and Greenberg, M., *British Trade and the Opening of China 1800 to 1842* (Cambridge 1951).
14. Tripathi ibid. pp. 9–10.
15. See Marshall, op. cit.
16. The crisis is explained in depth in the early chapters of Phillips, C. H., *The East India Company* (Manchester 1940).
17. Richards, J. F., 'The Indian Empire and Peasant Production of Opium in the 19th Century' in *Modern Asian Studies*, 15 (Feb. 1981), 59–83.
18. Tripathi, op. cit., pp. 1–36 and Marshall, op. cit.
19. Tripathi, p. 11.
20. Tripathi, p. 11.
21. There are extensive records of Palmer's career, in the Bengal Commercial Records and the Bengal Public Consultations. Palmer's own papers, in the Bodleian Library, Oxford are another valuable source of information.

22. Phillips, op. cit., chs. 8 and 9.
23. Marshall, ch. 4.
24. The best accounts of these expeditions are to be found in Bassett, D. K., 'British Commercial and Strategic Interest in the Malay Peninsula during the late 18th century' in *Malaysian and Indonesian Studies: Essays presented to Sir Richard Winstedt on his 85th Birthday*, eds. Bastin, J. and Roolvink, R. (Oxford 1964). Bassett, D. K., 'Thomas Forrest, an 18th Century Mariner' in *J.M.B.R.A.S.*, 34, 2 (1961), 106–22.
25. The importance of military and strategic considerations at this time have been highlighted in Tarling, N., *Anglo-Dutch Rivalry in the Malay World* (Queensland 1962) and Kennedy, B. E., 'Anglo-French Rivalry in S.E. Asia 1763–1793' in *J.S.E.A.H.*, 4, 2 (Sept. 1973), 199–215.
26. Tregonning, K. G., 'The Founding and Development of Penang 1786–1826' (unpublished PhD. thesis, University of Malaya 1958).
27. Bassett, D. K., 'Anglo-Malay Relations 1786–1795' in *J.M.B.R.A.S.*, 38, 2 (1965), 197–223. Also see Webster, A., 'The Origins of the Straits Settlements: British Trade and Policy in the Malay Archipelago 1786–1824' (Ph.D. thesis, University of Birmingham 1984). Chapter 2 discusses the inadequacies of Penang's geographical position.
28. Of particular importance was a report by a certain Major Kyd to the Bengal Council, 2 Aug. 1795 (Fort William, 28 Sept. 1795), *S.S.R.* G/34/7 I.O.L.
29. Indeed Raffles used his authority to pursue a deliberate policy of expanding and entrenching British commerce throughout South-east Asia. See Bastin, J. 'Raffles and British Policy in the Indian Archipelago', *J.M.B.R.A.S.*, 27, 1 (May 1954), 84–119.
30. Richards, J. F., 'The Indian Empire and Peasant Production of Opium', op. cit.
31. This consensus has been developed through the work of a number of historians, particularly Wright, H. R. C., 'The Anglo-Dutch Dispute in the East 1814–24' in *Economic History Review*, 3, 2 (1950–51), 229–39; SarDesai, D. R., *British Trade and Expansion in South-East Asia 1830–1914* (Bombay 1977); Marks, H., *The First Contest for Singapore* (Nijholt, Gravenhage 1959).
32. See the Palmer papers, Eng. Lett. C.86 Bodleian Library, Oxford.
33. A particularly interesting account of Palmer's connection with Syed Hussein is to be found in Wurtzburg, C. E., *Raffles of the Eastern Isles* (London 1954), pp. 500–30.
34. Minute of Governor Bannerman of Penang (undated), *Dutch Records* I/2/29 Vol. 28 I.O.L.
35. Details of this connection are to be found in papers relating to the case of Edward Swale Portbury vs George Charles Lindsay, 1815. *Records of the Supreme Court* C.H.C.A. (Calcutta High Court Archives), Calcutta, West Bengal.
36. Knight, G. R. 'John Palmer and Plantation Development in Western Java' in *Bijdragen*, 131, 2/e (1975), 309–37. The article also shows that Palmer had a close commercial and financial connection with Deans, Scott and Co., a British agency house based in Java.
37. See Tarling, N., 'The Palmer Loans' in *Bijdragen*, 119, 2 (1963), 161–88.
38. Deposition of Luis Barretto, partner in the agency house of Joseph Barretto, 16 Nov. 1803 in the case of Thomas Asken vs Gavin Hamilton and Alexander Aberdein, 1803. *Records of the Supreme Court*, C.H.C.A.
39. The case of Portbury vs Lindsay (note 35).
40. Tarling, *Anglo-Dutch Rivalry*.
41. Phillips, *The East India Company*, ch. 7.
42. Op. cit.
43. Phillips, op. cit., p. 46, for a description of the 'Investment'.
44. Tripathi, op. cit., p. 120.
45. Tripathi, ibid., pp. 122–3.
46. Tripathi, ibid., pp. 126–7 and 132–3. The Nepal War lasted from late November 1814 until 1816, and the war with the Marathas lasted for the whole of 1812.
47. Tripathi, ibid., p. 123.
48. Tripathi, ibid., p. 136.
49. Tripathi, ibid., p. 137.
50. Tripathi, ibid., p. 137.
51. Greenberg, *British Trade and the Opening of China*, p. 85.
52. Import Warehousekeeper, J. Trotter to George Udny, Acting President of the Board

of Trade, 19 July 1818, *Board of Trade Proceedings*, Vol. 346, Aug. 1818. West Bengal Archives, Calcutta. A copy of this was sent to Governor-General Hastings.

53. Crawford, J., 'A Sketch of the Commercial Resources and Monetary and Mercantile System of British India with suggestions for their Improvement by means of Banking Establishments' (1837) in Chaudhuri, K. N., *The Economic Development of India under the E.I.C.* (Cambridge 1971).

54. The Bengal Commercial Reports are kept in the I.O.L, London.

55. Bengal Commercial Reports 1817/18, Range 174, Vol. 29, I.O.L.

56. Bengal Commercial Reports 1818/19, Range 174, Vol. 30, I.O.L.

57. Palmer to Brown (sent between March and June 1818), Eng. Lett. C.86 p. 289, Bodleian Library, Oxford.

58. Raffles was closely associated with Charles Grant, probably the most influential Director of the time.

59. See note 31.

60. 'Substance of a Memoir on the Administration of the eastern islands by Sir Stamford Raffles', *Raffles Papers*, Eur. Mss. D/742/39 I.O.L.

61. Marks, op. cit., p. 69.

62. SarDesai, op. cit., p. 34.

63. Marks, op. cit., SarDesai, op. cit.

64. Hastings' Minute, Nov. 1818, *Dutch Records*, I/2/29, Vol. 28, I.O.L.

65. See note 64, ibid.

66. See quote, p. 162–3 above.

67. For a more detailed account, see Wake, C. H., 'Raffles and the Rajas' in *J.M.B.R.A.S.*, 68, 1 (May 1975), 47–73.

68. Marks, op. cit., pp. 50–1.

69. Marks, ibid., p. 51.

70. Turnbull, C. M., *A History of Singapore 1819 to 1975* (Oxford 1977), p. 11.

71. Wong Lin Ken, 'Singapore: Its Growth as an Entrepot' in *J.S.E.A.S.*, 9, 1 (March 1978), 50–84.

72. For an insight into these long-term developments, see Khoo Kay Kim, *The Western Malay States 1850–73: The Effects of Commercial Development on Malay Politics* (Kuala Lumpur/OUP 1972).

APPENDIX I

The Export Trade from Bengal to the Malay Archipelago 1796 to 1826 (The Private Trade)

All figures below are in Sicca Rupees. Exports to the Malay Archipelago appear under the general heading of 'Penang and the Eastward', in the Bengal Commercial Reports of 1796 to 1826, from which these statistics were taken. Figures for the export trade to Java are also incorporated into (ii).

Year	(i) Total of Bengal's Export Trade to the World (Value)	(ii) Bengal's Export Trade to 'Penang + the Eastward' and Java (Value)	(ii) as a % of (i)
1796/97	15157185 (estimate)	910430 (estimate)	
1797/98	16156362 (estimate)	910430 (estimate)	
1798/99	11741612 (estimate)	910430 (estimate)	
1799/1800	24450404	2206227	9.0%
1800/1801	26662002	2570640	9.6%
1801/1802	28018661	2171382	7.8%
1802/1803	34975883	3331968	9.5%
1803/1804	35288304	1978098	5.6%
1804/1805	35347781	2366409	6.7%
1805/1806	35634550	3480416	9.8%
1806/1807	39712927	1734394	4.4%
1807/1808	37176696	2454308	6.6%
1808/1809	26753585	2488012	9.3%
1809/1810	32272530	2166552	6.7%
1810/1811	33450988	2969007	8.9%
1811/1812	33374689	3601668	10.8%
1812/1813	30918179	2847289	9.2%
1813/1814	35497688	2740753	7.7%
1814/1815	41017352	3530288	8.6%
1815/1816	49988116	3351434	6.7%
1816/1817	55156128	2015981	3.7%
1817/1818	55274395	2665536	4.2%
1818/1819	50776900	1970476	3.9%
*1819/1820	NOT AVAILABLE	5810935	NOT AVAILABLE
1820/1821	58032610	5938200	10.2%
1821/1822	65949510	4957661	7.5%
1822/1823	67003440	5549895	8.3%
1823/1824	62798331	4625177	7.4%
1824/1825	56108031	3010094	5.4%
1825/1826	56778626	2069980	3.7%

* After 1819/1820 both the Company's trade and the Private Trade are combined as one figure.

Source: Bengal Commercial Reports
1796 to 1826
174/13 to 174/37

APPENDIX II

The Opium Export Trade from Bengal to the Malay Archipelago 1796 to 1826 (The Private Trade)

All figures are in Sicca Rupees, and indicate the value of exports.

Year	(i) Opium Exports from Bengal to the World	(ii) Opium Exports to Penang and then Eastward from Bengal	(iii) Opium Exports from Bengal to Java	(iv) (ii) + (iii)	(v) (iv) as a % of (i)
1796/97	1331255	604800	NONE RECORDED	604800	45.5%
1797/98	1077961	376619	NONE RECORDED	376619	35.0%
1798/99	1255579	337268	NONE RECORDED	337268	27.0%
1799/1800	2880593	1215172	NONE RECORDED	1215172	41.7%
1800/01	NOT AVAILABLE	NOT AVAILABLE	NOT AVAILABLE	NOT AVAILABLE	NOT AVAILABLE
1801/02	2751915	916105	NONE RECORDED	916105	33.3%
1802/03	3943951	1035666	NONE RECORDED	1035666	26.3%
1803/04	4188225	913989	NONE RECORDED	913989	21.7%
1804/05	6412283	1503158	NONE REQUIRED	1503158	23.3%
1805/06	5866888	2125209	NONE RECORDED	2125209	35.7%
1806/07	4712611	1162365	NONE RECORDED	1162365	25.0%
1807/08	6331952	1478072	NONE RECORDED	1478072	23.3%
1808/09	5838855	1545525	NONE RECORDED	1545525	26.3%
1809/10	6487483	1476141	NONE RECORDED	1476141	22.7%
1810/11	7939103	1406220	264300	1670520	21.0%
1811/12	7719798	1768780	459705	2228485	28.6%
1812/13	6353422	1442175	205685	1647860	25.6%
1813/14	7293946	1247655	233225	1480880	20.4%
1814/15	9176506	1249670	342145	1591815	17.2%
1815/16	8239631	1545721	598332	2144053	26.3%
1816/17	8720372	1145981	365408	1511389	17.2%
1817/18	8041327	924362	323335	1247697	15.6%
1818/19	8234950	1037185	91720	1128905	13.7%
1819/20	6060969	677352	1508739	2113091	35.7%
1820/21	12055894	1519652	1722249	3241901	26.9%
1821/22	9119220	958461	1154630	2113091	23.3%
1822/23	14208153	1454682	1570225	3024907	21.3%
1823/24	10539345	1853670	967245	2820915	27.0%
1824/25	9082732	1738604	420325	2158929	23.9%
1825/26	8268393	906953	181885	1088838	13.2%

Source: Bengal Commercial Reports

APPENDIX III

The Opium Export Trade from Bengal to China 1796 to 1826 (The Private Trade)

All figures are in Sicca Rupees, and indicate the *value* of exports.

Year	(i) Total of Bengal's Opium Export Trade to China (Value)	(ii) The Opium Export Trade to China as a % of Total Opium Export
1796/97	539325	40.5%
1797/98	586064	54.3%
1798/99	103084	9.0%
1799/1800	1428716	50.0%
1800/1801	NOT AVAILABLE	NOT AVAILABLE
1801/1802	1386166	50.2%
1802/1803	2710470	68.5%
1803/1804	2918294	68.5%
1804/1805	4478460	69.9%
1805/1806	3294578	56.2%
1806/1807	2637230	55.8%
1807/1808	4607280	73.0%
1808/1809	4058874	69.4%
1809/1810	4689248	72.5%
1810/1811	5815507	73.0%
1811/1812	4542968	75.2%
1812/1813	4311383	68.0%
1813/1814	5574277	76.9%
1814/1815	7117764	86.2%
1815/1816	5806912	70.4%
1816/1817	6856385	78.7%
1817/1818	6331569	78.7%
1818/1819	6850839	83.3%
1819/1820	3498188	57.8%
1820/1821	8585311	71.4%
1821/1822	6787154	74.6%
1822/1823	10961631	76.9%
1823/1824	7590920	71.9%
1824/1825	6667349	73.5%
1825/1826	7105544	86.2%

Source: Bengal Commercial Reports.

APPENDIX IV

The Export Trade in Cotton and Silk Piece Goods from Bengal to the Malay Archipelago 1796 to 1826 (The Private Trade)

All figures are in Sicca Rupees. As with opium, exports of piece goods to the Malay Archipelago, appear under the general heading of 'Penang and the Eastward'. Figures for the export trade to Java are also included.

Year	(i) Cotton and Silk Piece Goods Exports from Bengal to the World	(ii) Cotton and Silk Piece Goods Exports to Java	(iii) Cotton and Silk Piece Goods Exports to Penang + the Eastward	(iv) (ii) + (iii) Total for Malay Archipelago	(v) (iv) as a % of (i)
1796/97	7426752	NONE	274456	274456	3.7%
1797/98	5748617	NONE	336870	336870	5.9%
1798/99	1850030	NONE	521902	521902	28.2%
1799/1800	12001199	NONE	703341	703341	5.9%
1800/1801	NOT AVAILABLE	NOT AVAILABLE	NOT AVAILABLE	NOT AVAILABLE	NOT AVAILABLE
1801/1802	16591309	NONE	833224	833224	5.0%
1802/1803	18594676	NONE	1474559	1474559	7.9%
1803/1804	16169478	NONE	703751	703751	4.4%
1804/1805	11085509	NONE	544975	544975	4.9%
1805/1806	11849670	NONE	103994	103994	0.9%
1806/1807	13340738	NONE	330257	330257	2.5%
1807/1808	11588949	NONE	707679	707679	6.1%
1808/1809	5479147	NONE	649244	649244	11.9%
1809/1810	11141674	NONE	579135	579135	5.2%
1810/1811	13119535	108887	789589	898476	6.9%
1811/1812	10756519	273106	541910	815016	7.6%
1812/1813	9412758	340201	354973	695174	7.4%
1813/1814	14960404	148145	473689	621834	4.2%
1814/1815	24042545	122989	936078	1059067	4.4%
1815/1816	13156587	378392	404900	783292	6.0%
1816/1817	16599943	116698	189282	305980	1.8%
1817/1818	13234725	225237	643172	868409	6.6%
1818/1819	11524356	81753	361356	443109	3.9%
1819/1820	11666071	475246	89496	564742	4.8%
1820/1821	10840652	637295	395496	1032791	9.5%
1821/1822	11029537	1153608	685379	1838987	16.6%
1822/1823	11066798	660586	441996	1102582	10.0%
1823/1824	8252566	458486	600920	1059406	12.8%
1824/1825	7544751	96498	327088	423586	5.6%
1825/1826	6995003	318271	105543	423814	6.1%

Source: Bengal Commercial Reports

5

Tribesmen, Government and Political Economy on the North-West Frontier

R. O. CHRISTENSEN

This chapter is about the economic aspects of the interrelations between the independent tribes of the North-West Frontier and the British-Indian government. Its main point is that the course of change in the tribal economy must be understood not so much in terms of the conventional factors of production, as in terms of tribal political culture and the policy objectives of the government.

The tribes in question occupy a peripheral position. They were, indeed, never incorporated into British India, but have continued to live beyond the administrative border of the North-West Frontier, a border already roughly established when the British annexed the Punjab in 1849. The border defines not only a political-administrative division, but also an ecological and cultural division. Put broadly, the trans-border tribes are politically independent, possess a mountainous habitat, and maintain a way of life based on the principles of the *Pakhtunwali* (the tribal 'code of honour'). The cis-border tribes, on the other hand, are 'settled' in the sense both that they are under government administration and that they are generally sedentary agriculturists inhabiting the river basins of the region. They are also widely thought of as having lost many of the cultural traits associated with adherence to the *Pakhtunwali*.[1] In the view of the independent tribesmen, the 'settled' tribes have virtually ceased to be true Pakhtun, having become peasants not very different in their way of life from those of the Punjab.

The position of the trans-border Pakhtun tribes, like that of many other tribal societies, is economically and politically marginal.[2] Their territory is poor in revenue-yielding resources, is relatively inaccessible to would-be invaders, and affords good terrain for partisan guerrilla warfare by the tribesmen. No government has ever attempted to establish its administration over the tribes, because of the high costs (fiscal and military) that would be incurred in doing so. Yet for governments of the region relations with the tribes have always been a matter of importance, partly because of the strategic position of their territory, which forms the mountain buffer separating Afghanistan from the plains of the Indus river system. Moreover, although the tribes have never been integrated politically into any state system, for a combination of ecological and political reasons most of them have come to be economically highly dependent on both the 'settled' population and the government. Indeed, the position of the tribes may be described as one which combines political independence with economic dependence – a position which it has not always been easy for either the tribes or the government to maintain.

The relationship between the tribes and the government is crucial to any understanding of the processes of change in the tribal economy and society during the century of British frontier administration. This is not to argue simply that British policy 'caused' whatever change occurred; but there is much evidence to support the proposition that historically interaction with external forces – usually states – has been the main factor in generating change in tribal societies.[3] Yet one prolific writer on the Pakhtun tribes has taken a quite different view. The anthropologist Akbar Ahmed has consistently argued that until very recently external government has had no impact on the socio-economic organisation of the independent tribes. In the past, Ahmed maintains, tribal–governmental relations have served to reinforce the traditional tribal way of life expressed in the principles of the *Pakhtunwali*. It has only been since the early 1970s – as a result of policies pursued by the Pakistani administration, and the opening up of employment opportunities for many of the tribesmen in the Gulf – that change has begun to become evident.[4] This argument assumes the existence of a static, 'ideal-type' model of Pakhtun society which the tribesmen have been able to maintain in the face of external forces.

Ahmed's view is not without substance. By the close of the British period the North-West Frontier was considered to be economically one of the most 'backward' regions of India.[5] And there is little to suggest that there had been any fundamental change in the structure of the tribal economy in the previous century. But the absence of such a structural transformation does not mean that the socio-economic organisation of the tribes was merely static. Certain important quantitative changes – notably the growth of population, of income, of commerce, and employment opportunities – did occur during the nineteenth and early twentieth centuries, prefiguring those economic processes described by Ahmed as being of only very recent origin. If these changes failed to constitute development (in whatever sense of that problematic word), the explanation lies not in the lack of impact by the British government, but in the character of government policy and the way external forces were mediated by tribal values and political organisation. In short, the 'backwardness' of the tribal economy is largely a problem of political economy.

ECOLOGY AND POLITICAL CULTURE IN TRIBAL ECONOMIC ORGANIZATION

A common – and superficially quite plausible – way of explaining tribal socio-economic organisation is in terms of ecology. Indeed, the influence of the physical environment on tribal culture seems self-evident.[6] A rugged terrain, climatic aridity and a largely un-cultivable land area – all have been taken to account for the tribes' relative poverty, their dependence on the sedentary, agricultural population of the administered districts, their rejection of external government and their militant defence of their political independence. Thus a stereotyped picture has emerged of barren hills producing wild and predatory tribes in a state of permanent rebellion against the outside world.[7]

This rather oversimplifies matters. For one thing, the tribal areas of the North-West Frontier do not form a homogeneous physiographic entity. There are many variations in local ecological conditions, and associated with these are co-variations in types of socio-economic organisation. In the valley of Swat, for example, the availability of water for irrigation and of fertile land in the valley floor has allowed the development of a fairly intensive agricultural economy; and unlike other tribal areas, Swat has always been a net exporter of rice, wheat, *ghi* and other foodstuffs.[8] Certain tribes, by virtue of their location on commercial routes, have become specialists in the local or regional carrying trade. Others, again, have engaged in such activities as forestry, mineral extraction and small-scale manufacturing (notably in firearms), depending on local environmental factors and resource availability. In so far as ecology has shaped the tribal economy, it has been in the way the economic organisation of each particular tribe has to varying degrees been the outcome of adaptation to the ecological niche it occupies.[9]

Nevertheless, some of the best known and most 'ideal-typical' of the independent tribes (these would include the Afridis, Mohmands, Orakzais, Darwesh Khel Wazirs and Mahsuds) do in certain aspects of their economy approximate to the stereotype. These tribes are generally engaged in both pastoralism and cultivation, activities which are mainly for subsistence and which account for most of tribal income. Several of them practise a variety of transhumance, migrating with their flocks and herds to upland pastures in the summer and back to lowland pastures in the cooler months. These migrations enable tribal members to avoid the climatic extremes of sub-freezing temperatures in the mountains in winter, and the intense heat of the plains in summer. Migration is also a way of making optimal use of scarce land resources, since it means that limited pasturage does not become over-grazed. Cultivation is generally *barani*, but in some places, where valleys open out to form small alluvial basins, irrigation is possible. The most important point about the economy of these tribes is its lack of self-sufficiency in subsistence requirements, and the tribes' consequent dependence on the outside world. The shortfall in tribal subsistence production is difficult to estimate, but in most cases it is likely that between a fifth and a quarter of tribal income had to be obtained from external sources. During the British period, large numbers of tribesmen spent at least part of the year engaged in petty trade or working as agricultural labourers in administered territory. In addition, there were those sources of income provided by the government, to be discussed below.

It should be mentioned that the popular view of the tribes as predators on the sedentary-agricultural population finds little support in the evidence. Only one or two tribes or tribal sections (e.g. the Mahsuds and the Zakha Khel Afridis) carried out raids with any degree of regularity, and these usually had little economic significance, being acts of hostility towards the government rather than a means of securing an income. According to returns for the period 1920/21 to 1941/42 (the only years for which figures are available), the mean annual cash value of property stolen by the independent tribes on the entire North-West Frontier was less than Rs. 57,000. This average conceals the fact that by far the greater part of raiding in this period occurred during the disturbances which followed the third Anglo-Afghan war, or was connected with the insurgency in Waziristan. In several years there were no raids at all in most of the frontier districts.[10] In ecological terms, the relation of the independent tribes with the sedentary population of the administered districts has been one of symbiosis or interdependence, rather than predation.

More generally, the relationship between ecology and economic organisation is not quite as simple as it initially appears. Certainly, given a static and low-level agricultural technology, such factors as the availability of water and soil fertility set the limits of what is possible in the sphere of production. But within these limits, ecology is not the only determining factor. Political organisation and the tribal value-system have also played a very significant part in patterning economic activities and the deployment of resources. The absence of any centralised system of government among the tribes and the strongly-held desire to remain independent of external polities have given rise to and been reinforced by an ethic which stresses egalitarianism, self-help and the maintenance of honour, an ethic embodied in the *Pakhtunwali*. While it could be argued that these cultural features are closely related to ecological conditions, a more convincing approach is to treat them as independent variables influencing important aspects of tribal economic organisation in their own right.

The influence of political culture and the *Pakhtunwali* on the tribal economy is evident in two general respects. First, there is the obligation on tribal members to uphold group and personal honour; and the ability to do so requires the possession of adequate means of defence, since feuds and other types of violent conflict are often intense and chronic. Consequently, available investment resources have tended to be channelled towards the acquisition of arms and ammunition rather than towards the improvement of productive capacity.[11] The prevalence of feuding has been a disincentive to investment in another way, by deterring tribesmen involved in conflict from engaging in cultivation. The man working his plot of land was an easy target; and common tactics in feuds were to burn the crops of an enemy or destroy his irrigation channels. According to one frontier official, Evelyn Howell, there existed in Tirah and Waziristan 'the traces of terraced fields ... to show that once men grew corn where now there is no tillage'; a vivid testimony to the economic consequences of insecurity of life and property.[12]

The second aspect of the influence of values and political culture on the tribal economy is the aversion to types of activity considered dishonourable, or to deviations from the ideals of conduct prescribed by the *Pakhtunwali*. To many tribesmen, such activities include both trade (the occupation of Hindu *banias*) and agriculture (the occupation of the sedentary population of the administered districts). The aversion to these activities is, of course, relative rather than absolute. Most tribesmen are engaged for at least part of the year in some form of agricultural activity. And, as noted, certain tribes have been able to exploit their location by specialising in commerce. But those tribesmen who can afford to, leave such matters to others. Much of the trade in tribal territory was carried out not by the actual members of the tribes, but by men of client status who (until 1947) were Hindus and Sikhs. And most menial tasks — such as the carrying of water, the gathering of wood-fuel and the cutting of forage grass — have been left to women. Even for those tribesmen engaged in trade and cultivation, these have rarely been full-time occupations; and for the majority much of the annual economic cycle has been spent in under-employment.

Thus the low productivity of most of the tribal economy of the North-West Frontier has been the consequence not only of a poor resource-base, but also of the way in which available resources have − or have not − been used. And this in turn may be seen as the result of the priorities established by tribal values and political organisation. As one report put it:

> Unproductive though a great part of tribal territory may be under existing conditions, too much stress can be laid upon the economic factor [i.e. an unfavourable ecology]. Its importance is we think greatly exaggerated, with picturesque legends of hungry hills that breed more than they can feed. But poverty has not prevented the tribesmen from paying fantastic prices for their armament or kept down the price of human life or of women in tribal circles. It is in fact only certain sections of whom it has been literally true to say that they must raid in order to live.[13]

There could be few clearer statements in rejection of the simple environmental determinist explanation of tribal economic organisation. In short, the economy of the independent tribes has to a large extent been patterned by the higher value placed on the defence of honour than on the accumulation of wealth, and by the tribesmen's preference for investment in rifles rather than in ploughs.

The cultural-ecological approach outlined here also puts a question-mark over the conventional factor-mix analysis of economists. While it could be shown that all three productive factors − land, labour and capital − have historically been in short supply on the North-West Frontier, such statements of factor availability do not provide a very adequate basis on which to assess actual or potential economic change and development. A far more fruitful line of analysis is to examine the ways in which adaptation to ecological conditions and the political culture of the tribes have influenced the utilisation of factors. Thus, the deployment of land as a productive factor (that is, excluding large areas of uncultivable scrubland and scree with little or no productive potential) is closely related to both specific environmental features and culturally determined tribal preferences. Similar points can be made about the deployment of labour and capital. When considerations of honour and defence meant that labour was idle for much of the year and available capital was directed to non-economic ends, there is little to be gained from regarding the tribesmen merely as members of that much-mentioned species *homo economicus*. This is not to suggest that they are entirely unresponsive to economic forces, but they are very much a political species as well.

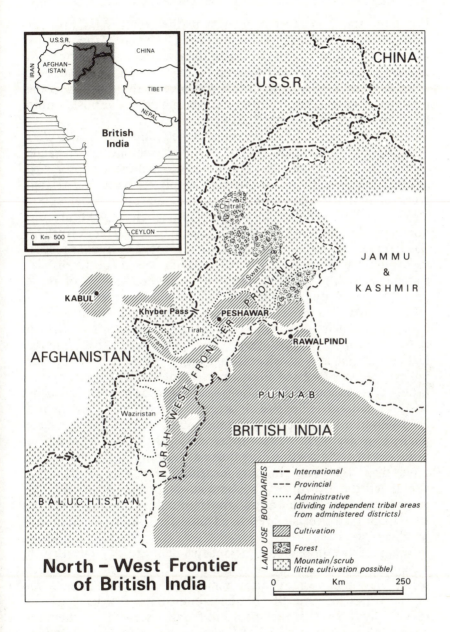

North – West Frontier
of British India

Map labels:

USSR · CHINA · AFGHANISTAN · IRAN · TIBET · NEPAL · British India · CEYLON · 0 Km 500

CHINA · U.S.S.R. · JAMMU & KASHMIR · Chitral · Swat · KABUL · Khyber Pass · Tirah · PESHAWAR · Kurram · RAWALPINDI · AFGHANISTAN · NORTH–WEST FRONTIER PROVINCE · Waziristan · PUNJAB · BRITISH INDIA · BALUCHISTAN

Legend:

LAND USE BOUNDARIES

–·– International
– – Provincial
·········· Administrative
(dividing independent tribal areas
from administered districts)

▨ Cultivation
Forest
Mountain/scrub
(little cultivation possible)

0 · Km · 250

THE BRITISH IMPACT:
GOVERNMENT POLICY AND ITS ECONOMIC CONSEQUENCES

From the start, the British interest in the North-West Frontier was predominantly military-strategic. Throughout the century after the annexation of the Punjab at least a quarter of the strength of the Indian Army was stationed on the frontier, and the most conspicuous aspect of the British presence in the region was the establishment of a chain of cantonments and defensive posts within and just beyond the administrative border.

In fiscal terms it was always accepted that the North-West Frontier was and would remain a deficit region. The revenue yielded by the administered districts never remotely approached government expenditure on military supply, defence and related construction work (including roads and railways), tribal allowances and militia pay, and so on. This deficit expenditure undoubtedly had a considerable (though unquantifiable) effect on the frontier economy. The establishment of British rule tended to promote growth in other ways. Much was made in official statements of the benefits resulting from the creation of more peaceful conditions on the frontier. While the economic side-effects of *pax Britannica* should not be exaggerated – and besides, tribal insurgencies continued right until the last years of British rule – it probably contributed to an expansion of cultivated area in the administered districts. More important was land revenue policy. Before 1849 the Sikhs had claimed a half-share of the produce as revenue, which seems usually to have been levied by coercive methods. The British greatly reduced the demand, to a level below that in most other regions of India; and this low revenue pitch, together with the rise in agricultural prices, did much to bring about the growth of commercial farming in Peshawar and other districts.[14] Thus military expenditure and revenue policy stimulated the growth of trade and cultivation in British administered territory. There was no growth of manufacturing industry; what manufacture existed remained almost entirely of the domestic handicraft type.[15]

What of the impact on the independent tribes? The British view was that improving economic conditions on the frontier would play an important part in achieving the long-run integration of the tribes into the life of the administered districts, and so reduce any threat that they posed to frontier security. In the mid-nineteenth century a policy of *laissez-aller*, of giving the tribes free access to markets in British territory, was regarded as sufficient. It was, noted Reynell Taylor of the Wazir tribesmen in 1852, far better that they should wander through our well-stocked bazaars, talk with strange merchants, acquire a taste for clean clothes, roofed houses, and sweetmeats, and experience the advantages of a warm market themselves, by finding a ready sale for their own cattle, tobacco, and other hill produce, than that they should be shut up in the hills to gaze on the luxuriant but indifferently protected vallies [*sic*] of the plain, and with no better employment than to plan highway robbery and assassination, if not more active hostility.[16]

A few years later it was remarked of the Afridis that

these mountain barbarians are beginning to be influenced by self-interest and civilization.[17]

The wealth which has been thrown amongst these tribes by trade with us was unknown to them under Sikh or Dooranee rule.[18]

Whether tribesmen themselves shared this mid-Victorian faith in the beneficial effects of commerce as an agent of peace and progress seems doubtful. Certainly, the descriptive evidence suggests that there was a significant growth in trade between the independent tribes and the administered districts in the second half of the nineteenth century. But it is unlikely to have transformed tribal economic organisation very greatly.

The opening up of trading opportunities to the tribes did not provide them with a vent for surplus. Very little tradeable surplus existed. Although several thousand tribesmen appear to have been engaged for part of the year in selling such products of tribal territory as hides and skins, timber and firewood, and fruit and nuts, this trade was very small-scale and served mainly to enable the tribesmen to purchase foodstuffs and manufactures (particularly cotton cloth) not produced in tribal territory. With the exception of Swat, however, the main feature of tribal commerce was the net visible deficit with the administered districts.[19] Given the cultural and resource-endowment constraints described above, commercial growth failed to stimulate any noticeable movement of factors into production for trade. Nor can it be regarded as an important source of growth in tribal income. Trade accounted for only a small proportion of total tribal income (probably no more than 5 per cent), and whatever growth occurred was more a symptom than a cause of improving income.

Market forces, then, provide only a partial explanation of the growth of the tribal economy during the British period. Yet growth there was. Perhaps the main indicator of this growth was the increase in the independent tribal population. This increase is quite impossible to measure with any degree of accuracy, since the census estimates of tribal population – based on little more than rough guesses by the frontier authorities – are very unreliable. These estimates do, however, indicate a demographic growth in the tribal areas commensurate with that in the administered districts. In 1911 the population of the tribal population approximately doubled. The natural rate of popu-almost 2.4 million.[20] It is likely that in the century of British rule the tribal population approximately doubled. THe natural rate of population growth may have been even higher, since there are indications that in the second half of the nineteenth century fairly large numbers of tribal families migrated to and settled in British territory.[21] This steady demographic increase could not have occurred without a corresponding increase in total (though not necessarily *per capita*) tribal income.

A second indicator of the growth of income among the tribes was the increase in the quantity and the improvement in the quality of firearms possessed by them. As noted above, a rifle is regarded by the tribesmen as a priority investment, and since the purchase of a good weapon could take several years' individual savings, the growth in tribal armament is an important symptom of greater tribal prosperity. In the mid-nineteenth century only a small minority of tribesmen owned firearms, and these were all smooth-bore muskets. A century later, over half the tribesmen were armed, mostly with high-velocity precision rifles.[22] Nothing demonstrates more clearly than this expenditure on more up-to-date weapons – which probably constituted the largest single type of investment by the tribes – the precedence given to political over economic considerations. The intriguing question, though, is: how could the tribesmen afford to expand and improve their arsenal, when the resource-base was narrow, their productive technology was static, and their population was growing?

The answer is to be found largely in the character of the political relationship between the tribes and the government.[23] The most persistent problem which the British had to confront on the North-West Frontier was how to establish a stable framework for tribal 'management'. The problem, that is, was one of how to gain an adequate measure of political influence among the tribes so as to obtain their co-operation in arrangements for frontier security – or at least, to prevent their hostility towards the government. British policy towards the tribes was, in effect, a variant of 'indirect rule', adapted to tribal political organisation.

The most important of the management techniques employed by the British was to provide the tribesmen with sources of income. Perhaps the best-known of these was the payment of allowances to the tribes in return for entering into agreements for the safeguarding of military-commercial routes (such as the Khyber) and the protection of their respective parts of the frontier. These payments were often described by contemporaries as 'blackmail', but a less tendentious view would be that they represented a relatively cost-effective method of providing for frontier security (given such possible alternatives as the extensive use of military force in tribal territory). Whether the allowance payments had much impact on the tribal economy is doubtful, however. The total payments to the tribes in the 1930s — by which time the system had been extended to nearly all tribes — were less than Rs. 900,000 annually, and they can have formed only a small increment to tribal spending power. Their purpose, anyway, had never been economic, but political: to purchase tribal goodwill, and in particular to win over tribal leaders to acceptance of government policy.[24]

A far greater contribution made by the government to tribal income was through the employment of tribesmen as soldiers in the Indian Army and as militiamen in the various irregular forces established on the North-West Frontier. This employment reflected a complementarity of interests. From the point of view of the government, it formed part of the arrangements for the political integration of the tribesmen and was a way of utilising their martial skills and inclinations. From the point of view of the tribes, it provided their members with an income, military training and an 'honourable' occupation. During the three decades or so before World War I, the 'Pathans' (Pakhtun) became one of the most favoured of the 'martial races' of India. The figure of trans-border tribesmen serving in the Indian Army rose from less than 2,000 just after the second Anglo-Afghan war, to a peak of over 7,500 in 1915 (see chart).[25] At the same time there was the formation of several frontier corps (the Khyber Rifles, the Tochi Scouts, the Kurram Militia, and so on) which absorbed many thousand more tribesmen. Not all the earnings of these men were injected into the tribal economy, but the contribution of military income to tribal income was nevertheless considerable and probably accounted for most of the growth described. In the case of the most heavily recruited of the tribes, the pay of the soldiers and militiamen and the pensions of retired soldiers may well have constituted as much as a quarter of tribal income from all sources.

This increasing dependence on military employment placed the tribes in a vulnerable position, however. The growth of their income had become contingent on their ability to persuade the government that it was worth obtaining their political goodwill through enlistment. During World War I this arrangement broke down. Disaffection and

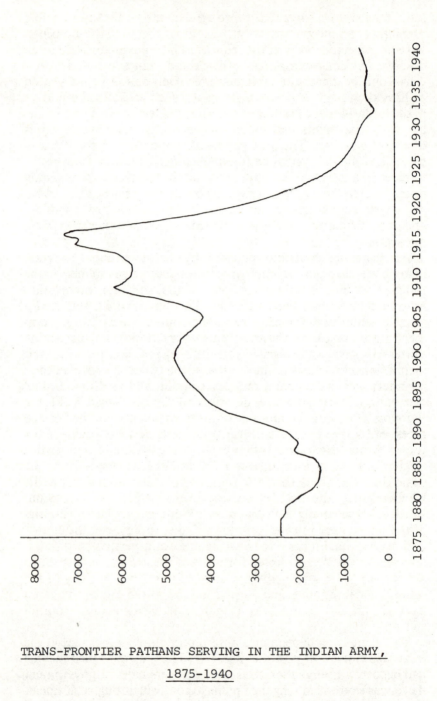

TRANS-FRONTIER PATHANS SERVING IN THE INDIAN ARMY,

1875-1940

dislike of trench warfare led to the desertion of many tribesmen and the discharge of many others. Former soldiers fought in large numbers on the Afghan side in the Anglo-Afghan war of 1919, and formed the core of anti-government dissidence among the tribes in subsequent years. Enlisting the tribesmen ceased to have any political or military value: 'The presence of trans-border Pathans in the regular army is from a purely military point of view an embarrassment instead of a source of strength.'[26] Besides, financial retrenchment and the consequent reduction in size of the Indian Army greatly restricted the possibilities of re-opening tribal recruitment. By the late 1920s there were fewer than 1,000 independent tribesmen who were regular soldiers, and the figure did not pick up again until well into World War II.

The rapid decline in military employment after 1915 imposed great strains on the tribal economy, which had considerable political repercussions. The large numbers of unemployed tribesmen – especially the younger men – were seen as a standing threat to the stability of the frontier arrangements by both the government and the established tribal leaders. The irregular forces on the frontier were maintained as a safety-valve measure based on 'the simple economic proposition that in order to live honestly the young men of the tribes must be given Government employment'.[27] But this form of employment represented only a partial solution to the political problem, and did not compensate for the sharp reduction in military income.

Otherwise, the pre-World War I strategy was abandoned, or even reversed. Instead of providing a significant share of tribal income through military employment, as a means of promoting political integration, the government devised schemes for employment that were conditional on the tribes' acceptance of encroachment on their independence. In Waziristan this was obtained by the military occupation in strength of tribal territory. During the late 1920s road-building projects and military supply contracts provided work for the Wazir and Mahsud tribesmen, which, according to a propaganda article in *The Times*, had greatly raised tribal living standards:

> Instead of being content with maize and water and homespun, the clansman wants white flour, cigarettes, tea, silken *pugris*, good cotton cloth, elaborate waistcoats, better shoes; and his women – 'What', said one despairingly, 'do they not want?'[28]

Rising consumer expectations solved no problems. By the mid-1930s the temporary boost to tribal income had come to an end, and the tribes of Waziristan had embarked on a full-scale insurgency under the leadership of the Faqir of Ipi. Elsewhere on the frontier, schemes to construct roads into tribal territory met with little success. When in the early 1930s Afridi leaders complained of the hardships being experienced by the tribe, the government responded with a proposal that recruitment into the Indian Army would be re-opened if a road suitable for military use were constructed into the heart of tribal territory. The proposal presented a difficult dilemma: should the tribesmen accept the offer of employment, and so compromise their political independence? or should they maintain their independence intact and suffer the economic consequences? Initially the proposal was accepted, and road construction began in 1935; but it had soon to be halted as tribal opposition grew.[29] In the last resort, the tribesmen set a higher value on political independence than on sources of income provided by government to limit that independence.

In the end, the course of relations between the tribes and the government revealed clearly the underlying weakness of the tribal economy – its lack of self-sufficiency and its failure to generate employment for a growing population. British rule stimulated few endogenous sources of growth among the tribes. Instead, the tribesmen had become increasingly dependent on the government for income and employment as part of a political bargain. After World War I the fragility of the bargain was exposed, as both sides came to realise the incompatibility of their respective political objectives. And the tribesmen, on their side, became conscious of their poverty in relation to the sedentary-agricultural population, and of the welfare costs of maintaining their political independence.[30]

In the closing years of the British period the problem of tribal 'management' was defined in slightly different terms from previously. 'Like all political problems', Sir William Barton argued, 'the Frontier problem is largely economic.'[31] This perception of the problem was not new, but it led to a shift in emphasis. The official catch-phrase became 'peaceful penetration', and attention began to be given to the development of the tribes' subsistence economy and the improvement of their welfare. In the late 1930s schools and hospitals appeared in certain parts of tribal territory, inoculation programmes were introduced, and agricultural grants were made.[32] These measures, small in themselves, formed the start of what was intended to be a very long-term policy of assimilation by raising economic conditions in the tribal areas. Development, as the 1946 five-year plan for the frontier explained, was at base a political exercise:

the objectives must be the ultimate development of the whole Tribal Areas to the same standards of civilization as those designed for India as a whole, in order to provide ... security from tribal aggression.[33]

The difficulty, though, was that the tribes were highly resistant to any policy perceived by them as a challenge to their way of life and political independence. If they accepted welfare measures, it was only on their terms:

Although the tribesmen themselves often welcome the introduction of measures clearly designed to promote their own welfare provided that the cost of these is not charged to them, their instinct to freedom to manage their own affairs is strong, and much patient and persevering work will be required to win them from their own suspicions.[34]

By 1946, in any case, there were more urgent political problems to be dealt with, and the impasse on the North-West Frontier was left to the Government of Pakistan to resolve. And that is another — though not exactly a different — story.

CONCLUSION

There are three general points to be made about the tribal economy of the North-West Frontier during the century of British rule. The first is that Ahmed's argument that tribal socio-economic organisation was unaffected by government policy, though not altogether wrong, is nevertheless misleading. True, there was no transformation of the tribal mode of production. Technologically, pastoral-agricultural activities seem to have remained static; the growth of commercial links with the administered districts provided at most a weak stimulus to production; and there was almost no growth of manufacturing. But external forces did bring about change in other respects. The government provided the tribesmen with military employment and other sources of income which generated considerable growth in the tribal economy. This allowed a steady demographic increase and also a rise in consumption standards, although quite a large proportion of income growth went into arms expenditure. It is likely that the degree of economic interdependence of the tribes with the sedentary-agricultural population grew appreciably.

Second, the pattern of and the constraints on change in the tribal economy have to be understood very largely in terms of two sets of political factors: tribal political culture and organisation, and the policy objectives of the government. Adherence to the principles of the *Pakhtunwali* has meant both that the tribes have not for the most part engaged very extensively in subsistence farming (though ecological factors are also important in this respect), and that resources available for investment have been diverted from economically productive uses to the accumulation of weaponry. The vigorous defence of political independence explains the rejection by some tribes of employment schemes that were conditional on their acceptance of the presence of external government in their territory. The British, for their part, provided the tribesmen with military employment because by tribal values such employment was honourable, and because it integrated the tribesmen into the arrangements for frontier security. The tribesmen recruited as soldiers and militiamen were never regarded as a resource being utilised in an economically efficient way, but above all as men who required an occupation because otherwise their martial skills would be used against the government. But when, during and immediately after World War I, this arrangement collapsed, much of the political logic of the tribal recruitment policy was destroyed and tribal military income was sharply curtailed. The government provision of income to the tribes, in short, was a function of the assessment of its political value.

This leads to the final point, that the economic consequences of British policy towards the tribes have to be understood in the rather broader context of political priorities on the North-West Frontier. In so far as the government had an interest in the economic condition of the tribes, it was only as an incidental aspect of the primary concern to achieve frontier security. Relations with the tribes were never perceived in any but political terms until the last decade or so of British rule. Equally, the level of tribal economic development was never an issue before the 1930s. The tribesmen themselves seem often to have made a virtue of their relative poverty, as a sign of their hardiness and their distinctness from the more prosperous sedentary-agricultural population. Only in the late British period was the problem of relations with the tribes re-formulated in a way which stressed the importance of economic conditions; and by then the political matrix of these relations, which largely determined the possibilities for introducing measures to improve tribal production and welfare, was too well-established to be dismantled. The problem of development is, after all, historically of very recent origin, and it is perhaps ahistorical to judge the course of change in the tribal economy and the impact of British policy by mid-twentieth century criteria.

NOTES

1. See Akbar S. Ahmed, *Pukhtun Economy and Society: Traditional Structure and Economic Development in a Tribal Society* (London, 1980), ch. 4 and *passim*.
2. Cf. Ernest Gellner, *Saints of the Atlas* (London, 1969), pp. 2–3; also David M. Hart, 'The Tribe in Modern Morocco: Two Case-Studies', in E. Gellner and C. Micaud (eds.), *Arabs and Berbers: from Tribe to Nation in North Africa* (London, 1973), pp. 25ff.
3. For an overview which cites a wide range of studies, see A. M. Khazanov, *Nomads and the Outside World* (Cambridge, 1984).
4. Ahmed, *Pukhtun Economy*, op. cit., chs. 1, 3, 10, 11 and *passim*; also 'The Arab Connection: Emergent Models of Social Structure among Pakistani Tribesmen', *Asian Affairs*, n.s. 12 (1981), 167–72.
5. See, e.g. G. L. Mallam, *Five-Year Post-War Development Plan for the North-West Frontier Province and Tribal Areas* (Peshawar, 1946), pp. 1–6.
6. See, e.g., David Dichter, *The North-West Frontier of Pakistan: a Study in Regional Geography* (Oxford, 1967), pp. 3ff.
7. For an early example of this view, see Richard Temple, *Report Showing the Relations of the British Government with the Tribes, Independent and Dependent, on the North-West Frontier of the Punjab, from Annexation in 1849 to the Close of 1856*, in *Selections from the Records of the Government of India* (Calcutta, 1856).
8. Capt. A. H. McMahon and Lt. A. D. G. Ramsay, *Report on the Tribes of Dir, Swat and Bajour* (1st edn. Calcutta, 1901; new edn. Peshawar, 1981), p. 49. See also Fredrik Barth, *Political Leadership among Swat Pathans* (London, 1959), pp. 5–6, 79.
9. For a pioneering analysis, see Fredrik Barth, 'Ecologic Relationships of Ethnic Groups in Swat, North Pakistan', *American Anthropologist*, 58 (1956), 1079–89.
10. *Report on the Administration of the Border of the North-West Frontier Province*, 1921/22 to 1941/42.
11. Cf. Sir William Barton, *India's North-West Frontier* (London, 1939), p. 265.
12. Evelyn Howell, *Mizh: a Monograph on Government's Relations with the Mahsud Tribe* (1st edn. Simla 1931; new edn. Karachi, 1979), p. 97.
13. *Report of the Tribal Control and Defence Committee 1931* (Delhi, 1931), p. 10.
14. H. R. James, *Report on the Settlement of the Peshawar District* (Lahore, 1862), p. 56; E. G. G. Hastings, *Report of the Regular Settlement of the Peshawar District of the Punjab* (Lahore, 1878), p. 188; *Report on the Administration of the North-West Frontier Province 1901–03* (Peshawar, 1903), p. 30.
15. *Census of India, 1921*, vol. 14, NWFP (Peshawar, 1922), p. 26; Mallam, *Post-War Development Plan*, op. cit., p. 6.
16. R. G. Taylor, *District Memorandum: Derah Ishmael Khan*, in *Selections from the Records of the Government of India* (Calcutta, 1852), p. 83.
17. *General Report on the Administration of the Punjab and its Dependencies 1860–61* (Lahore, 1861), para. 164.
18. Note by Lt.-Col. H. B. Edwardes, Commissioner, Peshawar Division, 19 March 1860, file of the Office of the Commissioner, Peshawar Division, no. XXXIV/F/8.
19. See, e.g., the statement on the trade between Peshawar District and neighbouring independent tribal areas in L. W. Dane, *Final Report of the Settlement of the Peshawar District* (Lahore, 1898), p. 21.
20. *Census of India, 1911*, vol. 13 (Peshawar, 1912) and *Census of India, 1941*, vol. 10 (Delhi, 1942).
21. See, e.g., D. C. J. Ibbetson, *Report on the Census of the Panjab Taken on the 17th of February 1881*, vol. 1 (Calcutta, 1883), pp. 63, 86.
22. Annual *Statement of Fighting Strengths and Armament of Independent Tribes on the North-West Frontier, 1907–47*, compiled by the Office of the Chief Commissioner/ Governor of the NWFP.
23. The term 'political' in this context has much the same meaning as that given it by British-Indian administrators, who, Macaulay remarked, 'always use the word "political" as synonymous with diplomatic'. Quoted in T. C. Coen, *The Indian Political Service* (London, 1971), p. 5.
24. *Report of the Tribal Control and Defence Committee*, loc. cit.

25. These figures are derived from the *Annual Caste Return of the Native Army in India* (title varies), 1874–1940. There is certainly some margin of error in the figures; the method of compilation seems to have varied over time also. The chart does, nevertheless, provide a fair guide to levels of tribal recruitment.
26. *Report of the Tribal Control and Defence Committee*, op. cit., p.55.
27. Report on the Administration of the Khyber 1920–21, in file of the Office of the Chief Commissioner, NWFP, no.5/18 of 1921.
28. 'The Changing Frontier: Check to Wazir Blood Feuds', *The Times*, 31 March 1930.
29. *Report on the Administration of the Border of the North-West Frontier Province 1934–35* (Peshawar, 1935), pp.9–10.
30. See, e.g., Application by the Tribes of the Khyber Agency to the Governor, NWFP, no.39/72 FRP.
31. Barton, *India's North-West Frontier*, loc. cit.
32. See, e.g., *The Border (N-WFP) 1939–1940* (Peshawar, 1941), pp.23–5.
33. Mallam, *Post War Development Plan*, op. cit., p.1.
34. Loc. cit.

6

Colonial Education Policy and Manpower Underdevelopment in British Malaya

MARTIN RUDNER

The introduction of modern education in British Malaya followed as a by-product of colonial rule. Colonial administration carried in its wake considerable European investment in trade and primary industry along with a substantial influx of Chinese and Indian immigrants to the new towns, tin mines and rubber estates. If the indigenous Malay agricultural community lay largely outside these economic developments, they were at least due special political treatment by virtue of the principles of protectorate and indirect colonial rule upon which the British rationalised their presence in Malaya. Thus, even more than other instruments of colonial policy, education was obliged to give expression to Britain's differential commitments to the Malays on one hand, and to alien Chinese and Indians on the other, while at the same time ensuring an adequate supply of educated manpower for government service and the commercial economy. The education systems that emerged during the colonial period reflected this divergence of goals between differential communal commitments and manpower training, where ethnic pluralism was very largely coterminous with the dualistic pattern of economic development.

Before the coming of the Europeans, Malay education centred on village schools operating at low levels of institutionalisation.[1] No significant centre of Islamic theology, or schools of thought, arose in peninsular Malaya. At the same time, alien communities resident in Malaya operated their own educational establishments in their native languages. Schools set up by Chinese and Indian traders, whose settlement in Malaya dated from the eighteenth century and earlier, were run essentially as Malayan adjuncts of their respective homelands' education systems. When the Portuguese conquered Malacca in 1511, a school was opened for local Eurasians under Roman

Catholic auspices. By the turn of the nineteenth century Malayan education had already been crystallised along lines linking ethnicity to language, culture and religion, with each group's schools enjoying autonomy in management and curriculum.

EARLY COLONIAL EDUCATION INSTITUTION-BUILDING

English education began in Penang in 1816 as a result of efforts by the Church of England and with financial support from the East India Company, then responsible for administering British outposts in Malaya. In 1823 Sir Stamford Raffles, founder and administrative architect of Singapore, endowed on behalf of the East India Company the establishment of an English school for all races in the new settlement of Singapore − some 23 years before annual education grants were offered in England.[2] While English schools operated with official sponsorship and finance in the British-ruled Straits Settlements of Penang, Malacca and Singapore, Chinese and other vernacular schools were left to themselves. From the very beginnings of British rule in the Straits Settlements, the structure of education was therefore divided according to linguistic and communal streams having separate organisation, financial provision and orientation. The pattern for the next 150 years of education institution-building was thus set.

Despite Raffles' parting injunction that 'education must keep pace with commerce in order that its benefits may be assured and its evils avoided', subsequent progress in educational development in nine-teenth-century Singapore proved almost painfully slow. Neither the Colonial administration nor the newly-established mercantile communities were prepared to underwrite the expansion of schooling. Following the extension of British rule through the Malay peninsula, Christian missionary societies spread from the Straits Settlements to open English-language schools in the main towns of the Malay States.[3] Faced with a rapidly expanding demand for English-educated clerks and subordinate staff for both government service and business, local administrations also set up a small number of government-financed English schools in the Malay States of Perak and Selangor during the 1880s and 1890s.

Meanwhile, traditional Malay education underwent a radical structural and secularising transformation under the impact of 'indirect' colonial rule.[4] Many village Malays viewed with suspicion sponsored secular-oriented vernacular schools. The emergent Westernised elite, on the other hand, expressed a preference for more extensive instruction in English and 'European' subjects (e.g. mathematics) among the Malays. The Colonial authorities, for their part, conceded that there existed a considerable appetite for education among the Malays, but characteristically declined to divert additional public funds from investment in economic infrastructure to the social services.[5]

Chinese- and Indian-language schools in Malaya developed according to the private capacities of their respective communities. In spite of the fact that Chinese constituted nearly half the non-European population of the Federated Malay States (FMS) at the turn of the twentieth century, except in rare instances State administrations declined all responsibility for vernacular education other than in Malay. The official attitude maintained that the Chinese and Tamils, as transients in Malaya, did not merit public finance for their own language schools. This line of argument was reinforced by a declared fear that vernacular education for non-Malays would strengthen racial barriers and inhibit social integration.[6] Denied government finance, the Chinese proceeded to build up their own vernacular primary and later school systems throughout Malaya, financed by voluntary contributions not all of which came from upper income groups. Some of these Chinese vernacular schools were organised and managed by individuals, some by groups, most charged fees and virtually all were China-oriented in curriculum.

The structure of education administration reflected this irregular pattern of institution-building. Even after federation each of the Malay States enjoyed near autonomy in the conduct of education policy. The education policies of the FMS treated schooling essentially as a matter of administration rather than as a programme of public instruction. This was by way of contrast with the Straits Settlements of Singapore, Malacca and Penang, where from 1901 a professional Director of Public Instruction effectively controlled the Colony's education system. In 1906 the FMS and Straits Settlements Departments of Education were merged under a single professional Director of Education based in Singapore. Since the greater part of Malay schooling was located in the Malay States, the vernacular system obtained few direct benefits from this administrative reorganisation compared to the Straits Settlements-centred English schools. Then in 1916, the continuing deterioration of standards in Malay vernacular schools impelled the government to appoint an Assistant Director of Education (Malay) with special responsibility for Malay schools in the FMS and Straits Settlements. With education administration as with much else, the Chinese were left to fend for themselves.

THE EDUCATION OF AN ANGLOPHONE ELITE

From 1903 the policy of the colonial administration was to 'encourage', through government subsidies, private philanthropic organisations to undertake the provision of English schooling. Although this policy relieved the colonial governments of a considerable portion of the direct costs of education, and especially English schooling, the latter still received favourable financial treatment compared to other language streams. Thus in 1937 the Straits Settlements government directed 71.4 per cent of its education budget towards English schooling, notwithstanding the considerably greater enrolment in vernacular schools. Similarly the FMS in that same year allocated 48.3 per cent of its public expenditure on education to English schools alone. This distribution was typical of government spending for education in all the pre-war Malay States and Straits Settlements.

Judged by conventional criteria, the overall quality of English schooling was much superior to that of the other vernacular streams. Only the English stream offered opportunities for local post-secondary education at Raffles College and at the Straits Settlements and Federated Malay States Medical School (1905), later renamed the King Edward VII College of Medicine. A proposed merger of both these institutions into a university college with British affiliation, as a first step towards establishment of a Malayan university, was aborted by the Japanese conquest of Malaya in 1942. Yet, by virtue of curriculum, language of instruction and organisational linkages, access to higher and professional education in pre-war Malaya remained very largely limited to graduates of the English stream.

Though designed to create a Westernised, English-speaking cadre of government officers and clerks, English education was definitely not seen as an agency for broader social modernisation. Indeed, on the contrary, British colonial administrators had early on warned against any general provision of English schooling. In the words of Frank Swettenham, then Resident of Perak, the most advanced Malay State:

> One danger to be guarded against is to teach English indiscriminately ... I do not think it is at all advisable to attempt to give the children of an agricultural population an indifferent knowledge of a language that to all but the very few would only unfit them for the duties of life and make them discontented with anything like manual labour.[7]

For the first four decades of the twentieth century FMS education policy sought to strike a balance between the provision of sufficient English schooling to satisfy urban manpower and colonial administrative needs, while avoiding unwanted social changes among the local population. Though open to all ethnic groups, English education remained very restricted in the number of school facilities and enrolments.

Government ambivalence towards the provision of English education was especially pronounced with respect to the Malay community. English education among Malays remained a prerogative of scions of Rulers and chiefs, for whom special provision to learn English had been made, and for the few others able or willing to overcome imposing cultural-religious barriers to attend alien, infidel schools.[8] In order to avert possible 'economic dislocation and social unrest', government policy deliberately limited the provision of English education for Malays, despite the Colonial commitment to enhance Malay participation in administration.[9] Yet English had become a virtual prerequisite for entry even into minor government service posts, thereby excluding the great majority of Malays.

Veiled criticism by the Rulers of the Malay States of the low level of Malay participation in administration led, in 1905, to the establishment of an English-language residential grammar school, on the British model. The Malay College at Kuala Kanguar was originally conceived as a training school for Malay boys from any social class for public service, but shortly evolved into the educational preserve of Malay royalty and aristocracy – the 'Malay Eton'.[10] Enrolments at Malay College remained constant at about 150 boys of gentle birth, and generous financial provision was made to provide offspring of the traditional Malay ruling class with a proper preparation for entry into the higher-level cadres of the colonial bureaucracy.

The post-World War I trade recession led the colonial administration to try to economise on expatriate salaries by further extending the English education of the Malays. In 1924 the first two English schools were opened in non-urban Malay districts. This departure from past policy of concentrating English education in the towns encountered serious misgivings on the part of British education officials in Malaya, including R. O. Winstedt, then FMS Director of Education. The Malay aristocratic elite was similarly apprehensive lest English schooling in the rural areas undermine traditional values and disrupt the peasant social order.[11] Nevertheless, fiscal requirements dictated education policy, and further led to improvements in English-language instruction in Malay vernacular schools. These measures brought about a considerable increase in Malay enrolment in English schools and in their rate of participation in government service in the 1930s, though both remained predominantly non-Malay in ethnic composition.

If English education and its attendant employment opportunities still remained beyond the reach of most Malays, neither did it touch the bulk of Malayan Chinese population. Although English school fees were not high — indeed these covered but a fraction of their total cost to government — they were well beyond the means of most poor Chinese. At the same time, many Chinese were antipathetic towards English schooling and its bureaucratic orientation, preferring instead their own Chinese traditions. English education appealed mainly to the locally-born, urban, middle-class segment of the Chinese community, who tended to regard English schools as a means of obtaining colonial good graces as well as entry into government service and the professions. Of the 91,534 Chinese children enrolled in schools in British Malaya in 1938, only 27,064 attended English schools, overall a small proportion of their eligible school age group.[12]

Along with a minority of Malayan Chinese, English education also attracted the better-off segment of the other major non-Malay immigrant community, the Indians (and Ceylonese) who had been brought to British Malaya during the early expansionary period to meet the personnel requirements of government departments. Together with their Chinese counterparts these 'middle-class' Indians comprised the great majority of English school enrolment in British Malaya through the 1920s and 1930s.

The deliberately narrow provision of English-medium education for urban and upper-income groups limited its developmental impact upon Malayan society as a whole. Rather than functioning as an agency for social integration, modernisation and development, English schooling served instead to create a privileged Westernised, English-speaking elite geared to administrative office-holding and the free professions. This Anglophone product of the English-language education stream was set apart from the bulk of Malayan society, culturally divorced from the vernacular population and alienated from its social, economic and political environment.[13] It was this cultural gap between the elitist Anglophone caste and the vernacular masses which contributed, as much as anything, to the social distance that characterised ethnic and class relations in pre-World War II British Malaya.

MALAY SCHOOLING FOR RURAL POVERTY

The development of the Malay-medium school system up to the outbreak of the Pacific War gave expression to the fundamental ambivalence of colonial policy towards the Malays. British administration was committed to promoting participation of the Malay ruling class in the colonial government, but was *pari passu* concerned to preserve intact the fabric of traditional Malay society. To reconcile the contradictory educational implications of these divergent goals, Malay education was divided between English and vernacular streams. The former served as an agency of elite socialisation and recruitment while the latter formed an instrument of agrarian social control and Malay cultural preservation.

Malay vernacular education was intended to contribute to moral and physical betterment, without distracting the Malay peasantry from their traditional agrarian preserve. Intellectual creativity was to be confined to traditional rural horizons:

> The aim of the Government is not to turn out a few well-educated youths, nor a number of less well-educated boys, rather it is to improve the bulk of the people, and *to make the son of the fisherman or peasant a more intelligent fisherman or peasant than his father had been, as a man whose education will enable him to understand how his lot in life fits in with the scheme of life around him.*[14]

Colonial policy towards Malay vernacular schooling was generally welcomed by British commercial interests as a device for teaching indigenes the 'dignity of labour' while avoiding 'trouble' through 'over-education'.[15]

The early expansion of Malay vernacular schooling was haphazard and slow. Vernacular school facilities were generally meagre, the quality of instruction poor, the curriculum of little relevance to peasant needs. Many Malay parents were in any case unwilling to send their children, especially girls, to secular, albeit Malay-language schools sponsored by an alien colonial government. Efforts at educational reform introduced by R. J. Wilkinson, Federal Inspector of Schools (1903–6), led to a temporary invigoration of Malay schooling.[16] However, the subsequent period witnessed a general deterioration in Malay education, notwithstanding a continued growth in enrolments.

The crisis in Malay education prompted a reversion to a more explicitly conservative policy. The newly created post of Assistant Director of Education (Malaya) was assigned to R. O. Winstedt, who thereupon visited Java and the Philippines to examine the vernacular and 'industrial' education provided by their respective 'native schools'. What he saw impressed Winstedt as to the prospects of excluding purely 'academic' subjects from the vernacular curriculum and emphasising instead such 'practical' arts as basket-making and horticulture. The stress was always on 'the dignity of manual labour'.[17]

The education reforms introduced at Winstedt's instance institutionalised the 'rural bias' in Malay vernacular schooling. Whereas access to English education would continue to be limited to a select privileged few, the bulk of the Malay population were to be educated in rural-oriented Malay-language elementary schools. The number of years of elementary schooling was reduced, and renewed emphasis was placed on manual and agricultural subjects. Basket-making became virtually the symbol of the 'new' Malay education policy.

Although the rural bias in Malay education presented an illusion of reform, in effect it deprived the rural Malays of the substance of educational progress. To be sure, Winstedt desired to reorient vernacular schooling away from the type that 'merely produced boys who think they ought to be clerks but are insufficiently educated'.[18] But his 'rural bias' implicitly denied the very desirability of intellectual pursuits. The conservative thrust of Winstedt's reforms committed the Malay vernacular school system to the training of peasants for subsistence agriculture, and little else.[19] This benign custodial outlook in education tended to reinforce the prevailing colonial presumption that the Malay peasantry should be retained, and improved, in their traditional *Kampong* environment and saved from the disruptions of modernisation.

A major feature of this educational policy reform was the establishment of a proper teacher training college for the Malay vernacular stream. The Sultan Idris Training College was opened in 1922. Like its aristocratic counterpart, the Malay College, SITC drew its students from throughout British Malaya, and subjected them to the unifying experience of an English mode of education. Yet there were fundamental differences in enrolment and socialisation patterns between the two. While the Malay College educated the scions of the Malay ruling class for careers in the English-speaking, urbane world of the civil service, SITC trained the sons of peasants and fishermen to return to Malay-language village schools. The Malay College produced an Anglicised elite of administrators, SITC nurtured a distinctively Malay intelligentsia.[20]

The spread of Malay education under colonial auspices fomented a resurgence of the (non-governmental) religious school network. Then as now, Islam played a major role in the definiton of Malay culture. At the turn of the century, Cairo-educated religious reformers, the 'Young Faction', set up new-style *medrashas* as part of their quest to purify Islam and render it compatible with contemporary social developments.[21] Borrowing from Egypt and the West, the curricula of these *medrashas* attempted a synthesis of modern secular knowledge and the fundamental principles of Islam. Students were drawn to *medrashas* from both town and country, teachers came from intensely nationalist Java as well as from the Arab world, while numbers of graduates went on to Cairo for higher education. From the *medrashas* came forth a counter-Malay elite, whose intellectual affinities with Egypt and Java shared the current anti-colonialist, pan-Malay mood.[22]

Opinion among this nascent nationalist counter-elite was highly critical of the vernacular education offered Malays in government schools:

> We do not deny that education is necessary for freedom, but we do not believe that education which is given in countries under colonial rule can contain the seeds of freedom. The knowledge that is given to peoples under foreign influence has no purpose other than to impoverish their intellects and teach them to lick the soles of their masters' boots.[23]

While the *medrashas* enjoyed a rapid expansion up to 1913, the reformist views of the 'Young Faction' encountered resistance from the Malay communal establishment. By way of reaction, the Malay establishment wielded its religious and communal authority in favour of government vernacular schools. The 'rural bias' of Malay vernacular education came to reflect the shared vested interests of Malay aristocracy and colonial control.

By the late 1930s enrolments in Malay vernacular schools had expanded more than 15-fold over the 1900 figure, and exceeded 100,000. Nevertheless, this represented fewer than a fifth of the eligible school-aged Malay population of British Malaya. So far as the mass of rural Malays was concerned, the educationally sound principle of instruction in the vernacular language became a negative and intellectually stultifying experience. In its way, colonial education policy may have reflected a genuine feeling of solicitude for Malays. But Malay language education did not acquire either a development goal or a 'higher' cultural-maintenance goal, such as preserving an Oriental culture or even containing European influence. Rather, vernacular schooling for Malays aimed expressly at keeping the peasantry in their station, while teaching the disciplines of industry, punctuality and obedience to authority. This was a static, mundane, even anti-developmental conception of education. Indeed, the establishment and success of the elite Malay College constituted a confession of failure of the purely vernacular stream. In its social conception and economic utility, Malay vernacular schooling constituted an immobiliser of roles, and entailed a veritable 'education for poverty'.[24]

IMMIGRANT EDUCATION AND CULTURAL IRRIDENTISM

The education of the Chinese and Indian populations of British Malaya, apart from those few having access to English schools, remained almost entirely outside the responsibility of colonial government policy. Several attempts were made by the colonial authorities during the 1920s and 1930s to modify Chinese and Indian schooling in terms more compatible with British Malaya. Official concern was directed at the content of the vernacular curricula, and especially their orientation towards overseas states and nationalisms. Yet there was no question of accepting public responsibility, especially financial responsibility, for Chinese and Indian education.

Most privately and communally established Chinese schools originally followed a traditional pedagogical regime imported from Imperial China. The Chinese Revolution of 1911 found strong support among the Malayan Chinese, and it was not unnatural that the revolutionaries' zeal for educational reforms extended to their overseas compatriots.[25] With the beginnings of the National Language movement in China, *kuo yu* (Mandarin) came to be adopted as the language of instruction in most overseas Chinese vernacular schools as well. This facilitated adoption of a curriculum focusing exclusively on the culture, geography and history of China, frequently with a strong republican and nationalist bent. To British officials in Malaya, Chinese education sounded of subversion, pure and simple.[26] Moreover, the arrival of radical left-wing teachers and school managers from China brought many Chinese vernacular schools under Communist influence.

The Republican Government of China retained an abiding interest in Overseas Chinese education.[27] To forestall any loss of cultural identity among Chinese emigrants the Chinese authorities endeavoured to integrate Overseas Chinese schooling into Nationalist Chinese education policy. Chinese Government inspectors were dispatched to inspect Overseas Chinese schools, administrative procedures were laid down, textbooks prescribed, annual reports to Nanking requested and a regular system of grants-in-aid instituted. The overall effect was to institutionalise the China-orientation among Chinese vernacular schools in British Malaya, as elsewhere.

An increasingly radical and anti-western Chinese nationalism, transmitted through vernacular schools, moved the colonial administration from indifference to concern over the education of Malayan Chinese. After taking office as Governor of the Straits Settlements and High Commissioner for Malaya in 1929, Sir Cecil Clementi set about 'Malayanising' the Chinese community and severing their allegiance to China. The Malayan Kuomintang (Chinese Nationalist

Party) was banned (May 1930), and those Chinese leaders and others considered unassimilable, were deported.[28] At the same time the colonial authorities concluded that Chinese educational socialisation patterns were at the core of the problem, so that the brunt of the Malayanisation campaign was to be borne by an incipient schools policy.

A proposal was put forward for the abolition of Chinese vernacular schools and their replacement by so-called 'National Schools' which would be government financed and free to all communities, and in which the language of instruction would be Malay. No Chinese content whatever was to be provided in the curriculum. Most Chinese perceived this National School proposal as a direct threat to their cultural heritage and social status. Strenuous objections against forced assimilation to what most Chinese considered to be an inferior and economically retrogressive Malay language culture led the government to abandon the proposal. An alternative suggestion for universal and free education in English was stillborn, only to be resurrected again in the 1950s.

In the absence of genuinely national norms for Malayan education, the emergent schools policy offered financial inducements in order to bring under control Chinese vernacular education. Chinese schools were given direct grants-in-aid per pupil enrolled from the 1920s, on condition that they accept government inspection and supervision. Most Chinese schools initially declined government aid and attendant control, preferring their independence. However, the Depression of the 1930s drove many schools to apply for government grants, so that by 1938 well over half those receiving a Chinese vernacular education in the FMS and Straits Settlements were enrolled in aided schools. Although motivated primarily by political rather than educational considerations, the limited provision of financial aid, coupled with inspection and supervision, denoted the beginnings of a positive government commitment towards the education of Malaya's Chinese.

Government aid to eligible Chinese schools pertained only to the FMS and Straits Settlements. None of the five Unfederated Malay States accepted responsibility for Chinese-language education, even though Johore alone had over 10 per cent of total Chinese school enrolment in 1938. School enrolments among Malayan Chinese reached approximately a third the eligible age group before the Second World War. Enrolments in Chinese schools in the FMS and Straits Settlements in 1938 (91,534) greatly exceeded the total enrolled in English Schools (26,974). The Chinese school network in British Malaya offered both primary and secondary-level instruction, with access to higher education available back in China. Notwithstanding the colonial authorities' effort to Malayanise education through limited grants, the institutional orientation of Chinese education in effect insularised Chinese-educated manpower within the traditional occupational structure and cultural perspectives of the immigrant community.

Vernacular education for Indians in Malaya was rather less acutely political. FMS authorities looked favourably upon Tamil-language schooling as a means of promoting a needed immigration of Indians for Malaya's expanding plantation industry. A Labour Code enacted in the FMS in 1912 compelled rubber estates with ten or more children of school age to provide and staff free vernacular schools for their Indian labour force. Government subsidies were available for this purpose. The comparatively few Indian schools located in towns obtained limited direct government grants. This arrangement assured the Indian population, most of whom lived on rubber estates, at least a rudimentary elementary education in their vernacular.[29] No facilities existed in British Malaya for post-primary schooling in Tamil or other Indian languages. Indian vernacular education remained intellectually deprived, with little potential for genuine manpower development. Rather, it served more as a palliative for the immigrant manual labour force.

EDUCATION AND DEVELOPMENT IN BRITISH MALAYA

Education in British Malaya evolved distinctive institutional forms, marked by the following characteristics:

(*a*) The propensity of each community, Chinese, Indian and Malay, to have recourse to its own language schools. With few exceptions there was little crossover between language streams. The only language stream attended by all communities were the English schools, so that inter-ethnic educational integration was effectively limited to an Anglophone elite.

(*b*) The tendency of each language stream to provide its own pattern of educational socialisation according to its particular institutional outlook. English education was directed towards creation of a class of officials grounded in Anglophone thought and values. By way of contrast, Malay vernacular schooling reflected colonial feelings of solicitude for Malays, but aimed at preserving their traditional peasant condition. Chinese schools, for their part, maintained a strong China-orientation, while Indian schools were expressly intended to make immigrant Tamil labourers feel 'part of India'. Divergent patterns of educational socialisation, reflecting differential occupational and normative orientations, in effect reinforced the identification of ethnicity and language with economic role and social stratification.

(*c*) The policy of encouraging the private running of schools made for a minimal level of curricular commonality and educational integration in British Malaya. Private schools constituted a major part of the school system in all language streams, except for the Malay. Public expenditure on education seldom exceeded 1.5 per cent of total revenues, and government grants to schools were generally limited and haphazard. The virtual autonomy of private schools in British Malaya created powerful vested interests in the institutional *status quo* which militated against efforts at educational reforms.

(*d*) The divided structure of authority over education in British Malaya made for regional as well as communal linguistic inequalities in the provision of school facilities. Administrative responsibility for education was fragmented among the governments of the Straits Settlements, the (four) Federated Malay States individually and in federation, and the five Unfederated Malay States. Public responsibility for and support of education varied in the different jurisdictions. The resulting unevenness of educational development engendered deficient standards of manpower development.

The character of education in British Malaya constituted a divisive factor, serving to reinforce existing communal and social barriers. Later colonial policy initiatives were to founder upon these discontinuities in education institutionalisation.

Public expenditure on education reached 1.5 per cent of total FMS revenues by 1902. This budgetary proportion was seldom exceeded up to the Second World War. This low fiscal priority for education, characteristic of colonial education policy, made for a correspondingly low level of educational development for British Malaya. Educational retardation was indicated by the relatively low rate of school enrolments before the war, less than a quarter the total eligible age group.[30] The result was a comparatively low rate of literacy among adult (age 15 +) Malayans of all communities, only 41 per cent for males and a mere 7 per cent of females in 1931.[31] While the problem of illiteracy was doubtless compounded by immigration, this widespread underdevelopment of human resources and its segregation along ethnic – linguistic – occupational lines underscored the educational impoverishment of colonial Malaya.

The Japanese conquest of Malaya in 1942 signalled the beginning of the end of colonial dominion over education, as over other public institutions. British rule was no longer incontestable. In education, English and Chinese language schooling were terminated by the Japanese occupation, and Japanese substituted. Malays were given expanded opportunities in administration, reinforcing their nationalist aspirations.

The political turmoil following the post-war British return to Malaya had a further unsettling effect on the existing education system.[32] Malay resistance to British plans for a reconstructed Malayan Union; labour unrest culminating in a Communist-led insurgency ('The Emergency'); and the Communist revolution in China all had an impact on social expectations and demands on education policy on the one hand, and on governmental determination to utilise education policy as an instrument of social control on the other.

In 1949, leaders of the ethnic communities and the British administration accepted the notion that Malaya required an educational system which had an integrative, national focus, while being responsive to the country's ethnic and linguistic pluralism. The following year the government commissioned an inquiry into Malay education, which went beyond its terms of reference to make far-reaching recommendations on education policy generally.[33] These recommendations would have had the effect of reconstituting Malayan education around English and, in a limited way, Malay-language schooling, while disestablishing Chinese and Tamil. This served to plunge education into the vortex of ethnic politics in Malaya.

Whereas the recommended policy changes found favour in the colonial administration, they received little support from the Malays, who were concerned about the subordination of Malay-language schooling to English. The Chinese and Indians, however, were bitterly opposed. Indeed, the education question galvanised the Chinese to political action as never before. In response, the government invited a second inquiry into Malayan Chinese education. Its report recommended that education in Chinese be continued with public support, but that a new curriculum be designed to give Chinese-language schooling a Malayan orientation.[34] (No official inquiry was launched into Tamil education, though the Indian community proceeded to submit its own report and recommendations to the administration.) The result was an effort at compromise. The colonial government proposed to establish a 'national' education system which would be publicly-financed and offer plural language schooling around a common, integrative curriculum; however, English would remain the educationally dominant stream. This compromise solution pleased neither ethnic nor nationalist sentiments, and in the event fell victim to the budgetary stringencies resulting from the trade recession of 1954.

The building of a national education system in Malay(si)a had to await the election of the country's first government in 1955 and its transition to independence. That story has been told elsewhere; suffice to note here that the educational reforms introduced beginning in 1956 have contributed significantly to Malaysian economic and social development.[35] Yet the education system inherited by the elected, independent government suffered from the legacy of structural deformity, diffuse scholastic standards, and chronic underinvestment. Enrolment ratios which underwent a brief spurt immediately after the war regressed during the last years of colonial rule.[36] At the end of the colonial period Malay(si)a was still acutely under-educated in relation to the country's level of economic attainment. This lag in educational development was to leave its imprint on high-level manpower constraints, on social and ethnic inequality, and on regional disparities for some time afterwards.[37]

NOTES

1. On the organisation of education in pre-colonial Malay society, see R. O. Winstedt, *Malaya and its History* (London, Hutchinson's University Library, 1956), pp. 130–1, and Chai Hon-Chan, *The Development of British Malaya, 1896–1909* (Kuala Lumpur, OUP, 1964), pp. 226–7.
2. This school underwent a long series of fluctuations in organisation and function until 1903, when it was made into a government sponsored secondary school, renamed Raffles College in 1928. According to Winstedt, the history of Raffles College was 'an epitome of the stumbles and falls of education in Malaya', op. cit., p. 132. See also E. Wijeysingha, *A History of the Raffles Institution, 1823–1963* (Singapore, University Education Press, 1963).
3. On early British contact with the Malay States and the transformation of British interest from non-intervention to protection, see Chai Hon-Chan, op. cit., pp. 1–37; W. Roff, *The Origins of Malay Nationalism* (New Haven: Yale University Press, 1967), Chap. 1; K. G. Tregonning, *The British in Malaya*. The Association for Asian Studies: Monographs and Papers XVIII (Tucson, University of Arizona Press, 1965); F. A. Swettenham, *British Malaya, An Account of the Origin and Progress of British Influence in Malaya*, rev. ed. (London, George Allen & Unwin, 1948).
4. Rex Stevenson, *Cultivators and Administrators. British Educational Policy Towards the Malays 1875–1906* (Kuala Lumpur, OUP, 1975).
5. Cf. Sir Frank Swettenham, *Report on the Protected Malay States for 1892*, C. 7228, p. 26: 'What we spend on education at present is too small a proportion of our revenue, but until the railways under construction are completed, I fear we cannot greatly increase the expenditure on other services'.
6. *The System of Education in the Federated Malay States*, p. 11. Whatever the merit of this latter argument in principle, the failure of government to provide adequate English (or Malay) school facilities for all non-Malay children and its tolerance of privately financed non-Malay education places doubts on its validity. Note that in 1902 the Conference of Residents agreed to the provision of vernacular education in Tamil 'with the object of making the FMS, from the point of view of the Indian immigrant, an outlying part of India' (ibid., p. 11). Here expedience, the need to encourage immigrant labour for the expanding plantation industries, triumphed over principle.
7. *Annual Report for Perak for 1890*, C. 6576, p. 18

8. Cf. High Commissioner, *Federal Council Proceedings* (1920), p. 1365.
9. R. O. Winstedt, *Education in Malaya* (London, 1924). The quoted phrase 'economic dislocation and social unrest' was to become the conventional slogan in official publications rationalising the denial of English education to the Malay community-at-large.
10. As early as 1905 the Resident of Perak was able to note that 'This school is exclusively for boys of gentle birth' (*Annual Report of Perak for 1905*, p. 12).
11. *Federal Council Proceedings* (1924), p. B57.
12. According to the 1931 Census of Malaya, covering the FMS, UMS and Straits Settlements, there were some 417,000 Chinese in the age group 5–14 years; see T. E. Smith, *Population Growth in Malaya* (London, Royal Institute for International Affairs, 1952), pp. 12–13. Tables VIII, X.
13. For a discussion of the attitudes towards education of English-speaking elites in colonial and post-colonial societies, and their general resistance to the expansion of English educational opportunities, see D. Adams and R. M. Bjork, *Education in Developing Areas* (New York, David McKay, 1969), pp. 94–7.
14. *Annual Report on the Federated Malay States for 1920*, p. 13. Emphasis added, M. R.
15. *Federal Council Proceedings* (1915), p. B67.
16. For a study of Wilkinson's attitudes towards Malay schooling and his resultant educational reforms, see Roff, op. cit., pp. 130–5.
17. 'Report by Mr. R. O. Winstedt, Assistant Director of Education, Straits Settlements and FMS, on Vernacular and Industrial Education in the Netherlands East Indies and the Philippines', *Straits Settlements Legislative Council Proceedings*, Council Paper No. 22 of 1917 (Henceforth: *Winstedt Report on Vernacular Education*), pp. C96–118.
18. *Winstedt Report on Vernacular Education*, p. C118.
19. Winstedt's policies have been subject to considerable debate. For a favourable view of the 'new world of vision ... opened to the Malay', viz. gardening and basket-making, see e.g. J. S. Nagle, *Education Needs of the Straits Settlement and Federated Malay States* (Baltimore, 1943), p. 142, while Roff, op. cit., pp. 139–41 provides a detailed critique of Winstedt's 'rural bias'. Winstedt's antipathy to Malay intellectual development did not prevent him from buidling a personal reputation as a scholar of Malay literature and history.
20. For a detailed study of Malay schooling and elite creation see Roff, op. cit., Ch. 5, esp. pp. 142–3.
21. On the 'Young Faction', or *Kaum Muda*, and their rivalry with the established religious theoarchy, the *Kaum Tua*, see W. Roff, 'Kaum Muda – Kaum Tua: Innovation and Reaction Amongst the Malays' in K. G. Tregonning, ed., *Papers on Malayan History* (Singapore, *Journal of South-east Asian History*, 1962), pp. 162–5; Gordon P. Means, 'The Role of Islam in the Political Development of Malaysia', *Comparative Politics* (Jan. 1969), 273–4.
22. On the role of the *medrashas* in engendering an anti-colonialist, Pan-Malay elite, see Roff, *The Origins of Malay Nationalism*, p. 66.
23. Tengku Abdullah Ahmad, 'Apa Kah Faedah Merdeka' (What is the Advantage of Freedom?). Serual Azhar (Oct. 1924), pp. 492–3, cited in Roff, *The Origins of Malay Nationalism*, pp. 89–90.
24. Cf. Gunnar Myrdal, *Asian Drama* (London: Allen Lane, 1963), pp. 1737–41.
25. On Malayan Chinese and the 1911 Revolution see L. E. Williams, *Overseas Chinese Nationalism. The Genesis of the Pan-Chinese Movement in Indonesia 1900–1915* (Glencoe, Free Press, 1960), p. 171; Png Poh Seng, 'The Kuomintang in Malaya, 1912–1941', *The Journal of South-east Asian History* (March 1961), 6–9.
26. V. Purcell, *The Chinese in South-east Asia*, (London: OUP, 1965), p. 280.
27. Shortly after re-establishing a united China in 1928, the Kuomintang regime convened a National Education Conference. This indicated a departure from the past practice of Chinese governments which had ignored the education of Overseas Chinese. Instead it took upon itself the task of ensuring that all Chinese everywhere obtain a national education. The conferences resolved that Sun Yat-sen's Three Principles be made the philosophical underpinnings of Overseas Chinese education. Cf. Ch'en Ta, *Immigrant Communities in South China* (New York, 1940), pp. 157–60; Yoji Akashi, 'The Nanyang

Chinese Anti-Japanese and Boycott Movement, 1908–1928', *International Conference on Asian History*, (Kuala Lumpur, 1968), Paper No. 4, p. 25.

28. Over a half million Chinese labourers were repatriated during the early 1930s, ostensibly because of the lack of employment resulting from the Depression. However, demands by Chinese that the unemployed be allowed to settle in Malaya's abundant virgin land and plant rice, thus using their agricultural talents and saving on the country's import bill, went unheeded. Cf. R. Elegant, *The Dragon's Seed: Peking and the Overseas Chinese* (New York: St. Martin's Press, 1959), pp. 59–61.

29. On Indian education in British Malaya see J. N. Parmer, *Colonial Labour Policy and Administration* (New York, Association for Asian Studies, 1960), pp. 124–5.

30. IBRO, *The Economic Development of Malaya* (Baltimore: Johns Hopkins Press, 1955), p. 440, and Smith, *Population Growth in Malaya*, pp. 12–13.

31. UNESCO, *World Illiteracy at Mid-Century*, Monographs on Fundamental Education, IX (Paris, 1957), p. 63.

32. On post-war turmoil in Malaya see Martin Rudner, 'Financial Policies in Post-War Malaya: The Fiscal and Monetary Measures of Liberation and Reconstruction', *The Journal of Imperial and Commonwealth History* (May, 1975) and 'The Political Structure of the Malayan Union', *Journal of the Malaysian Branch, Royal Asiatic Society* (1970); James de V. Allen, *The Malayan Union* (New Haven: Yale, 1967); Michael R. Stenson, *Repression and Revolt: The Origins of the 1948 Communist Insurrection in Malaya and Singapore* (Athens, Ohio: Ohio University Center for International Studies, 1969); Anthony Short, *The Communist Insurrection in Malaya, 1948–1960* (New York: Crane Russak, 1975).

33. Federation of Malaya, *Report of the Committe on Malay Education* (Kuala Lumpur: Government Printer, 1951), known as the Barnes Report, after the chairman of the Committee, L. J. Barnes of the University of Oxford.

34. Federation of Malaya, *Chinese Schools and the Education of Chinese Malayans: the Report of a Mission invited by the Federation Government to Study the Problem of the Chinese in Malaya* (Kuala Lumpur: Government Printer, 1951), known as the Fenn-Wu Report after its co-chairmen Dr. William P. Fenn of the United States and Dr. Wu Teh-yao, a United Nations official.

35. On the development of education in independent Malay(si)a, see Chai Hon-Chan, *Education and Nation-building in Plural Societies: the West Malaysian Experience* (Canberra: Australian National University, 1977); R. O. Tilman, 'Education and Political Development in Malaysia', *Yale University South-east Asian Studies*, Reprint Series No. 27; Francis Wong and Ee Yiang Hong, *Education in Malaysia* (Hong Kong: Heinemann, 1971); Martin Rudner, 'The Economic, Social and Political Dimensions of Malaysian Education Policy', in Kenneth Orr, ed., *Appetite for Education in Contemporary Asia* (Canberra: Australian National University, 1977).

36. The enrolment ratio, that proportion of the eligible age group actually enrolled in schools, was estimated to have reached an historic peak of 63% (Member for Education, *Federation of Malaya, Legislative Council Proceedings*, 19 Sept. 1951) for the colonial period in 1951, and subsequently declined steadily to only about 58% by 1954 (International Bank for Reconstruction and Development, *Economic Development of Malaya*, Singapore: 1954).

37. Charles Hirschman, 'Educational Patterns in Colonial Malaya', *Comparative Education Review* (Oct. 1972) calls attention to the long run effects of colonial education policies on ethnic imbalances, social inequality and regional disparities in independent Malaya. On independent Malaysian education policy and development strategies see Martin Rudner, 'Education, Development and Change in Malaysia', *South-east Asian Studies* (Kyoto) (June 1977).

7

The East African Sisal Industry, 1929–49: The Marketing of a Colonial Commodity during Depression and War

N. J. WESTCOTT

The iniquities of the world's commodity markets have for long been the subject of criticism. The following account describes the efforts of one group of tropical primary producers to secure a fair return for their produce in the face of an uncertain world market and an imperially-dominated economy during the hard times of the 1930s and 1940s. It suggests that there was little producers could do to affect the long, or even short run fluctuations of the world economy. Government intervention merely brought existing conflicts of economic interest within the government machine, adding to them the divergent and contradictory interests of the imperial government, and tended to work in the interests of the politically, rather than the economically, dominant group; and although the structure of Britain's imperial economy could operate to the detriment of producers, it could also be exploited by politically powerful producers for their own benefit.

Sisal is now a forgotten commodity, yet 40 years ago it was not only the backbone of Tanganyika's economy but was also, with other hard fibres, a strategic commodity essential to the harvesting of the world's grain crops. Its history during these years therefore illuminates many of the structural problems of all colonial commodity industries and suggests that, at least in the case of sisal, many of the received wisdoms about the role of metropolitan capital and the workings of the imperial economy are too simplistic to provide a satisfactory explanation of how things worked.[1] This is particularly so when we try to understand the effects of the sterling area, exchange controls, and bulk purchase arrangements for colonial commodities introduced during the war. This chapter argues that while these initially operated to the detriment of East African sisal growers, they were able to use their political leverage to turn them to their own advantage and, with the cooperation of the Colonial Office, try to use them to overcome the marketing problems they had suffered during the depression. In the event the more ambitious plans foundered on the opposition of the London merchants and the USA, but sisal producers were nevertheless able to exploit to the full the post-war commodity boom, as some other African producers were not. The fact that settler and plantation producers were able to benefit from the market more than African peasant producers was a result of the former's ability to use their political strength in the colonial state to determine the marketing structure for their crops. Finally, this chapter helps to explain how one colonial industry was able to continue to develop and ultimately prosper despite the difficult economic circumstances of the depression and war.

I

The historical development of the East African sisal industry created an economic structure unlike that of almost any other colonial agricultural industry. The forms of production were similar to those of other plantation industries, but the financing and marketing were distinctly different.

Sisal growing established itself in East Africa during the rapid expansion of settler agriculture in the early years of this century. Of the various estate crops tried by white farmers, sisal proved one of the more successful, being easy to grow, resilient and economic. It grew in areas too dry or poor for more profitable crops like coffee, and, provided there was adequate labour, was cheap to produce and easy to process. Introduced by settlers and requiring expensive processing by machine before it could be marketed, sisal naturally evolved as an estate crop, the profits being too low and the work of cutting and transporting too hard to attract African peasant producers. In German East Africa and Kenya the settler producers were also able to secure government assistance in keeping local Africans available to labour on their estates.[2]

The First World War seriously disrupted production in German East Africa, renamed Tanganyika by the British, where the bulk of East African sisal was grown. Many German estates were subsequently sold to new British and Greek settlers, Asian businessmen (such as the Karimjee Jivanjee company) and a few plantation companies (such as Amboni Estates) owned by British and Continental interests. Germans were allowed to return in 1924 and several bought back their estates.[3] The majority of growers were therefore independent producers on small estates producing a few hundred tons a year. Besides those in the Kenyan highlands, they were concentrated in Tanganyika's Northern Province and along its Central Line railway. Over half of East African production, however, came from large estates producing over 1,000 tons a year each, concentrated along the Tanga railway line and in the Southern Province. Some of these large estates, notably Amboni, Ruvu and Kikwetu, were tied to London sisal merchants, such as Wigglesworth & Co., or in the case of German estates to the Usagara Co. These merchants helped finance the estates and dealt with the shipping and marketing of the sisal from the moment it left the producer. The other estates relied on agents and shippers, such as Arbuthnot Latham, Dalgetty, Gilliats and Ralli Brothers, to buy their sisal or transport it on their own account (for a fee) to London where it was offered to merchants who sold it to the rope and twine spinners for the best price they could get. The only exception was Karimjee Jivanjee who until 1940 marketed their own and some other Asian-produced sisal in London.[4]

Sisal exports grew rapidly during the 1920s from 22,000 tons in 1923 to 62,000 tons in 1929, encouraged by prices of £30 to £40 a ton. Three-quarters of East African sisal was produced in Tanganyika, where it accounted by value for over one-third of all exports. Like other primary producers, however, East Africa's sisal growers suffered badly during the depression. Prices collapsed to between £10 and £20 a ton, not so much because of excess supply – the market continued to absorb an ever-increasing amount of hard fibre during the 1930s – but because sisal prices were dragged down by the world trend. Spinners with large stocks of fibre could hold off the market until growers and shippers were both desperate to sell at any price for cash to cover their running costs. There was also increasing competition from the large Dutch-run sisal estates in Java producing a superior quality fibre and from the peasant producers of henequen in Mexico and manila in the Philippines whose lower costs enabled them to undercut East African producers. Providing only a quarter of world hard fibre supplies, East African growers were price-takers and had to cut their costs accordingly.[5]

In East Africa, production costs varied enormously. Large efficient estates, such as Amboni, were able to make profits throughout the depression. Karimjees merely broke even, but the small high-cost producers could barely make ends meet.[6] A response to this situation was the formation in 1930 by Major William Lead (owner of Mazinde, a large locally-owned estate) of the Tanganyika Sisal Growers' Association (TSGA), soon joined by every grower in the territory and imitated by a sister association in Kenya. Representations to government secured lower freight rates and port and storage charges, and a 50% wage reduction was organised among its members.[7]

Marketing costs proved more difficult to cut. Many smaller producers thought their sisal passed through too many hands, each taking its 1−2% commission, between leaving the estate and reaching the spinner. Direct sales from grower to spinner would benefit both − though obviously not the shippers or merchants. In 1931 the TSGA tried to establish its own marketing organisation in London, but failed because of opposition from Wigglesworth's, who represented or marketed 25% of Tanganyikan production.[8] Instead, in 1934 some growers built a twine and cordage mill at Tanga to by-pass London altogether and sell direct to the farmer. This, however, foundered on the intense opposition of the British spinners who threatened to boycott East African sisal altogether and persuaded the Colonial Office to threaten a penal import duty to protect the 20,000 jobs in the British spinning industry.[9]

Many producers were therefore forced to borrow money from their shippers and bankers to keep going: by 1931 the industry had debts amounting to some £1 million, on a total investment of £6−7 million. Several growers were forced to sell out to larger companies or were taken over by their creditors. The largest Kenyan estate, Dwa Plantations, passed to its London receivers (Hogg, Bullimore & Co.), while the largest locally-registered British company in Tanganyika, Bird & Co., was taken over by Sisal Estates Ltd., a holding company tied to Gilliat's. The Usagara Co. also accumulated a number of German estates.[10]

To maintain the level of cash income, reduce costs per ton and pay off their debts, growers and shippers alike sought to maximise production. East African production consequently rose to 130,000 tons in 1939. This scramble to cut costs and increase production inevitably caused a deterioration in quality which, in a fiercely competitive market, made East African sisal more difficult to sell. Merchants bought sisal on the basis of estate marks, reputable estates like Amboni receiving a premium and disreputable ones, declared 'ineligible marks', being bought only at a discount. Since merchants then graded the sisal and sold to spinners solely by grade, producers of 'ineligible marks' − mainly Greek and Asian growers − suspected the merchants of making unfair profits at their expense. These small growers also suspected that the violent fluctuations in price were the result of merchants' speculations and blamed the dramatic price collapse on shippers who 'couldn't hold their water for five minutes' to get producers a better price. Thus, while big growers and merchants blamed the small growers for bad quality and weak selling, small growers blamed the marketing system itself.[11]

By 1935 the London merchants themselves were so concerned about continuing low prices that they began discussing a scheme to force prices up by restricting world production (as had been done with other commodities), but the talks were abandoned when the market revived in 1936 and prices rose above £20 a ton. A marketing campaign to increase British imports of East African sisal did succeed in increasing imports from 5,000 tons in 1931 to 37,000 tons in 1935, but most East African sisal still went to markets on the Continent.[12] The recovery of 1936 also stimulated the interest of several Far Eastern merchant companies. Four new estate companies were floated in London to run sisal estates on the south-east Asian 'managing agency' basis, three managed locally by Jardine Matheson's East African subsidiary and all connected with established Eastern merchant houses such as R.C. Treatt and Francis Peek.[13] Throughout the 1930s, therefore, metropolitan interests were increasing their stake in the East African sisal industry. By 1939, 25% of production was controlled by London interests (directly or indirectly), 28% by Continental interests (mainly German, Dutch and Swiss) and 47% by local interests, half of them Asian.[14]

In 1938 prices slumped again. In response the merchants suggested establishing a futures market for sisal, but the East African growers preferred to send Lead to London to investigate direct sales to the spinners through a single London selling organisation. The merchants managed to persuade him that their expertise in marketing was indispensible, but with Eldred Hitchcock, a London director of Bird & Co., Lead did set up a London Sisal Growers' Association (SGA) to represent producers' interests there. Although financed from East Africa, the SGA was open to London shippers and merchants who thereby came to have a powerful say within it.[15] Back in East Africa, Lead decided that growers must strengthen themselves against metropolitan domination with the help of the local administration. A new Tanganyikan Sisal Ordinance strengthened the TSGA-dominated Sisal Board, but it was not until the war brought wholesale government intervention in sisal marketing that East African growers were able to use their local political power to strengthen their position in the market.[16]

II

During the first two years of war the government took complete control over the marketing of sisal, not so much because of British war needs as because of the collapse of East Africa's traditional sisal markets.

Before the war 54% of East African sisal was sold to Continental Europe, 36% to Britain and the Empire and 10% to North America. In 1939 Britain and France agreed to absorb Germany's share, but in 1940 France, Belgium and Holland all fell and even the American market was described as dead. Combined with the drastic restriction of shipping this caused a massive accumulation of stocks in East Africa, amounting by December 1941 to 70,000 tons. The Colonial Office approached other hard fibre producers to negotiate a world restriction scheme but although the Dutch were cooperative the Mexicans were not and no agreement was reached.[17]

East African producers therefore looked to the imperial government for help. When the war started the new Ministry of Supply established a Hemp Control, staffed by London fibre merchants (including Wigglesworth's), to buy all the hard fibre Britain needed at a 'fair' price of costs plus a standard profit.[18] In East Africa a Sisal Control was created to purchase, inspect and grade as much sisal as the Ministry of Supply requested. Lead, appointed first Sisal Controller, worked through the two East African growers associations so that, while the London Control was dominated by merchants, the East African one was firmly in the hands of producers.[19]

Initially the Ministry required only 62% of East African production, the rest being sold by merchants on the open market. This was not easy because of the lack of markets and shipping, so in February 1940 Lead came to London to secure more shipping facilities. He failed and stocks continued to accumulate.[20] By September the Colonial Office saw no option but to force East Africa to restrict production unilaterally and in December producers reluctantly agreed to cut output by 25% to 100,000 tons. Kenyan growers wanted this reduction to be made by closing down all the ex-German estates. These, all in Tanganyika, accounted for 18% of production and had been taken over in 1939 by other Tanganyikan growers who were doing very nicely out of them and preferred an all-round cut. The British Government eventually vetoed the Kenyan idea, fearing retaliation against British assets in Germany, and agreed to cut Kenyan production to 26,000 and Tanganyikan to 74,000 tons a year. Quotas for each estate were based on past performance, which favoured the old-established large estates and enraged small growers who were trying to enlarge their production. For them a 25% reduction meant bankruptcy and the TSGA was on the verge of a split when restriction was unexpectedly ended.[21]

Restriction harmed the industry by preventing new planting and investment, but also had its silver lining. In return for restricting production, Hitchcock (Chairman of the SGA and the growers' chief negotiator in London) persuaded the Ministry of Supply and Treasury to buy the whole 100,000 tons at its guaranteed price, together with 23,000 tons of unsold pre-restriction stocks at a lower price. The

Ministry of Supply were reluctant to lumber themselves with more sisal than Britain needed, and the merchants were dead against what they saw as virtual nationalisation of marketing, wanting to keep some sisal to sell on the free market when it revived. But Hitchcock firmly believed 'the more control the better' and wanted the Ministry to sell East African sisal direct to America, where the market was reviving.[22] He was supported by Melville, the Colonial Office representative sent to Washington to persuade the USA to help save colonial producers from bankruptcy by buying their surplus commodities. Melville reported that:

> London sisal merchants (except Wigglesworth) have been since the beginning of the war completely out of touch with the US market. My impression of them in any case is that they are dead from the neck up ... the [London] Sisal Control is a caucus of merchants whose ideas are heavily colored with the particular interests of the firms to which they belong. They are as touchy as ballerinas and as jealous of each other as tom cats. I am quite sure that Colonial interests will suffer if they are allowed too big a say in the marketing of the whole East African output.[23]

Merchants resented Colonial Office interference in things they felt it did not understand,[24] but on this occasion the Colonial Office and Hitchcock won their case against the Hemp Control and merchants because the Treasury desperately needed the dollars Britain could earn from selling Ministry of Supply sisal to the USA, and instructed the Ministry to buy the whole crop. The financial needs of the imperial Exchequer overrode the sectional interests of 'metropolitan capital'. Individual shippers and merchants now ceased to have any marketing function at all. Their role was simply to store and transport the sisal, for which they received a one or two per cent commission because the government wished to maintain where possible the 'normal channels of trade'.[25]

Disputes between Ministry, merchants and growers over prices and grading were now brought within the administrative machine. Even at the time it was clear that both merchants and growers were throughout 'jockeying for position in the post-war period', merchants and shippers trying to retain their pre-war control, the local growers trying to break it.[26]

The price of sisal under the Ministry of Supply contract was the subject of heated negotiations between the growers and the Ministry. These revolved around the enormous differences in costs of production between estates and the problem that the average pre-war price had been uneconomic for many small inefficient estates. Production costs varied from £11 to £19 a ton f.o.b. so that the Ministry's 1939 offer of £19 a ton c.i.f. London provoked immediate protests from Hitchcock who claimed this was uneconomic and persuaded them to increase it to £26, equivalent to £19 a ton f.o.b. East Africa. Although costs began to rise steadily, efforts to get a further increase were countered by the Ministry's argument that without its contract growers would be unable to sell their sisal at all, and at the present price all could break even and some could make handsome profits. Certainly nobody went bankrupt, though profits in 1940 averaged only 6%. Government purchase through the Sisal Control did at least provide all growers with a regular and predictable income, enabling many to liquidate the debts built up during the depression and free themselves from outside control.[27]

The Sisal Control also took grading out of the hands of the merchants and put it in those of its own inspectorate in East Africa. Sisal was sold to the Ministry solely by grade, despite protests from merchants and those estates whose marks had previously commanded a premium. But the result was a great improvement in quality, especially among small Greek and Asian estates hitherto notorious for producing large quantities of low-grade sisal which supposedly depressed the market.[28] In all this the growers could generally rely on the support of the Colonial Office which, despite its personal distrust of Hitchcock's unscrupulous negotiating methods, recognised that a better return for growers could only benefit colonial economies and administrations. Thus, by manipulating government control, growers were already strengthening their position before the market changed in their favour at the end of 1941.

III

The situation was transformed by Japan's entry into the war in December 1941. Java and the Philippines were soon overrun and Allied hard fibre supplies thereby halved to under 245,000 tons a year, half of which came from East Africa. British sisal stocks were soon 'desperately low' and the USA were so short that Washington insisted sisal be given the absolute first priority for production in Tanganyika since 'sisal could be got from nowhere else ... they had got to have sisal'.[29] With an unlimited American demand, East Africa achieved a dominant market position which it retained until the 1950s. But there was no free market during the war, when most sisal was bought by governments and distributed by the Combined Raw Materials Board. The market change was therefore not reflected in producer prices but in the government assistance to increase production.

Three things were needed: shipping, labour and machinery. The Americans provided shipping to take sisal direct to the USA despite

DSCP-H

obstruction from the traditional Conference Lines' monopoly in East Africa. The local administrations did all they could to increase labour supply to the estates and eventually, on instructions from the War Cabinet, resorted to labour conscription for sisal work. Machinery was more difficult because much of the existing stock was worn out or German-made and new equipment could only be obtained (for dollars) from the USA. After a special American mission to East Africa, however, the British administration agreed to sanction all the dollar imports the sisal growers requested. This succeeded in increasing production from 106,600 tons in 1941 to 139,300 in 1945, most of the increase coming from the small Greek and Asian growers.[30]

The assistance did not stop growers' costs of production increasing, however, and their struggles with the Ministry of Supply over the terms of their contract continued. In 1943 they demanded a £5 increase in price to cover the rising cost of labour and machinery, and the Treasury eventually conceded £4. The following year growers demanded a further £5.7.0 to ensure that the most marginal producer could cover his costs. The Treasury objected that this would inflate the profits of efficient producers and wanted to pay high- and low-cost producers different prices. But with the Americans breathing down their necks for every last ton of sisal and the SGA insisting that the small high-cost growers accounted for 41% of production, the Government finally agreed an increase to £30 a ton f.o.b.[31]

By 1944 the end of the war was also coming in sight and the growers began to seek ways of ensuring that their prosperity did not end with the war. They feared a fall in demand and an increase in Far Eastern production that would cause a collapse of the post-war market and an end to government purchase that would restore the merchants to their pre-war position. They therefore wanted the new contract to be fixed for five years, arguing that the industry needed longer-term stability to recover from the depression; as Hitchcock said:

> for too long the East African sisal industry has been one of the sub-economic primary industries of the Colonial Empire. Its soundness is of great importance not only for war production but to the economic structure and prosperity of East Africa.[32]

Although it was reluctant to commit itself to paying the same price after the war when free market prices might fall, the Ministry of Supply noted that free market prices were currently double the agreed contract price and that such a contract would secure British control over a major part of world hard fibre supplies. The Treasury agreed that:

in the absence of any long-term arrangement there must be
continual pressure for B.E.A. prices to follow those which are
being paid by the U.S.A. [on the free market] ... We should
make whatever arrangements we can to guard against future
demands for a higher price.[33]

Both sides therefore agreed that the contract should last until two
years after the end of the war with Japan, the price (£30 a ton) to
be adjusted upwards only on the basis of proved increases in
costs.[34]

In 1945 the war ended but Far Eastern production was slow to
revive and the free market price remained around £60 a ton. In 1946
the growers requested a price increase of £18.9.0 to cover increased
costs and improve labour conditions. In negotiations, however, they
increasingly based their case on the argument that they should receive
the 'world value of their product'. The Board of Trade (as the
Ministry of Supply had become) replied that they considered 'they
were still dealing with an essential commodity which it would not
be proper to sell at the highest price the market would stand', and
the Treasury did not think the British taxpayer should subsidise labour
welfare in East Africa. The Colonial Office attacked the Board for
'its policy of exploiting the Colonies', and did its utmost to ensure
'that UK buying Ministries do not abuse their monopolistic powers
in reaching price settlements with colonial sellers'.[35]

But the real issue was the control of supplies not price. The Board
was desperate to secure adequate supplies of sisal for Britain and
the Dominions, because without it grain crops could not be harvested
and Britain, already short of food, would starve. Sisal also had to
be secured from sterling sources. If producers had been free to sell
anywhere most East African sisal would have gone to the USA for
higher prices and the Board would have been forced to compete in
dollar markets for inferior Mexican and Philippine substitutes.
Buying the whole East African production and using it to supply all
Empire needs prevented a drain on the sterling area's slender dollar
resources and even, through US sales, augmented them. As Hitchcock
noted, 'At present the sterling area gains both as to quantity and price
at the expense of the producers', and Melville admitted to Tanganyika
that 'every ton of sisal sold brings in additional dollars'.[36] Under
pressure from the Colonial Office, the Board of Trade admitted to
the Treasury that if Britain was to get the supplies she needed,

some concession must be granted ... if they had asked to cancel
the contract ... I am doubtful if we could have resisted them.
They could then certainly have obtained prices much in excess
of those they now ask for ... The existence of the contract

has enabled us, and will still enable us to get sisal very substantially more economically than we could otherwise do.[37]

The Government therefore agreed to the growers' price demand for 1946 and in 1947, when the world price rose to £96 a ton, conceded a further £20 bringing the East African price to £78.9.0. Producers also secured a guarantee that they could sell 30,000 tons to non-Empire markets in America and on the Continent.[38]

The East African growers were now making enormous profits because the Sisal Control, run by the growers' associations, passed on all price increases to the producers. The Tanganyikan administration considered an export tax to cream off some of this surplus but decided against it because the TSGA was too powerful and because they persuaded themselves the profits were not inflationary as long as they were reinvested in imported machinery. The Colonial Office nevertheless encouraged growers to set aside part of the increase for a price stabilisation fund.[39]

The Government sisal contract was due to end in 1947, but those growers who were trying to prevent merchants regaining control over marketing wanted to prolong it until they had agreed an alternative marketing scheme. Once the British Government had agreed to pay something near the free market price they were happy to continue the contract, as were the Board of Trade who could thereby continue to control supplies without having to compete in dollar markets. The merchants' protests went unheeded and the contract was renewed for a further year with another £10 increase. Unfortunately this infuriated the Americans who had been looking forward to getting free access to East African sisal as soon as the contract ended. They accused Britain of surreptitiously reintroducing imperial preference in a Trusteeship territory, and only agreed not to raise the matter in the UN when Britain promised to end the contract in 1948.[40] Thereafter a relatively free market was restored and over half East African sisal was sold to non-sterling buyers in Europe and America. Prices rose dramatically to over £160 a ton in 1951 before falling back to around £70 a ton during the 1950s as world production rose to meet demand.[41]

IV

The ending of the contract brought to an untimely end a debate over future marketing that had been going on within the industry since before the war. To understand this stuggle between the merchants, in alliance with the large externally-controlled estates, and the predominantly small independent growers, in alliance with the

Colonial Office (with the Tanganyikan administration standing rather helplessly between the two camps), it is necessary to follow the marketing debate from the early years of the war.

As early as February 1941 Hitchcock had discussed a price stabilisation scheme involving buffer stocks with Lord Keynes at the Treasury. Hitchcock continued to pursue this idea with the Colonial Office, convinced that after the disastrous experience of the 1930s, 'primary commodities cannot be left entirely to competitive commercialism'.[42] The Colonial Office representative at the Anglo-American discussions on the reconstruction of the post-war world economy, Gerard Clauson, agreed that 'Sisal is almost ideally a commodity suitable for "buffer stock" treatment, either through an international scheme or through a more modest single selling agency'. However, the discussions on reconstructing world trade came to nothing with the failure to establish an International Trade Organisation, and commodity producers had, as before, to fend for themselves.[43] The sisal industry's importance both to Britain and Tanganyika made the Colonial Office and the Tanganyikan administration vitally concerned with its welfare but, as the Governor admitted, the growers were too politically powerful to be coerced and 'an effective scheme must spring spontaneously from the industry itself and command the support of the majority of those concerned'. They could therefore do no more than encourage the industry to 'seek its post-war salvation by its own efforts'. Unlike the mining companies, there was never any question of nationalisation.[44]

The first two stabilisation schemes were proposed by London-based growers. That of Mr Bosanquet, a director of many Malayan planting companies, aimed to eliminate weak selling by eliminating the small inefficient growers, but was clearly unacceptable to the TSGA and KSGA where those growers had a powerful voice. The other, by Mr Bovill (of Bovill Matheson & Co., the local offshoot of Jardine's), suggested a mild form of single selling agency in London, which was equally unacceptable to the merchants and shippers.[45] That these schemes were proposed and discussed in London by the SGA and CO without reference to East Africa aroused growers' fears that 'London wanted to dominate our affairs from that end', whereas 'post-war marketing and international negotiations were important matters in which the Senior Partner (the TSGA) will insist on having the last word'.[46]

These fears were exacerbated by Hitchcock who arrived in East Africa 'breathing fire and fury against "the blood-sucking bankers" of the London Association'.[47] In 1941 Lead, the dominant force within the East African industry, died of cancer and Hitchcock transferred himself from London to Tanganyika where he tried to assume Lead's mantle. Like many small men of great ability, Hitchcock was pugnacious and quarrelsome. He was unquestionably the most able individual in the industry and a brilliant negotiator, but his ferocious and sometimes unscrupulous pursuit of what he saw as the industry's (and his own) best interests alienated not only the London merchants and their clients but some of the independent growers as well. Even so, by 1946 he had achieved an ascendency within the TSGA based on the solid support of the Greek and Asian growers and some of the independent British estate owners.[48]

In London Hitchcock had quarrelled with the merchants and the SGA (which accused him of speculation whilst Chairman) and this added a certain acrimony to the dispute between the TSGA and the London SGA which festered throughout the war. Since the East African growers held the purse-strings they eventually forced the disbandment of the merchant-infiltrated SGA and replaced it with a new London Committee elected solely by the East African producers. This created a 'unique position among London representatives of Colonial industries', as all other London commodity associations were run by the metropolitan interests alone.[49] The producers were beginning to flex their new-found muscles.

The growers next sought to strengthen themselves in East Africa by persuading the local governments to pass new Sisal Ordinances perpetuating the Sisal Control's powers to purchase, inspect and grade all sisal but transferring them to the producer-controlled Sisal Boards. Tanganyika's was passed in December 1945 after a long wrangle over two controversial clauses. The TSGA was given a majority on the reformed Sisal Board but it was not allowed to elect its own chairman, mainly because if the choice was left to the growers, 'the frightful possibility looms that their choice might light on Mr E. F. Hitchcock', which the authorities considered 'very unwelcome ... if not a calamity'. Instead the Governor appointed R. W. R. Miller, Tanganyika's Director of Agriculture, Lead's successor as Sisal Controller and an old friend of the TSGA.[50] The other disagreement was over a clause allowing the Board to enforce a statutory monopoly selling agency in East Africa when the government contract ended. The clause was supported by Hitchcock and a majority of the growers but opposed by the minority of externally-controlled estates. The Government finally agreed to allow it only if a two-thirds majority of production within the TSGA approved any scheme introduced under the clause.[51]

Hitchcock promptly organised a Committee to draw up a plan for an East African sisal marketing board to by-pass the shippers and merchants by selling directly to the spinners, and including a price stabilisation fund. The income from all sisal sales would be pooled and all growers paid a uniform price. This was greatly to the advantage of the small and lower-quality producers but not to the 'premium mark' estates such as Amboni. In essence the scheme sought to prevent a recurrence of the traumas of the 1930s by preserving the sort of marketing system evolved during government purchase. As the Committee reported, this was

> not a scheme to restrict production or to hold up stocks in order to create artificial prices, but the sale of production will be handled in an orderly manner, and in times of crisis growers will have a responsible body able to deal with the marketing problems of the industry as a whole.[52]

Such a scheme was strongly encouraged by the Colonial Office which, as the industry were told, 'favoured schemes of planned administration and cooperative effort on the part of producers. There was political sympathy for ensuring prosperity and security for the weaker members of industries'.[53] It was also supported by the Board of Trade who believed it would make it easier to secure UK and Dominion supplies of fibre, and knew that 'a "sudden" free market would mean no sisal at all for the UK – and how the 1949 grain crops would be harvested at home it is impossible to foresee'.[54]

The shippers and merchants, however, were implacably opposed to any such scheme because it would reduce their own role and profits. Wigglesworth also believed that 'no system of collective selling can achieve the skill of a merchant who knows how to sell in the best market'. Collective marketing in their eyes meant bad marketing and the ruin of the East African industry, just as the Mexican henequen industry had been ruined by a state-run bulk sales organisation in the 1930s. Such arrangements might work on a rising market but were disastrous when markets fell. The merchants' opposition was naturally reflected by the metropolitan-run estates, led by Wigglesworth's local representative, Sydney Tranter, who represented nearly 40,000 tons and therefore had a powerful voice in the industry. The merchants supported their case by offering very attractive terms to growers who agreed to let them market their sisal.[55]

As the marketing debate dragged on through 1947 and 1948 the Colonial Office became increasingly impatient with the industry, 'always squabbling among themselves', and wanted the local administrations to enforce the desired marketing arrangements. Melville believed the merchants were the main obstacle because they 'refuse to recognise that nineteenth century trading methods are out of fashion and that for better or worse [they] have got to conform to the pattern of the new planned economy'.[56] The Tanganyika government were more hesitant. They preferred Tranter to Hitchcock and feared, even 'in the imperial interest', to coerce such politically powerful producers. They were also aware that

> the Wigglesworth group would never obtain more than one-third of the votes without the support of a few producers (Wilkins, Boscawen etc) who in reality favour the scheme but whose personal animosity to Hitchcock will not allow them to support it.[57]

Until they could be certain of a two-thirds majority for the scheme both Hitchcock and the Colonial Office wanted to continue the government contract. But pressure from the USA and fear that the contract would be challenged as contrary to the UK's Trusteeship obligations for Tanganyika finally forced the TSGA to vote on the marketing scheme in May 1948.[58] Only 22 out of 98 growers opposed it, but those few accounted for 41.5% of total production and thus prevented the scheme's implementation. Hitchcock's scheme fell at the final hurdle.[59]

Other than proposing a last minute compromise (which failed) Kenya had been peripheral to the marketing debate, though growers there tended to favour the scheme. After the vote it therefore established its own marketing board and sought to renew its bulk-purchase contract with the Board of Trade, later negotiating another with the US Government.[60]

In Tanganyika the frustrated majority, including almost all the Greek and Asian growers and accounting for 50% of production, went ahead with an alternative scheme for their own collective marketing organisation (TASMA). This operated successfully in London, and meant that the real losers of this extended struggle were the shippers and London-based growers who were tied to them.[61] The boom years that followed in the early 1950s were the result of a world shortage of sisal, more to do with the slow recovery of Far Eastern production than the action of East African growers. But the struggle over marketing at least ensured that growers secured the maximum possible profit from the seven fat years and many growers made their fortunes in these years.[62]

V

This tale is relevant in a number of ways to contemporary debates about commodity marketing and price stabilisation.

The sisal industry is an example of the successful development of capitalist production in a third world country. To an extent it followed the pattern of 'enclave development' experienced elsewhere (though the patterns of production and labour use have not been discussed here), but it does not fit satisfactorily any of the existing models of 'underdevelopment' or of metropolitan control over colonial production. There was clearly a fragmentation of capital between diverse local and metropolitan groups, none of which was dominant and all of which had distinctly different interests. At times the marketing system approximated closely to almost 'perfect competition' with a large number of relatively small producers, shippers and merchants competing against each other; not that this proved any advantage during the depression. Most of the profits from production (when there were any) were also retained in East Africa where they were either consumed or reinvested.

The producers were naturally very concerned about the instability of the market and repeatedly sought ways to secure a fair and regular return. The experience and discussions of these years showed that sisal producers could not control the market, but that they could succeed in securing for themselves the maximum return the market would yield, unlike many African producers at that time. In seeking security against market fluctuations Wigglesworth represented the ultimate in accepting market instability and playing the market for the best return it could give. Hitchcock on the other hand wanted to insulate growers from the fluctuations of the market through bulk-selling and price stabilisation but had only partial success.

Yet it is clear that East African sisal growers were able by the late 1940s to avoid exploitation by either merchants or the imperial government. The form of production and marketing was unlike that anywhere else in the British Empire. Dominion producers were more in control of their produce on international markets and, supported by independent governments, were more effective in bargaining for a fair return than most colonial producers. In the Far East the managing agency system ensured the direct control of production by metropolitan interests. Elsewhere in Africa, peasant producers were at the mercy of European merchants or colonial marketing boards until, with the development of cooperatives and political muscle, African peasants were able to secure a better return for themselves. Settlers most nearly approximated the pattern of the sisal industry, but they never ran their own marketing organisation in London as the sisal growers did.

By the luck of the wartime market and by using their political leverage to its utmost, East African producers were able to reverse the trend towards greater metropolitan control which had characterised the depression. The imperial government had become deeply involved during the war, but was clearly divided within itself and never simply supported the interests of metropolitan capital. The various factions within it allied at different times with different sections of the industry to secure what they saw as their own interests, with the Treasury defending sterling, the Board of Trade its sisal supplies and the Colonial Office vigorously championing the interests of colonial producers.

Since independence the sisal industry has been unable to exert the political influence it used to, either in London or Dar es Salaam, to the detriment of the industry. It no longer receives the privileged treatment with regard to the import of scarce foreign machinery or the supply of labour, for example, which enabled it to grow during the 1940s. Single channel marketing was finally enforced in 1973. But the market had changed with the arrival of an even cheaper substitute in synthetic fibres and it is therefore impossible to judge whether its introduction at an earlier stage would have helped the producers.

NOTES

1. The literature is too large to list, but e.g. E. A. Brett, *Colonialism and Underdevelopment in East Africa, 1919–1939* (London, 1973); N. Swainson, *The Development of Corporate Capitalism in Kenya, 1918–1977* (London, 1980); and for a different area and ideological perspective, P. T. Bauer, *West African Trade* (Cambridge, 1954). For help in collecting the information on which this paper is based I am grateful to the Director and staff of the Tanzania National Archives (TNA), Dar es Salaam, and the Public Record Office, Kew (for the Colonial Office (CO) papers), and Mr J. Hugh Leslie of Wigglesworth & Co. I am also grateful to Professor Fieldhouse and other members of the DSA seminar for comments on an earlier draft of this paper.

2. V. Harlow and E. M. Chilver (ed.), *History of East Africa*, vol. II (Oxford, 1965), 219–36; J. Iliffe, *A Modern History of Tanganyika* (Cambridge, 1979), pp. 146–7. The problems of production are discussed elsewhere. Here I shall concentrate on the questions of financial control and marketing.

3. Iliffe, *Tanganyika*, pp. 261–3.

4. 'List of Registered Sisal Estates', 1940, TNA 29113/57D. K. M. Stahl, *The Metropolitan Control of British Colonial Trade* (London, 1951), pp. 248–72. Information from Wigglesworth's and Mr Anver Karimjee. Wigglesworth's also represented the one major sisal estate in Portugese East Africa, which exported some 3–4,000 tons a year.

5. 'Sisal Production in British East Africa', Note by CO, 16 Sept. 1943, CO 852/517/5. (I have used the new CO 852 classification, omitting original file numbers, for the sake of brevity.) Discussions with London sisal merchants, C. H. Dale, 20 Sept. 1930, TNA 11475/I/93. Stahl, *Colonial Trade*, pp. 146–7, 271; C. W. Guillebaud, *The Sisal Industry of Tanganyika* (Welwyn, 1958), pp. 18–25; G. W. Lock, *Sisal* (London, 1962), pp. 323–5.

6. 'Memorandum on the Sisal Industry and Taxation', E. F. Hitchcock, Dec. 1941, TNA 30015/I/117. 'Tanganyika's Merchant Princes', *Caltex Star* 3:9 (Sept. 1959), 4–7 (kindly lent me by Mr Karimjee).

7. Correspondence in TNA 11475/I and TSGA Report for 1937, TNA 19475/I. Iliffe, *Tanganyika*, p. 352.

8. Provincial Commissioner Tanga to Chief Secretary (CS), 19 Sept. 1931, and Lead to CS, 3 Nov. 1931, TNA 11475/I/239, 247.

9. Sir Eldred Hitchcock, 'The Sisal Industry of East Africa', *Tanganyika Notes and Records*, 52 (1959), 11. Brett, *Underdevelopment*, pp. 170–3.

10. Hitchcock, 'Sisal Industry', 10–12. Stahl, *Colonial Trade*, pp. 249, 258–64.

11. Note of TSGA meeting with Government, 13 Dec. 1930 and Report of TSGA Committee, TNA 11475/I/118, 188; TSGA Committee meeting, 16 Sept. 1938, TNA 22472/161. Hitchcock to J.M. Keynes, 19 Feb., and Hitchcock note of 16 April 1941, CO 852/432/6. 'Memorandum on the Sisal Industry', N. Bosanquet (SGA), 11 Dec. 1942, CO 852/432/8. Stahl, *Colonial Trade*, p.271. A. Wigglesworth, *A Retrospect, 1895–1935* (London, 1935), p.7.

12. Correspondence in CO 852/2/7 (1935). *Sisal Review* (London), Jan. and March 1938. Brett, *Underdevelopment*, p.151. J.F.W. Rowe, *Primary Commodities in International Trade* (Cambridge, 1965), pp.136–55.

13. Stahl, *Colonial Trade*, pp.249–60. *Sisal Review*, 1938.

14. Hitchcock to Marlow, 4 May 1944, CO 852/6/9/4.

15. Correspondence in TNA 22472; TSGA meeting, 21 Oct. 1944, TNA 29513/I/57. 'Cooperative marketing', memorandum by E.W. Bovill, March 1943, CO 852/517/8. *Sisal Review*, Sept. 1938.

16. Wakefield to CS, 6 June, and Sisal Board meetings, Dec. 1938, TNA 22472. *Sisal Review*, Jan. 1939.

17. Hitchcock to Lead 9 Sept. 1940, TNA 27674/III/247; Hitchcock to Bretherton, 28 May 1947, TNA 29513/II/189; CO to Melville, 18 Dec. 1941, CO 852/431/12; negotiations in CO 852/311/8 and CO 852/431/10.

18. Goldberg (MoS) to Figg (CO), 8 Aug. 1941, CO 852/431/11. J. Hurstfield, *The Control of Raw Materials* (HMSO, 1953), p.258.

19. Tanganyika, *Agricultural Report*, 1939, p.2. Stahl, *Colonial Trade*, p.258.

20. TSGA meeting, 21 Oct. 1939, TNA 19417/II/11. Correspondence in CO 852/311/8 and 9.

21. CO to Governor, 21 Sept. 1940, and other items in TNA 27674/III; material in TNA 29113 and TNA 29513/I. Hitchcock to Figg, 1 July 1941, CO 852/432/6.

22. Notes of meetings and correspondence in CO 852/311/10 (1940) and CO 852/431/11 (1941).

23. Melville to Caine, 25 Sept. 1941, CO 852/431/11.

24. Believing there were 'several government officials, entirely ignorant of business but ideologically at war with non-socialist enterprise in all forms' and whose 'ignorance was total' in regard to sisal marketing. I am grateful to Mr. Aschan of Wigglesworth's for his reminiscences of this period.

25. Correspondence in CO 852/431/11 and 12. The Ministry sold surplus sisal to the USA on a 'no profit no loss basis'.

26. Minute by Carstairs, 16 April 1943, CO 852/517/6.

27. TSGA meeting (Tanga), 6 May 1940, TNA 19417/II/22; memorandum by Hitchcock, Dec. 1941, TNA 30015/I/117. Correspondence and meetings, Jan.–Feb. 1941, CO 852/432/6. Report by Sir J. Foley, 1944, CO 822/117/46748/2. Stahl, *Colonial Trade*, p.258.

28. TSGA Report for 1943, TNA 29513/I/33. Minute by Carstairs, 16 April 1943, CO 852/517/6; Killham to Hempo, 9 Jan. 1944, CO 852/609/1.

29. CO to Governor Tanganyika, 3 April 1942, CO 852/431/13; Note for Secretary of State, 14 Sept. 1943, CO 852/517/5. Record of EA Governors' Conference meeting, 22 Nov. 1943, CO 822/107/46506/E; TSGA meeting, 11 Nov. 1943, TNA 29513/I/31. The British Navy converted entirely to sisal ropes during the war.

30. TSGA Annual Reports, 1944–6; N.J. Westcott, 'The Impact of the Second World War on Tanganyika, 1939–1949' (PhD thesis, Cambridge, 1982), pp.87–93 for full references.

31. See CO 852/517/6 and CO 852/609/1.

32. Governor's Deputy to CO, 9 Feb. 1944, CO 852/609/1.

33. Shillidy (MoS) to Helsby (Treasury), 7 Aug. 1943, and Helsby to Shillidy, 18 Aug. 1943, CO 852/517/7.

34. Shillidy to Carstairs, 11 March 1944, CO 852/609/1.

35. Correspondence and meetings, 1946, CO 852/609/3. Minutes by Melville, Jan. 1947, CO 852/925/1.

36. Hitchcock to Bretherton (BoT, 20 Jan. 1947, and Melville to Proctor (Treas), 13 Feb. 1947, CO 852/925/1. Melville to Sandford (CS), 11 March 1947, TNA 16682/I/7a. Melville to Leslie (Tanganyika), 8 Jan. 1948, CO 852/925/2.

37. Bretherton to Proctor, 20 May 1946, CO 852/609/3.
38. Flett (Treas) to Shillidy, 28 Feb. 1947, CO 852/925/1. Hitchcock to Bretherton, 28 May 1947, TNA 16682/I/30E.
39. Minutes by Hadow and Governor, April 1947, TNA 16079/V/746−7. CO to Governor Tanganyika, 8 March 1947, CO 852/925/1.
40. Correspondence in CO 852/925/2. US Consul Nairobi to CS, 3 Sept. 1947, and CO to Governor, 26 March 1948, TNA 16682/I/113 and 149.
41. Guillebaud, *Sisal Industry*, pp. 27−32.
42. Keynes to Leith Ross, 26 Feb. 1941, CO 852/432/6. Hitchcock to Marlow, 4 May 1944, CO 852/609/4.
43. Minute by Clauson, 22 Dec. 1942, CO 852/432/8. Clauson to Jackson (Governor Tanganyika), 9 Dec. 1943, CO 852/517/8. Rowe, *Primary Commodities*, pp. 155−61. R. N. Gardner, *Sterling−Dollar Diplomacy* (Oxford, 1956), pp. 365−80.
44. Jackson to Stanley, 14 Aug. 1943, and minute by Bull, 6 Oct. 1943, CO 852/517/8.
45. Bosanquet memorandum, 11 Dec. 1942, CO 852/432/8. Bovill memorandum, March 1943, and minute by Clauson, 28 Oct. 1943, CO 852/517/8.
46. TSGA meeting (with Chairman of SGA), 21 Oct. 1944, TNA 29513/I/57.
47. Clauson to Battershill (Governor Tanganyika), 20 July 1945, CO 852/609/5.
48. Information gleaned from CO 852/609/4 and TNA 29513/I and II. Obituary in *TNR* 52 (1959), 1−3. Rumour has it he was the brother of Alfred Hitchcock, the film-maker.
49. Minute by Monson, 22 Dec. and Clauson to Jackson, 28 Dec. 1944, CO 852/609/4. Stahl, *Colonial Trade*, pp. 269−72.
50. Correspondence and minutes in CO 852/609/4, 5 and 6.
51. TSGA meetings, 1944−5, TNA 29513/I and II, Tanganyika, The Sisal Industry Ordinance, 1945.
52. 'Report of the Joint Marketing Committee to the Members of the Tanganyika and Kenya Sisal Growers' Associations' (March 1948); printed copy in the University Library, Dar es Salaam (hereafter Report of JMC).
53. JMC meeting with CO and BoT, 16 Sept. 1947, Report of JMC, p. 35.
54. Ibid., and minute by Miller, 6 April 1948, TNA 16682/I/154.
55. 'Minority Report submitted by Mr J. H. S. Tranter', Report of JMC, p. 84. Creech Jones to Battershill, 12 July 1948 (enclosing record of CO meeting with merchants on 11 May). TNA 16682/I/220. A. Wigglesworth, *The Future of the Sisal Industry in East Africa* (London, 1946; kindly lent me by Mr Leslie).
56. Melville to Surridge, 11 July 1947, and Melville to Sandford, 24 April 1948, TNA 16682/I/77 and 173.
57. Minute by Miller, 6 April 1948, and Leslie to Lockhart, 30 June 1947, TNA 16682/I/31 and 154.
58. CS Tanganyika to CO, 20 and 26 April 1948, TNA 16682/I/166.
59. TSGA Special meetings, 30 March and 31 May 1948, TNA 29513/III/204 and 213.
60. M. Yoshida, 'Agricultural Marketing Reorganisation in Postwar East Africa', *The Developing Economies*, 9 (3), 1973, 252. Material in CO 852/1165/1 (1950).
61. TSGA to CS, 10 July 1948, TNA 16682/I/218.
62. Little remains of the extravagances of the sisal barons in those years except a few municipal halls and a lot of anecdotes.

8

Colonialism and the Economy of the Gold Coast 1919–45

BARBARA INGHAM

There are two inter-related themes running through our account of
the Gold Coast economy in the inter-war period. The first concerns
the experience of the Gold Coast as a primary producer, highly
dependent on a single crop, cocoa, whose price on world markets
began to decline in the early 1920s, recovered briefly in the latter years
of that decade, but then slumped dramatically in the 1930s – a decline
which ended only with the post-World War II commodity boom.
The second theme concerns the status of the Gold Coast economy
in the inter-war period, viz. that of a dependent colony of Britain.
As a consequence of falling prices, all primary producers experienced
a decline in their capacity to import during the inter-war period. But
the ways in which they coped with this problem depended to a large
extent on whether they could operate with a degree of independence
in the international economy. Countries like Australia could impose
tariffs as their external indebtedness rose in the 1920s, and this period
saw a rapid increase in tariffs throughout the world. Eventually, as
the crisis worsened, 'independent' primary producing countries such
as Australia drew on overseas balances, sold gold and depreciated
their currencies. For Britain's dependent empire, which included the
primary producing countries of West Africa, the situation was
different. A major plank of colonial policy was that such countries
should balance their budgets without recourse to outside assistance.
Moreover unilateral action on tariffs was ruled out. Ruled out too
was an independent monetary policy, since monetary systems were
offshoots of the British one, local currencies exchanging with sterling
on a pound for pound basis. Thus West Africa had a very limited
range of policy options for coping with the reduced import capacity
which resulted from falling export prices. The impact of such
measures as were adopted, and especially their place within the
broader framework of colonial economic policy, forms the subject-
matter of this chapter.

Part I looks at the performance of the Gold Coast economy between 1919 and 1945 in terms of a standard market model in which the central feature is overproduction of cocoa. It is argued that 'overproduction' in this case did not imply an absence of economic calculations on the part of the producers themselves. We also note that although the Gold Coast cocoa farmers undoubtedly lost out during the inter-war period, and especially in World War II, this was not true of all groups in the economy. Gold mining, for instance, was relatively prosperous in the 1930s. Employment opportunities for many categories of professional and skilled workers appear to have been on the increase throughout our period. There were favourable movements in the real wages of the urban working population. And though it is difficult to get information on the performance of the non-cocoa rural economy, a 'retreat into subsistence' (Hopkins) seems unlikely for the Gold Coast. Moreover we argue that by 1939 it is likely that a number of important changes had been experienced in the distribution of income on the Gold Coast, away from the traditional rural centres of prosperity based on the cocoa economy, and in favour of the professional classes and urban skilled and unskilled workers.

The implications of these changes in economic and political bargaining power, for recent debates concerning decolonisation (Flint), are debated in Part II, where we address the broader question of colonial economic management and the effects this may have had on the Gold Coast economy of the inter-war period. *Prima facie* there are reasons to expect increased 'exploitation' of the Gold Coast economy at this time, viz. in Britain a strong preference for exports over essential imports, in order to create employment at home, and a variety of other pressures exercised for the generation of privately profitable investment opportunities. One is led, in fact, to look for increasing evidence of economic imperialism in the Gold Coast in the inter-war period, as manifested in such things as preferential tariffs, monopolistic concessions for metropolitan-based interests and the manipulation of property rights (especially laws relating to land tenure). Moreover, such issues also constitute a strong argument for extending the period under consideration beyond 1939, to cover the years of the Second World War. How did Britain secure from the dependent empire those goods and services deemed necessary to the war effort? There was widespread disruption of economic activity in the colonies, and large-scale changes in prices and incomes. Does this shed any new light on the practicalities of colonialism at that time, less than two decades away from Gold Coast independence? How did the reduction in imports, a significant element in the wartime experience of many Third World countries, affect the

Gold Coast's home production of consumer and capital goods? What about the marketing boards which according to some have had the most far-reaching consequences, going well beyond the colonial era?

In answer to these and other questions we argue that official indifference in the 1920s to the Gold Coast's economic problems gave way in the 1930s, and especially during World War II, to a significant degree of exploitation. The Gold Coast was increasingly managed according to Treasury objectives for the British economy. The 1930s, and World War II itself, also saw important changes in Britain, in political attitudes towards West Africa. This was the decolonisation movement, ideas on which are argued in recent writings to have been strongly articulated in Britain well before the outbreak of war in 1939. In this chapter we examine, therefore, the extent to which new political ideas were associated with changes in colonial economic policy. Decolonisation has long been associated in people's minds with the concept of planned economic development and state intervention, the beginnings, according to some, of that unhappy legacy of public intervention in sub-Saharan Africa which stultifies the development efforts of the present day. What evidence is there to support the view that arguments for decolonisation, as articulated in the inter-war period, were associated in Colonial Office thinking with a much enhanced role for the state as an agent of material progress?

Finally, Arthur Lewis argued a number of years ago that what he termed 'The Greatest Depression', that is the years 1913 to 1948, had had a profound and deleterious effect on tropical exporting economies. The Gold Coast was one of a small number of tropical countries which had grown quite rapidly by contemporary standards between about 1870 and 1914. If that growth rate had been maintained during the inter-war period and World War II, the Gold Coast, like certain other tropical exporting economies, would have been significantly wealthier, 'unrecognisably affluent' according to Lewis. Thus the experience of the Gold Coast in the inter-war period has a broader significance, in terms both of the study of tropical development, and of the impact of colonialism on material welfare at that time.

I THE PERFORMANCE OF THE ECONOMY, 1919–1945

Writing of the inter-war period, Kindleberger expressed the dilemma of a present-day economist confronting those momentous years. How does one explain, in the face of massive inter-war instability, the failure of an economic system to respond to deal with the trouble, either automatically, through the microeconomic mechanism of adjustments in supply and demand, or through macroeconomic response through monetary and fiscal systems, or through policy reactions in which the automatic economic forces set in motion are reversed or supported in the interests of stability ... The initial force may be contained in two ways – automatically or by policy decision – and to explain its consequences one has to account both for the failure of automatic forces in the economy to act, and for the failure of decision-making machinery.[1]

The economic system to which Kindleberger refers was the world system of trade and payments between the United States, Europe and the periphery which had operated from about 30 years or so before World War I, down to 1914. We are concerned, in the Gold Coast, with a peripheral economy and for peripheral countries, major exporters of raw materials, foodstuffs, and minerals, it is the implications of the severe downward fluctuations in the prices of primary products during the 1920s and 1930s which is of central importance. More particularly the phenomenon of falling prices accompanied by rising output stands even now as a largely unresolved issue.

Why, in the face of falling world prices, did the output of primary products from the periphery continue to rise in the 1920s and 1930s? In principle there were (at least) three possible reasons: (*a*) 'target income' whereby producers tried to maintain living standards in the face of falling world prices, by increasing their production; (*b*) 'lagged response' in which increased output in one period is the response to higher prices and hence investment in a previous period; (*c*) 'supply shifts' as output responded to some secular change in costs or producer preferences. Thus in support of the latter explanation, Arthur Lewis argued that primary production in the inter-war period was 'excessive' in relation to demand in industrialised countries, as a result of major supply-side changes since the 1880s, the opening up of new countries, migration, capital investment and improvements in transport, particularly railway building.[2]

There is, unfortunately, no measure of agreement among researchers as to where the balance of truth lies, given these three possibilities. In large part this reflects very real difficulties in formulating the theoretical alternatives (which concern producers' motivations and responses) in ways which are amenable to empirical investigation. We return to this important issue in discussing cocoa exports in the Gold Coast case.

In the archetypal open primary-producing economies of the inter-war period, highly dependent on export earnings and highly susceptible to external influences, all the key economic indicators relative to national economic performance reflected to a greater or lesser degree movements in the foreign trade sector. A priori reasoning would lead us to expect increased unemployment, higher taxation and reduced public spending, falling real wages (due to rising import prices), rising rents, and a general decline in the internal exchange economy in peripheral countries between the wars. Whether or not this was the case in practice is an issue to which a number of researchers have addressed themselves in recent years. The result has been that hitherto received wisdom on the relationship between the export sector and overall domestic performance now appears as something of an unresolved issue. Some peripheral economies, and particularly some groups within those economies, may have benefited more than is commonly realised, during the depression years.

The researcher who is trying to build up a picture of the Gold Coast economy between the wars has very little in the way of sources at his disposal. For statistical information there are the Colonial Office reports, and the reports of various commissions on West Africa appointed from London. To this may be added the reports of the Legislative Council Debates and the Censuses of 1921 and 1931. For the rest, there are individual accounts which range from the authoritative *African Survey* of Lord Hailey, or A. W. Cardinall's *The Gold Coast, 1931* to the more idiosyncratic reports and recollections of various colonial officers, administrators, traders and travellers. Inevitably, a picture which relies heavily on the above sources will be biased towards the colonial economy: government revenue and expenditure, foreign trade and transport, mining, commerce, manufacturing and wage employment. It will be relatively weak on all that pertains to the indigenous economy, such things as agricultural output and investment, local trade, self-employment and the personal incomes and savings deriving therefrom. In consequence there are no satisfactory estimates of national income available for the inter-war period.[3]

Table 1 summarises available statistical information on the Gold Coast economy between 1918 and 1950. Beginning with government revenue and expenditure, the break in trend at the end of the 1920s is clearly discernible. The bulk of government revenue was derived from import and export duties, as such it reflected the prosperity of the export sector: rising slowly through the 1920s, but falling dramatically at the end of that decade. It declined until 1935 — indeed the 1934 revenue was barely half of the 1927 revenue. Then the upturn which started in 1935 progressed steadily through the second half

TABLE 1

The Gold Coast Economy 1918–1950

	Revenue and Expenditure			Trade			
	Government Revenue £'000	Government Expenditure £'000	Surplus and Deficit	Imports £'000	Exports £'000	Balance of Visible Trade	Net Barter Terms of Trade
1918	845	1086	− 241	3256	4472	1216	54.8
1919	1935	1471	464	7946	10814	2868	61.1
1920	2985	3189	− 204	15152	12352	− 2800	81.4
1921	2220	5704	− 3484	7661	6942	− 719	48.6
1922	2462	3493	− 1031	7900	8335	435	68.0
1923	2828	2696	132	8448	8959	511	57.7
1924	2896	4847	− 1951	8315	9914	1599	55.5
1925	3005	4487	− 1482	9782	10890	1108	65.4
1926	3200	4642	− 1442	10285	12104	1819	72.0
1927	3987	4472	− 485	13770	14350	580	82.8
1928	3771	4286	− 515	12220	13824	1624	88.0
1929	3389	3789	− 400	10082	12677	2595	75.0
1930	2663	3482	− 819	8953	11287	2334	78.3
1931	2278	2622	− 344	4803	9300	4497	55.0
1932	2654	2375	279	5605	8348	2743	68.4
1933	2654	2168	486	5543	8048	2505	57.1
1934	2760	2204	556	4848	8117	3269	58.9
1935	3231	2401	830	7956	9971	2015	66.7
1936	3733	2845	888	11656	12636	980	77.8
1937	3748	3194	554	19228	16218	− 3010	95.7
1938	3717	3340	377	10380	15425	5045	60.9
1939	3704	3581	123	10626	16235	5609	68.2
1940	3844	3859	− 15	7631	14323	6692	68.9
1941	4118	3547	571	6268	13548	7280	56.3
1942	4135	4093	42	9877	12550	2673	59.0
1943	4286	4504	− 218	10167	12631	2464	39.6
1944	5418	4452	966	9828	12314	2486	33.3
1945	7145	5957	1188	10954	15743	4789	37.7
1946	7535	6546	989	13220	20303	7083	50.0
1947	10209	9902	307	22590	27415	4825	64.2
1948	11601	11404	197	31378	56115	24737	98.7
1949	18058	14059	3999	45416	49927	4511	74.0
1950	20840	17750	3090	48129	77407	29278	107.5

TABLE 1 contd.

The Gold Coast Economy 1918–1950

	Output & Employment				Wages and Prices				
	Rail-ways No. of W'krs '000 Afri-cans	Gold-mining No. of W'krs '000 Afri-cans	Gold Exports Vol. '000 oz	Cocoa Exports Vol. '000 tons	Daily Cost of Food per head shill-ings	Urban Wage Index 1921-100	Railway Wage Index 1918-100	Cocoa Price £/ton F.O.B.	Average Price to the Farmer (Nowell Commi-ssion)
1918	2.5	10.8	–	–	3.00	–	100.0	–	–
1919	2.8	11.0	360	176	2.81	–	85.0	47	–
1920	3.5	9.8	230	124	5.77	–	101.7	81	–
1921	3.7	10.3	221	133	4.64	100	116.2	35	–
1922	4.0	12.1	228	159	3.54	124	110.5	36	–
1923	4.1	10.0	225	200	3.33	116	121.6	32	–
1924	4.9	10.3	232	223	3.05	119	112.3	32	–
1925	4.9	9.1	218	218	2.90	120	118.1	37	–
1926	4.6	8.2	220	230	3.00	128	128.4	39	–
1927	5.3	7.8	189	210	3.03	124	113.4	55	46.80
1928	6.1	7.8	179	225	2.83	125	100.8	49	34.02
1929	3.5	7.4	225	238	2.85	122	175.7	40	30.79
1930	4.6	–	272	190	2.88	122	135.9	36	16.58
1931	4.0	7.9	273	244	2.91	127	143.5	22	16.03
1932	3.8	8.8	286	233	2.85	131	–	23	15.35
1933	3.8	10.4	294	236	3.01	–	124.8	21	10.96
1934	3.7	15.1	351	230	2.96	–	126.7	17	13.24
1935	4.0	23.5	371	268	2.87	140	118.3	19	15.41
1936	4.1	27.0	434	311	2.40	142	118.9	24	–
1937	4.2	27.3	558	236	2.56	141	120.0	42	–
1938	4.6	30.5	677	263	2.47	147	112.8	17	–
1939	4.7	33.7	793	280	2.31	–	–	18	–
1940	4.7	33.8	858	223	2.74	–	–	20*	–
1941	4.7	34.5	815	218	3.12	–	–	18*	–
1942	5.1	30.1	786	123	3.16	–	–	19*	–
1943	5.2	21.7	630	187	–	–	–	18*	–
1944	6.1	22.7	534	202	–	–	–	19*	–
1945	–	25.4	475	232	7.55	–	–	30*	–
1946	–	30.1	646	236	7.81	–	–	40*	–
1947	5.4	31.1	568	180	8.11	–	248.0	92	–
1948	5.8	30.1	671	214	8.84	–	216.0	197	–
1949	5.5	29.5	656	263	8.93	–	235.2	129	–
1950	5.7	31.0	705	267	9.10	–	250.0	204	–

Notes   Starred Figures are Estimates of the Cocoa Control Board
(Figures for 1940–1947 inclusive)

Source   Colonial Reports, Gold Coast

of the 1930s and during the war years. Much of this latter improvement was due to the rising fortunes of the gold-mining industry, for cocoa remained relatively depressed until the post-World War II commodity boom.

Government expenditure was rising through the 1920s, but a long decline commenced in 1930. It did not recover its 1928 level until the middle of World War II. Ordinary or recurrent expenditure showed little change throughout the 1920s and 1930s, though it started to rise at the outbreak of war. Extraordinary expenditure and development expenditure together constituted the government's capital expenditure, the distinction being that the extraordinary expenditure was financed out of accumulated surpluses, whereas development expenditure, which related primarily to harbours and the railways, was financed out of loans raised abroad. Capital expenditure remained consistently high during the 1920s but declined dramatically in the 1930s, with development expenditure ceasing altogether. There was a slight recovery in capital expenditure in 1936–39, but this was curtailed by the outbreak of war. Wages and salaries paid by the colonial government, as a percentage of total government expenditure, also rose in the 1930s. Personal emoluments were a major component of government current expenditures.

With the exception of two isolated years, 1919 and 1923, there were budget deficits annually between 1918 and 1931. These deficits were financed either from accumulated reserves or from loans raised in London. But beginning in 1932 budget surpluses became the norm. Apart from 1940 and 1943, budget surpluses occurred annually until the mid-1950s.

On foreign trade the notable features are the depressed export earnings between 1921 and 1923, and between 1931 and 1936. Earnings from cocoa exports were in decline well beyond 1936. But gold exports compensated to some extent thereafter. As increases in world demand brought rising gold prices through the 1930s, gold exports increased in volume and value terms, surpassing the value of cocoa exports in 1938.

Movements in the economy-wide net barter terms of trade are recorded in Table 1. 1921–1925, 1931–1935, and 1942–1947 are periods of markedly unfavourable terms of trade. The war years were special in that they brought exceptionally rapid rises in import prices. Cocoa farmers in the inter-war period and World War II suffered an even more dramatic downturn in fortune than did the export sector as a whole. The cocoa price index declined far more sharply than did the economy-wide export index. Finally, in all but three years and despite external vicissitudes, trade surpluses were recorded annually between 1918 and 1945. In the post-war period this was to lead to the famous 'sterling balances' accumulated in London by the colonial empire.

Employment is a key indicator of economic performance but, in the context of tropical Africa in the inter-war period, its value is severely limited by lack of information on the level of activity in the internal exchange economy. Nevertheless, it is worth looking at the other recorded categories of employment, and perhaps hazarding some guesses at likely movements in the local economy. Outside the cocoa and local agriculture, the main categories of employment on the Gold Coast during our period were gold-mining and the railways (Table 1). Between 1924 and 1931 African employ-ment in gold-mining fell, but then rose rapidly throughout the 1930s. In 1931 it employed about 8,000 Africans. By 1945 it employed some 25,000 Africans. (The estimated male population of working age in 1945 was of the order of 1.2 million.) On the railways African employment rose steadily from 1918 to 1928. Between 1928 and 1929 it was halved. In the mid-1930s, though making a modest recovery, railway employment never regained the momentum of the 1920s, due to the cessation of investment and increasing compe-tition from road transport (Table 2). The achievements documented in Table 2 are a tribute to the personal efforts of Governor Guggisberg, discussed more fully in section II below. This table also shows the genesis of a problem of his own making. By the time he left the Gold Coast in 1927, he had overseen the construction of over 3,000 miles of new roads, at a cost of £1.2m. But the effects of improved roads on the viability of the railways he had sponsored were already becoming evident, and Guggisberg was obliged even-tually to issue a statement to the effect that no new road could be countenanced if it covered the same route as a railway.

TABLE 2

Year	Miles of Railway Open	Miles of Motorable Roads
1921	276	2241
1922	334	–
1923	379	–
1924	394	3977
1925	394	–
1926	457	5110
1927	480	5527
1928	495	–
1929	500	6111
1930	500	6738

Source: A. W. Cardinall, op. cit. *The Gold Coast, 1931*

The employment implications of the Guggisberg's Ten Year Development Programme, with an annual average expenditure of £2.5m between 1921 and 1927, must have been significant – especially for construction and associated activities in the south where much of the expenditure was concentrated. When development and extraordinary expenditure dwindled in the 1930s, this employment was lost to the economy. On the other hand, current expenditure was maintained during the 1930s and two areas within this category even increased during that decade, current expenditure on health and education. In the field of education much of the increase was associated with the expansion of the college at Achimota, launched in 1927 with the help of an annual government grant, and in full swing by 1938. Similarly, the increase in recurrent expenditure on health was associated with another project undertaken in the 1920s and becoming fully functional in the 1930s, viz. the hospital at Korle Bu. But current expenditure on health and education by 1938 still amounted to little more than £½ million per annum, and its employment effects were relatively limited.

If we turn to employment in agriculture, the 1948 census, which was the first to offer reliable evidence on occupation, estimated that about 72% of the male population were wholly engaged in agriculture. Between one-quarter and one-fifth of the male agricultural population were classified as cocoa farmers, including labourers, porters, etc. The remainder were involved in the production and transport of a variety of local foodstuffs, plus rural crafts and services. This is the local exchange economy about which we know so little.

Taking first the question of employment in cocoa farming, there are no figures on the numbers employed in the industry between the wars, so inference must be drawn from data on cocoa output. The question of supply response in cocoa farming is discussed in more detail below. Briefly, it is unlikely that there was any fall in the number of cocoa farmers during the period 1918–1945. Instead the evidence points to a significant increase since, despite falling prices, the volume of cocoa exports virtually doubled between the end of the first and second world wars. Reasonable assumptions lead to the conclusion that increased labour inputs were involved in the expansion of exports.

On the local exchange economy, output data are lacking, thus employment figures cannot be derived even indirectly. In the absence of other evidence it is tempting to argue, as Hopkins and others have done, that employment in the local economy in West Africa was tied to the fortunes of the export sector, declining in the depressed trade conditions of the inter-war period.

The poor terms of trade in the period 1930–1945 had a serious effect on the internal market. In general it can be said that when the export trade was depressed fewer cattle were sent south, fewer kola nuts were imported into the savannah, fewer craft products were sold, fewer labourers were employed and so fewer foodstuffs were produced for exchange.[4]

Though not departing substantially from this line of argument, one or two qualifications need to be made for the Gold Coast case. First, as far as exports are concerned, the thriving gold industry represented a departure from generally depressed trading conditions and no doubt had favourable repercussions on local output and employment in the 1930s. Second, certain categories of employment – those in skilled and semi-skilled occupations, in government service, transport and commerce – may well have increased both in the 1920s and in the 1930s, though from an admittedly low base. We have already mentioned the increased recurrent expenditure on health and education in the 1930s. To this may be added the enlarged functions of municipal authorities in urban areas, the development of telephone and telegraph services, the increase in post office savings accounts, improved harbour facilities, the developments in road transport and increases in the ownership of motor vehicles, all of which were features of the Gold Coast economy in the 1930s.

Although one should not set much store by the 1931 census figures, since they were recognised even at the time as containing a large number of inaccuracies, nevertheless they are broadly indicative of the sort of trend suggested for certain skilled and semi-skilled occupations, when compared with the returns for 1948.[5]

Data on wages and prices between 1920 and 1945 are patchy, but the broad trends may be discerned. As far as prices are concerned, import prices are available for the whole of our period (Table 1). Broadly speaking the trend was downward until 1936, with a rapid acceleration from 1939 to 1950 due to war-time shortages, and further shipping problems in the immediate post-war period.[6] Data on the

TABLE 3

Occupations of the African Population (Males) Census Years 1931, 1948

Occupation	1931	1948
Professional and Technical	2,064	4,168
Commercial	48,388	93,204
Transport and Communication	4,260	11,650
Fishery, Farming, etc.	76,122	77,595
Blue Collar	43,641	44,979

prices of domestically-produced goods and services are not available, and this affects the compilation of a cost-of-living index. Altogether this is a difficult area. One series which is available for the whole of our period, and which reflects both imported and domestic food prices, is the daily cost of feeding a prisoner in establishments under the control of the Prisons Department of the colonial administration. These data, reproduced in Table 1, indicate a fall in food costs of about 20% between 1927 and 1939. But between 1942 and 1945 the cost of food doubled. This rapid rise in the cost of living between 1939 and 1945 is also shown in Birmingham's index reproduced below (Table 4).[7]

TABLE 4

Index of Real Wages of the Unskilled Labourer in Accra

	Index of Money Wage	Cost of Living Index	Index of Real Wage
1939	100	100	100
1941	122	151	81
1945	122	186	66
1946	139	198	70
1947	183	212	86

Birmingham's index, like the aforementioned food cost series, relates to urban areas and was therefore heavily biased towards the rising cost of imports. The increase in the rural cost of living index, during World War II and its aftermath, may well have been less dramatic insofar as it was influenced by the availability of domestically produced foodstuffs.[8]

On wages, information is available for the period 1918–1939 for workers employed in the gold-mining industry and on the railways. Real wages for skilled and unskilled workers on the railways rose 50% during the 1920s. Although there was a decline in the early 1930s, real wages on the railways were some 37% above the 1920 level at the outbreak of World War II (Table 5 below, compiled from Colonial Reports). Gold mining presented an even more favourable picture, with both money and real wages rising during the 1930s as mining companies recruited more labour to take advantage of the rising gold prices. Finally, an index (Table 1) constructed from official data on the wage rates of urban skilled workers who were in government employment – nurses, teachers, clerks, dispensers – shows a rise of 40% between 1921 and 1938 in the real remuneration of these occupational groupings.

TABLE 5

Index of Real Wages, African Workers on the Gold Coast Railways

Year	Money Wage	Index of Money Wages 1918 = 100	Cost of Food Index	Index of Real Wages 1918 = 100
1918	3.55	100.0	100.0	100.0
1919	3.02	85.0	93.7	90.7
1920	3.61	101.7	192.3	52.9
1921	4.13	116.2	154.7	75.2
1922	3.93	110.5	118.0	93.6
1923	4.32	121.6	111.0	109.5
1924	3.99	112.3	101.7	110.5
1925	4.19	118.1	96.7	122.1
1926	4.56	128.4	100.0	128.4
1927	4.03	113.4	101.0	112.3
1928	3.58	100.8	94.3	106.9
1929	6.27	175.7	95.0	184.9
1930	4.83	135.9	96.0	141.6
1931	5.10	143.5	97.0	147.9
1932	–	–	95.0	–
1933	4.43	124.8	100.3	124.4
1934	4.50	126.7	98.7	128.4
1935	4.20	118.3	95.7	123.7
1936	4.22	118.9	80.0	148.6
1937	5.39	120.0	85.3	140.6
1938	4.01	112.8	82.3	137.0
1939	–	–	77.0	–
1940	–	–	91.3	–
1941	–	–	104.0	–
1942	–	–	105.3	–
1943	–	–	–	–
1944	–	–	–	–
1945	–	–	251.7	–
1946	–	–	260.3	–
1947	8.81	–	270.3	91.7
1948	7.67	–	294.7	73.3
1949	8.36	–	297.7	79.0
1950	8.88	–	303.3	82.4

Source: Colonial Reports, Gold Coast

What broad conclusions can be drawn about the performance of the Gold Coast economy between 1919 and 1945, from the statistical evidence which has been brought together so far in this section? Briefly, for the colonial economy, orientated towards exports and public investment, the evidence supports the idea of a break in the trend of activity in the 1930s, with a sharp decline in cocoa prices, a drop in government revenues and a cessation of government investment. The break is marked by a switch from deficit budgeting before 1931 to surplus budgeting thereafter. But the contrast between the 1920s and the 1930s should not be overdrawn. The cocoa price, except for isolated years, had already begun to experience a decline in the early 1920s. Throughout the period 1920–1945 the cocoa farmer was under very real pressure from the world decline in primary product prices. On the other hand, the gold-mining industry, under the influence of rising gold prices, was expanding in terms of output and employment throughout the 1930s. For this and other reasons we must qualify, for the Gold Coast, Hopkins' thesis of a 'retreat into subsistence' in West Africa in the 1930s.[9] Employment for some categories of skilled workers was almost certainly increasing, so also was spending on education and health, and there were favourable movements in the real wages of urban workers, railway employees and those employed in the gold-mining industry. There are strong grounds for suggesting that by 1939 a change had already taken place in the distribution of income and potential political bargaining strength, in favour of the professional classes and the urban skilled workers. Overall, per capita income may or may not have increased. Dr Teal suggests an increase of some 50% in per capita income between 1919 and 1939, but there are problems with his methods of estimation.

During the Second World War the economy of the Gold Coast came under increasing pressure from rising import prices. Unfortunately the war years are even less accessible to the researcher at present than is the period up to 1939 (cf. Robert Pearce's contribution elsewhere in this volume). Some of our statistical series omit the war years altogether, and for the time being it is necessary to keep an open mind on many issues. This is especially so in relation to movements in the internal exchange economy and the effects these may have had on domestic prices during World War II. These issues are discussed more fully on p. 257 below, in terms of new income-earning opportunities afforded by the War, and the activities of the West African War Council.[10]

We can now look in more detail at the fortunes of those who undoubtedly lost out during the inter-war period in the Gold Coast, viz. the cocoa farmers. Cocoa presented an unhappy combination of expanding output and relatively slow-growing demand between the wars, which weakened the cocoa price and dramatically reduced the fortunes of the peasant farmers. It followed a world-wide trend for primary products in which output continued to increase after World War I, quite out of step with the normal peacetime demands from European consumption and production. According to Lewis, in a view shared by Kindleberger, the experience with primary products was the decisive factor in the troubles of the world economy in the inter-war period:

> it was this insecurity in the markets for primary commodities which was so decisive in converting the crisis of 1929 into a major depression. This is the answer to the fundamental question which any survey of this period raises. Its misfortunes were due principally to the fact that the production of primary commodities after the war was somewhat in excess of demand. It was this which by keeping the terms of trade unfavourable to primary producers, kept the trade in manufactures so low, to the detriment of such countries as the U.K. even in the twenties, and it was this which pulled the world economy down in the early thirties. (W.A. Lewis, *Economic Survey, 1919–1939*, p. 196)

The extent to which the problems of the inter-war period stemmed from over-production of primary products is widely known to be a controversial matter. Others have preferred to indict instead the deficiencies of the gold exchange standard, or the degree of international indebtedness, or the instability of national monetary and banking arrangements. Nonetheless the significant empirical feature, which is the inverse relationship between price and supply for primary products in the inter-war period, remains. How does this look, on the ground as it were, from the standpoint of the Gold Coast cocoa economy?

The nature of the cocoa farmers' response involves a number of issues which are inter-related. What motivated farmers to supply more output in the face of falling prices? Can their behaviour be reconciled with market principles? And how did increases in supply come about? Was it through increases in productivity? Did it involve a switch of labour inputs from other activities? Did it imply some opening up of new areas and increases in numbers through migration? Although it is not possible to give definitive answers to these questions, some pointers can be derived from a range of empirical material. For purpose of exposition it is helpful to deal with the answers under three headings: changes in supply in the very long run, the long-run supply function and the short-run supply function.

It was Arthur Lewis who argued that the increase in output of primary products between the two world wars was part of a *very long run shift in supply* which had begun about 1850 (op. cit., p. 191). Two forces were at work here. First there was technological progress, especially in developed countries like the United States, where productivity in agriculture increased at an annual rate of 1.5%

between 1870 and 1930. Second, and more important according to Lewis, there was an increase in the numbers involved in primary production through migration from Europe to the newly-settled areas. Migration was instrumental in pushing out the agricultural frontier in the newly-settled areas. Elsewhere, in tropical areas which did not experience European migration, it was the opening up of new areas through developments in transport and communications which permitted the rapid increase in output of primary products. The very long run shifts in supply, together with unchanged or slow-growing demand in the inter-war period, according to Lewis resulted in the dramatic decline in the terms of trade for primary products relative to manufactures, which precipitated the inter-war Depression.

With one or two adaptations, the Gold Coast cocoa economy fits well into the picture Lewis has drawn of the very long run. Fortunately the origins and development of the cocoa industry have been well researched.[11] Briefly, cocoa production was insignificant before 1890. Between 1894 and 1936/7 it grew rapidly. At the 1936/7 peak 300,000 tons were exported, though by that date the fungus disease which was to devastate the older cocoa-growing areas was already becoming evident. The pattern of cultivation was an extensive, labour-intensive one. Farmers, whether 'migrant' or 'sedentary', cleared and occupied successive forest lands taking cocoa cultivation northwards and westwards, and in the process radically transforming the hitherto underutilised forest belt. As time went on, and knowledge of market opportunities spread, new tribal groups came into the cocoa economy. Hired labour, much of it migrant labour from adjoining territories, also became increasingly important in the industry. The development of railways and coming of motor transport similarly encouraged the extension of the margin of cultivation, as cocoa spread outwards to the Brong Ahafo border with the Ivory Coast. Unfortunately there is no evidence to suggest any significant improvements in productivity through time. Techniques of production largely carried over from subsistence agriculture provided for the needs of the new cocoa industry, and these techniques remained substantially unchanged throughout the period of inquiry.

Turning now to the question of the *long-run supply function* for cocoa, the first piece of research to address this question directly was Ady's paper on trends in cocoa production in British West Africa, published in 1949.[12] Ady set out to discover the determinants of changes in the *capacity* of the cocoa industry through time, viz. the rate of replacement of bearing trees. Assuming a constant tree mortality rate, this was identified with the rate at which farmers planted new trees. Using data on Gold Coast cocoa output and price between 1920 and 1940, a strong positive correlation was observed between cocoa output and price when the price variable was lagged nine years. The nine-year lag was assumed to represent the period of time taken for a tree to reach full bearing capacity. The conclusion was that

> Changes in the magnitude of cocoa exports from the Gold Coast in the period 1930–1940 were to be explained largely by the effect on planting some nine years earlier of changes in cocoa prices. (Ady, ibid., p.390)

In other words, the expanding output of the early 1930s was the result of a relatively prosperous cocoa industry in the period 1920–1924.

In terms of new plantings, the investment decision was shown to be entirely positive and orthodox, i.e. in line with observed price changes. Later studies by Ady (and others) confirmed these findings using data for the post-World War II period under statutory cocoa marketing.[13] What was termed the 'long-run supply function', output and lagged price, showed a strong positive relationship, though a twelve-year lag was now suggested to operate between price and output – a change brought about by changes in the variety of cocoa planted.

A major shortcoming of these studies, though one which was fully recognised by the researcher involved, is that they failed to come to grips with the question of the *short-run supply function*. Although price has been shown to determine the capacity of the industry via new plantings, actual output in any one year depends, among other things, on the harvesting and marketing decision. How then does one explain the strong inverse relationship which characterised current cocoa price and output in the Gold Coast in the inter-war period? Why did farmers continue to harvest and market the crop in increasing quantities, when faced by falling prices? One possibility is that farmers had become accustomed to a certain cash income, and alternative employment opportunities with their associated transfer earnings were of negligible importance. Thus Ady argues that

> No index need be included in the analysis for the rate of transfer earnings ... Other cash crops had ceased to be serious competitors of cocoa by 1920 ... Alternative crop prices enter neither the short nor the long run analysis ... This is also true of urban occupations, for the peasant farmers did not engage in urban pursuits ... similarly wage-rates for mining labour had no influence, since the tribes from which such labour is forthcoming are from areas hundreds of miles away, and not those of the cocoa villages closer at hand. (op. cit., 1949, p.393)

In such circumstances we can envisage that farmers, in an attempt to compensate for falling prices, would actually increase output in order to maintain the standard of living to which they had become accustomed.

Alternatively it could be argued that in circumstances where alternative employment opportunities outside cocoa were zero, then at any one time the transfer earnings of labour in harvesting and marketing an orchard crop like cocoa are the earnings from labour devoted to tree planting. The fall in the price of cocoa makes investment less profitable, i.e. it lowers the transfer earnings. The 'cost' of labour in producing current output falls accordingly. If this fall in labour costs is greater than the fall in the price of cocoa, then it may still be profitable, and therefore rational, to produce more output.

To conclude on the questions posed earlier, concerning the cocoa farmers' supply response: cocoa output in the inter-war period was strongly influenced by very long-run changes, not so much in techniques of production as in changes in such things as the availability of land, knowledge of market opportunities, new forms of transport and labour mobility. Fundamental supply shifts, coupled with relatively slow-growing demand, resulted in increasingly unfavourable terms of trade for cocoa producers in the inter-war period. At all times, however, their behaviour can be shown to be reconcilable with market principles. Investment decisions, leading to changes in the capacity of the industry, responded to market forces, and the short-run harvesting and marketing decision can also be shown to be rational, under certain assumptions concerning the level of transfer earnings. 'Market failure' in relation to primary production in the inter-war period, at least as far as the Gold Coast cocoa farmers were concerned, does not imply an absence of economic calculations on the part of the producers themselves.

Economic calculations notwithstanding, Table 6 demonstrates the very real hardship suffered by the cocoa farmers from 1927 onwards. Over a ten-year period, the price received by the farmer, after allowance had been made for transport and brokerage charges, declined from £47 per ton in the 1927/28 season to £15.4 per ton in the 1935/36 season. In the following season the cocoa price improved but the revival was short-lived; a further drop at the beginning of the next season, 1937/38, led farmers into the famous cocoa hold-up which resulted in the appointment of the Nowell Commission. There had been cocoa hold-ups before, as early as 1903, and notably in 1930/31. But this one was generally recognised to be different.[14]

TABLE 6

Cocoa Season	Output[1] '000 tons	Average total price to the agricultural community[2]	Average up-country transport cost (head-loading and lorry)	Average price to the farmer
		£ per ton	£ per ton	£ per ton
1927–28	210	48.40	1.6	46.80
1928–29	225	35.42	1.4	34.02
1929–30	238	31.99	1.2	30.79
1930–31	190	17.78	1.2	16.58
1931–32	244	17.23	1.2	16.03
1932–33	233	16.55	1.2	15.35
1933–34	236	12.16	1.2	10.96
1934–35	230	14.34	1.1	13.24
1935–36	268	16.51	1.1	15.41

Source: Cmnd. 5845 (1938) Nowell Commission, for Cols. 3, 4, 5.

Notes: 1. roughly equivalent to export volume. No significant domestic consumption.
2. F.O.B. export price less brokerage and other charges at the ports.

The main difference between the hold-up of 1937–38 and its predecessors lay in the depth of support on which it was able to call. Whereas in earlier years hold-ups had failed because the sectional interests of the various groups involved failed to coincide for a brief length of time, in 1937–38 the interests of the most important elements remained complementary throughout the season. (Southall, ibid., p.110)

If, as has been argued by some, colonial policy had undergone a sea-change by 1939, then the role that the 1937–38 cocoa hold-up played in this turnabout for colonial policy may be a matter of some significance.

II COLONIAL POLICY AND THE GOLD COAST 1919–1945

Studied as an aspect of British economic policy between the wars, colonial policy towards the dependent empire, of which the Gold Coast formed a small but significant part, has been shown to present some unifying themes. First and foremost, in the inter-war period, there was the Treasury view that the colonies should pay their own way. In the 1920s this was manifested in a large measure of distrust and reservation, on the part of the Treasury, about the policies which emanated from the Colonial Office between 1918 and 1929, successively under Secretaries of State for the Colonies, Milner and

Amery. I.M. Drummond (*Imperial Economic Policy, 1917–1939*), has labelled Amery, Milner and others with certain ideas in common, the imperial 'visionaries' of the inter-war period.[15] It was they who favoured Empire developments principally as a solution to Britain's own problems in the inter-war period. Particularly, they advocated more government assistance for empire migration, and increased capital exports. Migration would directly assist the British unemployment problem. Capital exports would boost the capital goods industries in Britain. Colonial development, aided by migration and investment in transport, education, health and research, would ultimately benefit Britain through higher imports, provided that an appropriate preferential tariff structure could be devised. Colonial development of course meant increased output of primary products. The traditional division of labour between Europe and the colonies was envisaged as continuing, albeit at lower costs.

From the end of the First World War, the imperial visionaries argued for colonial development in the face of Treasury opposition, the latter claiming that colonial borrowing would encourage overspending and raise interest rates. Nevertheless, some limited impact was made on the dependent empire in the 1920s. For the first time Africa began to figure prominently in Colonial Office thinking. Milner helped to establish the London School of Tropical Medicine. A Colonial Research Committee was appointed to advise on agricultural research, and small sums of money were made available. A Bill was introduced into parliament guaranteeing loans to be raised by East African governments. Finally, in 1929, the Secretary of State for the Colonies in the second MacDonald Government, Sidney Webb (Lord Passfield), introduced the Colonial Development Bill which authorised regular grants to aid colonial development.

According to Drummond, the 1929 Act was the last expansionary theme in colonial economic policy before 1940. In the 1930s Treasury opinion reasserted itself, and the dependent empire was seen as an aspect of Britain's budgetary problem. Dependent colonies were to be managed in such a way as to minimise demands on the Exchequer, and to improve the position of sterling. For the colonies this meant reduced expenditures and increased taxation, trade surpluses and reduced capital inflows. Some extensions were also made to the preferential tariff system, with British goods paying lower rates of duty in certain parts of the dependent empire. Quotas were introduced to exclude Japanese textiles from some colonies.

The outbreak of war in 1940 intensified the control which Britain exercised over the dependent empire, and brought into sharper focus the exploitative nature of the relationship between the centre and the periphery. Stringent currency controls were imposed by the Bank of England on all transactions within the sterling area. Colonial imports were restricted both to save currency and to economise on shipping space. As a result sterling balances accumulated in London, amounting to some £3.5 million by the end of the war, effectively constituting a 'forced loan' to bolster Britain's payments position.

The marketing boards, as they came to be called, were introduced into the dependent empire in 1939 largely as the result of a long-standing official desire for more orderly marketing of colonial peasant crops. The marketing boards quickly became indispensable as wartime economic agencies, controlling the supplies of raw materials. This was one instance where British domestic economic planning spilled over into the colonies during World War II. There were others. For instance in 1940 the Colonial Development and Welfare Act extended the 1929 Act in terms both of the scale of assistance offered, and of the type of projects which could be supported. Furthermore, colonial governments were urged to prepare development programmes for a period of years ahead, as a condition for the granting of assistance.

The Gold Coast

When we come to look at the policies pursued by the colonial administration on the Gold Coast between the wars and during World War II, a working hypothesis might run as follows. In the 1920s the Gold Coast was of limited interest to the British Government; as Drummond (op. cit.) argues, it was simply 'a locus for a little employment-generating government expenditure'. In such circumstances a Governor, like Guggisberg on the Gold Coast, might pursue policies broadly in line with the mood of the Colonial Office, though from time to time he could expect opposition if there was any tendency on his part to 'overspend'. From 1930 onwards, however, the picture changed as Treasury orthodoxy reasserted itself. The Gold Coast Colony had to be managed with the claims of sterling as a prime objective of Treasury policy. In the Gold Coast of the 1930s capital expenditure declined, development expenditure ceased altogether, and the economy operated within the constraints of a budget surplus. Despite falling export proceeds sterling balances accumulated, and the direction of trade became increasingly biased towards Britain. Thus in many respects the 1930s was the most unfortunate era in colonial economic relationships. The Gold Coast was increasingly managed according to Treasury objectives for the British economy, giving way ultimately, during the Second World War and its aftermath, to a significant degree of exploitation. During the war large sacrifices were demanded of peasant producers and urban wage earners, most of whom had, in any case, a very marginal standard of existence.

The question we now ask is how and to what degree economic policy on the Gold Coast was influenced by the decolonisation movement in the inter-war period. Flint has reminded us that informed groups in Britain and overseas had been arguing strongly for the economic, social and political advancement of colonial peoples throughout the 1930s. He refers not only to the officials in the colonial office, but also to members of parliament, the Fabian Colonial Bureau, British trade unions, the Anti-Slavery and Aborigines Protection Society, academic and university opinion.[16]

Flint has argued, moreover, in his broader thesis, that consideration of policies of decolonisation were entirely British in inspiration (with no other colonial power in Africa contemplating such steps before 1958) and that these British ideas antedated the outbreak of war. He goes on to argue that this was not the reaction of an 'exhausted' imperial power realising its own weakness, but contemplated as means of strengthening British economic and international influence, and that the element of nationalism played no part in these developments – the emergence of nationalist political parties seeking mass support was the *result of decisions to decolonise* and a creation of imperial policy.

> It could be taken for granted that anything in the shape of direct election ... would be out of the question for some time to come. Britain could not decolonise to mere compradors, the new elite would have to demonstrate that it had genuine support from the masses at large.[17]

To what extent did economic policy on the Gold Coast reflect the burgeoning in Britain of a new philosophy of self-government for the colonies? There is a measure of support for this hypothesis. For instance, in the area of social welfare there were important developments from the mid-1930s onwards indicative of changes in attitudes on the part of the colonial government. The Report of the Education Committee of the Gold Coast, 1937–1941, formed the basis of an expanded educational policy. Although the Gold Coast had the highest percentage of children in any African colony receiving full-time education, nevertheless in 1939 only 1,000 children were attending Gold Coast secondary schools. The new educational policy involved a commitment to universal education of six years' duration and provision for expanded secondary education. Official attitudes towards the urban working classes also changed, with adequate trade union legislation being made a condition for the granting of assistance under the 1940 Colonial Welfare and Development Act.

Another important change in colonial policy from the late 1930s onwards was the emphasis on government intervention in the development process and the espousal of planning techniques. There is undoubtedly an important link here between the ideas of planned economic development, and new attitudes towards political change in West Africa, both of which appear to have been articulated well before the outbreak of World War II. Secretary of State Macdonald had linked the idea of political advance with social and economic development through state action, in speeches in 1938 and 1939. An important measure of material progress must precede the granting of self-government, an idea which received further reinforcement from Lord Hailey's *African Survey*.[18]

According to Flint, 'the new sentiments, taken together, amounted to an almost total reversal of the attitudes of the 1920's and early 1930's'.[19] Furthermore, if Flint is right that a consensus on planned decolonisation had been reached as early as 1943 between politicians in Britain and potential West African nationalists, then the emergence and development of certain groups or classes during the inter-war period is of great importance. These are the groups or classes which in the event were to spearhead the post-war nationalist movement on the Gold Coast, the professional and salaried classes supported by urban wage-earners.

Nevertheless, when colonial policy on the Gold Coast is subjected to more careful scrutiny, it appears that whatever the demands of decolonisation might have been, the Colonial Office was very often reluctant to don the mantle of interventionism during our period. For purposes of more detailed analysis of colonial policy on the Gold Coast, we can divide the years 1919–1945 into two phases. The first, from 1919–1930, largely corresponds to the quite exceptional Governorship of Guggisberg (1919–1927) and his ambitious Ten Year Development Programme. The second phase, 1930–1945, was ushered in by a 60% fall in the value of cocoa exports. This phase illustrates the combined and somewhat contradictory nature of the decolonisation movement, which *prima facie* required massive investment to promote material advance, together with the Treasury's requirements for retrenchment in the adverse economic conditions of the 1930s and World War II, and the innate 'market orientation' of Colonial Office thinking.

The Guggisberg Era

During the Governorship of Gordon Guggisberg, from 1919 to 1927, the Colony embarked upon an ambitious Ten Year Development Programme, with proposed expenditures of £24m on projects in transport, communications, water supply, drainage, electric power, agriculture and education (Table 7).

This was a quite remarkable break with the traditions of colonial economic management and Guggisberg is remembered to this day as having brought to the Gold Coast pronounced liberal attitudes in the area of long-term economic development. In political terms, however, Guggisberg appears to have been highly conservative. Again this illustrates the trap of too readily associating 'development' with 'decolonisation' in the official mind.

TABLE 7

The Guggisberg Era: The Ten Year Development Programme

	Original Plan 1919	Revised Plan 1922	Revised Plan 1927
Harbours	2,000,000	1,840,000	3,551,000
Railways	14,581,000	6,076,000	5,948,000
Roads	1,000,000	750,000	1,619,000
Water Supplies	1,790,000	1,208,000	634,000
Town Improvements	1,850,000	300,000	740,000
Hydraulics	2,000,000	200,000	199,000
Public Buildings	1,100,000	1,000,000	2,273,000
Posts and Telegraphs	90,000	422,000	336,000
Maps and Surveys	200,000	120,000	200,000
Agriculture and Forestry	–	–	252,000
Takoradi Town	–	–	669,000
Miscellaneous	–	100,000	225,000
	£24,611,000	£12,016,000	£16,646,000

From Kimble, D., *A Political History of Ghana, 1850–1928*, Oxford 1963.

By the standards of the time Guggisberg inherited an already prosperous dependent Colony. During the First World War, despite disruptions and shipping shortages, the peasant cocoa crop had come to dominate the export earnings of the Colony. The immediate post-war years of 1919 and 1920 were boom years for external trade, and in his first year of office the Governor enjoyed a revenue surplus of over £1½ million. Non-agricultural African employment was on the increase, especially in mining, and parallel increases were also to be noted in internal exchange activity and the volume of money.

The Ten Year Development Programme which Guggisberg introduced within months of taking office broke sharply with accepted ideas which emanated at that time from the Treasury in Britain.

The idea that 'countries' which had been pronounced to be political entities without knowing anything about it had a *right* to receive injections of capital was one that lay in the future, as far as the British were concerned. Although considerable achievements grew out of this situation, to the eternal credit of colonial officials working on shoe-strings, it was a modest interpretation of Chamberlain's doctrine of 'developing the estate'. The purpose of good administration tended to be better administration, rather than economic development by the Colonial Power. Development was a marginal rather than a central activity; within the limits of British Treasury doctrine it could never be otherwise. (Wraith, in *Guggisberg*, op. cit., p. 99)[20]

Guggisberg's Programme was financed in three ways: by loans raised on the London market (£4m. at 6 per cent in 1921, and £4½m. at 4½ per cent in 1925), from accumulated balances, and from revenue. Being thus financed from the colony's own resources, it did not contradict the doctrine of colonial self-sufficiency.

The long-run objectives of the plan were to improve communications in order to get agricultural produce to market, and to provide for a higher level of national wealth out of which improved education and technical training might be financed. The overarching goal of the Programme appears to have been improved educational standards. Successful implementation, however, depended almost entirely on a prosperous export sector, and in particular, on high prices for the peasant export crop, cocoa. Unfortunately, following on from the boom years of 1919 and 1920, cocoa prices remained depressed throughout the period 1920–1945. Indeed, apart from isolated years, 1927, 1928 and 1937, cocoa prices showed a marked decline as the period proceeded. Inevitably, there was retrenchment. Proposed developments in hydro-electrics, town improvements and the railways were either abandoned or cut back. By the end of the governorship in 1927 only about £16½m. had been committed out of the planned £24m. expenditure.

In 1927 Guggisberg was retired from the Gold Coast, and on leaving was told that there were no other appointments vacant, 'curious circumstances for a man who had been the most popular and successful Governor of his day' (Wraith, op. cit.). His strange career illustrates the complexities of the colonial relationship during the inter-war period. Although personally appointed by Milner, and apparently held in esteem by Amery, the attitude of the Colonial Office to Guggisberg was always ambivalent. Within three years of his taking office the pattern was set, as Guggisberg strongly dismissed the views of the Secretary of State's own Committee on West African Trade and Taxation. Reporting in 1922, the Committee had concluded that the Gold Coast Colony, along with Nigeria and Sierra

Leone, was 'incurring expenditure in excess of that revenue' which it had 'a reasonable prospect of obtaining from existing taxation'. Investment was being undertaken on 'too lavish a scale and with too great rapidity'.[21] Even in the relatively prosperous trading conditions of the 1920s the Colonial Office was recommending that the Governments concerned should 'submit their expenditure to drastic revision, and (where possible) remit taxation' (ibid). In his reply to the Secretary of State, the Governor stressed the need to maintain development expenditure, for 'unless the Gold Coast spends every penny it can justly afford on extending its present lamentably inadequate facilities for transport, education and sanitation, its progress must and will be so hopelessly retarded as to give real cause for discontent, unrest, and failure to compete with other countries'.[22] The arguments were repeated throughout his Governorship. The Colonial Office was cautious; the Governor was determined to press ahead in the fields of education, transport, public health and other infrastructural investment.

Surprisingly, perhaps, the investment which Guggisberg initiated, and which may have played a role in the circumstances of his departure, appears to have continued for a significant length of time after 1927. Governor Slater who succeeded Guggisberg in 1927 recommended to the Secretary of State a policy of consolidation, and the official Statement of Expenditures indicates that capital expenditure on the Gold Coast did not peak until 1930. The collapse of the cocoa price in the season 1930/1931, rather than the departure of Guggisberg, marked the beginning of retrenchment in capital expenditure. There is however an interesting postscript on the question of official attitudes towards the Guggisberg Programme, in Colonial Office policies for the post-war reconstruction period. In 1941 the Colonial Office set out preliminary ideas for coping with the economic problems of the dependent empire after the cessation of hostilities. In a thinly-veiled reference to Guggisberg, some 14 years after his departure from the Gold Coast, C. L. M. Clauson attacked the 'unco-ordinated and badly conceived development' which followed on World War I in the Colonial Empire when 'Large sums of money were borrowed at high rates of interest to construct public works of various kinds – railways, harbours etc. – some of which have been a burden rather than a help to the territories which constructed them ever since. It is obvious that this must not occur again'. By 1941 the economic requirements of decolonisation were being debated in official circles, and the Colonial Development and Welfare Act was on the statute book. Nevertheless Guggisberg and his 1920s programme of 'public works' still appear to have been regarded in a highly unfavourable light.[23]

1930–1945

From the standpoint of colonial economic management, the striking contrast between the 1920s and the years which followed was the change in budgetary style as Treasury views came to dominate colonial policy. According to Drummond (op. cit.) we can best understand colonial policies of the time if we think about sterling, debt service, the budget and unemployment. 'Sterling' involved the management of the dependent empire to improve sterling's position in terms of the UK exchange rate and reserves. 'Debt management' meant that the government tried to ensure that colonial borrowers would not over-commit themselves and would be able to pay their UK debts. The 'budget' was the UK budget. Colonies must pay their own way without outside assistance. 'Unemployment' was British unemployment, implying particular help for exports of British capital and old staples such as textiles.

Thus on the Gold Coast in the 1930s the budget deficits which had characterised every year but two since 1918 were translated into budget surpluses. Borrowing to finance development was at an end. Significantly this change in policy, agreed between the Gold Coast Governor and the Secretary of State in 1930, came at a time when the cocoa price was still credible and Gold Coast reserves relatively healthy, following a high cocoa price in the 1929 season.[24] Further restraint on government spending was signalled when the cocoa price did indeed decline dramatically in the 1933 season. Not until 1945 did public spending in real terms return to its 1921 level.

The implications of Treasury policy for foreign exchange and the capacity to import were equally unhelpful to the Gold Coast in the depressed trading conditions of the 1930s. Despite a massive decline in earnings from cocoa exports, the Gold Coast economy continued with its characteristic surplus on visible trade, accumulating reserves in London which in effect constituted an interest-free loan to Britain.

In commenting upon the likely effects of these policies in West Africa in the 1930s, we must be wary of judging those who carried them out in terms of economic processes which were only imperfectly understood at the time. After all, as Kindleberger reminds us, there were very few public figures in the 1930s even in the USA, who had domestic remedies which 'made sense in modern terms' (op. cit., p. 24). Nevertheless it seems clear that the pursuit of objectives such as those suggested by Drummond would have ruled out an effective counter-cyclical policy on the Gold Coast in the 1930s, and that the requirement for the colony to pay its own way in spite of falling customs revenues was unlikely, in the circumstances, to offer much hope of respite from the vicissitudes of trade.

Much of what was happening at the macro-level on the Gold Coast at this time was not perceived directly by the average Gold Coast citizen. If Treasury policies were 'exploitative' it was a form of exploitation which was only indirectly felt. Price-fixing of the major export crop, cocoa, was a different matter altogether. As we have noted earlier, low cocoa prices had led over the years to a number of cocoa hold-ups, the most serious of which had brought the appointment of the Nowell Commission which reported in 1938. Low cocoa prices in the 1930s were generally perceived by cocoa farmers to be the outcome of exploitation by European merchants, in which the colonial government acquiesced.

During the war years, however, despite the most stringent official policies there was no serious political opposition on the Gold Coast. At first sight this is remarkable, in view of previous experience and the severity of controls. For instance, spending outside the sterling area was stopped entirely in order to maintain Britain's currency reserves. Local investment could take place only if it made use of local and not imported capital goods and materials. All imported goods were increasingly scarce because of the need to economise on shipping space.

Strict controls were exercised over the production and export of raw materials and foodstuffs, particularly after the fall of Malaya and the loss of supplies from the Far East. On the Gold Coast this meant that the Ministry of Food (subsequently the West African Cocoa Control Board) undertook the bulk purchase of the cocoa crop. Prices were to be fixed 'at a low level' on the grounds that

(*i*) this was a crop in 'surplus supply', as compared with other crops such as oilseeds, palm oil and rubber, which had become scarce following the outbreak of war with Japan;

(*ii*) the supply of labour to alternative 'military works' needed to be encouraged; and

(*iii*) a 'careful watch' was needed on inflation, in circumstances where the supply of domestically-produced and imported consumer goods was severely restricted.[25]

In consequence, throughout the war years, the Gold Coast cocoa farmer received a price for his crop roughly equivalent to that obtaining in the worst years of the depression, viz. £18 per ton.

That severe wartime restrictions did not evoke strong protest on the Gold Coast may be attributed to a number of factors. First there was British wartime propaganda, which emphasised the need to protect the interests of different races within the dependent empire, by the defeat of Nazi Germany. This view can be found expressed in speeches by Secretary of State MacDonald from 1939 onwards.

Those in Britain who espoused the decolonisation movement were quick to point out the implications for the economic development of Africa when the allied victory should eventually come.

Second, though the cocoa farmers undoubtedly lost out during the Second World War, as indeed they did in the 1930s, this was probably not the case for the Gold Coast population as a whole. The immediate impact of the war was to increase market opportunities for locally-produced foodstuffs and raw materials as British and later U.S. troops were stationed on the Gold Coast, which became an important staging post on the route to the Far East.

In 1943 a West African War Council was established, covering the four West African colonies of the Gold Coast, Nigeria, Gambia and Sierra Leone. The War Council had a two-fold function: to ensure that British and American troops had sufficient local foodstuffs, and that exports of commodities in short supply attained certain pre-determined targets. Price support schemes were introduced, and significant increases were recorded on the Gold Coast in the output from local farms of vegetables, cereals, pig-meat and poultry. Production targets were established for important raw materials such as manganese, bauxite, timber, copra and palm products. Foods such as millet and rice to feed the local population also enjoyed a price support system. Thus although firm statistical evidence is lacking for the war years, it is highly likely that outside the cocoa economy, agriculture and associated local activities were relatively prosperous. Employment generally, other than in gold mining, most probably increased significantly as government expenditure doubled between 1939 and 1945. Particular emphasis was placed on developments in transport, and the airport at Accra was also extended. There is evidence too of an acceleration in the pace of urbanisation.

A third factor explaining the relative political stability of the Gold Coast under wartime controls, when compared now with the immediate post-war years, is the behaviou: of domestic prices. In 1947/48 the urban riots took place which led to the appointment of the Watson Commission. These riots took place against the background of rapidly increasing prices for domestically produced goods, especially local foodstuffs in urban areas. At this time cocoa farmers were enjoying the benefits of the post-war boom in commodity prices, and their enhanced income-earning opportunities placed pressure on domestic prices. During the war, by way of contrast, although import prices were rising rapidly, the prices of domestically produced goods and services on which urban wage-earners depended were held in check, both by the increased output of staple foodstuffs and by the relatively depressed purchasing power of the cocoa economy. Thus it appears that by 1939 it was largely the urban groups who held the key to the willingness or otherwise of the people of the Gold Coast to accept the restraints which colonial economic policy placed on them.

The outbreak of war led Britain to adopt economic policies which, by any objective standard, must have inflicted considerable damage on the economy of the Gold Coast. But there was a more positive side to colonial policy at that time, as witnessed in the activities of the West African War Council. The WAWC, under Lord Swinton, had a very wide brief in economic matters. In addition to the price support schemes already mentioned, which aimed to increase the output of locally-produced foodstuffs, the WAWC was called upon to devise policies in the areas of export price stabilisation and marketing, the activities of merchants, the development of local industries, tariffs and land policy. Lord Swinton's memorandum, 'Economic Policy in the West African Colonies', submitted to the War Cabinet in 1943, made specific reference to the altered political circumstances of the time, in which it was explicitly stated that although Britain was responsible for the development of the social, political and economic institutions of West Africa, this was only until such a time as the people 'can safely assume the responsibilities of government themselves'.[26] Yet in practice, little that was absolutely new emerged from the WAWC. Primary production was still to be the mainstay of the economy, though producers were to be encouraged to attend to local consumption as well as to exports. Local industries should be developed, though in an interesting new departure it was suggested that where such industries required large amounts of imported capital, their location, scale, and degree of local participation should be controlled through a Government licensing system. In agriculture, however, no such encouragement should be given to large-scale units employing foreign capital. The longstanding policy which discouraged the alienation of land by European-owned plantations was to be upheld.

The West African War Council was dissolved after the end of the War, and no attempt was made to replace it by any new body with similar aims, i.e. to increase and diversify the output of local foodstuffs, and to co-ordinate economic policy between the three colonies. As an example of greater state involvement in terms of planning, co-operative marketing and price stabilisation the WAWC has some historical significance, but it was short-lived, and indicates that the Colonial Office was in no sense wholly committed to a more active role in the economic modernisation of the Gold Coast, despite the message of decolonisation. Once the requirements of wartime economic control were relaxed, the colonial government appears to have been quite willing to revert to its previous role.

CONCLUDING REMARKS

The inter-war period in West Africa, more especially the period of World War II, is a little-researched area. This is to be regretted, since the study of these years can be expected to illuminate important aspects of the long-term development of the region, including producers' motivations and responses, at a time of great political and social change. These years saw important changes in Britain in political attitudes towards the dependent empire. It was also the period in which the fortunes of certain sections of the rural population of West Africa underwent a dramatic decline.

This study has suggested for the Gold Coast

(*a*) that the years 1930–1945 do have the combined and contradictory effects of the decolonisation movement, which *prima facie* required massive investment to promote material advance, and the Treasury's requirements for retrenchment in the adverse economic conditions of the 1930s and World War II. But there is scant evidence that the Colonial Office actively sought an interventionist role on the Gold Coast during the period in question. If indeed we accept Flint's view, that policies of decolonisation were British in inspiration, and that these ideas antedated the outbreak of war, we must nevertheless conclude that economic policy on the whole was at variance with the demands of political change throughout the period.

(*b*) that the rising fortunes of those classes – professional, salaried and urban wage-earners in the inter-war period – who were to spearhead the post-war nationalist movement, are of some importance. Largely this was the outcome of overproduction of cocoa in the inter-war period, which shifted income away from the traditional rural centres of prosperity based on the cocoa economy, and in favour of the professional classes and urban skilled and unskilled workers. The rapid process of urbanisation of the Gold Coast during the inter-war period was a development of great significance, though it appears to have been a process which was only imperfectly understood and appreciated at that time by the colonial government.

NOTES

Earlier drafts of the paper benefited from comments received at Workshops of the 'Third World History and Development' Study Group. I am grateful too, for comments from colleagues Colin Simmons, Gregory Anderson and Robert Millward at the University of Salford, and for the research assistance of Robert Ward.

The term 'Gold Coast' throughout, refers to the Colony, Ashanti and Northern Territories, governed as the Gold Coast according to Orders in Council, 1901.

1. C. P. Kindleberger, *The World in Depression, 1929–1939* (London, 1973). For an antidote to his essentially Keynesian approach see M. Friedman and A. Schwartz, *A Monetary History of the United States, 1867–1960* (Princeton, 1963), with its conclusion that the monetary policy of the United States was responsible for the Depression. This latter book evokes interest because of its broader implications for the role of the market. Lines of research being pursued in relation to the inter-war period are to be found in K. Brunner ed., *The Great Depression Revisited* (Rochester N.Y., 1981).
2. W. A. Lewis, *Economic Survey, 1919–1939* (London, 1949).
3. Szereswski estimated the Gold Coast National Income between 1891 and 1911, and offered projections on this basis to 1960 (*Structural Changes in the Economy of Ghana, 1891–1911*, London 1965). The fundamental problems associated with Szereswski's procedures were discussed in my book *Tropical Exports and Economic Development* (1981). Szereswski's GDP data have now been updated for the period 1911 to 1950 in an unpublished Ph.D. thesis (Francis Teal, School of Oriental and African Studies, University of London, 1984) showing an increase in GDP per capita between 1919 and 1939, from 108 Million Cedis (1968 prices) in 1919, to 163 Million Cedis (1968 prices) in 1939. Unfortunately in these estimates many of the problems associated with Szereswski's work, in particular his calculations of domestic private consumption and gross capital formation, remain unresolved. I am grateful to Mr. J. H. Frimpong-Ansah for drawing my attention to Dr Teal's work.
4. A. G. Hopkins, *An Economic History of West Africa* (London, 1973), p. 253.
5. According to Cardinall, who was the chief census officer, more inaccurate information was returned on the subject of occupations than for any other inquiry. For instance, no clerks were returned from the mining area, though it was obvious that mining companies had clerks in their employ. A. W. Cardinall, *The Gold Coast, 1931* (Government Printer, Accra, 1931), pp. 169–70.
6. More generally on the problem of wartime inflation of import prices in primary producing countries see A. R. Prest, *The War Economics of Primary Producing Countries* (Cambridge, 1948).
7. W. Birmingham, 'An Index of the Real Wages of Unskilled Labourers in Accra, 1939–1959', *Economic Bulletin of Ghana*, 4, 1960.
8. On the question of the *availability* of domestically produced foodstuffs we are once again in the hazy area of the internal exchange economy. One point which has often been overlooked is that domestic foodstuffs linked, in a complementary fashion, to cocoa output, since food crops were used to provide shade for cocoa seedlings and young cocoa trees. As far as domestic *exchange* of staple foods is concerned, some fragmentary evidence for the 1930s and during the period of World War II was provided in a paper by H. P. White published in the mid-1950s, which looked at data on truck loadings gathered at a number of check-points, southwards from the Northern Territories and westwards from South Togoland and Trans-Volta. In the case of westbound traffic on the Senchi Ferry, records had been kept since 1929. Traffic on the Senchi Ferry declined between 1932 and 1935 but rose rapidly thereafter, including during the period of World War II. Trade increases, though less dramatic, were also noted on the Volta ferries during World War II. H. P. White, 'Internal Exchange of Staple Foods in the Gold Coast', *Economic Geography*, 32, April 1956.
9. A. Hopkins, *An Economic History of West Africa*, ibid.
10. An impressionistic account of these new opportunities and their effects on the internal exchange economy is to be found in Fortes' address given at Chatham House in 1944. In this he argued that West Africa's role as a port of call for convoys to the Middle and

Far East was bringing about significant social and economic changes in the local economy.

> The war has made possible previously undreamt of development of new agricultural and manufactured products in West Africa. Restriction of overseas supplies, coupled with considerable local demand emanating from the army, aerodrome staffs and transit ocean and air traffic has been the main stimulus. In addition to timber for construction and for export, large quantities of shingles, creosoted poles and lately furniture, have been produced in the Gold Coast.

M. Fortes, 'The Impact of the War on British West Africa', *International Affairs*, 21 (2), April 1945, 217.

11. P. Hill, *The Migrant Cocoa Farmers of Southern Ghana*, op. cit.; J.M. Hunter, 'Akotuakrom: A Devastated Cocoa Village in Ghana', *Institute of British Geographers – Transactions and Papers*, 29, 1961. M. Johnson, 'Migrants' Progress', *Bulletin of the Ghana Geographical Association*, 9, 1964.

12. P. Ady, 'Trends in Cocoa Production', *Bulletin Oxford University Institute Statistics*, Dec. 1949.

13. P. Ady, 'Supply Functions in Tropical Agriculture', *Bulletin Oxford University Institute Statistics*, 1968.

14. R.J. Southall, 'Polarisation and Dependence in the Gold Coast Cocoa Trade, 1890–1938', *Transactions of the Historical Society of Ghana*, 1, 1975.

15. I.M. Drummond, *Imperial Economic Policy, 1917–1939* (London, 1974) and *British Economic Policy and the Empire, 1919–1939* (London, 1972).

16. J. Flint, 'Planned Decolonization and its Failure in British Africa', *African Affairs*, 82, 328, July 1983. For example, Professor Reginald Coupland, in his influential book *The Empire in These Days* published in 1935, argued for an end to tropical exploitation and the beginnings of economic development, 'wisely planned, firmly controlled'. Moreover, this economic objective had as its political counterpart the termination of British rule – though it is clear that what Coupland had in mind was a large measure of self-government rather than total independence from the British Crown. Indeed it is claimed that his book contains the first serious suggestion from informed opinion in Britain for parliamentary self-government in West Africa.

17. Flint (ibid.), p. 405. In contrast to Flint's ideas we may set the views of Hopkins, first put forward in his paper, 'Economic Aspect of Political Movements in Nigeria and in the Gold Coast, 1918–1939', *Journal of African History*, 7, 1966, and in his later *Economic History of West Africa*, op. cit., pp. 254–8. Hopkins offered a thesis on the significance of the inter-war years, which broadly speaking runs as follows: the depressed state of trade during this period had a profound effect on the nature and organisation of political opposition to colonial rule and the rise of African nationalism. Between the end of World War I and 1930, economic problems in Nigeria and on the Gold Coast became acute. Moderate Africans with reformist policies, albeit ones which were wholly within the imperialist framework, tried to assist farmers and businessmen but they were overtaken by events. Between 1930 and 1945 there was a dramatic downturn in the fortunes of Africans, manifested in unfavourable terms of trade, declining government revenues and falling real wages. Out of this came a new political alliance which overturned moderate reformist ideas, and joined radical nationalist leaders with farmers, traders and urban wage-earners in calling for the overthrow of the imperialist system. From this alliance came the post-war movements which were to reject colonialism and bring independence to Nigeria and the Gold Coast. Independence movements were in no sense creations of the colonial masters. Rather, the growth of nationalism, in response to the economic vicissitudes of the inter-war period, 'sought and won the political kingdom' (Hopkins, ibid., 1966).

18. The idea that economic and social development must precede political change is strongly associated with Lord Hailey. His *African Survey*, however, did not appear until 1939, by which date Colonial Office ideas on development appear to have been already well established.

19. Flint, op. cit., p. 394.

20. The Guggisberg era, though fascinating, is largely neglected by researchers. Most

writers rely heavily on David Kimble's *Political History of Ghana, 1850–1928* (Oxford 1963) and R. E. Wraith, *Guggisberg* (London, 1967).

21. *Report of the Committee on Trade and Taxation for British West Africa, Sessional Paper VII, 1921–2.*
22. Despatch from the Governor to the Secretary of State, Aug. 1922.
23. I am grateful to Mr. J. H. Frimpong-Ansah for drawing my attention both to the attitude of Governor Slater (the relevant documents include CO98/57, 8 March 1930) and to the implied criticism of Guggisberg in Clauson's document of 1941, CO967/13, 31 March 1941.
24. CO98/57 (8/3/30), ibid.
25. *Report on Cocoa Control in West Africa and Statements on future policy*, Cmd. 6554, 1944, para. 25.
26. *Economic Policy in West African Colonies*, Memorandum by the Resident Minister, CO554/132/33712/1 Feb. 1943.

9

The Colonial Economy:
Nigeria and the Second World War

ROBERT PEARCE

An article sent in May 1943 from West Africa to the *Daily Mail*
in London contained a quotation from a British District Officer:
'Truth is that we have no colonial policy. For years we have drained
West Africa of her wealth without putting anything back. We have
allowed vested interests to do much as they liked.'[1] The permanent
officials at the Colonial Office decided that much of the article
was unanswerable − 'It is a fair comment' − and that nothing
could be done to stop publication of an admittedly embarrassing
piece of work.[2] The Whitehall establishment had in fact recently
been made all too aware of the absence of clearly defined objectives
in colonial policy. In September 1941 Prime Minister Winston
Churchill explained that though the Atlantic Charter, in which the
British and Americans made known their respect for the right of
people to choose their own government, had been intended to refer
primarily to those states taken over by Nazi Germany, the British
Government had made declarations on the colonies which were
'complete in themselves, free from ambiguity' and entirely in
harmony with the spirit of the Charter. Yet the search for these
statements, provoked by a parliamentary question, proved more than
a little discomfiting. They were found to be neither complete nor
unambiguous but 'scrappy, obscure and jejune'. 'Declarations on
Colonial Policy seem to have been mainly conspicuous by their
absence', noted the Secretary of State for the Colonies, 'and where
any have been made, they are vague in the extreme'.[3]

Students of colonial policy in the inter-war years will do well to
take heed of this cautionary tale: we may all be too apt, like Churchill,
to make confident statements without being aware of 'the true
nakedness of the ground'.[4] Almost all official statements on the
Colonial Empire in the inter-war period stressed the large number
and diversity of the colonies, and thus the impracticability of devising
one policy towards them all: the goal was normally defined vaguely

as being 'good government' or 'freedom'. Britain was acting as a trustee for the local inhabitants, but the nature of this trusteeship – and whether it would be temporary or permanent – was never explained. Trusteeship was in fact rather moral justification for British rule than a coherent policy to be pursued, and 'self-government', when the term was used at all, usually referred to local self-government; in other words indirect rule through tribal admin-istration, black 'independence' (a word studiously avoided) being an issue about which no one need think seriously until the next century or the one after that. Responsible self-government for white settlers in Africa was a much more important – and troublesome – issue, and one of the functions of the doctrine of trusteeship in the inter-war years was to veto settler self-government, though the doctrine itself being largely negated by the reality of settler power.[5]

With no clearly defined overall aims, and with no attempt by the Colonial Office to force the individual colonies into a pre-conceived mould, each colony was free within limits to go its own way, the initiative lying with the Governor on the periphery rather than the politician and his advisers at the centre. Indeed even within a colony there could be divided authority and significant divergence of practice, the classic example being between north and south in a Nigeria that had been unified in name only in 1914. And even when account of such divisions has been taken, the searcher after policy must tread warily, for often statements of intent in particular areas of administration, like education, were but an elaborate fiction that bore little or no resemblance to what was happening in the real colonial world.[6]

British policy statements spoke confidently if not complacently about improving economic standards in the colonies, but in practice the varied efforts of individual District Officers, often acting on their own initiative, were what mattered.[7] The Whitehall requirement was simply that the colonies balanced their budgets and dispensed with grants-in-aid, the level of income and expenditure being a totally secondary issue. It was expected that the colonial government would ensure law and order and provide roads and railways and rudimentary social services to the limit that local revenue could afford, while private European capital and enterprise could do the rest.[8] The prime concern of the colonial authorities was efficient administration. Shortages of money and of British officials meant that the pre-existing tribal institutions had to be utilised as agencies of administration, and it was recognised that rapid and unregulated economic develop-ment would undermine the way of life which made such institutions effective. Various schools of thought coexisted in British colonial Africa on this topic: in southern Nigeria, for instance, the emphasis was usually put on development and adaptation, while in the north a non-interventionist form of indirect rule grew up, viewing tradition and continuity as ends in themselves and aiming more to preserve than to develop. Generally speaking, there was an ambivalence amongst the British about the desirability of 'westernising' Nigeria. Higher standards, progress, materialism, modern ideas of competition and individualism – against these was raised a stark warning, 'What shall it profit a man if he gain the whole world and lose his own soul?'[9] In such attitudes we see not only the rationalisation of a practical administrative system into something philosophically desirable, and not only a means of perpetuating British supremacy by perpetuating colonial backwardness, but also a reflection of a perhaps unconscious public-school distaste for an increasingly industrialised and democratic Great Britain. After all, it has long been recognised that while the British official in the colonies was sympathetic and fair with tribal Africans, who respected time-honoured traditions, he found it very difficult to co-operate with the educated elite.[10]

During the Second World War much was to change. Pressure from the United States, together with the ideological requirements of a war against Nazi racialism and imperialism, meant that overall British colonial policy was at last defined, responsible self-government becoming the accepted objective, while at the same time Britain aimed to mobilise 'all the potential resources of the Colonial Empire ... for the purposes of war'.[11] Colonial governments had to stimulate and regulate production on a scale and in a manner hitherto unknown, and they themselves were subject to an unprecedented degree of direction from Whitehall.

Recent books have charted the scope of these changes in metropolitan policy, but little has so far appeared on the colonial reality.[12] The aim of this present paper is to examine colonial economic policy and practice in Nigeria from 1939 to 1945, this crucial period in which attitudes and actions were substantially modified and yet which has been either neglected or largely misunderstood in the standard literature. E. J. Usoro, writing on the Nigerian palm oil industry, manages to ignore the war years altogether;[13] A. G. Hopkins brackets the war within the 1930–45 period and minimises its special and distinguishing features;[14] while a recent book by Bade Onimode is so concerned to convict colonialism in general for 'persistent, pervasive and savage exploitation ... continuous wholesale rape and mutilation' in Nigeria that it does not cavil to analyse in any depth the crimes of particular phases.[15] Historians have perhaps painted too gloomy a picture of the Nigerian economy during the war.[16] The colonial government believed – or at least hoped – that British and Nigerian war-time economic needs would turn out to be complementary and that the war provided an excellent opportunity for improving the economic standing of the colony: imported goods were in short supply but there were compensating uses of adversity, including a more self-sufficient and diversified economy.[17] The Governor of Nigeria, Sir Bernard Bourdillon, announced in September 1942 that 'the large majority of the inhabitants of Nigeria are definitely better off than they were before the war',[18] while in 1945 an academic judged that the war might well prove to have been 'the outstanding instrument of social progress in West Africa for fifty years'.[19] This paper will question such views and, more generally, seek to analyse the development of economic policy and practice as adapted to war-time necessities in Nigeria and in the general context of economic change.

I

The two World Wars make for easy periodisation, and it is very convenient to talk about '1919–39, the colonial situation' and to dub these years the 'classic age' of colonialism.[20] Yet economically this was a period of contrasting fortunes, so much so that we may well agree with Anthony Hopkins' division of the inter-war years by the onset of the depression in 1930. Hopkins contrasts the period before 1930 (which broadly speaking was a time of rising prosperity, favourable terms of trade for West Africa, and co-operation between rulers and ruled) with the years 1930–45 (which saw depression, unfavourable terms of trade, growing discontent, and the origins of the mass nationalism that was to end formal empire).[21] The approach is neat, orderly, schematic. On this latter period he has written that 'Retrenchment was the theme, safety first the motto, and indirect rule the philosophy cut to suit the narrow cloth of the time'.[22] He has no doubt that not only the 1930s but also the war years are to be included in this division. Such generalisations cannot of course take account of the diversity of the whole of colonial West Africa, and they tell only part of the story of Nigeria's economy between 1930 and 1945.

The economic function of colonialism has been to expand the world market economy, opening up underdeveloped areas to world trade. The colonial powers aimed to use their colonies as markets for manufactured goods and to extract primary products in return, taxation and to a less extent forced labour encouraging farmers to shift from subsistence to export production. Colonial governments did not, as is so often claimed, pursue a policy of pure *laissez-faire*: they constructed roads, harbours, and bridges; they built railways and ran them; they encouraged new export crops and the adoption of more productive agricultural techniques; they instituted a system of produce inspection for exports; they made some progress in combating livestock diseases; they provided some rudimentary health and education services, to the limit that local revenue could support.[23] But though it might seem to some Tory politicians that Britain was practising 'rank Socialism' in the colonies,[24] this concern with the economic infrastructure never, in the inter-war years, amounted to a 'managed economy'. Colonial governments undertook these duties reluctantly – because no one else would do them – and hoped that they were providing the basic pre-conditions that would attract private enterprise. There was little attempt to diversify colonial economies, most territories being dependent on a small number of primary products, nor any effort to stimulate secondary industries. In West Africa production was largely in the hands of smallholders, while marketing was controlled by expatriate firms whose monopoly Africans were unable to break.

Nigeria's economy was in many ways typical. Coal had been mined at the Government Colliery at Enugu since 1915 and tin was extracted from mines on the Jos Plateau by private firms, but the economy was overwhelmingly agricultural, groundnuts being the staple product in the north, cocoa in the south-west, and palm kernels and palm oil in the south-east. Though proportions fell in the 1930s and 1940s, it was not unusual in the prosperous 1920s for palm produce to constitute half of the value of all Nigerian exports. The range of imports was great, and there is some evidence that cheap imported cloth and metalware competed with and even ousted local handicrafts.[25] Nigerian imports included a very large, though declining, percentage of goods from Britain (70.5% in 1929, 54.0% in 1939), while an increasing percentage of exports went to Britain (44.1% in 1929, 59.5% in 1939).[26] From 1900 to 1929 export volume increased by 500%, but from 1930 to 1945 the volume grew by only 20% and *per capita* output was probably stationary, increased production on the whole being due less to new agricultural techniques than to the greater area of land brought under cultivation, a sign of 'growth without development'.[27]

The depression of the early 1930s hit the staple export industries hard. Prices paid to producers plummeted (e.g. palm oil producer prices fell from £24.20 in 1928 to £5 per ton in 1934; groundnuts fell from £12.90 per ton in 1928 to £2.70 in 1934). The total value of Nigerian exports fell from £16,927,000 in 1928 to £8,560,000 in 1933, while the net barter terms of trade decreased from 86 in 1928 to 48 in 1934 and the income terms of trade from 40 in 1929 to 25 in 1931 (1953 = 100).[28] The severity of the economic storm in Nigeria revealed the inadequacy of traditional colonial policies, for the colonial government was ill-equipped to do other than reduce its expenditure and wait for better days.

Perhaps the most obvious trait of colonialism in the inter-war years was financial orthodoxy. The highest priority was given to the need to balance expenditure by recurrent revenue; second in importance was the creation of reserves to meet 'normal' contingencies, the depression itself being classified as decidedly abnormal; and so expansion came only a poor third.[29] Given the prevailing pre-Keynesian orthodoxy in Britain and the fact that the colonial government in Nigeria was administratively top-heavy, the onset of depression was greeted predictably.[30] Government revenue fell and therefore government expenditure had to be reduced accordingly. There occurred what I. F. Nicolson has described as 'the gruesome spectacle of the skeleton administration tightening its belt'.[31] Services were reduced, the government took an extra 10% of the taxes collected by the Native Administrations, and there was an official levy on salaries.[32] There was recovery, as world prices rose, but this was short-lived; and in 1938 a renewed slump hit Nigeria. Groundnuts, which had been fetching £10 a ton in Kano in December 1936, raised only £3.12 in December 1938, a fall of 68.7%. Even the profits of the United Africa Company, which had risen steadily from £428,386 in 1933 to £1,811,099 in 1937, fell back in 1938 to £699,916.[33]

In 1939 Nigeria was, as the Governor informed the Secretary of State, a country of 'very real poverty'.[34] The revenue of the government, per head of the population from all forms of taxation, was a mere 29.2p per annum (compared with £1.97 in Malaya, £1.04 in Ceylon, and £0.61 in the Gold Coast; only Nyasaland, of British colonies with a population of over one million, saw a lower yield, at £0.21). After income had been spent on servicing debts, on military expenditure, pensions, and gratuities, a mere 17p per head was available in Nigeria for administration, internal security, and social and developmental services. 2.7p per head was spent on health every year and 1.9p on education. Medical facilities had been extended in the inter-war years (in 1920 there were 16 dispensaries and 18 hospitals; in 1930 there were 89 dispensaries and 46 hospitals; and in 1940 there were 350 dispensaries and 85 hospitals[35]), but it was clear to the Governor that there was a 'staggering loss of life and efficiency' caused by preventible diseases.[36] The number of children getting some form of education, mostly in schools unassisted by the government, increased from 143,977 in 1926 to 319,476 in 1938, but the total number of boys and girls under the age of 16 was estimated at around 7,750,000 in 1942.[37] Bourdillon believed that housing conditions were 'absolutely shocking' in Lagos and that British efforts to eliminate slums compared very unfavourably not only with French but also with Italian efforts in Abyssinia.[38] There seemed to be no way of improving matters simply by modifying old policies, for Nigeria was caught 'in a vicious circle. We cannot develop this country without spending more money on our undeveloped services, and we cannot get that money until the country develops first'.[39] There are thus signs that at the end of the inter-war years the government of Nigeria was dissatisfied with the old ways: in April 1939 Governor Bourdillon urged the Colonial Office to abandon the doctrine of colonial self-sufficiency, for the future of Nigeria seemed likely to be one of stagnation unless the British Treasury were prepared to inject capital into the colonies.

The growth of this dissatisfaction in Nigeria, which parallels similar developments in Britain, should lead us to be wary of exaggerating the impact of the war in inculcating new attitudes.[40] But what had not occurred before September 1939 was the translation of an emotional desire for a colonial new deal into policy and practice. This is revealed in particular by a study of the Nigerian palm oil industry, where it was official policy to proceed very gradually.

Overall agricultural policy was well voiced by Bourdillon in 1937: the British had to go slowly and should see their task not as forcing the producer to adopt new techniques but as encouraging him to want to adopt them.[41] This viewpoint, an integral part of the philosophy of indirect rule, had the corollary that inefficiency and backwardness had to be tolerated:

> The fetish-ridden Igala with their drink-sodden priest-king ... must be as exasperating to the administrator as they are interesting to the anthropologist, but I remain convinced that we have chosen the right path. Reform will come, slowly indeed, from within; to impose it too quickly from the outside would be to leave the heart of the people unchanged and to produce a veneer with rottenness seething underneath it.[42]

Indirect rulers, believing that change had to be regulated and to be voluntarily accepted, did not put a premium on growth; and in retirement Bourdillon himself judged that a future indigenous government might well condemn the British for not having planned 'for the people against their own inclinations'.[43] This is a verdict that well illustrates the impact of the war years; for at the end of the inter-war years, especially on palm oil, he had other ideas.

It had been traditional palm oil policy to leave production in peasant hands and to restrict the scope of European firms. The clash between Sir Hugh Clifford and Lord Leverhulme over European plantations is well known, and Sir Bernard Bourdillon had similar suspicions of big business.[44] He believed that the United Africa Company fixed prices at the lowest levels that would 'satisfy the producer and persuade him to go on producing', and sometimes too low to effect this object,[45] and in the 1938 controversy over the European 'Cocoa Pool' his sympathies were very much for the producers and against the mercantile buying agreement: he believed, with the Nowell Commission, that the way forward lay with the growth of co-operative societies.[46]

In 1936 it was discovered that though the colonial government had made consistent *ad hoc* decisions it had no clearly defined policy in regard to palm oil plantations. There was not even a file on the subject: instead it had been relegated to a file on bananas.[47] In the same year the UAC obtained an area of over 6,000 acres at Ajagbo-dudu for a palm oil plantation, without the Governor even hearing of the scheme, and it was therefore decided that henceforth no alienation of land, however small, to non-natives for agricultural purposes was to be allowed without the express approval of the Governor.[48] By this time the UAC had 13,595 acres under palm production, and it seemed very doubtful that they would get more – better, according to the Colonial Office at least, to abandon the export of palm oil altogether if the industry could only be preserved by the adoption of European plantations.[49] This veto complemented the official stress on organic rather than stimulated change; but, in a far from ideal world, no viable policy existed.

The external factor which threatened traditional palm oil policy was competition from the Dutch East Indies, where plantations were in existence and methods of extraction more efficient. Controversy on this issue had blown hot and cold for decades.[50] In the late 1930s there were renewed alarums from merchants at Sumatran and Malayan competition.[51] In May 1939 Lord Trenchard, chairman of the UAC, pointed out the dangers to the Nigerian palm oil industry of competition from the Far East, stressed the need to improve methods of cultivation and extraction, and offered the Nigerian government as a gift 250 Miller (i.e. hand) presses (a figure which he increased to 300–400 when telling the tale to the Colonial Office) each worth £18, the use of which would, he insisted, increase output for the producer by 30%. But Governor Bourdillon rejected the offer.[52]

Officialdom believed that the way ahead for palm oil lay with a gradual development of traditional practices. In 1939 the Director of Agriculture, J. R. Mackie, pinned his hopes on a system of small, native-owned 'plantations' instead of reliance on the wild oil palm. He wished to see more efficient methods of production, with the cultivation of high-yielding palms and – eventually – a system in which the farmer had a palm plot and a food plot, with livestock feeding under the palms and manuring the foodcrop. This arrangement, based upon that used in coconut plantations in Fiji, was not an immediate prospect but 'should not be an unattainable ideal in Nigeria'.[53] (In fact, in 1939 such plantations covered less than 7,000 acres.[54]) Extraction would be improved by an increased use of hand-presses, to be provided cheaply or even freely, with the possibility in future of using mobile power units and small power mills. (Traditional methods of extraction yielded about 55% of oil content, hand-presses 65% and mills up to 93%.[55]) Mackie also intimated that a full-scale Oil Palm Research Station might be set up in Nigeria in the near future. In conclusion, however, he felt constrained to note that 'Progress must inevitably be slow for the next few years ... and it seems likely that during the next year or two it will be very slow indeed'.[56] It can clearly be seen that though there was a palm oil policy it was neither radical nor urgent – and nor indeed was it viable, for disappointing yields from older palm plantations soon led to the suspension of propaganda aimed at the encouragement of palm plantations.[57] It should also be noted that the Governor's rejection of free hand-presses from the UAC was only compatible with his own government's policy in view of the gradual and long-term nature of its objectives.

Yet within a few days of the start of the Second World War, the hitherto spurned UAC hand-presses were accepted by the colonial government with alacrity, with a Pioneer Mill thrown in for good measure – a small but symbolic detail.[58] As we shall see, the war delivered 'both a shock and a tonic' to the colonial economy[59] and removed the ambivalence that existed in a government which, though critical of overall economic progress, had done very little to reform or reinvigorate its own policies.

II

The loss of the Central European market, enforced by exchange controls forbidding exports to areas outside the sterling bloc, together with shipping shortages, threatened Nigeria with economic catastrophe. It was thus to the colony's benefit that the British government agreed to buy the total production of Nigeria's three main export crops: palm produce, groundnuts, and cocoa (much of which had to be destroyed for lack of shipping space). But after April 1942, and the loss of the vital war production of Britain's eastern colonies, especially Malaya, it was very much in Britain's economic self-interest to maximise Nigerian production. The market was now totally assured and virtually bottomless – a welcome contrast after the vagaries of the 1930s and a pre-condition that rendered feasible a greater degree of economic planning than ever before – and so the West African Cocoa Board, set up by the Colonial Office in 1940, was expanded to form the West African Produce Control Board. This body, through its local arm, the Nigerian Supply Board, had the task of co-ordinating the production of local foodstuffs and raw materials and the importing of needed commodities, and was responsible for the marketing of cocoa, groundnuts, and palm produce. There was a Standstill Agreement on marketing, preserving the *status quo ante bellum*,[60] and the WAPCB employed expatriate firms as agents, these firms even helping to fix the prices that were paid to producers. This was not the producers' organisation recommended by the Nowell Commission but, effectively, a dealers' monopoly – the Cocoa Pool, extended to cover other crops, under another name.[61] The war certainly dealt a blow to the development of co-operatives. Bourdillon recommended that the co-operatives should be allowed to market a quota of 7% of the total cocoa crop, an amount equal to that exported by German firms in the pre-war years, but though he pressed this proposal on the Colonial Office for several months he was ultimately forced to accept defeat.[62] Past performance also tended to determine the provision of export licences for those products not covered by the WAPCB.

Yet the major reason why the war has been bracketed with the depressed 1930s is not the marketing arrangements as such but the low prices paid to producers and the unfavourable terms of trade. The Ministry of Food set the price of cocoa (grade II) at £16.50 per ton in 1939–40, whereas in the previous season producers had received £22.25.[63] Cocoa was bought at considerably lower than world prices, and yet between 1939 and 1945 profits on the sale of Nigerian cocoa yielded £2,700,068 for Britain.[64] The case was similar with Nigeria's other exports. For several years the Ministry of Food wished to raise the prices paid to producers for palm produce and groundnuts, believing that higher prices would stimulate production, but the governments of West Africa insisted that, on the contrary, higher prices would lead to lower output and inflation, since consumer goods were in short supply; and price increases, when granted, were lower than the Ministry had desired.[65] Such unpaid profits constituted, in effect, 'a forced loan in aid of the war effort',[66] and since import prices were not subject to the same restrictions the terms of trade turned decisively against the Nigerian producers (see table).

Thus the terms of trade were worse during the war than in the worst years of the depression. If we examine the index of real producer income for the export staples (which has to be calculated in relation to a less than perfect consumer price index) we find a similarly

	Net Barter Terms of Trade	Income Terms of Trade
1939	46	30
1940	42	25
1941	37	26
1942	38	24
1943	30	19
1944	35	21
1945	39	23

Source: G. K. Helleiner, *Peasant Agriculture*, Table IV-A-6, p. 500. 1953 = 100.

gloomy but pronounced pattern. Real producer income for cocoa farmers stood at 36.6 in 1933, their worst year of the depression, but in 1943 it slumped to 32.7 (with 1948 at 100). For palm oil production real producer income for the worst years of the depression and the war were 47.8 and 38.8 respectively; for palm kernels 58.1 and 46.8; for groundnuts 59.6 and 20.8.[67] There seems here to be clear statistical justification for the periodisation adopted by Hopkins, and for his equation of the escalation of nationalism with increased economic hardship.

There are several ways in which Nigerians suffered as a result of the war. Lack of shipping, and indeed the reorientation of the British economy to war production and the necessity to restrict imports that had to be paid for with 'hard' currencies, meant a shortage of imported consumer goods. Available indices show a significant decline of such imports in the early years of the war, though by 1945 pre-war totals had in some cases been equalled or exceeded.[68] The number of bicycles had decreased between 1938 and 1941 by 74%; footwear shows a 65% drop for the same period. Cotton piece goods between 1938 (itself a very poor year for such imports) and 1941 declined by 14%, while the cost of this smaller imported volume was higher − £1,835,000 compared with £1,656,000. In all, the volume of imports, 1940−45, fell by 38% compared with the previous six-year period, while over the same years the import price grew by a startling 95%.[69] This increased cost and diminished volume helped fuel an inflation that the government proved powerless to stop. The Nigerian government did its best: it increased and encouraged local savings, in order to take money out of circulation; it successfully instituted fuel rationing and also prosecuted many believed guilty of extortion, but no comprehensive system of rationing was possible in a country like Nigeria where communications were poor, where no accurate census of population existed, and where numerous re-sales were an economic feature of daily life.[70] It was also found impossible to eliminate the black market, wherein the 'debased commercial standards' of the Syrian community were said to have found full scope.[71] As a result the Cost of Living Index rose from

100 in September 1939 to 147 in April 1942 and 174 in October 1943.[72] Nnamdi Azikiwe, the editor of the *West African Pilot* and the leading nationalist figure of the time, argued in June 1940 that the already 'disgraceful standard of living' in Nigeria was being aggravated and judged in September 1941 that 'Everywhere, men live on the border-line of poverty and in some cases poverty is even the rule of their existence'.[73]

There were other ways too in which the war had harmful effects. The level of efficiency of social services declined, especially since the colonial government was severely under-manned at this time.[74] Education was certainly a casualty. Teachers were released for military service, and the colleges at Yaba, Ibadan, and Umahia were for a time taken over by the military. The Director of Education described the position in 1940 as 'deplorable'. Since it was in many cases being found impossible to pay the salaries of well-trained and experienced teachers, untrained men on far lower salaries were taking their place.[75]

The war also led, between 1942 and 1944, to the conscription of labour to work in the Nigerian tin mines. The Ministry of Supply, the sole buyer and seller of Nigerian tin, insisted on conscription to improve output when Britain's eastern supplies were cut off by the Japanese. Increased production may have been thought necessary for the war effort, but the use of these men, in the particular conditions in which they were forced to work, seems a clear case of exploitation. Bill Freund has argued that the 'forced-labour years were perhaps the most dramatic and awful episode in the history of tin-mining in Nigeria'.[76] Around 100,000 men were conscripted for four months, 18,000 conscripts working at any one time. After a journey of often several hundred miles to the Jos Plateau, over 50% of those medically examined were found to be unfit for work; and of those who were fit around 15% deserted before their four months had ended. The colonial administration was unable to make adequate provision for the men, so that accommodation was poor, food inadequate, and medical treatment (in the words of Governor Bourdillon) 'hopelessly weak'.[77] The colonial authorities reviewed the situation in July 1942, and it seemed possible that the whole programme might be abandoned, but Whitehall insisted that it should carry on. The Nigerian government thereafter attempted to improve wages and food distribution, but their efforts do not seem to have been markedly successful. Bourdillon's successor as governor, Sir Arthur Richards, professed to be more than satisfied with affairs.[78] But there was no diminution in the death rate among labourers, official figures showing 721 deaths (8.7 per 1,000) between October 1942 and December 1943.[79] Production itself was disappointing.

The initial target of 20,000 was never reached, production rising from 16,638 tons in 1941 to only 17,107 in 1942 and 17,463 in 1943.[80] Conditions were similarly poor, if not worse, for the 4,000 men conscripted to build a dam at Tenti. Mortality rates were so high amongst the Tiv — 134 died in less than six months — that eventually all Tiv labourers had to be repatriated.[81] The good intentions of the colonial government, in instituting minimum wages and food rations and in increasing the supervision of labour officers, had not prevented the scheme — improvised at Whitehall dictation — from becoming a nightmare.

There were also anomalies in the purchasing of Nigerian goods for export. Cocoa farmers had to deliver their crop directly to the shippers to receive the full control price, with consequently high transport costs and loss of time. Most farmers in fact let middle men transport the crop and themselves received less than the already low control price.[82] Wild rubber had also often to be taken long distances to buying centres. An investigating body in 1943 found that Nigerians were often cheated of the full value of their produce at those centres, run by the agents of European firms, which were not inspected by Forestry Officers. A parcel of rubber bought for 90p when a Forestry Officer was in the district soon fetched 75p and then 50p. In one verified case rubber (accurately valued at 86p, the product of two weeks' work) was taken 60 miles to a buying centre, where it raised only 50p. At some centres wild rubber was graded at a lowly C3 without being properly examined, while C1 plantation rubber was often bought as A1. The only alternatives to accepting these unfair prices were to transport the rubber even further afield to those centres that paid the proper prices, perhaps through the use of middlemen, or to seek other means of livelihood.[83]

It has even been argued that the war led to a diminution of food production. Subsistence agriculture was disrupted in several ways — by recruitment for the Nigeria Regiment of the Royal West African Frontier Force, by conscription for the tin mines, by the diversion of production towards materials for Britain's war effort, by the drift from countryside to towns. Since there were fewer people growing food, each of whom was able to produce only a relatively small surplus, and since a lack of imported goods meant less incentive to producers, surely less food must have been available.[84] The argument has not been empirically verified but seems plausible enough. In similar vein Hopkins has argued that because of the all-important terms of trade even the domestic economy suffered in West Africa during the war. In his view the amount of money spent on domestic goods and services 'fluctuated with the level of receipts from exports, given that the proportion of earnings exchanged for imports remained more or less constant for the greater part of the colonial period'.[85] There was thus no possible refuge for colonies in the vortex of the international market economy.

III

There seems little reason to believe that during the war, as Hopkins implies, the terms of trade were determinants of Nigeria's internal economy. After all, there was a shortage of consumer goods for at least several years of the war and so the proportion of earnings spent on domestic goods would probably have risen.[86] Primary producers were worse off according to the terms of trade, but most farmers did not depend on exports for their livelihood, the bulk of commerce in Nigeria being internal.[87] There was an expansion in the amount of money in circulation (from £5,857,000 in 1939 to £15,386,000[88]) which not only boosted savings and fuelled inflation but also gave a fillip to the local economy. In fact war-time exigencies, and colonial policy, led to an important expansion in Nigeria's economy, which had perforce to become more self-sufficient and diversified.

In the export sector the expansion was the result of Britain's war needs, and colonial policy in this sphere took its lead from London, but it was none the less important for this. Tin exports rose from 10,486 tons in 1938 to over 17,000 in 1942 and 1943; and if tin production did not reach expectations, rubber production exceeded them. In January 1942 the UAC predicted that maximum annual output would be 6,000 tons, but in fact rubber exports rose from 2,778 tons (all from plantations) in 1939 to 9,395 tons (plantation and wild rubber) in 1944. Columbite exports rose from 831 tons in 1943 to 1,975 tons in 1945, by which time Nigeria was the world's leading supplier.[89] The development of new export sources of revenue, which continued to be valuable after the war, constituted an important measure of diversification for a Nigerian economy which in some sectors was exhibiting new powers of productive capacity. Coal production at Enugu rose from 323,266 tons in 1938–9 to 668,158 in 1944–5.[90] Cotton production increased.[91] Also there were new secondary industries designed to obviate the need for imports. Rope output increased from 8,400 yards in 1940 to 4,000,000 in 1944.[92] Local manufacture of bricks and tiles was boosted by the war, and so was that of soap at Apapa: output at Unilever's West African Soap Company increased from 3,072 tons in 1940 to 10,643 tons in 1945, during which time a loss of £5,335 was converted into a profit of £29,596, this 'miraculous transformation' being due entirely to the special circumstances of the war.[93] The timber industry was stimulated by construction work for the Services, a pilot saw-mill at Aponum being added to the existing mills at Lagos and Sapele, where in 1945 the UAC established a plywood factory with government support and approval.[94] Instead of the 'creaming' of Nigerian forests for quality timber like mahogany for export, a more systematic policy of forestry utilisation began during the war.[94] Forestry officers, voicing colonial policy, stressed the necessity of 'controlled scientific exploitation' proceeding 'hand in hand with regeneration'.[95] Partly as a result of this 'turning-point in Nigerian forest history'[96] it was found possible to export timber and frame houses ready for erection to the other West African colonies.[97] Only the absence of suitable machinery prevented the setting up of a factory to make sacks, import of which was partly offset by increased raffia work in the north.[98] Locally spun silk was expanded, kapok was used to manufacture lifebelts, and there was a greater use of local charcoal and gum arabic.[99] The Chief Commissioner of the Eastern Provinces referred in 1942 to 'the prodigious development of local trade and industry',[100] while the number of wage-earners in Nigeria increased from around 183,000 to 300,000.[101]

The war also led to a new emphasis in colonial policy on improved communications.[102] In the period beginning with the fall of France in June 1940 and ending with Allied victory in North Africa in February 1943, Nigeria was strategically important as a staging-post for Middle East supplies and was the scene of considerable military activity. In consequence the Public Works Department had never been so busy. These two and a half years saw the construction of 17 entirely new aerodromes; major extensions and improvements to the nine existing aerodromes; 205 miles of new road construction to all season standards; 180 miles of new dry season track; extensive major improvements, including the strengthening of bridges, on over 1,900 miles of existing roads; the construction of numerous military camps and barracks in Nigeria and the export of standard huts to Sierra Leone.[103] By the end of 1942 the Electricity Branch of the PWD had installed 19,000 new lighting points, involving 68 miles of overhead low tension distribution lines, 10.6 miles of overhead high tension lines, and 4.2 miles of underground cable.[104] By the end of 1942 the estimated cost of all public works completed or in hand totalled £2,968,000.[105] In addition the number of telephone exchanges increased from 40 in 1940 to 59 in 1945, during which period the number of post offices grew from one to 113.[106]

Nor does it seem likely that food production declined during the war, except perhaps in 1944—5. It was certainly colonial policy to make sure that it did not. In January 1939 the Director of Agriculture, J. R. Mackie, judged that if properly developed Nigeria could supply 'almost every product which could be grown in the tropics' and become virtually self-supporting;[107] and as Director of Food Production he told the Governor, at the end of 1940, that 'From the African point of view there is more food in Nigeria than ever before, and it is cheap'.[108] During the next few years, despite poor rainfall in 1942, Mackie remained satisfied with the position: one healthy sign was the increased transportation of produce from one area of the country to another, for instance oranges and gari from the east to the north and yams *vice versa*.[109] Governor Bourdillon, who had been unable to tour the country because of pressure of work until the arrival of Lord Swinton as Cabinet Minister Resident in West Africa in 1942, was relieved at the standards he found. After a trip to the north he told the Legislative Council that he had obtained 'plentiful and unshakeable evidence' at first hand that the standards of nutrition had risen considerably during the war, the people in general having a much more varied diet.[110] The Emir of Ilorin told Bourdillon that his people had never been more prosperous, the only black spot being the very high cost of imported cloth.[111]

Conclusive evidence to support or refute these contentions is not at present available. We need more local studies on the lines of Tiffen's work on Gombe Emirate, which does happen to point to increased prosperity during the war.[112] What is certain is that a shortage of imported foodstuffs for Europeans, whose numbers were dramatically swelled by servicemen, led to the domestic production of such items, a proportion of which − but probably only a very small proportion − went to the local population. The Agricultural Department, founded in Southern Nigeria in 1910 and being originally concerned with the increased production of export crops, now had a greatly extended function, increased food production being one of its top priorities. Before the war 72,000 lbs of butter and 22,000 lbs of cooking fat had been imported into Nigeria every year: now Nigeria's first dairy was set up at Vom, the headquarters of the Veterinary Service, and the second at Kano. In 1942 the decision was taken to extend the Vom scheme to include dairies in the Pankshin Division of the Plateau Province.[113] As a result butter production rose quickly from 600 lbs to 30,000 lbs a month. Butter production in the northern provinces reached 325,000 lbs in 1942.[114] This increased production benefited mainly Europeans, but the construction of the dairies was also undertaken because 'a local industry of permanent value will be established'.[115] The PWD produced the equipment to make a proportion of the milk into cheese ('of cheddar-like quality'), and Vom also saw Nigeria's first piggeries, about 2,200 lbs of fresh pork being produced every month by early 1941.[116] Production of potatoes rose from 50 tons in 1939 to 1,100 tons in

1942. Vegetable production increased, and sugar was produced in large quantities − several hundred tons a year − with imported crushers. Wheat was grown in the north and mills erected for grinding it into flour. The growing of rice was also encouraged: before 1939 10,000 tons of rice had been imported every year, but between 1940 and 1945 only 8% of this total was imported. During the same years, owing to the development of local resources, only 2% of the quantities of dried fish previously imported, largely from Scandinavia, were brought into the country. Production of fruit drinks increased from 13,000 bottles in 1941 to 77,000 in 1942.[117] In fact it was found possible to export some surplus food from Nigeria to the other West African colonies.[118]

A detailed report on Nigerian production drew from the Colonial Office expert Dr. Tempany the comment that the war had

> stimulated production and ... created internal demands for produce which did not previously exist. It illustrates to my mind very forcibly how in paying attention to export products and failing to organise internal exchange of produce full advantage has in the past not been taken of the potentially very great opportunities that exist for raising the standard of living. It seems to me essential that after the war the healthy stimulation of internal trade which has occurred ought to be maintained.[119]

It seems clear therefore that any effort to determine the standard of living in Nigeria simply by reference to the supposed touchstone of the terms of trade, without attention to the internal economy and to colonial policy, is doomed to failure. Nor should we forget that, despite an admitted degree of specialisation in some sectors, most cash-crop producers had a diversified means of support.[120] Perhaps even to talk of the 'proletarianisation' of wage-labourers in this period[121] is a misformulation which ignores the variety of skills the workers enjoyed and exaggerates the degree to which the method of production determined the mode of existence.[122]

IV

New attitudes on the part of the colonial government in Nigeria during the Second World War are easily discernible. Stretch our inter-war generalisations though we may, they will no longer fit the contours of the new dispensation. Financial orthodoxy and retrenchment are no longer the predominant themes. Bourdillon now decided that previous policy had been 'narrow and short-sighted'[123] and 'wrong'[124] and commented scathingly on 'the fetish of a balanced budget'.[125] Never again, he believed, should inadequacy of local funds be sufficient excuse for failing to pay a government labourer or employee an adequate wage.[126] His government was soon to authorise wage increases for the staff of the Native Administrations even though, especially in the eastern provinces, this totally disrupted NA finances.[127] On the outbreak of war he reacted not by cutting back services and taking a greater share of taxation but by insisting that 'all our development work should go on'[128] and arranging to borrow money from the financial reserves of the NAs.[129] Old and orthodox colonial policies were flatly rejected, the conversion being prompted by the pent-up frustration that had accumulated during the depressed 1930s, by the revolutionary situation that existed in 1940 and that not only concentrated the mind but encouraged bold measures, and by the pervasive economic thought of Maynard Keynes, whose influence on colonial circles was exercised indirectly, perhaps through the writings of Professor W.M. Macmillan and Lord Hailey.[130]

Bourdillon showed a willingness to finance annual budget deficits that would have been unthinkable ten years earlier, and some of his war-time proposals were well in advance of what the Colonial Office were prepared to sanction. One of his proposals in 1940, to give government aid to enable an African company to establish a flour-grinding mill at Kano in the teeth of UAC competition, drew from an official the shocked comment that 'what the Governor is proposing is directly opposite to the principles on which we have been working for a hundred years', namely to allow British capital and British enterprise to develop backward countries.[131] Bourdillon was thought to have 'become obsessed ... with an anti-UAC complex'.[132] More significant for colonial policy were the Nigerian government's new attitudes to production, and these were endorsed by the Secretary of State. No longer had change to be organic and voluntarily accepted by Nigerians: instead it was to be stimulated to the maximum degree possible. Production Teams were set up to control and allocate transport and to direct intensive propaganda towards the increased production of desired products: demonstration plots were started, seeds were distributed, prices were guaranteed, and transport and storage were provided where possible. The Governor told his officers that any suggestions for increasing output, 'however wild and unorthodox they may seem', would be welcomed. He added that they should go on 'nagging at the producers and those who have influence over them until you and they are heartily sick'.[133] The aim of the war-time groundnut campaign in the north was 'all-out production ... A very considerable degree of compulsion is practical in some areas'.[134] No longer was there any reluctance over using the most modern and productive techniques, and there were concerted attempts to put the Oil Palm Research Station near Benin on a proper footing. The Nigerian government's expenditure on the Station rose from £588 in 1938–9 to £9,443 in 1945–6 (both amounts not counting salaries), and over £500,000 was requested from the Colonial Development and Welfare Fund.[135] In 1944 the British West African governments pooled their resources to establish the West African Cocoa Research Institute.[136]

The Nigerian government attempted to manage the colonial economy during the war. Its failures are clear. It was slow to see the need for a full-scale Labour Department, which was not created until October 1942, after serious trouble.[137] It did not stop inflation, which high government spending did something to create. But on balance, in the words of A.R. Prest, the 'indictment, if it can be so called, is ... hardly a formidable one'.[138] Inflation was much steeper in India, Egypt, Iraq, Trinidad, and elsewhere, and there is reason to conclude that the price rise in Nigeria would have been greater without the measures that were taken by the government.[139] Certainly there was hardship among wage-earners, but the government did grant a Cost of Living Allowance for its own workers, awarded in July 1942 and backdated to October 1941, at a level which became the norm for private employers too. The government appointed a committee, including prominent Nigerian labour spokesmen, which used detailed and exhaustive means to determine a cost of living index; and although these efforts were rendered in part illusory by the necessity of fixing 1939 prices somewhat arbitrarily, the index was really as accurate as could be devised.[140] Lord Swinton believed that the award was in excess of what was either necessary or expected,[141] while some trade union leaders argued that the COLA was 'a gross underestimation of the considerable upward movement of prices since the outbreak of war';[142] but probably the increase was as fair as any that could have been made, and the government's only adjustments to the committee's recommendations were in an upward direction.[143] Educated opinion in Lagos certainly believed that the level of COLA was acceptable.[144] It was explicit colonial policy to prevent a deterioration of real wages and – despite the inevitable controversy about the accuracy of statistics – it does seem that the Nigerian government was more successful than its counterparts in the other West African colonies.[145] W.M. Warren has argued that between 1939–40 and 1946–47 money wages were able to keep pace with or even to exceed steeply rising price levels.[146] This may have been so, but the price index continued to rise after the 1942 COLA, and although Bourdillon promised periodic readjustments his successor,

Sir Arthur Richards, resisted revision until 1945, when the so-called general strike forced him to set up a commission of enquiry. Only a short-sighted governor could put the real discontent that existed down to the intrigues of extremist politicians and money-lenders, and only the 50% COLA recommended by the commission allowed real wages to be made good at the end of the war.[147] In the meantime, from 1943 to 1945, hardship in Nigeria was probably at its peak.[148]

The Nigerian government was not without concern for the welfare of its colonial subjects during the war. This is shown by legislation like the Workmen's Compensation Ordinance, hailed by Azikiwe as the 'Working Man's Magna Carta',[149] but in particular by war-time plans for a brighter future – for jam tomorrow. For the first time, colonial policy had become forward-looking, and for the first time the colonial government had the means to plan positively. Inadequate government revenue had in the past been a major restraint upon growth, vetoing developmental schemes; but during the war gross central government revenue rose from £6,113,000 to £13,200,000,[150] a rise due not only to increased customs yields but to the fact that revenue from direct taxation more than doubled.[151] In fact a notable feature of the war was the taxation for the first time in Nigeria of those European companies operating there: hitherto the firms had paid all their tax to the British Exchequer. Company Tax was introduced in 1939 at a rate of 12½%, rising to 20% in 1940 and 25% in 1941.[152] If the war increased the profitability of expatriate firms in Nigeria, at least colonial policy ensured that the country would share in the profits.[153] Personal income tax rates were also raised affecting British officials and wealthier Lagosians, and for the first time there was token direct taxation of women in the Colony, 1½% on incomes over £200.[154] The war saw for the first time what one expert has called 'a modern progressive income tax' in Nigeria.[155] In consequence government expenditure rose from £6,499,000 in 1939–40 to £10,693,000 in 1945–6, an increased share of which was by the end of the war being devoted to development expenditure.[156] This extra local revenue, together with the prospect of grants from the Colonial Development and Welfare Fund, meant that the Nigerian government was able to draw up a Ten-Year Plan of Development and Welfare – a tangible sign of the reorientation of colonial policy that had taken place during the war – costing £55,000,000, £23,000,000 of which would be granted from the Colonial Development and Welfare Fund.[157] It was a Plan which gave high priority to the betterment of health (including the provision of uncontaminated urban and rural water supplies, as well as extended medical treatment) and education and which aimed at improved standards, modernisation, and higher productivity. Agricultural, veterinary, and forestry services were to be expanded; a new department of Commerce and Industries was to be set up, with an export and an internal section, part of its job being to establish palm oil factories — a proposal 'regarded as being one of the most important of all the schemes in this general plan'.[158] The colonial government would not merely encourage but 'induce' agricultural change, and legislation was to be passed to stimulate whatever measures were capable of enforcement.[159] There was to be no return, in policy or practice, to the *status quo ante bellum*. It is not surprising that the ending of forced labour in the Jos tin mines did not see the ending of official supervision of mining conditions.[160]

Another major feature of the post-war world was the use of marketing Boards from 1947. Initially financed with the surplus funds of the West African Produce Control Board, this was also clearly of war-time derivation.[161] So too was the continuation of currency restrictions — due to Britain's 'dollar gap' — which restricted colonial access to accumulated sterling balances and exacerbated a shortage of imported capital goods that dampened post-war economic growth.[162]

V

The years of the Second World War in Nigeria provide plenty of material for a partisan approach — in fact for several such approaches. Thus we can bracket the war in the 1930–45 period (if we take account of the terms of trade) or with the years 1940–60 (if we take account of the expanded demand for Nigeria's produce, the accelerated pace of economic activity, and the enlarged aims and scope of colonial policy). But it is important to remember that such approaches, which are seemingly alternatives, are not in fact mutually exclusive, for historical reality has a habit — discomfiting or reassuring, according to taste — of transcending our neat semantic categories and of reconciling verbal incompatibilities. The determined attempt to refute 'bourgeois mystifications' and to combat 'intellectual pimping for imperialism'[163] — or indeed to glorify the record of colonialism — can produce its own one-sided viewpoint, together with a vituperative — or romantic — style which will appeal only to those already emotionally converted: it may even disguise a fundamentally sound interpretation with unnecessary hyperbole. The war provides a pot-pourri wherein the ideologically engagés, or those with a penchant for balance-sheets, can pick whatever they wish to support their thesis.

A balanced approach would stress the exploitation in the tin mines and contrast this with the model villages constructed for the Enugu coalminers: semi-detached rent-free cottages were provided, built of brick instead of mud, each with electric light and a small vegetable garden. The Colonial Office publicity section vaunted these 'model homes'; but high costs, which increased from an estimated £62,700 to an actual £104,000, meant that the scheme, though beneficial in itself, was too expensive to be adopted elsewhere.[164] War-time price-fixing arrangements meant that producers of staple exports did not receive the 'true' value of their produce; but on the other hand this scheme did cushion farmers from the immediate impact of war and make for a greater degree of stability in export prices and volume than in the inter-war years. Between 1928 and 1938 export prices fluctuated by an annual average of 18.5%; from 1939 to 1945 the annual price fluctuation was 10.6%,[165] while higher prices would almost certainly have added to inflation. Marketing arrangements may have cemented the predominant position of the expatriate firms, yet they also made the firms subject to the control of the British government − and in November 1939 Bourdillon judged that it was due to the Ministry of Food that groundnuts from Niger Province were 'for the first time in history' raising a proper price from the United Africa Company's buyers.[166] Taxation of the companies, which was raised to 37½% in 1946 and 40% in 1950,[167] now benefited the local government.

The war boosted the proportion of Nigerian exports going to Britain, but this was increasing anyway, and had little long-term effect on the trend of Nigerian imports.[168] More significant were changes in the Nigerian economy itself, with the stimulation of more productive agriculture techniques and a degree of secondary industrialisation. Yet during the war those industrial enterprises which were fostered displayed 'an almost entire neglect of elementary safety precautions'. The expert Orde Browne urged that the authorities should not presume upon 'the well recognised nimbleness of the African combined with his lack of clothing' and that safety measures should urgently be taken.[169] Nor were such industrial undertakings structurally significant for the Nigerian economy as a whole. After the war there was only minor emphasis on the development of secondary industries in the Ten-Year Development Plan; and despite the fact that the war had tended to diminish their relative significance, the basic staple export crops still dominated the economy. Similarly the money available from the Colonial Development and Welfare Fund may have been a sign of new aspirations, but the scheme was hindered by a post-war shortage of capital goods and the effect of these grants on the Nigerian economy seems to have been of only marginal importance: buoyant world prices for Nigeria's primary products after the Korean war were what really allowed development before independence.[170] We should thus be aware of a substantial measure of continuity, from the pre- to the post-war periods, in Nigerian economic history.

Colonial policy in Nigeria must be seen in the light of intractable economic realities. The revolution in colonial policy was not mirrored in the economy; and yet of this revolution itself there should be no doubt. There had been signs on the eve of the war, in Governor Bourdillon's dissatisfaction and that of others, of a wish for a colonial new deal. Bourdillon had called for the ending of colonial self-sufficiency and for the injection of pump-priming capital. But no change in official policy came about before the war, and Bourdillon himself was clinging to ideas of 'organic' development and was all too aware that economic growth could mean economic exploitation by privately-owned European firms. It was the war which swept away this ambivalence. Colonial officers had never had such a clear mandate. They were to stimulate those products needed for Britain's war effort and at the same time to make the Nigerian economy as self-sufficient as possible in order to save valuable shipping space. It was the war which established the overall contours of colonial policy, as can be seen by the impact of the loss of the Far Eastern colonies in 1942, and it was the British government which laid down fiats, as with conscription for the tin mines, for the Nigerian administration to obey. Lord Swinton, as Resident Minister from 1942, brought the authority of the Cabinet to West Africa. But the colonial government was not slow at following the lead and developed some expertise not only at stimulating production but at fostering rudimentary welfare services; and in general colonial policy aimed to mitigate the hardships that war created. Its new developmental concerns were grafted onto its traditional *raison d'être* as a preserver of law and order, a function that had to be exercised by new techniques. During the war in fact the very nature of colonialism began to change. The scope of its activities became more extensive and its grasp more professional. The social ramifications of attempted economic management were endless: the government had to enter the fields of industrial relations, setting up arbitration machinery, of food distribution, of price controls, of rationing of certain goods, of press censorship, of the assessment of rents, of public relations generally. The way was being prepared for the post-war boom in recruitment to the Colonial Service, and especially to its technical branches. Colonialism was becoming a professional interventionist agency designed to manage the economy and regulate the life of its citizens.

The development of colonial policy during the war in many ways prepared for post-war economic development. The resources of the colonial government in Nigeria would henceforth be devoted with more wholeheartedness and a greater measure of expertise to increasing export and domestic production, and there was a recognition of the interrelatedness of welfare and development. The official mind had been converted to the utility of economic management and stimulated production, and also to their necessity, in order to appease Nigerian and international critics. The experiences of the 1939–45 period had convinced the Nigerian government of the useful possibilities of economic development under colonialism. (Nigerian nationalists too believed that economic progress would be made in the final years of British rule. Nkrumah, with his doctrine of seeking the political kingdom first, had no counterpart in Nigeria.) But the methods employed would have to change. The special conditions of war, which render the 1939–45 period *sui generis*, made forced labour in particular and compulsion in general viable propositions, but henceforth voluntary means would have to be used. The willing co-operation of the Nigerian people would have to be won more successfully than had been achieved during the war.[171] Unless the progressive, development-minded Africans could be taken into partnership with the colonial government, there would be confrontation and deadlock — as in the general strike of June and July 1945 — rather than development.

The makers of colonial policy in the early post-war years thought that only if the educated elite of Africans would work with the British, could the modernisation of colonies like Nigeria become a reality, despite the fact that their support could only be bought by the transfer of political power and the ending of formal British rule. The retirement of the diehard Governor Sir Arthur Richards at the end of 1947 inaugurated a policy of 'nation building' in Nigeria. Economic progress, foreshadowed by developments during the Second World War was, in theory at least, to be the flowering of a nationalism that was not repressed but conciliated by the colonial authorities. The replacement of the old indirect rule by local government on British lines, and thus of tribal chiefs by the educated elite as collaborators with the British, was an integral part of this new policy.[172] The strategem behind this policy was, it has been argued, the notion that Britain's connections with Nigeria could be reconverted from formal to informal empire.[173] No doubt the hope did persist that British influence could be sustained to some degree by a voluntary transfer of power, but more than this one probably should not say. War-time experiences erected a poor structure to support the cerebral edifice of neo-colonialism. The war had certainly transferred the initiative in colonial policy-making from the colony to London, a pre-condition for neo-colonial theories. But the economic experiences of Nigeria and of other colonies during the war, while exhibiting some capacity for growth, were scarcely such in themselves to convince the disinterested that the book was worth the candle. Nor, if the war years are anything to go by, should we necessarily accept the conventional judgement that economic considerations determined the nature and direction of colonial policy as a whole. But on post-war policy there is much more to be said.

NOTES

I wish to thank Barbara Ingham and Colin Simmons for their incisive comments on an earlier draft of this chapter.

1. CO 554/133/33738, copy of intercepted cable to *Daily Mail*, 11 Oct. 1943.
2. CO 554/133/33738, ibid., minute by Dawe, 15 Oct. 1943.
3. Pearce, R.D., *The Turning Point in Africa: British Colonial Policy, 1938–48* (London, Cass, 1982), pp. 24–7.
4. Pearce, R.D., ibid., p. 26. The quotation is taken from a minute of 1 Sept. 1942 by Under-Secretary of State Harold Macmillan.
5. Pearce, R.D., ibid., p. 6.
6. See Clive Whitehead, 'Education Policy in British Tropical Africa: the 1925 White Paper in Retrospect', *History of Education*, 1981, 10 (3), 195–203.
7. Lumley, E.K., *Forgotten Mandate* (London, 1976), p. 27.
8. CO 852/291/8, minute by Clauson, 30 Sept. 1940.
9. CO 583/96/2062, minute by A.J. Harding, 15 Jan. 1920.
10. Pearce, R.D., 'Governors, Nationalists, and Constitutions in Nigeria, 1935–51', *Journal of Imperial and Commonwealth History*, May 1981, 10 (3), 290; Sylvia Leith-Ross, *Stepping-Stones* (London, 1983), p. 131.
11. Macmillan, H., *The Blast of War* (London, 1967), p. 167.
12. Louis, W.R., *Imperialism At Bay* (Oxford, 1977), *passim*; Lee, J.M. and Petter, M., *The Colonial Office, War, and Development Policy* (London, 1982), *passim*; Pearce, *Turning Point in Africa*, Chs. 2–4.
13. Usoro, E.J., *The Nigerian Oil Palm Industry* (Ibadan, 1974), p. 74.
14. Hopkins, A.G., *An Economic History of West Africa* (London, 1973), pp. 254–67.
15. Bade Onimode, *Imperialism and Underdevelopment in Nigeria* (London, 1982), p. 237.
16. See Hopkins, *Economic History of West Africa*, pp. 254–67, and Helleiner, G.K., *Peasant Agriculture, Government, and Economic Growth in Nigeria* (Illinois, 1966), pp. 18–21.
17. Sir Bernard Bourdillon, 'War-time Reactions in Nigeria', *Crown Colonist*, April 1941.
18. *Nigerian Legislative Council Debates*, 7 Sept. 1942.
19. Meyer Fortes, 'The Impact of War on British West Africa', *International Affairs*, 21, April 1945, 206.
20. E.g. by Rhoda Howard, *Colonialism and Underdevelopment in Ghana* (London, 1978), preface.
21. Hopkins, *Economic History of West Africa*, pp. 183–4.
22. Hopkins, ibid., p. 185.
23. Ibid., p. 183; Ekundare, R.O., *An Economic History of Nigeria, 1860–1960* (London, 1973), p. 174.
24. CO 583/146/75, minute by Ormsby-Gore, 18 Jan. 1927.
25. Hopkins, *Economic History of West Africa*, pp. 250–1; Freund, W.M., 'Labour Migration to the Northern Nigerian Tin Mines, 1903–1945', *Journal of African History*, 22 (1981), 181.
26. Helleiner, *Peasant Agriculture*, Tables IV-A-15, IV-A-14.

27. Ibid., pp. 5, 18; Ekundare, *Economic History of Nigeria*, pp. 200–1; Onimode, *Imperialism and Underdevelopment in Nigeria*, p. 62.
28. Helleiner, *Peasant Agriculture*, Tables II-B-2, II-B-4, IV-A-1, IV-A-6.
29. Brett, E. A., *Colonialism and Underdevelopment in East Africa* (London, 1973), pp. 141–8. For a classic statement of inter-war financial orthodoxy, see Bourdillon's speech to the Uganda Legislative Council, 5 Dec. 1932, in CO 685/18.
30. In 1936–7 an analysis of expenditure in the British African dependencies revealed that outlay on administration accounted for 29.3–50.5% of total revenue expended; Nigeria had the lowest figure, but also record debt charges, accounting for 21.4% of its expenditure, while pensions cost another 11.5%: see Lord Hailey, *African Survey* (London, 1938), p. 1433.
31. Nicolson, I. F., *The Administration of Nigeria, 1900 to 1960* (Oxford, 1969), p. 227.
32. Gailey, H. A., *Sir Donald Cameron, Colonial Governor* (Stanford, 1974), pp. 101–6.
33. 52nd Ordinary General Meeting of the African and Eastern Trade Corporation, 23 March 1939, archive of the United Africa Company, London. I am most grateful to Pleydell, G. J., of the Public Relations Department of UAC for facilitating my access to these papers.
34. CO 859/48/12901/1, Bourdillon to Secretary of State for the Colonies [hereafter S of S], 5 April 1939. Figures quoted are for 1936, a good year.
35. *Nigeria Handbook* (London, 1953), p. 123; cf. Onimode, *Imperialism and Underdevelopment in Nigeria*, p. 67.
36. CO 859/48/12901/1, Bourdillon to S of S, 5 April 1939.
37. See Ekundare, *Economic History of Nigeria*, p. 357; CO 657/53, Bourdillon to S of S, 19 Nov. 1942; Helleiner, *Peasant Agriculture*, Table I-A-6.
38. CO 554/129/33669, Bourdillon to S of S, 24 Oct. 1941.
39. *Nigerian Legislative Council Debates*, Bourdillon, 4 Dec. 1939.
40. Pearce, R. D., *Turning Point in Africa*, pp. 17–20.
41. Pearce, R. D., ibid., p. 7.
42. Papers of the Chief Secretary's Office, Nigerian archives, Ibadan [hereafter CSO] 26/31105 vol. II, His Excellency's Inspection Notes, 31 Aug. 1937.
43. Bourdillon's review of Forde, D. and R. Scott, *The Native Economies of Nigeria*, in *African Affairs*, 46 (182), Jan. 1947, 54.
44. For extracts from the Clifford–Leverhulme and Bourdillon–Trenchard correspondence, see my forthcoming 2-volume collection of documents, *Colonialism in Nigeria*, to be published by Frank Cass.
45. CO 554/122/33650, Bourdillon to S of S, 16 Feb. 1939.
46. *Report of the Commission on the Marketing on West African Cocoa*, Cmd. 5845 of Sept. 1938, esp. pp. 151, 171; *Report of a Committee appointed in Nigeria to examine Recommendations by the Commission on the Marketing of West African Cocoa*, Sessional Paper no. 20 to 1939. See also Bourdillon to Trenchard, n.d. but Feb. 1938, Trenchard Papers, RAF Museum, Hendon, and Beer, C. E. F., *The Politics of Peasant Groups in Western Nigeria* (Ibadan, 1976), pp. 224–32.
47. CSO 26/31021 vol. I, minute by Maybin, 31 March 1936.
48. Ibid., Shelton, L. H., to Sec. of the Southern Provinces, 1 June 1936; minute by the Governor, 27 July 1936. See also Bourdillon to Trenchard, 29 Sept. 1936, Trenchard Papers.
49. Ibid., Whiteley to Maybin, Sept. 1936; CO 852/35/2, minute by Clauson, 2 Oct. 1936.
50. See Stibbs, T. P. C., 'Aspects of the Colonial Office Administration of the Trusteeship Concept with special reference to Kenya and Nigeria, 1919–1943', unpub. Oxford D.Phil. thesis, 1979, p. 140 *et seq.*
51. CO 852/35/2, Assoc. of West African Merchants to Bourdillon, 4 June 1936. See also 'The Oil Palm Industry' by Knox, T. M.; lecture given to the British Association in Dundee, 4 Sept. 1939, UAC archive.
52. CO 554/122/33650, Trenchard to Bourdillon, 18 May 1939; Note of an Interview with Lord Trenchard, 24 July 1939. Trenchard's figure of 30% was an exaggeration. Bourdillon disliked the fact that the presses were to advertise the UAC and believed that official distribution of them would damn the government by association.
53. CSO 26/31071/s.3, 'The future of the palm oil industry' by Mackie, June 1939.

54. Knox, 'The Oil Palm Industry'.
55. Helleiner, *Peasant Agriculture*, p. 101.
56. CSO 26/31071/s.3, 'The future of the palm oil industry' by Mackie, July 1939.
57. CO 657/58, *Statement of Agricultural Policy*, Sessional Paper no. 16 of 1946, p. 16.
58. Bryce, G. to Chief Secretary, 11 Sept. 1939, Mackie Papers, Rhodes House.
59. Wilson, C., 'The economic role and mainsprings of imperialism', p. 87 of Duignan, P. and L. H. Gann (eds.), *Colonialism in Africa, 1870–1960*: vol. 4, *The Economics of Colonialism* (Cambridge, 1975).
60. CO 852/650/14, 'British Colonial Exports, 1939–45', by Meyer, F. V., Aug. 1946.
61. Munro, J. F., *Africa and the International Economy, 1800–1960* (London, 1976), p. 171; Olorunfemi, A., 'Effects of War-time Trade Controls on Nigerian Cocoa-Traders and Producers, 1939–45: a case-study of the Hazards of a Dependent Economy', *International Journal of African Historical Studies*, 13 (4), 1980, 678.
62. Beer, *Politics of Peasant Groups*, p. 27.
63. Olorunfemi, 'Effects of War-time Trade Controls', p. 678.
64. *Report on Cocoa Control in West Africa, 1939–43, and Statement of Future Policy*, Cmd. 6554 of 1944, and *Statement on Future Marketing of West African Cocoa*, Cmd. 6950 of Nov. 1946.
65. CO 852/650/14, 'British Colonial Exports' by Meyer, p. 34.
66. Hopkins, *Economic History of West Africa*, p. 266.
67. Helleiner, *Peasant Agriculture*, Tables II-B-2, II-B-3, II-B-4.
68. Ibid. Tables IV-A-11 and IV-A-13.
69. Ibid. Calculated from Table IV-A-2. See also *Statistical Abstract for the British Commonwealth for each of the ten years 1936 to 1945*, Cmd. 7224 of Oct. 1947, pp. 121–4.
70. For the measures taken by the government, see CO 852/507/18, *Memorandum on the Organisation and Control of War Time Production*, 1943.
71. CO 554/132/33718/1, CO memo on economic policy, Aug. 1943.
72. Ananaba, W., *The Trade Union Movement in Nigeria*, (London, 1969), p. 31.
73. *West African Pilot*, 5 June 1940, 15 Sept. 1941.
74. See Pearce, R. D., 'Morale in the Colonial Service in Nigeria during the Second World War', *Journal of Imperial and Commonwealth History*, 11 (2), Jan. 1983, 175–96.
75. Fajana, A., 'The Evolution of Educational Policy in Nigeria, 1842–1939', unpub. Ph.D. thesis, University of Ibadan, 1969, p. 501; CO 859/22/1940, 'Notes on the Effect of the War on School Facilities in Nigeria' by Quinn-Young, C. T., Jan. 1940; Ogunlade, F. O., 'Yaba Higher College and the Formation of an Intellectual Elite', unpub. MA. thesis, University of Ibadan, 1970. See also Olusanya, G. O., *The Second World War and Politics in Nigeria, 1939–1953* (London, 1973), pp. 66–8.
76. Bill Freund, *Capital and Labour in the Nigerian Tin Mines* (London, 1981), p. 149. See the whole of his ch. 5 for an analysis of war-time conscription.
77. CO 554/139/33764. Report by Major Orde Browne on Visit to West Africa, 1944; see also Souter, D. N., 'Colonial Labour Policy and Labour Conditions in Nigeria, 1939–1945' (unpub. Oxford D.Phil. thesis, 1980), esp. pp. 174–5.
78. CO 583/270/30569/1, Richards to S of S, 11 May 1944: 'There is no doubt that the average conscript labourer has never been so well fed as when working on the mines. It is perhaps worth mentioning that even before the various amendments were made, the prescribed rations so noticeably improved the physique of most of the conscripts that some employers thought it worth their while to provide a similar diet for their more permanent voluntary labour'. CO 583/270/30569, Richards to S of S, 29 Feb. 1944: the Governor believed that the labourers had worked 'well and cheerfully' and that all concerned deserved 'a word of praise'.
79. Freund, *Capital and Labour*, p. 147.
80. Freund, ibid., p. 148.
81. CO 554/139/33764, Report by Orde Browne, 1944; Souter, 'Colonial Labour Policy', pp. 174–5.
82. Olorunfemi, 'Effects of War-time Trade Controls', p. 681.
83. CO 852/515/7, 'Rubber in Nigeria and in British Cameroons', Memo addressed to the Ministry of Supply by the West African Rubber Mission, 15 May 1943.
84. Souter, 'Colonial Labour Policy', pp. 87–8; see also Elliott Berg, J., 'Real Income Trends

in West Africa, 1939–1960', p. 212, in Herskovits, M. J. and M. Harwitz (eds.), *Economic Transition in Africa* (London, 1964). For a counter theoretical argument, see Onitri, H. M. A., 'Nigeria's Balance of Payments and Economic Policy, 1946–1960' (unpub. Ph.D. thesis, University of London, 1963), p. 46.

85. Hopkins, *Economic History of West Africa*, p. 253.
86. Hopkins, ibid., p. 267: Hopkins, himself notes that there is some evidence that after 1945 the domestic market grew even faster than the export sector.
87. See Cook, A. N., *British Enterprise in Nigeria*, (new edition, London, 1964), p. 240; and CO 583/136/48391, 'Co-operation in Nigeria: Palm Oil Factories' by Faulkner, Sept. 1925.
88. Helleiner, *Peasant Agriculture*, p. 194.
89. Helleiner, ibid., Table IV-A-8. See also CO 852/451/6, 'Rubber Production Territories not party to the International Rubber Regulation Agreement', 12 Jan. 1942.
90. *Report of the Commission of Enquiry into the Disorders in the Eastern Provinces of Nigeria, November, 1949*, colonial no. 256 of 1950, p. 57.
91. Ekundare, *Economic History of Nigeria*, p. 170.
92. Souter, 'Colonial Labour Policy', p. 53.
93. Fieldhouse, D. K., *Unilever Overseas: Anatomy of a Multinational* (London, 1978), p. 369. Bauer, P. T., *West African Trade* (2nd edn, London 1963), p. 140N, notes that the total taxable profits of trading companies (excluding mining, banking, and shipping) rose from £871,000 in 1939–40 to £7,100,000 in 1948–9. On expatriate firms generally, see Mars, J., 'Extra-Territorial Enterprises', pp. 43–135 in Perham, M. (ed.) *Mining Commerce, and Finance in Nigeria* (London, 1948).
94. *Nigeria: the Making of a Nation* (HMSO, 1960), pp. 13–14; CO 852/540/7, 'Purchase in the United States of Plywood Machinery for Nigeria', Jan. 1945: *The Colonial Empire* (1939–1947), Cmd 7167 of July 1947, p. 38.
95. Capt. L. Nichols, 'Notes taken on Tours of Inspection', 5 July 1945, papers of L. Nichols, Rhodes House.
96. *Nigeria Handbook*, p. 198. See also 'Timber: Historical Background', 9 Sept. 1966, no author, UAC archive.
97. *Nigeria: Making of a Nation*, pp. 13–14.
98. See correspondence in CO 852/370/11 and also *A Colony's Effort, compiled by the Nigerian Government*, n.d., p. 17.
99. *A Colony's Effort*, p. 12.
100. CO 657/55, 'Annual Report on the Eastern Provinces of Nigeria for the year 1942' by Shute, G. G., p. 2.
101. *Nigeria: Making of a Nation*, p. 14.
102. For the state of transport in Nigeria on the eve of war, see Smith, F., *Transport in Nigeria*, July 1939, and *Comments of the General Manager, Nigerian Railway, on Mr Frederick Smith's Report of July 1939*, UAC archive.
103. Walker, H. E., 'Notes on Activities of Public Works Department', papers of Sir Hubert Walker, Rhodes House.
104. Walker, ibid.
105. Walker, ibid.
106. Ekundare, *Economic History of Nigeria*, pp. 154–5.
107. Mackie to Chief Sec., 4 Jan. 1939, Mackie Papers.
108. Ibid., Mackie to Chief Sec., 13 Nov. 1940.
109. CO 852/468/4, memo by Mackie on food production and supply for Oct. 1941–March 1942; CO 852/524/1, memo by Mackie on food production, April 1942–Sept. 1942.
110. *Nigerian Legislative Council Debates*, Bourdillon, 15 March 1943; see also CO 583/262/30519., Bourdillon to S of S, 24 Jan. 1942.
111. CSO 26/03445 vol. VII, Note on a visit of H.E. to the Ilorin Province, Oct. 1942.
112. Mary Tiffen, *The Enterprising Peasant: Economic Development in Gombe Emirate, North Eastern State, Nigeria, 1900–1968* (London, 1976), pp. 61–5.
113. CO 852/371/12, Governor to S of S, 6 Nov. 1942.
114. CO 657/55, 'Annual Report on the Northern Provinces of Nigeria for the year 1942', by Sir Theodore Adams, p. 9.
115. CO 852/348/9, OAG to S of S, 19 April 1940.

116. CO 852/469/10, 'Schemes for the Production of Pork in Nigeria', n.d.; *Nigeria*, no. 22, 1944, pp. 14–15; *Nigeria: Making of a Nation*, pp. 13–14.
117. *Nigeria: Making of a Nation*, p. 13; *The Colonial Empire (1939–47)*, pp. 88–9.
118. *Nigerian Legislative Council Debates*, 15 March 1943.
119. CO 852/524/1, minute by Dr H. Tempany, 23 April 1943.
120. CO 852/510/24, memo on 'Nigeria' by Rawlings, H. J. of John Holt and Co., Nov. 1943.
121. Souter, 'Colonial Labour Policy', abstract.
122. Freund, 'Labour Migration to the Northern Nigerian Tin Mines', pp. 82–3.
123. CO 323/1695/7318A, Bourdillon to S of S, 19 Sept. 1939. Cf. CO 852/596/2, Richards to S of S, 15 Feb. 1945: 'As an officer of the Colonial Service of over 35 years' experience I feel bound to record the conviction which has been growing upon me that in its pronouncements of Colonial policy His Majesty's Government in the last 20 years has often paid only lip service to our obligations and has often not really faced up to the extremely difficult and embarrassing problems which have been before us'.
124. CO 583/262/30519, Bourdillon to S of S, 31 Aug. 1942.
125. Ibid., Bourdillon to S of S, 21 Jan. 1942.
126. Bourdillon, ibid.
127. Pearce, R. D., 'Morale in the Colonial Service in Nigeria', op. cit., pp. 184–5.
128. Mackie to Financial Sec, 19 Oct. 1940, Mackie Papers.
129. For this decision, see CSO 26/35989 vol. I.
130. CO 859/48/12901/1, Bourdillon to S of S, 5 April 1939.
131. CO 852/291/8, minute by Clauson, 30 Sept. 1940.
132. CO 852/290, minute by Parkinson, C., 9 Nov. 1940.
133. Bourdillon to Mackie, May 1943, Mackie Papers.
134. CO 852/514/1, Note of meeting between Resident Minister and the Governor of Nigeria, 18 March 1943.
135. 'Palm Oil Research State' by Mackie, n.d., Mackie Papers; see also Eicher, C. K., 'The Dynamics of Long-Term Agricultural Development in Nigeria', p. 8, in Eicher, C. K. and C. Liedholm (eds.), *Growth and Development of the Nigerian Economy* (Michigan, 1970).
136. Ekundare, *Economic History of Nigeria*, p. 168.
137. Souter, 'Colonial Labour Policy', ch. 5.
138. Prest, A. R., *War Economics of Primary Producing Countries* (Cambridge, 1948), pp. 260–2.
139. Prest, A. R., ibid., p. 5; Onitri, 'Nigeria's Balance of Payments', p. 46.
140. *West African Pilot*, 28 Feb. 1942, 4 Mar. 1942, 9 Mar. 1942.
141. Swinton to Lord Cranborne, 9 Nov. 1942, Swinton Papers, II 5/5, Churchill College, Cambridge.
142. 'Comments by the Associated Union of African Civil Servants (Nigeria) on the Report of the Cost of Living Committee', 3 July 1942, Herbert Macaulay Papers, Box 35, Ibadan University Library.
143. *West African Pilot*, 25 July 1942.
144. Gerald Wormal, Director of Labour in Nigeria, to Rita Hinden, 16 Oct. 1942, quoting the views of Abayomi, K. Papers of the Fabian Colonial Bureau, FCB 82/2 3–4, Rhodes House.
145. Berg, 'Real Income Trends in West Africa' (see note 84).
146. Warren, W. M., 'Urban Real Wages and the Nigerian Trade Union Movement, 1939–60', *Economic Development and Social Change*, 15 (1), Oct. 1966, 21–36.
147. Pearce, R. D., 'Governors, Nationalists, and Constitutions', pp. 296–7; *Enquiry into the Cost of Living and the Control of the Cost of Living in the Colony and Protectorate of Nigeria*, colonial no. 204 of 1946.
148. Olusanya, *Second World War and Politics in Nigeria*, pp. 62–6, 87–9.
149. *West African Pilot*, 29 March 1941.
150. Helleiner, *Peasant Agriculture*, Table V-E-3.
151. Ibid. See Table V-E-4 for customs duties and Table V-E-5 for direct tax.
152. From Governor's speeches to the Legislative Council.
153. Fieldhouse, *Unilever Overseas*, p. 361.
154. Mba, N. E., 'Women in Southern Nigerian Political History, 1900–65' (unpub. Ph.D.

thesis, 1978, University of Ibadan), pp. 414–19. I am grateful to Susan Martin for providing me with a reference to this thesis. See also Cheryl Johnson, 'Madam Pelewura and the Lagos Market Women', *Tariqh*, 7, 1, 1–10. The women's reluctance to accept taxation probably owed less to the hardships they were already undergoing than to their dislike of the principle of female taxation and their fear that rates would escalate. Mba, p. 414, notes that within a few minutes of first hearing of the Income Tax (of females) Ordinance the market women subscribed 100 Naira to campaign against the tax.

155. Ekundare, *Economic History of Nigeria*, p. 114.
156. Ibid., pp. 116–17; Helleiner, *Peasant Agriculture*, pp. 233–4.
157. CO 657/53, *A Ten Year Plan of Development and Welfare for Nigeria*, Sessional Paper 24 of 1945. For the insubstantial statistical basis of such development plans, see Morgan, D. J., *The Official History of Colonial Development*, vol. 2: *Developing British Colonial Resources, 1945–1951* (London, 1980), p. 68.
158. *Ten-Year Plan of Development and Welfare*, para. 174.
159. CO 657/58, *Statement of Agricultural Policy*, Sessional Paper 16 of 1946, pp. 1, 3, 5.
160. Freund, *Capital and Labour*, p. 151.
161. *Statement on Future Marketing of West African Cocoa*, Cmd 6950 of Nov. 1946, p. 5.
162. See Morgan, D. J., *Developing British Colonial Resources, 1945–1951*, chs. 1 and 2.
163. Onimode, *Imperialism and Underdevelopment in Nigeria*, preface and p. 114.
164. CO 583/263/30544, OAG to S of S, 18 Mar. 1942; Governor to S of S, 10 Aug. 1942; 'New Homes in Old Africa' by Wormal, 'Model Villages for African Miners', press section notice, n.d.
165. Calculated as a percentage of the higher of the two magnitudes compared, from Helleiner, *Peasant Agriculture*, Table IV-A-2.
166. Bourdillon to Trenchard, 28 Nov. 1939, Trenchard Papers.
167. Onimode, *Imperialism and Underdevelopment in Nigeria*, p. 110.
168. Helleiner, *Peasant Agriculture*, Tables IV-A-13 and IV-A-15.
169. CO 554/139/33764, Report by Orde Browne on visit to West Africa, 1944.
170. Morgan, D. J., *The Official History of Colonial Development*: vol. 3, *A Reassessment of British Aid Policy, 1951–1965* (London, 1980), ch. 2.
171. *West African Pilot*, 20 Feb. 1943.
172. Pearce, R. D., *Turning Point in Africa*, ch. 6.
173. Louis and Robinson, 'The United States and the Liquidation of British Empire in Tropical Africa, 1941–51', p. 42, in Gifford, P. and W. R. Louis (eds.), *The Transfer of Power in Africa* (London, 1982).